THE
ULTIMATE
BOOK OF
WORDS
YOU SHOULD KNOW

DAVID OLSEN, MICHELLE BEVILACQUA, & JUSTIN CORD HAYES

adamsmedia
AVON, MASSACHUSETTS

Previously published in another form as *The Big Book of Words You Should Know* by
David Olsen, Michelle Bevilacqua, and Justin Cord Hayes, copyright © 2009 by
F+W Media, Inc., ISBN 10: 1-60550-139-5, ISBN 13: 978-1-60550-139-0.

Published by
Adams Media, a division of F+W Media, Inc.
57 Littlefield Street, Avon, MA 02322. U.S.A.
www.adamsmedia.com

ISBN 10: 1-4405-0483-0
ISBN 13: 978-1-4405-0483-9

Printed in the United States of America.

10   9   8   7   6   5   4   3   2

Library of Congress Cataloging-in-Publication Data
is available from the publisher.

INTRODUCTION

Peregrination. Skullduggery. Chicanery. Do these words sound familiar? If so, pat yourself on the back. You are, most assuredly, a genius of the highest order. But if you find yourself at an embarrassing loss for words, don't be upset. You're not alone. Learn a few of these, drop them into a conversation, and . . . *voilà*! . . . instant genius!

Chances are, you already use many of the words found throughout *The Ultimate Book of Words You Should Know*, but—if pressed—would not be able to offer a definition for them. Have no fear. Once you've read through this book, you'll not only use these words but will actually know what they mean as well, thus gaining confidence in your ability to impress others with your *prodigious* communication skills.

Are you struggling to pick up a foreign language? Think you can't learn one to save your life? *Au contraire!* Well, chances are you've even used at least a few of the expressions in this book. Many of them are *bona fide* foreign idioms that have been adopted wholesale into English. These words are *de rigueur* for the discerning conversationalist and will help you realize that you actually already are the *daedal* foreign speaker you hoped to be!

Have you ever been—or longed to be—a *Casanova*? Has someone ever accused you of being *quixotic*? Have you ever been embroiled in a *catch-22*? Are you interested in knowing how words like these came into being? Well, each of these words are derived from the name of a real—or fictional—person or from a real—or fictional—place. Read on to *augment* your knowledge of *etymology* and learn the words that you truly should know.

Whether you're attending a party, conversing with your coworkers, or trying to impress your friends and family, dropping these words into your everyday conversations will help you achieve *ebullience, eloquence,* and feats of *rhetorical effulgence.*

A

a capella *(ah kuh-PELL-a), music, adjective*

Singing without musical accompaniment. Used as an adjective, *a capella* often refers to a rhythmic and highly inventive vocal style.

> *The group's A CAPELLA rendition of "The Star Spangled Banner" was remarkably good, especially considering that the song is quite difficult to sing with musical accompaniment.*

abacus *(AB-uh-kuss), noun*

A device used to figure arithmetic equations by moving beads along rods.

> *Mrs. Danvers thought that the ABACUS, with its brightly colored beads, would entertain the first graders while illustrating the basic principles of addition and subtraction.*

abase *(uh-BASE), verb*

To humiliate or deprive of self-worth.

> *Melanie refused to ABASE herself for her boss over a simple clerical error.*

abash *(uh-BASH), verb*

To disconcert, humiliate, or shame. To *abash* is to make another feel uncomfortable or disconcerted, or to cause someone to lose composure.

> *The older boys had no qualms about ABASHING the new arrivals; it was an old tradition at the school.*

abate *(uh-BATE), verb*

To put an end to or reduce in intensity. To *abate* is to reduce or diminish something. Something that lessens or weakens is abating.

> *The flood waters ABATED when the rain stopped.*

abbess *(AB-iss), noun*

A head nun in charge of a convent; a mother superior.

> *The old ABBESS generally ran a strict convent, so on my birthday I was amazed to find she'd left a box of chocolates on my reading table.*

abbreviated *(uh-BREE-vee-ate-ud), verb*

Shortened.

> *Because the hour is late, I will limit myself to an ABBREVIATED version of my intended speech.*

abdicate *(AB-di-kate), verb*

To formally give up a position or responsibility. To *abdicate* means to step down from a high government office or other powerful position. Originally, the word referred primarily to royalty.

> *The King, as we all know, ABDICATED rather than give up the woman he loved.*

abduct *(ub-DUCT), verb*

To take a person away secretly and illegally, often by use of force; to kidnap.

> *My sister Ellen used to take such long showers that Dad would jokingly ask if she'd been ABDUCTED by aliens.*

abecedarian *(ay-bee-see-DARE-ee-un), noun*

A beginner; someone just learning the rudiments of a task, skill, job, etc.

> *Paul is an expert in a sea kayak, but when it comes to snow skiing, he's an ABECEDARIAN.*

aberrant *(AB-uh-runt), adjective*

Abandoning the correct, expected, or proper way of doing things; straying from the "right" or norm.

> *Alice's decision to quit college and tour the country on motorcycle seemed so ABERRANT to her parents that they asked her to get a psychiatric evaluation.*

aberration *(ab-uh-RAY-shun), noun*

Diverging from a moral standard or expected course. *Aberration* refers to a usually temporary departure from what is normal or expected. Something that deviates from a customary or natural course of action is an *aberration.*

> *Sally's poor work in the first part of October was hardly grounds for dismissal; it was an ABERRATION caused by serious problems at home.*

abet *(uh-BET), verb*

To encourage or assist a plan or activity. To *abet* is to entice or help, usually in a misdeed. An accomplice to a robbery *abets* the crime.

> *Though Michael did not participate in the actual kidnapping, he left himself open to charges of ABETTING the perpetrators by hiding them from the police.*

abeyance *(uh-BEY-unce), noun*

Temporary suspension; a temporary pause, especially in regard to a government or court's ruling.

> *To the embarrassment of the school administration, the local newspaper soon got wind of their decision to hold Chuck's expulsion in ABEYANCE and allow him to play in the championship game.*

abhorrent *(ab-HOR-ent), adjective*

Loathsome or contemptible. *Abhorrent* refers to something that is reprehensible or repulsive. That which is repugnant or detestable is *abhorrent.*

> *Julie found the book's recounting of the details of serial murders particularly ABHORRENT.*

A

abide *(Uh-BIDE), verb*
To withstand, patiently wait for, or tolerate. To *abide* is to tolerate or endure. *Abiding* also refers to the ability to withstand and/or persevere.

> *I could ABIDE my dinner companion's bigotry for only so long; by evening's end, I had to challenge him.*

abject *(AB-ject), adjective*
Reduced to a low state or condition; also, demonstrating hopelessness.

> *I gave up golf when I realized I was an abject failure on the green.*

abjure *(ab-JOOR), verb*
To renounce, repudiate, or reject one's word or professed beliefs. To *abjure* is to solemnly swear off or recant.

> *After some soul-searching following his financial and domestic problems, Brad ABJURED drinking and gambling.*

ablultion *(ab-BLOO-shun), noun*
Washing or cleansing the body as part of a religious rite; any cleansing, purification, or purging. *Ablution* is the washing away or cleansing of sin or spiritual uncleanness.

> *Pilate turned away from the crowd and called for a bowl of scented water with which to perform his ABLUTIONS.*

abnegate *(AB-ne-gate), verb*
To renounce, surrender, or deny privilege to oneself. *Abnegation* is the act of denying oneself something considered vital or important. Hunger strikes or long fasts are a form of *abnegation*.

> *The activist's fast lasted for forty-seven days; in an election year, such ABNEGATION draws headlines and attention from elected officials.*

abominate *(uh-BOM-ih-nate), verb*
To loathe or hate; to view with extreme hostility.

> *Miss Green ABOMINATED the notion of children working twelve-hour days, and sought legislation forbidding companies from hiring minor workers.*

aboriginal *(ab-uh-RIDGE-ih-nul), adjective*
Indigenous or native to an area; the first of its kind in a region. *Aboriginal* pertains most commonly to the aborigines in Australia. However, the most complete definition of the word is something that existed first in an area. The aborigines in Australia were that area's first inhabitants.

> *The General Assembly was presented with a petition on environmental matters signed by representatives of the world's various ABORIGINAL peoples.*

abortive *(uh-BOR-tive), adjective*
Unsuccessful or fruitless. Something that is *abortive* has failed to come to fruition. The word also refers to something that is partially or imperfectly developed.

> *Although it was the astronauts' failure to dock at the station that drew media attention, the ABORTIVE mission had many potentially more serious problems as well.*

abrade *(uh-BRADE), verb*
To wear away or rub off; to wear down in spirit. To *abrade* is to erode or break down. Sandpaper *abrades* the surface of wood.

> *The campaign had hoped for a hard-hitting, informative television commercial, but the ad—widely perceived as negative and mean-spirited—served only to ABRADE voter support.*

abrogate *(AB-ro-gate), verb*
To nullify or cancel. *Abrogation* is an official action used to formally and unilaterally conclude an agreement or deed. Something that has been repealed or abolished has been *abrogated*.

> *The United States ABROGATED the treaty after evidence appeared suggesting that the other nations had failed to honor the agreement.*

abscond *(ab-SKOND), verb*
To depart quickly and in secret, especially to avoid criminal charges. To *abscond* is to secretly flee the consequences of one's acts, particularly those acts leading to illicit gain. Prosecuting attorneys might accuse someone convicted of embezzling of *absconding* with company funds if the person left the firm shortly after the alleged crime.

> *The bank robbers immediately ABSCONDED with the money to Mexico.*

absinthe *(AB-sinth), noun*
A green alcoholic liqueur flavored with wormwood and having narcotic qualities.

> *Before the beverage was banned in the early part of this century, a great many Americans were addicted to ABSINTHE.*

absolution *(ab-suh-LOO-shun), noun*
The condition of having been forgiven or freed of guilt.

> *To Myron's dismay, the judge did not consider his having paid for the damage to the other party's car sufficient ABSOLUTION for the crime of driving while intoxicated.*

A

absolve *(ah-ZOLV), verb*

To formally pronounce guiltless or blameless. To *absolve* is to relieve of any responsibility for an actual or alleged misdeed. In the legal sense, absolution carries with it implication that the authorities no longer hold that the individual committed the misdeed.

> *The judge ABSOLVED the accused of any wrongdoing.*

abstain *(ub-STANE), verb*

To refrain from; to refuse to partake in; to go without voluntarily.

> *Maria, who had ABSTAINED from eating meat while in high school, was persuaded to try a cheeseburger on her graduation night.*

abstemious *(ab-STEE-me-us), adjective*

Consuming food and drink in moderation. Those who are *abstemious* restrict themselves to the bare necessities of life. In a larger sense, the word can refer to any austere or unassuming lifestyle.

> *Despite the hardships of his ABSTEMIOUS way of life, the monk radiated the confidence that comes with knowing one has chosen the correct path.*

abstinence *(AB-ste-nence), noun*

Voluntarily foregoing the indulgence of an appetite. *Abstinence* is the act of abstaining from food, drink, or pleasure. *Abstinence* may refer to denial of certain foods and drinks thought to be harmful to one's health; however, it can also refer to refraining from behavior considered immoral.

> *After years of indulgence, it was difficult for Evelyn to follow her doctor's order of complete ABSTINENCE from liquor.*

abstruse *(ab-STROOCE), adjective*

Complex and difficult to comprehend. *Abstruse* refers to something complex or specialized that requires special effort to grasp.

> *Scientists may understand Einstein's theory of relativity, but for most laymen it remains an ABSTRUSE collection of surrealistic ideas.*

abyss *(uh-BISS), noun*

An endless black void; an emptiness; a huge hole with no bottom.

> *After nine days of working on my term paper with no conclusion in sight, I felt more and more as if I were facing an ABYSS.*

academic *(ACK-uh-demm-ick), adjective or noun*
In addition to its noun form, which can mean "someone associated with a school" or "someone who is educated but lacks street smarts," *academic* refers to theories and speculations that have no practical or useful significance.

> *Janet is filled with all kinds advice on how to solve the world's problems, but all of her solutions are ACADEMIC, and thus, worthless.*

accede *(ak-SEED), verb*
To give one's consent. To *accede* is to signal one's acceptance of something. To formally accept a high position is to *accede*. Therefore, someone who accepts a position *accedes* to that office.

> *The college president eventually ACCEDED to the demands of the student demonstrators.*

accentuate *(ak-SEN-choo-ate), verb*
To intensify or accent. To *accentuate* something is to emphasize or stress it. To strengthen or heighten the effect of something is to *accentuate* it.

> *Brian's new glasses ACCENTUATE his nose unflatteringly.*

accept *(ak-SEPT), verb*
To take into possession. (See, for comparison, the listing for *except*)

> *I'm happy to ACCEPT your invitation to dinner, Claude.*

acclamation *(ack-luh-MAY-shun), noun*
Overwhelming approval, demonstrated by loud cheers, clapping, etc., rather than through a ballot.

> *The ACCLAMATION of the crowd made it very clear that Jack had won the talent show.*

acclimated *(AK-lih-may-tud), verb*
Having-adapted or become accustomed to.

> *At first Tami found college life lonely and stressful, but after a few weeks she became ACCLIMATED and never longed for home again.*

accolade *(AK-uh-lade), noun*
A mark of acknowledgment or expression of praise. Originally, an *accolade* was the ceremonial bestowal of knighthood upon a person, with a sword tapped on each shoulder. That which confers praise or honor is an accolade.

> *The firm's president had hung on his office wall many plaques, citations, and ACCOLADES.*

A

accord *(ub-CORD), noun*
A formal reaching of agreement. An *accord* is reached when a settlement or compromise of conflicting views occurs.

> *After a prolonged strike, with the issue of healthcare benefits was resolved, the representatives finally reached an ACCORD acceptable to both labor and management.*

accost *(uh-KOST), verb*
To greet or approach, usually in a confrontational way; to approach in order to confront.

> *I was having a wonderful time at Sara's wedding until Uncle George ACCOSTED me at the bar and demanded to know when I planned to get a real job.*

accoutrement *(uh-KOO-truh-mint), noun*
A superficial characteristic that, nonetheless, identifies a person, group, etc. *Accoutrement* also can refer to accessory items of clothing or equipment. In both cases, the word is usually plural.

> *Five televisions per household is just one of the ACCOUTREMENTS of American life.*

accrete *(uh-KREET), verb*
To accumulate or cause to become attached.

> *Dang it! Every time I park my car under a tree the candy apple red finish ACCRETES a layer of bird droppings!*

acculturation *(uh-kul-chu-RAY-shun), noun*
Alteration of one culture traceable to interaction with another. *Acculturation* describes the process of cultural influences as well as the means by which the culture of a particular culture is instilled in a human being.

> *While there are often severe adjustment problems among senior citizens who immigrate to this country, ACCULTURATION among younger children occurs remarkably quickly.*

Achilles' heel *(uh-KILL-eez HEEL), noun*
A vulnerable point. Achilles was a hero of the Trojan War who was vulnerable to harm only in his heel.

> *Bob was a hard worker, but he often lost jobs because of his Achilles' heel, his temper.*

acme *(AK-me), noun*
The highest point; summit.

> *Although his many fans might consider winning the Pulitzer the ACME of Marvin's writing career, in his mind nothing would ever match the thrill of seeing his first novel in print.*

acquiescence *(ak-wee-ESS-unce), noun*
The act of passive agreement or assent without objection. *Acquiesence* is the act of assenting or complying with another's demands. Someone who submits to another's will is *acquiescent*.
> *Hank, enchanted by first-time grandfatherhood, gave over to complete ACQUIESCENCE on his first day with little Laura.*

acquisitive *(uh-KWIZZ-uh-tihv), adjective*
Someone marked by a hunger to attain and possess things.
> *Fred stopped dating Laura after it became clear that she was disturbingly ACQUISITIVE.*

acrid *(AK-rid), adjective*
Biting or harsh in odor or taste; deeply or violently bitter. *Acrid* refers to anything unpleasantly sharp and pungent to the senses of smell or taste. *Acrid* can also be used to describe a bitter or harsh verbal exchange between persons.
> *Florence's ACRID remarks did not sit well with the board of directors.*

acrimonious *(ak-ri-MO-nee-us), adjective*
Mean-spirited, bitter, or ill-natured. *Acrimonious* refers to language or exchanges that are filled with animosity. Something characterized by sharpness or bitterness of speech is *acrimonious*.
> *Divorce is, we must remember, an expensive, emotionally devastating, and ACRIMONIOUS affair.*

acronym *(AK-ruh-nim), noun*
A word formed by combining the first letters of several other words. (Example: NOW is an acronym for the National Organization for Women.)
> *Cindy believed that-the secret to getting good grades on tests was to use ACRONYMS as memory aids.*

acrophobia *(ak-ruh-FO-bee-a), noun*
An abnormal fear of heights. *Acrophobia* refers to person's fear of high places; it is characterized by feelings of dread, danger, and helplessness.
> *Of course, his ACROPHOBIA ruled out any ride in the hot-air bolloon.*

acuity *(uh-KUE-uh-tee), adjective*
Keen, as in the mind or the senses; deft.
> *Although Professor Kane admitted that Jordan's chess ACUITY was impressive for one so young, he did not agree that the boy was ready to compete professionally.*

acumen *(uh-CUE-men), noun*
Keenness of judgment. *Acumen* refers to an ability to make quick, accurate decisions and evaluations. It is characterized by rapid discernment and insight.

> *After only two years as a restaurant owner, Clyde developed a remarkable business ACUMEN; in a supposedly "bad location," he had little trouble coming up with promotions that attracted customers.*

ad hoc *(ad HOK), adjective*
For a specific purpose or end; formed for immediate or present need. This Latin phrase translates literally to "for this purpose." Anything that is designed or set aside for a specific purpose may be referred to as *ad hoc*.

> *The council established an AD HOC committee to review textbook standards in face of the sudden complaints from parents.*

ad infinitum *(ad in-fi-NEYE-tum), adjective*
Without end. Literally, "to infinity." The phrase refers to things without end or to something that is limitless. In practical use, *ad infinitum* usually carries a sense of ironic overstatement.

> *Wilbur remarked wryly that he could probably discuss the treatment facility's weaknesses AD INFINITUM.*

ad lib *(ad lib), verb*
An off the cuff, spontaneous remark; also, to make such a remark.

> *I marveled at Erika's ability to AD LIB her way through the meeting, knotting as I did that she hadn't even read the annual report.*

ad nauseam *(AD NAW-zee-um), adverb*
To a sickening degree. This Latin phrase often is invoked when someone goes on and on about something and just doesn't know when to stop.

> *I know Helen loves her dogs, but she can go on about their exploits AD NAUSEAM.*

adage *(AD-ij), noun*
A short proverb or saying. An *adage* is a brief maxim. "A stitch in time saves nine" is an example of an adage.

> *The old man quoted ADAGES endlessly, which the reporter dutifully took doum in his notebook.*

adamant *(AD-uh-munt), adjective*
Unwilling to submit; stubborn and unyielding. Historically, *adamant* refers to a legendary stone of infinite hardness. (The word diamond shares the same root.)

> *Despite the objections of their families, Robin and Tim were ADAMANT about moving away from the town in which they had been raised.*

adapt *(uh-DAPT), verb*
To adjust; to make something or oneself fit in to particular circumstances; to conform. (See, for comparison, the entry for *adopt.*)

> *Jim and Daisy worried that the cross-country move would upset their teenage daughter, but as it turned out Melanie ADAPTED to their new home more easily than her parents.*

addendum *(uh-DEN-duhm), noun*
Something to be added; an addition.

> *The treaty included an ADDENDUM setting out the terms of troop withdrawal.*

addle *(ADD-ull), verb*
Depending on its context, *addle* can mean either "to cause something to spoil" or "to make confused."

> *You're going to ADDLE the milk if you keep forgetting to put it back in the refrigerator!*

adduce *(uh-DUCE), verb*
To cite as an example or justification. To *adduce* is to bring something forward for consideration. To cite an example or put forth a proposition is to *adduce.*

> *I would ADDUCE the following reasons in support of rewriting the club charter.*

adept *(uh-DEPT), adjective*
Proficient; expert; highly skilled. *Adept* refers to someone who is very good at performing a given task.

> *Hans, an ADEPT formulator of crossword puzzles, sometimes seems to me to have memorized the entire dictionary.*

adhere *(ad-HERE), verb*
To hold fast to, usually with a sense of honor or allegiance.

> *Even after his career in advertising forced him to move to New York City, Mason continued to ADHERE to the values of his strict Mormon upbringing.*

adherent *(ad-HERE-unt), noun*
Someone who adheres to an opinion. *Adherent* describes one who is devoted to or strongly associated with a cause or opinion.

> *The measure's ADHERENTS were outspent by its opponents.*

adjudicate *(ad-JOO-di-cate), verb*
To employ judicial procedure as a means of hearing and settling a case. To *adjudicate* is to have a judge or someone in authority reach a decision on some difficult point. It is usually reserved to describe processes of resolution within a legal setting.

> *Gentlemen, if this case is hard for you to argue, rest assured it is equally difficult for me to ADJUDICATE.*

adjunct *(AD-junkt), noun*

An unessential addition; an appendage or complement.

> *Fast cars and designer clothes are only ADJUNCTS to a comfortable lifestyle, Lyle argued, while health insurance is something a family simply can't do without.*

adjure *(ad-JOOR), verb*

To command solemnly as if under oath. To *adjure* is to command or enjoin solemnly, often under the threat of some sort of penalty.

> *The witnesses were ADJURED to avoid any contact with the accused.*

adobe *(uh-DOE-bee), noun*

A type of brick made of clay and straw; the clay used to form such bricks.

> *Our anthropology professor informed us that ADOBE huts are viable only in climates with very little rainfall.*

adopt *(uh-DOPT), verb*

To accept or take as one's own. (See, for comparison, the entry for adapt.)

> *After last year's car troubles, I've ADOPTED the philosophy that a good mechanic is worth every penny you pay him.*

adrenaline *(uh-DREN-uh-lin), noun*

A chemical produced in the body that gives one added strength and energy; epinephrine.

> *Having run up and down the basketball court for nearly and hour, Bob hoped for a burst of ADRENALINE to carry him through to the end of the game.*

adroit *(uh-DROIT), adjective*

Clever, expert, skilled with hands or feet

> *Basil Rathbone was an ADROIT swordsman.*

adulation *(ad-yoo-LAY-shun), noun*

Extreme praise, admiration, or flattery, especially of a servile nature. *Adulation* is generally taken to describe acclaim and admiration that is out of scope with its object.

> *Despite great hardship, upheaval, and death resulting from the violent tactics of the secret police, ADULATION of Stalin continued as though the country was paradise itself.*

adulterate *(a-DUL-ter-ate), verb*

To make impure or tainted. To *adulterate* is to reduce the quality of something— for instance, by substituting inferior ingredients. An unadulterated product is one that retains its original high quality and has not been tampered with in any way.

> *At the turn of the century, the sale of ADULTERATED dairy products in the U.S. caused a major scandal.*

adumbrate *(ADD-um-brate), verb*
To suggest or disclose something partially.
> *The factory workers were nervous when they learned the owner had ADUMBRATED a plan for layoffs.*

adventitious *(add-vin-TISH-us), adjective*
Arising or occurring sporadically or in unusual locations. *Adventitious* has a meaning similar to "accidental."
> *Every time I plant a garden, ADVENTITIOUS wildflowers pop up to ruin my design.*

adverse *(AD-verse), adjective*
Unfavorable; acting in opposition to. Also: tending to discourage. (See, for comparison, the entry for *averse*).
> *Despite ADVERSE circumstances, Jenny and I managed, after a month of looking, to find an apartment we could afford.*

advocate *(ADD-voe-kait), verb*
In its noun form, "advocate" is pronounced differently (ADD-vuh-kitt) and means "one who supports or defends the cause of another." As a verb, "advocate" is the act of pleading in favor of another.
> *If you need a recommendation, I'd be happy to ADVOCATE for you.*

aegis *(EE-jiss), noun*
From the Latin meaning "shield," an *aegis* is a controlling or conditioning influence. Also, control by one individual, group, organization, etc.
> *Tom tried to explain his illegal activity by claiming he was under the AEGIS of a crooked boss.*

aesthetic *(us-THET-ik), adjective*
Of or related to a sense of what is attractive or beautiful. Also: Related to sensation and feeling as contrasted with reason or logic. *Aesthetics* is the science that examines how people react to art and to beauty. Something that is aesthetically pleasing is in keeping with one's standards of scale, structure, clarity, and attractiveness.
> *It is not my place to comment on the AESTHETICS of the car; I am here to report on whether it won the race, which it did.*

affable *(AFF-uh-bul), adjective*
gentle; approachable; friendly.
> *We were all sad to see our old boss leave, but relieved that his replacement seemed like an AFFABLE person.*

A

affect *(uh-FEKT), verb*
To influence; to stir the emotions of; to produce an effect (in something). (See, for comparison, the entry for *effect*.)

> *The memory of my parents' hideous and protracted breakup AFFECTED my life profoundly, and made me vow to work harder at making my own marriage succeed.*

affinity *(uh-FIN-i-tee), noun*
A natural liking or affection for something or someone.

> *The king had an AFFINITY for those on his council who always said he was right.*

affirmative *(uh-FIR-muh-tive), adjective*
Positive in nature; factually valid. *Affirmative* is the opposite of negative; its use means the subject has vouched for and affirmed the correctness of a statement or idea.

> *When asked whether or not he lived at 1267 Main, the defendant answered in the AFFIRMATIVE.*

afflatus, *(uh-FLAY-tuss), noun*
From the Latin meaning "a breathing on," *afflatus* is inspiration that seems to come from divine origin.

> *Beethoven himself often attributed his genius to AFFLATUS, rather than to his own abilities.*

affliction *(uh-FLICK-shun), noun*
Suffering; a state of pain. An *affliction* is a state of miseryor disabling disease.

> *Carl's arthritis was at times quite painful, but he found the most remarkable ways to work around his AFFLICTION.*

aficionado *(uh-fish-ee-uh-NAH-doe), noun*
A devotee, someone who is enthralled with and supports a particular activity. The writer Ernest Hemingway helped to popularize this word of Spanish origin.

> *My dad can't get enough of it, but I've never really been a baseball AFICIONADO.*

agape *(ah-GAH-pay), noun*
In Christianity, divine love for humanity, or human love that transcends customary boundaries. *Agape* is the Greek word for love. Today, it is often used to describe an unselfish love that goes beyond sexuality or other worldly concerns.

> *The nurse's work among the poor and dispossessed seemed rooted, not in a well-meaning and temporary humanitarian instinct, but in a deeper and more profound AGAPE totally unfamiliar to most of us.*

aggiornamento *(uh-joarn-uh-MEN-toe), noun*
This Italian word means modernization, the concern with bringing something up to date.

> *The AGGIORNAMENTO of the 1930s-era office building is taking much longer than expected because of the edifice's antiquated wiring.*

agglomerate *(uh-GLAHM-uh-rate), verb*
To gather items into a ball or cluster.

> *Phil is so lazy he seems to think his job is just to AGGLOMERATE all the pieces of paper in the recycle bin.*

aggrandize *(uh-GRAND-ize), verb*
To raise the importance of or make to appear great. To *aggrandize* is to increase the prestige, influence, reputation, or power of a person or institution.

> *What had started out as a simple report quickly degenerated into meaningless self-promotion; Peter could not resist the urge to AGGRANDIZE himself.*

aggregate *(AG-ruh-git), noun*
As a verb, *aggregate* is pronounced differently (AG-ruh-gait) and means to collect into a whole. As a noun, *aggregate's* most common meaning is "sum total."

> *You've had some rough spots, but your AGGREGATE performance at this company has been first-rate.*

agnosticism *(ag-NOS-ti-sihz-um), noun*
The belief that it is impossible to know whether or not an ultimate cause (that is, God). exists. An *agnostic* is a person who is unable to conclude that there is or is not a God. By contrast, an atheist is a person who has concluded that God does not exist. (The two words are often confused.)

> *Frank, who had been raised in a deeply religious home, knew that it would hurt his parents to speak openly of his AGNOSTICISM.*

agrarian *(uh-GRARE-ee-un), adjective*
Relating to or concerning the land or farming.

> *It amazed the census taker that these farmers, living only a short drive from the big city, could maintain their small AGRARIAN community with so little difficulty.*

ague *(AG-you), noun*
A malarial fever marked by drastic fits of hot and cold sweats.

> *Our expedition down the Nile came to an abrupt halt when our navigator was struck with an attack of AGUE.*

aid *(aid), verb*
To help. (See, for comparison, the entry for *aide*.)
> *Please help our organizations efforts to AID these refugees.*

aide *(aid), noun*
An assistant or trusted helper.
> *She served as the senator's most important AIDE during his term in office.*

akin *(uh-KIN), adjective*
Showing a similar feature or quality. Two things that are comparable or related in some important way are said to be *akin*.
> *I feel that Harry's repeated falsification of his records is much more than a breach of policy: it is AKIN to outright perjury.*

alacrity *(uh-LACK-rih-tee), noun*
Eager, cheerful rapidity or promptness. Someone who is willing to extend themselves politely and quickly for another is said to show *alacrity*.
> *Jane made a special effort to show ALACRITY her first day on the job.*

albatross *(AL-buh-tross), noun*
A significant impediment, handicap, or burden. Also: a large pelican-like bird. The most common idiomatic use of *albatross* is the first sense given above.
> *In Coleridge's poem The Rime of the Ancient Mariner, a sailor shoots a friendly ALBATROSS and is made to wear the bird's carcass around his neck.*

albeit *(all-BE-it), conjunction*
A favorite word of pundits and editorial writers, *albeit* means simply "even though."
> *"I love chocolate," Kate said, "ALBEIT it makes me hyper."*

alchemy *(AL-kuh-mee), noun*
A medieval chemical philosophy in which the goal was to convert base metals into gold; also, any supposedly magical power of transformation or instant creation of wealth.
> *Staring at a printout indicating an 83-percent shortfall in projected income for the first three quarters, the president of the firm remarked bitterly that an ALCHEMY department would do the firm more good than its research and development team had.*

aleatory *(AY-lee-uh-tore-ee), adjective*
Of or by chance. Also, relating to luck . . . especially bad luck.
> *If you're honest with yourself, Bob, you'll have to admit that your current circumstances have more to do with your drinking than with the purely ALEATORY whims of nature.*

alibi *(AL-uh-bye), noun*

A story or circumstance that proves one is innocent of a crime or misdeed; a credible excuse or explanation of innocence.

> *Mike promised Craig he'd provide him with an ALIBI for the night of the bank robbery, but when the police questioned the men they found that the details of their stories didn't match.*

alienate *(AY-lee-uh-nate), verb*

To cause someone to lose affection for someone or something else.

> *If you keep taking advantage of Karen's generosity, you're going to ALIENATE a good friend.*

allay *(uh-LAY), verb*

To calm or help put aside fear or uneasiness.

> *My report will help ALLAY suspicions that our profits have been falling.*

allege *(uh-LEDGE), verb*

To accuse someone of something—usually wrongdoing—without proof.

> *Unless you can prove you didn't eat the last cookie, I will have to ALLEGE that you're the thief!*

allegiance *(uh-LEE-junce), noun*

Loyalty, particularly to a government.

> *Alex had promised his ALLEGIANCE to the family firm time and time again, but the new offer from their overseas competitor, he decided, was too good to turn down.*

allegory *(AL-uh-gore-ee), noun*

A story that seems simple on the surface but that uses symbolism and other techniques to convey a deeper meaning, usually one relevant to major ethical or social issues.

> *Dr. Seuss's Yertle the Turtle, a delightful children's story, is also an ALLEGORY about the dangers of fascism and megalomania.*

alleviate *(uh-LEEV-ee-ate), verb*

To make more bearable; to relieve.

> *The only thing that will ALLEVIATE the fatigue I'm feeling right now is a good night's sleep.*

alliterative *(uh-LIT-er-ah-tive), noun*

using the repetition of initial consonant sounds in language.

> *"Peter Piper picked a peck of pickled peppers" is an ALLITERATIVE tongue-twister.*

allocate *(AL-uh-kait), verb*
To distribute something for a specific purpose or to a specific person or group.
> *When mom ALLOCATES tasks, I'm always the one who has to take out the garbage.*

allude *(uh-LOOD), verb*
To make passing reference to. A person who gives a few details but does not describe an event openly and completely could be said to *allude* to that event. Similarly, someone who makes a brief reference to an incident in a certain novel is considered to have made an *allusion* to the work.
> *I am aware of the incident you are ALLUDING to, Mr. Mayor, but I am afraid you have been misinformed about the events of that night.*

alluring *(uh-LOOR-ing), adjective*
Tempting; possessing the power to entice.
> *Although Kim was following a strict diet, the chocolates were too ALLURING for her to resist.*

ally *(AL-lie), noun*
A confederate or fellow associate in a cause. Also, as a verb: to join with another in a common pursuit.
> *With Jones as my ALLY, I knew the project was more likely to be approved.*

aloof *(uh-LOOF), adjective*
Indifferent or uninterested; unsociable.
> *Chuck's ALOOF attitude at our dinner party made us wonder if our usually talkative friend was trying to tell us something.*

already *(awl-RED-ee), adverb*
Before or at some previously specified time.
> *My mother was ALREADY sitting in her place in church when I walked down the aisle.*

altar *(ALL-tur), noun*
A platform in a church or synagogue. (See, for comparison, the entry for *alter*.)
> *Father Miller stood and addressed us from the ALTAR.*

alter *(ALL-tur), verb*
to cause to change. (See, for comparison, the entry for *altar*.)
> *I could tell that the documents had been ALTERED; they featured two different sets of handwriting in two shades of ink.*

altruism *(aAL-troo-iz-uhm), noun*
Unselfish devotion to the well being of others.

> *Mother Theresa's life was marked by ALTRUISM toward the poor and suffering of the world.*

amalgamate *(uh-MAL-guh-mate), verb*
To blend into a coherent single unit. Originally, an *amalgamation* was the mixture of an alloy or metal with mercury. Today, to *amalgamate* is taken to mean to combine of a number of elements into a whole.

> *The two boards voted to AMALGAMATE the firms as soon as possible.*

amanuensis *(uh-man-you-WHEN-suss), noun*
A secretary, especially one whose principal duties involve copying manuscripts or taking dictation.

> *I didn't spend seven years in college to be an AMANUENSIS to a no-talent hack who calls himself a writer!*

amatory *(AM-uh-tore-ee), adjective*
Having to do with sexual love.

> *Jim hasn't stopped sulking since Helen repelled his AMATORY advances at the office Christmas party.*

ambidextrous *(am-bih-DEK-truss), adjective*
Capable of using both hands with equal skill. *Ambidextrous* is made up of two halves from old Latin words: "ambi," meaning both, and "dexter," meaning right. The idea is that an *ambidextrous* person is able to act as though he has "two right hands."

> *Since the juggler was AMBIDEXTROUS, she could start her routine with a circular motion to either the left or the right.*

ambience *(AWM-bee-awnce), noun*
A feeling or atmosphere associated with a place or individual. The distinctive air patrons may associate with a certain restaurant, for instance, can be a large part of its appeal; this atmospheric "feel" is called *ambience*.

> *The old mansion had the AMBIENCE of an elegant, refined gentleman unaccustomed to being hurried.*

ambiguous *(am-BIG-yoo-uss), adjective*
Unclear in meaning; open to more than one interpretation. (See, for comparison, the entry on *ambivalent*.)

> *The letter from my mother was AMBIGUOUS as to the date of the family reunion, so we will have to call her to get the specifics.*

ambivalent *(am-BIV-uh-lunt), adjective*

Uncertain or undecided. (See, for comparison, the entry on *ambiguous*.)

> *I'm AMBIVALENT as to whether we should invite Ralph to the party; he's a great storyteller, but he sometimes drinks too much.*

amble *(AM-bul), verb*

To walk in an easy or leisurely manner; to saunter or stroll. To *amble* is to go at an unhurried pace. Someone who explores a garden by walking through it slowly and reflectively at a comfortable pace could be said to *amble* through the garden.

> *The day's last customer AMBLED from one end of the shop to the other; no amount of staring from the clerk, it seemed, could make him come to the register.*

ameliorate *(uh-MEEL-yuh-rate), verb*

To improve or upgrade. To *ameliorate* is to make better or put right. When an unacceptable state of affairs is changed for the better, it can be said to have been *ameliorated*.

> *The ambassador's midnight visit was the first step toward AMELIORATING the poor relations between the two countries, and may actually have averted war.*

amenable *(uh-MEH-nuh-bul), adjective*

Agreeable (to an idea); open to suggestion or willing to heed advice. A person who yields to the suggestion or wishes of another is said to be *amenable* to the idea in question. The word carries a sense of tact and manageability rather than submissiveness.

> *We expected stiff opposition to the new benefits package, but once we took the trouble to explain it thoroughly the employees were quite AMENABLE.*

amend *(uh-MEND), verb*

To modify or update. (See, for comparison, the entry on *emend*.)

> *In light of the testimony we've heard tonight, Madame President, I'd like to AMEND my earlier remarks.*

amenity *(un-MEN-ih-tee), noun*

A pleasant manner or custom. Also: A component or feature that gives pleasure or satisfaction. While the primary meaning of *amenity* has to do with the customs of social interaction, its use in advertising and sales settings to mean "a convenient and desirable extra" has gained ground in recent years.

> *Chris's home, which was once spare, now featured all the AMENITIES: a sauna, a plasma TV, and even a new swimming pool in the back.*

amerce *(uh-MERSS), verb*

To punish, especially to punish with a monetary amount set by a court.

> *Barbara always watches her speed since she was AMERCED to the tune of a week's pay.*

amiable *(AY-me-uh-bul), adjective*

Possessing a pleasant, cordial nature. A person who has a happy disposition and is easy to get along with is said to be *amiable.*

> *Jeanne made it a point to speak to everyone at the party; she came across as quite an AMIABLE hostess.*

amicable *(AM-ih-kuh-bull), adjective*

Generally, "amicable" means "characterized by goodwill or peace," but the term is typically used to describe things most people don't consider particularly amicable.

> *The Hudsons' divorce is so AMICABLE that they often go out to dinner together.*

amity *(AM-uh-tee), noun*

Friendship, especially that expressed by two or more nations.

> *For decades, people of all nations have wished for AMITY between Israel and Palestine.*

amnesty *(AM-nuh-stee), noun*

Freedom from imprisonment for large numbers of people, initiated by a government.

> *The prisoners of war waited years for AMNESTY.*

amoral *(ay-MOR-uhl), adjective*

Without moral discretion or standards. To be *amoral* is to act as though the distinctions of right and wrong are nonexistent. A person who is *amoral* is neither moral nor immoral.

> *In the end, we find that war is not always "for the right," nor even "evil," but far too often a completely AMORAL exercise.*

amorous *(AM-er-us), adjective*

Strongly disposed toward love or sexuality. Someone who is *amorous* is preoccupied with thoughts of love, especially sexual love.

> *The young man's AMOROUS attentions merely annoyed Rose.*

amorphous *(uh-MOR-fuss), adjective*

Formless. *Amorphous* refers not only to physical shapelessness, but also to ideas, works of art or literature, and even personalities that are vague or poorly defined.

> *He did not make reasoned arguments in defense of his client, but rather an AMORPHOUS collection of unsupported claims that persuaded no one.*

amortize *(AH-muhr-tize), verb*
To settle a debt by means of installment payments. Also: To write off an asset's
value over a certain period. To *amortize* is to liquidate with periodic payments.
> *The debt will be completely AMORTIZED in two years.*

ampersand *(AM-per-sand), noun*
The symbol "&"; represents the word "and."
> *For the corporate logo she was designing, the graphic artist decided to use an
> AMPERSAND instead of the bulkier word "and."*

anachronism *(uh-NAK-ruh-niz-um), adjective*
The depiction of something as occurring or existing at a point in time it did not.
An *anachronism* is an intentional or unintentional representation of a historically
incorrect situation. A portrait of George Washington holding a pocket calculator
would be an example of an *anachronism.*
> *The author's weak grasp of Greek history is demonstrated by several embarrassing
> ANACHRONISMS in the book's very first chapter.*

anagram *(AN-uh-gram), noun*
A word game in which the letters of one or more words are reassembled to make a
new word or phrase.
> *Frank loves ANAGRAMS. His favorite for "William Shakespeare" is "I'll make a
> wise phrase!"*

analogous *(uh-NAL-uh-gus), adjective*
Similar to such a degree that an analogy may be drawn. An analogy is a similarity
or comparison between two items, ideas, or features; something is *analogous* to
something else when it can be shown to share a significant corresponding element
with it.
> *Historically, the American expansion westward to the Pacific is ANALOGOUS to the
> Russian expansion eastward across Siberia.*

anarchy *(AN-ar-key), noun*
The absence of government; a disordered and uncontrolled situation. Originally,
anarchy referred to a specific doctrine advocating voluntary associations among
individuals and arguing against any empowered government or rule of law. Today,
anarchy is generally used to describe a temporarily chaotic social situation in which
no central authority exists.
> *After the death of the Queen, many in the council feared a return to the ANARCHY
> of a decade earlier.*

anathema *(uh-NATH-eh-muh), noun*

A person or thing regarded as wrong in the highest degree; a loathsome entity. To say something is *anathema* to a person is to say that it is as detestable and unacceptable to him as it can possibly be. The word has its root in a kind of formal religious curse or denunciation.

> *The ambassador warned us ahead of time not to attempt to discuss the issue of dropping sanctions against the dictator; that subject is ANATHEMA to his government.*

ancillary *(AN-se-lare-ree), adjective*

Secondary or subordinate; serving an auxiliary or supportive function. An *ancillary* role is a role that does not "command the spotlight," but that may entail support duties of some importance.

> *He took a great deal of pride in his work, even though the pay was poor and most of his duties were ANCILLARY to those of the regional director.*

andante *(on-DONT-ay), noun and adjective*

Moderately slow tempo.

> *"Goodness, Sarah," exclaimed the music teacher, "it says 'ANDANTE,' but you don't have to play it like a dirge!"*

androgynous *(an-DROJ-ih-nuss), adjective*

Either specifically male nor female; appearing with both male and female characteristics.

> *Amy said her new short haircut was a breeze to maintain compared to the long mane she used to have, but I thought it made her look rather ANDROGYNOUS.*

anecdote *(AN-ik-doht), noun*

A short, interesting story, often amusing and biographical

> *The speaker filled his talk with funny ANECDOTES of his time in the U.S. Navy.*

anemic *(uh-NEE-mik), adjective*

Of or pertaining to a medical condition in which one's blood is deficient in red corpuscles; also, extraordinarily weak.

> *I made a few ANEMIC efforts to get some work done last night, but I couldn't really focus on the job at hand.*

anfractuous *(an-FRACK-chuh-wuss), adjective*

Full of windings and intricacies. This is a good word to describe extremely convoluted mysteries.

> *The ANFRACTUOUS plot of the recent spy movie turned me off so much that I don't intend to see the film's sequel.*

anglicize *(ANG-gli-size), verb*
To render into the forms of English or to make similar to English. To *anglicize* a word or name is to change it in a way that allows it to resemble other English words more closely. Many immigrants to this country anglicized family names (for instance, from Bodini to Bonney).

> *My grandfather came to this country in 1904 under the name of Mikhail Zarensky, which he ANGLICIZED to Michael Zare.*

anglophile *(AYNG-luh-file), noun*
One who is not British but who loves British culture and customs.

> *I know Jess is an Anglophile, but I will have to slaughter her with a bread knife if she makes me sit through one more silly British comedy!*

animadversion *(an-uh-mad-VER-zhun), noun*
Extremely harsh criticism that typically suggests the criticizer disapproves of what is being criticized.

> *The boss's ANIMADVERSIONS led to high staff turnover.*

animosity *(an-ih-MOSS-ih-tee), noun*
Intense hostility toward a person or thing, usually taking the form of action. *Animosity* is a bitter dislike directed at something or someone.

> *Clyde's first few months on the job were fine, but after he was transferred to a new department he came to harbor real ANIMOSITY toward his supervisor.*

animus *(AN-uh-muss), noun*
From the Latin meaning "mind" or "spirit," the word *animus* has two very different meanings. It can refer to a person's basic governing spirit, but it also can refer to prejudiced ill will.

> *Don's ANIMUS is one of calmness and peace since he took up practicing transcendental meditation.*

anneal (UH-neal), *verb*
To strengthen or toughen via difficult situations and experiences.

> *Far from making him despondent, Bill seems ANNEALED since his marriage ended.*

annunciate *(uh-NUN-see-ate), verb*
To proclaim or announce. *Annunciate* is a more formal, sometimes religiously oriented way to express the idea of proclaiming or announcing.

> *The ANNUNCIATION of the Virgin Mary figures importantly in Catholicism.*

anomaly *(uh-NOM-a-lee), noun*
A seemingly abnormal example; a deviation from established form. When
something differs markedly from the expected order of things, it is an *anomaly*.
> *Bill, who was raised in a family of avid golfers, is something of an ANOMALY: he thinks the sport is boring.*

anomie *(an-uh-MEE), noun*
In society, unrest or instability that arises from a collapse in values and systems of
order; for an individual, feelings of alienation, insecurity, and discontent, largely
do to one's loss or confusion over ideals or purpose in life.
> *There were some who speculated that the dismal state of the economy, combined with a general feeling of ANOMIE among citizens, could lead the country to revolution.*

anorexia nervosa *(an-uh-rex-ee-uh nur-VOH-suh), noun*
A disease in which the sufferer has a morbid fear of being obese and loses weight
by means of virtual starvation, refusing to stop even when nearly emaciated.
> *The late Karen Carpenter's was perhaps the most widely publicized case of ANOREXIA NERVOSA.*

antagonist *(an-TAG-uh-nist), noun*
The "bad guy" in a story, novel, film, etc. The character who opposes a story's main
character.
> *As an ANTAGONIST, you can't get any better than John Milton's version of Satan in Paradise Lost.*

antebellum *(an-teh-BELL-uhm), adjective*
Of or pertaining to the period preceding the American Civil War. *Antebellum*
translates from the Latin as "before the war."
> *Nostalgia aside, we should remember that for those held in slavery the ANTEBELLUM period was anything but romantic and chivalrous.*

antecedent *(AN-tih-see-dent), noun*
A trend, idea, fashion, historical event, etc., that came before. Also: An earlier
word to which a pronoun refers. (In the sentence "The car was painted blue,
though it had a huge red rust mark," car is the *antecedent* of it.)
> *Remember, writers: the ANTECEDENT always goes first in the sentence.*

antediluvian *(an-ti-de-LOO-vee-en), adjective*
Pertaining to the period prior to the Great Flood recounted in the Bible.
Figuratively, *antediluvian* has come to mean woefully out-of-date or extremely old-fashioned.

> *Rachel's ideas are outmoded, but those in Paul's report are practically ANTEDILUVIAN.*

anthropomorphic *(an-thro-puh-MORE-fik), adjective*
Attributing human characteristics to animals or other nonhumans.

> *Walt Disney knew that his ANTHROPOMORPHIC creations would be important to the success of his films.*

anticlimactic *(an-tee-klie-MAK-tik), adjective*
A disappointing decline in contrast to a previous rise; an average ending to a series of important events.

> *Mike got down on his knees and produced a small velvet box, only to reveal a tiny pewter thimble bearing a replica of the Golden Gate Bridge—which Elizabeth found ANTICLIMACTIC, to say the least.*

antinomy *(an-TIN-uh-me), noun*
Another word for "paradox," the apparent contradiction between two apparently equally valid ideas, statements, etc.

> *Yes, Sally, I think it's an ANTINOMY to say you hate how expensive that store is when you're always shopping there!*

antipathy *(an-TIP-uh-thee), noun*
A feeling of strong revulsion or dislike. *Antipathy* is a combination of the Greek forms "anti" (against or in opposition to) and "pathos" (having to do with one's feelings and emotions). Therefore, *antipathy* is a feeling of aversion.

> *I'm afraid my ANTIPATHY for light opera won't be changed by a single night out.*

antiquity *(an TI-kwi-tee), noun*
Ancient times, often used in reference to Greek and Roman civilizations.

> *The civilizations of ANTIQUITY have much to teach us today.*

antithesis *(an-TITH-i-sis), noun*
The opposite or highest possible contrast. *Antithesis* refers to the exact opposite of a given thing. *Antithesis* is also the name of a form in rhetoric in which two ideas are contrasted dramatically: "We will live as heroes or die in the attempt."

> *Mr. Brown—haggard, unkempt, and exhausted—looked like the very ANTITHESIS of the charismatic achiever we'd heard about.*

antonym *(AN-tuh-nim), noun*

A word having an opposite meaning to that of another word.

"Rapid" and "slow" are ANTONYMS.

apathy *(APP-uh-thee), noun*

The state of not caring, or seeming not to care, one way or the other how a situation resolves itself.

Because the characters weren't very convincing, their peril made me feel little more than APATHY.

ape *(AYP), verb*

To imitate someone else's characteristics, mannerisms, voice, etc.

Joey got suspended after he APED the teacher's pronounced limp.

apercu *(ap-er-SUE), noun*

From the French meaning "to perceive," an *apercu* is an immediate impression one gets from a person, situation, etc. Also, an *apercu* is a brief outline or synopsis.

The professor's APERCU of James Joyce's Ulysses just left me feeling even more confused.

aperitif *(uh-pair-uh-teef), noun*

An alcoholic beverage consumed before a meal.

The clock struck six o'clock and the guests at the dinner party were served APERITIFS.

aperture *(AP-er-churr), noun*

An opening, either natural or human-made, in something.

The APERTURES in the rock formation formed an exciting pattern of shadows on the desert floor.

apex *(AY-pex), noun*

The highest point.

The APEX of Dawn's career came when her novel was made into a miniseries starring Elizabeth Taylor as the heroine.

aphasia *(uh-FAY-zhuh), noun*

The inability, brought on by brain damage, to understand words and/or ideas.

After his car accident Marcus retained all of his physical faculties, but suffered minor APHASIA that made it difficult for him to speak coherently.

aphorism *(AYF-ur-iz-um), noun*
A short saying that illustrates an important principle or observation. An *aphorism* is a concise summation of opinion or received wisdom, for example: "You never get a second chance to make a first impression."

> *Early American readers found Franklin's Poor Richard's Almanac to be a rich repository of wit, political commentary, forecasts, humor, APHORISMS, and unapologetic gossip.*

aplomb *(uh-PLOM), noun*
A sense of self-possession and calm amidst chaos.

> *The police chief showed remarkable APLOMB amid the noise and confusion of the riot.*

apocalyptic *(uh-pok-uh-LIP-tik), adjective*
Having to do with revelation or prophecy. Also: presaging imminent destruction or disaster. In part because the final book of the Bible, Revelation, outlines prophecies of the end of the world, *apocalypse* has come to suggest a cataclysmic conflict of forces, and *apocalyptic* to reflect a sense of imminent mass destruction.

> *The novel's APOCALYPTIC ending may be appropriate, but it is still heartwrenchingly difficult to read of violence on this large a scale.*

apocryphal *(uh-POK-ri-fuhl), adjective*
Of dubious authenticity. A story that is fabricated long after the fact is considered *apocryphal*. (Similarly, several books of the Bible that are not universally accepted by all Christians form a body of work known as the *Apocrypha*.)

> *The story of Shakespeare's having shared a mistress with Richard Burbage is almost certainly APOCRYPHAL.*

apogee *(AP-uh-gee), noun*
Originally used to describe the distance at which an object circling the Earth is farthest away from the planet, *apogee* has come generally to mean "culmination" or "highest point."

> *"You know, Steve," Alison said, "it's a shame that the APOGEE of your life is being able to belch the entire alphabet."*

apoplectic *(ap-uh-PLECK-tic), adjective*
An "apoplexy" is a stroke, but *apoplectic* often is used to describe an extremely agitated state of rage.

> *Fred's carelessness can make me so APOPLECTIC that I just want to stomp him into jelly.*

aporia *(uh-PORE-ee-uh), noun*
Often associated with philosopher Jacques Derrida and his theory of deconstruction, *aporia* is the jaw-dropping feeling that occasionally overcomes us when we contemplate the world's paradoxes and mysteries.

> *Egg-laying mammals like the platypus fill me with APORIA.*

apostate *(uh-POSS-tate), noun*
One who renounces religious faith or, more generally, one who turns his or her back on previous loyalties.

> *Melinda's new stance on pro-life issues caused her church to label her an APOSTATE.*

apostolic *(ap-uh-STOLL-ic), adjective*
Of or relating to the New Testament apostles or their teachings.

> *The pastor's fiery, anti-American sermons surely would not be considered APOSTOLIC by church fathers.*

apotheosis *(uh-POTH-ee-oh-sis), noun*
A perfect example; the epitome of a person, place, thing, etc. Also, *apotheosis* can mean something or someone elevated to god-like status.

> *No, Bob, I can't agree that death metal is the APOTHEOSIS of rock 'n' roll.*

apparel *(uh-PAIR-ul), noun*
Clothing; something worn.

> *After sweating through class after class in the heavy wool uniform, I wanted to march to the principal's office and demand to know why shorts were considered inappropriate APPAREL for school.*

apparition *(ap-uh-RISH-un), noun*
A ghostly figure; something appearing to be a ghost.

> *The APPARITION waved its spectral hands and emitted a horrible moan.*

appease *(uh-PEEZE), verb*
To placate; to soothe or satisfy.

> *I only wore the dress to APPEASE my mother, who had made pointed comments all week about people who went to weddings dressed like slobs.*

appeasement *(uh-PEEZ-ment), noun*
Sometimes used in a negative sense—especially by political candidates— *appeasement* is an attempt to bring peace between people, groups, nations, etc.

> *Just because the candidate wants to open talks with that rogue nation doesn't make him guilty of APPEASEMENT.*

appellation *(ap-puh-LAY-shun), noun*
Title or name. An *appelation* is the formal name of something.
> *I wish you would stop calling me Doctor; I have never gone by that APPELATION.*

apportion *(uh-POOR-shun), verb*
To divide and distribute something in an equitable manner.
> *I don't think we'll have any trouble APPORTIONING the blame for this problem. There's plenty of blame to go around!*

apposite *(APP-uh-zit), adjective*
Though similar to the word "opposite," *apposite* means something that is relevant, pertinent, or appropriate to a given situation.
> *Your objections are extremely APPOSITE, but I wish you would let me finish describing my plan before you fill it full of holes!*

appraise *(uh-PRAZE), verb*
To estimate (an item's) value. (See, for comparison, the entry for *apprise*.)
> *This desk has been in our family for over a hundred years and I wouldn't dream of selling it—so there's really no use in getting it APPRAISED, is there?*

apprehension *(ap-ri-HEN-sun), noun*
Uneasiness about the future; suspicion of impending bad fortune. Also: The act of arresting or stopping. Another sense of *apprehension* is "idea or understanding."
> *A vague feeling of APPREHENSION came over Gordon as he stepped into the old house.*

apprentice *(uh-PREN-tiss), noun*
One who is learning a trade or art form by assisting a veteran practitioner or professional.
> *Uncle Jake offered to let me work as an APPRENTICE in his plumbing business for the summer, but I had no interest in water pipes.*

apprise *(uh-PRIZE), verb*
To notify; to cause to be aware of. (See, for comparison, the entry for *appraise*.)
> *Have you been APPRISED of the most recent news from home?*

arbitrary *(AR-bih-trer-ee), adjective*
Unregulated by law or reason; determined by impulse. *Arbitrary* refers to decisions made, not according to established procedures or laws, but purely through the discretion of an individual. It carries a sense of capriciousness or even lack of responsibility.
> *The rules you have laid down for this contest are completely ARBITRARY and have no basis in past tournaments.*

approbation *(ap-ruh-BAY-shun), noun*
Official approval or commendation.

> *Tim felt his boss's APPROBATION was even better than a raise since she was usually so hard to please.*

apropos *(ap-ruh-POE) adverb*
Opportunely; as an apt point. The structure is typically *apropos* of . . . , meaning "speaking of . . ." or "with regard to . . ." The word comes from the French for "to the purpose of . . ."

> *APROPOS of our vacation, it occurs to me that we haven't yet selected a hotel in Honolulu.*

aquiline *(ACK-wuh-line), adjective*
Resembling an eagle or curving like an eagle's beak.

> *Neil wasn't sure that it was a compliment when Julie described his features as AQUILINE.*

arbiter *(AR-bi-ter), noun*
A person selected to judge or mediate an issue in dispute. An *arbiter* is the person assigned to power to make a final decision. A person selected to rule definitively on a salary dispute, for example, would be an *arbiter*.

> *It is not my plan to ask an ARBITER to step in; I firmly believe you and I can settle this amicably between ourselves.*

arcadia *(are-KAY-dee-uh), noun (sometimes capitalized)*
This region of ancient Greece has come down through the centuries to refer to any region of rustic pleasure and quiet.

> *As the noise of the city retreated, Ben felt he had entered an ARCADIA of natural wonders.*

arcane *(are-CAIN), adjective*
Known only to a few; secret.

> *It's too bad, thought Yolanda, that my ARCANE knowledge isn't earning me any extra money. Maybe I can get on a game show.*

archaic *(ar-KAY-ik), adjective*
Relating to or resembling something from the past; antiquated.

> *Grandma refused to use our washing machine to clean clothes, insisting instead on her ARCHAIC washboard and bucket.*

archetype *(ARE-ki-tipe), noun*
The original upon which all subsequent versions are based, often used in its adjectival form, *archetypal.*

> *Robert Louis Stevenson's Long John Silver is the ARCHETYPE of the fearsome pirate captain.*

archival (are-KIE-vul)
Of or pertaining to important records or archives.

> *After the lab fire, the scientist was less disturbed by the loss of equipment and samples than by the destruction of the contents of his ARCHIVAL vault, a loss that set his work back at least six months.*

ardent *(AR-dent), adjective*
Intense, passionate, devoted; characterized by high emotion. *Ardent* people show great enthusiasm for causes and people close to them.

> *Barbara, an ARDENT stamp collector, has the most impressive collection of French stamps in the school.*

ardor *(AR-dur), noun*
Intense passion, desire, or emotion.

> *Since childhood, Michelle had studied animals with such ARDOR that her friends and family encouraged her to become a veterinarian.*

arduous *(AR-joo-us), adjective*
Requiring exceptional effort or care. Something is *arduous* if it is mentally or physically challenging, or if it pushes one to the limit of one's abilities.

> *Stacy has been preparing all week for the ARDUOUS marathon competition.*

argosy *(are-guh-SEE), noun*
Originally used to mean a large ship or fleet of ships, *argosy* is more commonly used to denote a rich supply of anything.

> *When the villagers walked into the deceased hermit's home, they found his domicile to be an ARGOSY of discarded bottles, cans, and comic books.*

argot *(are-GO), noun*
This French word denotes "secret" words and idioms used by particular groups.

> *With the advent of text messaging, it has become even more difficult to follow the ARGOT of teenagers.*

aromatic *(air-o-MAT-ik), adjective*

Possessing a pleasant odor. An *aromatic* flower is one that is pleasing to the smell. Many sweet-scented things share a certain chemical structure known as an *aromatic* compound.

> *The herbs lent what would have been an ordinary meal a satisfying AROMATIC touch.*

arrant *(AIR-ant), adjective*

Typically used with a negative connotation, *arrant* means thorough, complete, through-and-through, without qualification, etc.

> *Mindy considers Jack an ARRANT fool because he refuses to respond to her advances.*

arrogate *(AIR-uh-gate), verb*

To demand something for oneself or to take control without authority.

> *The way Nelson ARROGATES office meetings drives his co-workers crazy!*

arson *(AR-son), noun*

The act of destroying property with fire.

> *After Councilor Perry's campaign headquarters burned down, his supporters were quick to accuse their opponents of ARSON; in fact, one of their own neglected cigarette butts was to blame.*

art nouveau *(ART NEW-voh), noun*

From the French meaning "new art," "art nouveau" remains a popular form of design, which originated in the 1880s. It is characterized by wavy objects like flower stems, flowing hair, flames, etc.

> *That museum's collection of ART NOUVEAU jewelry makes it one of the town's best-kept secrets.*

artifice *(ART-ih-fuss), noun*

Sometimes referring simply to anything created naturally or by hand, *artifice* more often refers to trickery or deceit.

> *Tom Sawyer's ARTIFICE, which results in getting others to paint a fence for him, is one of the highlights of Mark Twain's Tom Sawyer.*

ascend *(uh-SEND), verb*

To climb or mount, especially a mountain.

> *Sir Edmund Hillary and Tenzing Norgay were the first to ASCEND Mt. Everest.*

ascertain *(ass-sur-TANE), verb*

To find out something by experimenting or by making inquiries.

> *Arriving to find the house locked and shuttered, I ASCERTAINED from the neighbors that my fiance had loaded up a moving van and fled the day before.*

ascetic *(uh-SET-ik), noun*
A person who chooses a life of constant and strict self-denial, usually as an act of faith. An *ascetic* is someone who foregoes the conveniences of society in order to lead a life of self-discipline and contemplation. *Asceticism* is the body of beliefs and philosophies by which ascetics live their lives.

> *At first Michael had doubts about his religious calling, but he eventually discovered that his tendency toward solitude and introspection were well suited to the life of an ASCETIC.*

ascribe *(uh-SKRYBE), verb*
To attribute or assign causal responsibility to a person or thing. *Ascribing* something to someone is acknowledging their responsibility or creation of it.

> *This work has been ASCRIBED to Rousseau, but his authorship now seems uncertain.*

aseptic *(uh-SEP-tick), adjective*
In addition to meaning "free from germs," *aseptic* describes someone who lacks emotion or vibrancy.

> *Jordan's ASEPTIC performance at the job interview is probably the reason he didn't get the job, despite his qualifications.*

asinine *(ASS-ih-nine), adjective*
Showing a very noticeable lack of intelligence and/or good sense.

> *I left halfway through the latest thriller because I could feel its ASININE plot depleting my brain cells.*

askance *(uh-SKANTS), adverb*
Sometimes used simply to denote the manner of looking obliquely at an object, person, or situation, *askance* often implies judgment or disapproval.

> *I looked ASKANCE at Philip when he left the store without paying for his bubble gum.*

asperity *(a-SPARE-ih-tee), noun*
Carrying with it a multitude of meanings, *asperity* most often refers to a harshness of manner. It also means "hard to endure."

> *The ASPERITY of the swamp's climate makes it unlikely anyone ever will settle there.*

aspersion *(uh-SPUR-zhun), noun*
False accusation; slander. To cast an *aspersion* on another is to make an unfair or untrue statement about his conduct or character.

> *I will not allow you to cast these ASPERSIONS on a man whose career has been so distinguished.*

aspiration *(ass-puh-RAY-shun), noun*
Goal; desire; something one wishes to achieve.

> *Marco, whose ASPIRATION was to be a concert violinist, practiced his instrument at least eight hours a day.*

assay *(UH-say), verb*
To test or examine; to check out.

> *My insurance company would not settle my accident claim until an adjuster had ASSAYED the damage to the car.*

assent *(uh-SENT), noun*
To agree that an opinion, view, or proposal is correct; to concur, corroborate, or acquiesce.

> *You forget, Mr. Jameson, that it is only with the ASSENT of the stockholders that the CEO can be ousted.*

assertion *(uh-SUR-shun), noun*
A positive statement or claim. An *assertion* is something claimed straightforwardly, without support of evidence or logical justification.

> *Your ASSERTION that my car was at the scene of the crime has no basis in fact.*

assiduously *(uh-SID-joo-us-lee), adverb*
Constantly; unceasingly in effort; persistently. Someone who is diligent and persistent is assiduous. Someone who works unremittingly and attentively works assiduously.

> *Karen worked ASSIDUOUSLY to complete her final project, but was still one day late.*

assignation *(as-ig-NAY-shun), noun*
A rather stuffy word for a rather "unstuffy" subject, an *assignation* is a secret meeting between lovers.

> *The ASSIGNATIONS between the countess and the stable boy caused tongues to wag throughout the town.*

assimilate *(uh-SIM-uh-late), verb*
In general, to assimilate is to absorb knowledge, food, etc., but you may hear it in regard to immigrants. In that sense, "assimilate" refers to the act of becoming similar to those already living in one's new environment.

> *You're giving me so much new information that I'm having trouble ASSIMILATING all of it.*

assuage *(uh-SWAJE), verb*

To ease; to make less severe; to mitigate.

> *Gary tried to ASSUAGE his grief at the loss of his lover by taking a long trip to Europe.*

astute *(uh-STUTE), adjective*

Skilled; quick to learn or grasp; shrewd; sharp-witted.

> *Carl was an ASTUTE investor who knew when to follow the crowd and when to ignore it.*

asunder *(uh-SUN-dur), adjective*

Into pieces or parts; separated.

> *The lightning bolt had torn the old hickory tree ASUNDER, and it now lay shattered and twisted in my grandparents' yard.*

atavistic *(at-uh-VIS-tic), adjective*

Having characteristics regressing to a more primitive type; resembling a distant relative.

> *I can't help thinking that when the men all congregate around the barbecue, some ATAVISTIC instinct from the stone age is at work.*

atrophy *(A-truh-phee), verb*

To shrivel or shrink from lack of use.

> *After sitting around on the couch all summer, my leg muscles had ATROPHIED so much that I had trouble walking to the mailbox!*

attenuate *(a-TEN-you-ate), verb*

To spread thin; to cause a decrease in amount, value, power, severity.

> *Jim's strategy was to ATTENUATE the impact of Joan's accusations of harassment by suggesting that she had somehow invited his overtures.*

attrition *(uh-TRISH-un), noun*

The gradual wearing down of something or the gradual reduction of a group. Often, you'll hear this word used in connection with a company that is trying to reduce its workforce.

> *The struggling company used a combination of early-retirement incentives and ATTRITION to reduce its workforce enough to continue to meet its payroll.*

au contraire *(oh kon-TRARE), noun*

On the contrary; the opposite.

> *"AU CONTRAIRE, you pompous fool," cried Jeanne; "I'm not playing hard to get at all, but rather despise you with all my heart!"*

au courant *(oh kuh-RONT), adjective*
Up-to-date; current.

> *Mary Ann prided herself on her ability to stay AU COURANT with the latest trends in fashion.*

au naturel *(oh nat-choo-RELL), adjective*
As is, without embellishment or adornment; also, nude.

> *Karen wanted to crawl under the table when her mother started showing her fiance the family photo album, which featured a number of embarrassing photo of her on the changing table, AU NATUREL.*

au revoir *(oh rih-VWAHR), interjective*
Goodbye; until we meet again.

> *I thought I had bid my last party guest "AU REVOIR," and was about to retire for the night, when I found Philbert passed out in the bathtub.*

audacious *(aw-DAY-shuss), adjective*
Brazen, daring, or fearless. *Audacious* refers to bold, unrestrained, uncompromising behavior. It often carries a sense of bending accepted rules or disregarding prevalent standards.

> *His AUDACIOUS behavior at the family reunion shocked even his brothers and sisters.*

auger *(AW-gur), noun*
A tool for drilling holes. (See, for comparison, the entry for *augur*.)

> *I couldn't use my father's drill because the AUGER was missing.*

augment *(og-MENT), verb*
To make bigger; increase; enhance.

> *The evening's program—a series of soliloquies from Shakespeare—was AUGMENTED by a short reading from Bradley's Notes on Hamlet.*

augmentation *(awg-men-TAY-Shun), noun*
The process of increasing in extent, size, or scope. The broadening, extension, or increase of something is that thing's *augmentation*.

> *He had hoped to bring in enough money with the second job, but even this AUGMENTATION of his income was not enough for him to meet the payments.*

augur *(AW-gur), verb*
To foretell future events, as though by supernatural knowledge or power; to divine; to indicate a future trend or happening.

> *The chairman's sour mood this morning does not AUGUR well for that budget proposal we made.*

aura *(OR-uh), noun*
A field of energy that some believe emanates from human beings.
I'm sure Paul will be a successful politician because he exudes an AURA of trust and dependability.

auspicious *(aws-PISH-us), adjective*
Promising; seemingly favorable or likrly to be accompanied by good fortune.
Auspicious is usually used to describe encouraging signals or reasons for optimism at the beginning of an undertaking.
The trip did not begin AUSPICIOUSLY; our car broke down within an hour.

auspices *(AWS-pis-uz), noun*
Support, encouragement, or patronage. *Auspices* is generally used with "under" To operate under the auspices of an organization is to act with that organization's encouragement or permission.
The emergency food shipments were delivered under the AUSPICES of the United Nations.

austere *(aw-STEER), adjective*
Severe in appearance or nature; self disciplined or strict to a high degree. An *austere* person is self-controlled and somber. That which is without ornamentation or luxury is austere.
The interior of the monastery presented an appearance of AUSTERE beauty.

auteur *(OH-ter), noun*
This French word meaning "author" was adopted in the 1960s by film critics who used it to put forth their theory that directors are the authors of their films. As such, many directors put a recognizable stamp on their movies. Generally speaking, an *auteur* is any artist with a distinctive style.
"Miles is so caught up with being an auteur that he's ruining the production!" Marla complained.

authoritarian *(aw-thor-uh-TARE-ee-un), adjective*
Describes a form of social control in which the government demands the absolute, blind assent of its citizens.
The eerie, AUTHORITARIAN world of George Orwell's 1984 continues to resonate today.

autism *(AW-tiz-um), noun*

A condition in which the sufferer has difficulty with or indifference to social contact, residing almost exclusively in his or her own world.

> *Often subjected to abuse and inhumane treatment two or three decades ago, those suffering from AUTISM are now more likely to receive a meaningful therapeutic regimen.*

autonomous *(aw-TAHN-uh-muss), adjective*

Being in charge of one's own life; independent of other influences; self-governing.

> *Peter had always struggled to remain AUTONOMOUS after leaving home, so it was no surprise to us that he chose to start his own business after graduation.*

auxiliary *(auk-ZIL-yuh-ree), noun*

Backup, reserve, extra.

> *"Don't panic," Mr. Forrest told his anxious staff after the office went black; "the AUXILIARY power will come on any minute now, and we'll be back in business."*

avail *(uh-VAYL), verb*

To be of benefit or use. Someone whose actions are to no *avail* acts in vain.

> *In November, we decided to AVAIL ourselves of the opportunity for a vacation.*

avant-garde *(ahv-ahnt GARD), adjective*

Relating to the latest trends, especially in the world of art; of a new or experimental nature. The term is French for "fore guard", or furthest from the line of battle. The *avant-garde* is the latest, most advanced work in a field, especially in the arts. As a noun, *avant garde* refers to the group doing this work.

> *Milton found keeping pace with AVANT-GARDE work in sculpture both challenging and rewarding for his own work.*

avarice *(AV-er-iss), noun*

Great desire for riches. *Avarice* is extreme greed. Those who hoard wealth compulsively can be said to be *avaricious*.

> *Although Matthew was an extremely successful businessman, AVARICE was certainly not in his nature.*

aver *(uh-VER), verb*

To assert the truthfulness of a statement.

> *I can AVER that your boyfriend is, in fact, a horse's butt.*

averse *(uh-VERCE), verb*

Holding a disinclination. (See, for comparison, the entry for *adverse*.)

> *I'm afraid the problem is not that Tom can't find a field of study he enjoys; it's that he's AVERSE to the idea of doing any work.*

aversion *(uh-VUR-zhun), noun*
Extreme dislike; loathing.

> *My AVERSION to soap operas leaves me with little to discuss at coffee breaks.*

avid *(A-vid), adjective*
Earnest; eager; passionate and committed.

> *Ralphie, an AVID Pittsburgh Steelers fan, owned posters, pennants, hats, socks, jackets, shirts, sweatshirts, and underwear bearing his team's logo and colors, but his wife had drawn the line at a tattoo.*

avocation *(av-uh-KAY-shun), noun*
While a vocation is a job, an *avocation* is a hobby.

> *As long as you treat your profession like an AVOCATION, you will not be successful.*

avoid *(uh-VOID), verb*
To shun; to stay removed from. (See, for comparison, the entry for *evade*.)

> *At all costs, AVOID the Chef's Surprise at Trudy's Whistlestop Cafe.*

avowal *(uh-VOW-uhl), noun*
An open admission or statement. To *avow* is to declare openly, so an *avowal* is an unconcealed declaration or confession.

> *He had run as a Democrat for over thirty years, so his AVOWAL of support for the Republican ticket shocked many supporters.*

axiomatic *(ak-see-uh-MATT-ick), adjective*
Something accepted to be self-evident.

> *"You don't have to tell me that life isn't fair," said Joan to her teenage son. "That's just AXIOMATIC."*

azimuth *(AZ-uh-muth), noun*
The distance in degrees in a clockwise direction from the southernmost point of a body.

> *The AZIMUTH between the main mast and the sea varied as the boat pitched in the waves.*

azure *(AZH-uhr), adjective*
The color of the sky on a clear day; sky-blue.

> *His AZURE eyes and charming manner may attract women initially, but his conceited personality keeps them from staying interested for long.*

doctrinaire
abstemious
levity hubris panacea
veracity cerebellum
labyrinth
criterion
nonagenarian
meticulous zither

B

verbiage quondam
colloquial
WOK palpable paginatio
incipient salutary
evity redact fervent
beleaguered yawnful
elixir beneficent
vamoose pragmatism

babbitt *(BAB-it), noun*
A person who clings to narrow-minded, materialistic ideals of the middle class. Sinclair Lewis' novel *Babbitt* has as its main character a man whose conventional ideals of success and business lead to self-satisfaction and indifference to higher human values.

Jerome may not be the most open-minded businessman, but he's no BABBITT.

babel *(BAB-uhl), noun*
When capitalized, this Hebrew word names the city in which the building of a tower is believed to have been halted due to a sudden inability to communicate. According to the Old Testament, workers suddenly found themselves speaking different languages. In lower-case, *babel* is a scene of noise and confusion.

I can't study in the student lounge anymore. The BABEL just won't allow me to concentrate.

baccalaureate *(bak-uh-LOR-ee-it), noun*
The degree awarded upon completion of an undergraduate course of study. A *baccalaureate*, also called a bachelor's degree, is the degree given to a college graduate. A *baccalaureate* is also a farewell address to a graduating class.

I received my BACCALAUREATE in 2003 from Brandeis University.

bacchanalian *(back-uh-NAIL-yuhn), adjective*
Drunken and carousing.

The fraternity brothers seemed to have an insatiable appetite for BACCHANALIAN revelry.

badinage *(BAD-in-azh), noun*
Witty, playful banter.

As their mutual attraction became clear, the BADINAGE between Mike and Sarah became increasingly suggestive.

bailiwick *(BAY-li-wick), noun*
Originally coined to describe an area controlled by a bailiff, the term *bailiwick* has come to mean any special domain.

I was exasperated by that so-called "customer service agent" because all she would ever say in answer to my queries was, "That's not my BAILIWICK."

balderdash *(BALL-der-dash), noun*
Nonsense; a ridiculous idea or suggestion. To say an idea is *balderdash* is to dismiss it as senseless, idle, or worthless. *Balderdash* is used almost exclusively to describe writing or speech.

He went as far as to suggest the works of Shakespeare had been written by Queen Elizabeth, as if further examination of that BALDERDASH would help his cause.

baleful *(BAIL-ful), adjective*
Ominous; signaling evil to come.

> *It always seemed to me that Mrs. Howard had a BALEFUL gleam in her eye as she passed out her absurdly difficult tests.*

ballistics *(buh-LISS-tiks), noun*
The study of projectiles and impacts.

> *Each of the scientists working on the missile project had extensive experience in BALLISTICS.*

balk *(bock), verb*
To hesitate and refuse to go forward; to prevent from accomplishing an aim; to stop oneself in order to consider whether or not to go on. In baseball: to perform an illegal maneuver in the delivery of a throw from the pitching mound; an instance of such an illegal delivery.

> *At first Mona BALKED at the suggestion that she apply for the position in management; she did not like the idea of working late hours.*

bamboozle *(bam-BOO-zul), verb*
To deceive; trick.

> *Fred was BAMBOOZLED out of $15,000 by a con artist, who convinced him to invest money in nonexistent real estate.*

banal *(buh-NAHL), adjective*
Trite; unoriginal.

> *Aaron always dismissed the insights of the other philosophers as BANAL, but I for one never heard him utter a single profound idea.*

bandy *(BAN-dee), verb*
To exchange or pass back and forth. Trading words or blows is often referred to as *bandying*. To exchange witticisms or insults is to *bandy them* about.

> *The two sides BANDIED threats and accusations for months, but it was clear that neither nation wanted war.*

baneful *(BAYN-ful), adjective*
Extremely harmful, ruinous, or destructive. Bane is anything that spoils or destroys utterly; *baneful,* then, means deadly and likely to cause ruin. The word is often used for dramatic effect and so is likely to describe that which should be considered deadly.

> *His BANEFUL influence on the younger man in the squad was the cause of all the misdeeds we are examining.*

barbarous *(BAR-ber-us), adjective*
Uncivilized or primitive; characterized by brutality or savagery. To say that
something or someone is barbarous is to say that it is crude and lacks refinement.
Barbarous treatment is uncivilized or even cruel and brutal.

> *Their captivity was marked by BARBAROUS living conditions, psychological abuse,
> and little or no news of outside events.*

baritone *(BARE-uh-tone), noun*
The second-deepest voice range on the scale, higher than bass and deeper than
treble.

> *Given his diminutive stature and shy demeanor, few suspected that Craig's powerful
> BARITONE would dominate the choir.*

barometer *(buh-ROM-uh-ter), noun*
An instrument that measures air pressure and aids in weather prediction.

> *After a lesson on meteorology, Mr. Cantelli put a BAROMETER up on the classroom's
> outer wall so that his students could practice predicting the weather.*

baroque *(buh-ROKE), adjective*
This French word refers to art, literature, music, etc. that is excessively, even
grotesquely, ornamental. It's so "over the top" that it can be striking. *Baroque* dates
from the seventeenth century, which gave birth to the form.

> *Paula decided not to buy the house because she feared its BAROQUE ornamentation
> would make it a difficult resell.*

barrage *(buh-ROZH), noun*
Concentrated outpouring or volley. A *barrage* is an overwhelming torrent of
something, usually words, blows, or projectiles. The word was originally used only
in a military sense.

> *The defense attorney subjected the witness to a BARRAGE of questions about the
> events of that night.*

basal *(BAY-suhl), adjective*
Fundamental and basic.

> *"The BASAL issue here," Donny said, "is what is right versus what is wrong!"*

basilica *(buh-SILL-ih-kuh), noun*
An oblong building used as a Christian church, especially one built in medieval
Italy with strong horizontal accents and little attempt at rhythmic internal design;
a building reminiscent of such a structure.

> *The highlight of our visit to Rome was our visit to St. Peter's BASILICA.*

bastion *(BASS-chun), noun*

A stronghold or bulwark for protection.

> *Because he is so shy, Peter uses his genius-level intellect as a BASTION to keep others at arm's length.*

bathos *(BATH-oss), noun*

Something excessively trivial, sentimental, or melodramatic; also, a ludicrous change from the high-minded to the commonplace.

> *The play's BATHOS made it hard for me to take it seriously, but June thought it was the most moving drama she had ever seen.*

bazaar *(buh-ZAR), noun*

A marketplace, especially one in the open air.

> *As Ned and I ambled through the BAZAARS of Casablanca, we kept an eye out for enemy agents.*

beatific *(bee-uh-TIFF-ic), adjective*

Having a saintly or angelic character or demeanor.

> *Charlie's BEATIFIC smile always makes me wonder what he's thinking about.*

beatitude *(bee-AT-it-tood), noun*

Highest possible blessedness or contentment. Also: Any of the declarations ("Blessed are . . .") made by Jesus in the biblical account of his Sermon on the Mount (usually capitalized). *Beatitude* comes from the Latin for "perfect happiness."

> *His translation of Christ's BEATITUDES cast new light on the familiar declarations.*

bedlam *(BED-lum), noun*

The popular name for London's Hospital of St. Mary of Bethlehem was "Bedlam." Since the hospital catered to the insane, *bedlam* has come to denote any place or scene of uproar and confusion.

> *I always do my best to stay focused on my work and to avoid the BEDLAM around the water cooler.*

bedraggled *(bee-DRAG-eld), adjective*

Harried or in a condition of disarray; unkempt; dirty and limp. A person who has just walked a long way through mud ana rain could be said to be *bedraggled*.

> *A group of BEDRAGGLED orphans stood outside begging by the flickering gaslight.*

befuddle *(bee-FUD-il), verb*

To confuse or perplex. To *befuddle* is to mystify or confuse, as with bewildering arguments or misleading statements.

> *His vague account of strange doings in the woods succeeded in BEFUDDLING the policemen, and probably saved him a traffic ticket.*

behemoth *(bih-HE-muth), adjective*
This Hebrew word appears in the Old Testament's Book of Job and refers to a large animal most biblical scholars believe was a hippopotamus. At present, "behemoth" describes anything that has monstrous size or power.

> *What the heck's wrong with Joe? Why did he buy that gas-guzzling BEHEMOUTH?*

belabor *(bih-LAY-burr), verb*
To go over and over a position excessively, even to the point of absurdity. Also, *belabor* can mean "to attack verbally."

> *As usual, you're making a jerk of yourself by BELABORING your point long after I've agreed with you.*

belated *(bee-LAY-ted), adjective*
Late or tardy; delayed. *Belated* refers to anything past due.

> *Jane sent a BELATED birthday card, but still felt guilty about forgetting her mother's birthday.*

beleaguered *(bee-LEEG-erd), adjective*
Embattled; constantly confronted with obstacles. To *beleaguer* is, literally, to beseige or surround with an army for the purpose of harrassment. When we say someone is *beleaguered*, we mean that he is beset with many troubles.

> *The BELEAGUERED financier even considered bankruptcy, but vowed to fight on.*

belie *(bee-LYE) verb*
To disprove or demonstrate to be false; to contradict appearances. To say something *belies* something else is to say that it gives evidence of a contrary state of affairs.

> *His unsteady walk and slurred speech BELIED his insistence of having consumed no alcohol at the party.*

belligerent *(buh-LIJ-er-ent), adjective*
Aggresive or pugnacious; eager to instigate a fight. *Belligerent* is rooted in the Latin word for "war."

> *Don became overbearing and BELLIGERENT with his employees after his divorce, causing many of them to resign.*

bellwether *(BELL-weh-THer), noun*
A leader, or something that indicates future developments. This term often is used in business, to discuss business trends.

> *We may have to change our plans. I'm afraid those dark clouds are a BELLWETHER of today's weather shifts.*

bemoan *(bih-MOAN), verb*

To regret passionately or to complain about an ill turn of events.

> *Joel could not stop BEMOANING the fact that he was only three numbers off of the Powerball jackpot.*

bemused *(bee-MYOOZD), adjective*

The quality of being bewildered, perplexed, or lost in reflection. A person who is preoccupied or confused by something is *bemused.*

> *Victor stared BEMUSED at the photograph of his father in full military dress—a man he had never thought of in quite that way.*

benchmark *(BENCH-mark), noun*

A standard by which to measure; the exemplary performance or criterion.

> *Anne's stunning oration on human rights was recognized in our debating society as the BENCHMARK performance for years afterward.*

benediction *(ben-i-DIK-shun), noun*

A formal blessing, an expression of good wishes. The most common sense of *benediction* has to do with the invocation of God's blessing at the end of a church service, but the word can also mean the expression of goodwill from one person to another.

> *As the priest pronounced the BENEDICTION, Julia looked around the pew for her coat but could not find it.*

beneficent *(buh-NEFF-uh-cent), adjective*

Related to performing acts of kindness and charity. *Beneficent* also can describe fortunate events.

> *The monsignor's quiet, BENEFICENT works have made him one of the most respected church leaders in the region.*

benevolent *(be-NEV-i-lent), adjective*

Marked by a tendency to do well toward others; kindly. A *benevolent* act is one in service to another. The word is derived from the Latin for "good wishes."

> *There is a BENEVOLENT side to Mark one would not expect to see in a man so apparently cold.*

benighted *(bee-NYT-ed), adjective*

Ignorant or unenlightened. Also: Lost in night or darkness. A person in intellectual or moral darkness is said to be *benighted.* A culture or time that is considered primitive or crude can also be said to be *benighted.*

> *It was a BENIGHTED era of superstition and folly, yet its problems were not all that different from ours.*

bequeath (*bee-QUEETH*), *verb*

Bestow by means of a will. *Bequeath* is often used metaphorically to describe something handed down to a group of people from those of a past era.

> *More than anything else, it is the language we speak, BEQUEATHED to us by Byron and Shakespeare and a legion of others, that binds us to the English and them to us.*

bereaved (bih-REEVD), *adjective or noun*

In a state of mourning; deeply sorrowful because of the loss of a loved one. As a noun, *bereaved* refers to the person in mourning (and is usually preceded by "the").

> *The most difficult part of Father Maurice's job was providing solace for the BEREAVED in his parish.*

beseech *(bih-SEECH), verb*

To entreat, implore, or request earnestly. *Beseech* is a formal verb used to request something. In contemporary use, it reflects either great (or even fawning) politeness or urgency of the highest order.

> *We BESEECH you, Mr. Prime Minister: think twice before committing the lives of so many of our countrymen to this cause.*

besiege *(bih-SEEJ), verb*

To submit a person to insistent demands from all sides; to crowd around; to harass.

> *Everywhere he went, the movie idol was BESIEGED by crazed fans looking for autographs and even pieces of his hair or clothing.*

besotted *(bih-SOTT-ed), adjective*

To besot is to make stupid or dull, especially due to drink. But the most common use of this word is its adjective form, which describes someone who is drunk. Also, *besotted* can describe anyone who has been made foolish by anything, such as love, money, a drive for power, etc.

> *I can't hang out with Will anymore because he's so ridiculously BESOTTED with Anna.*

bestial *(BESS-chul), adjective*

Of, pertaining to, or reminiscent of beasts. Something is *bestial* if it exhibits savagery or brutality.

> *The colonel's BESTIAL treatment of the prisoners of war was in violation of the Geneva Convention.*

bestow *(bih-STOW), verb*

To confer or give. One *bestows* an award, honor, or degree. The verb is usually followed by *on* or *upon*.

> *Though he lacked formal education, several universities had BESTOWED honorary degrees on Mr. Goldfarb.*

bête noire *(bett NWAHR), noun*

Something one does not like or finds fearful. *Bête noire* is French for "black beast."

Jean got A's in all subjects except geometry, her longtime BÊTE NOIRE.

betrothed *(bih-TROTHED), verb*

Engaged to be married. Also, as a noun: the person to whom one is engaged.

Marcia is BETROTHED to that handsome young captain she met in Miami.

bewail *(bih-WAIL), verb*

To express deep sorrow or regret over something, usually by weeping.

After his marriage ended, Chuck spent months BEWAILING his fate.

biased *(BYE-ussed), adjective*

Predisposed to a particular view or direction; prejudiced.

Mr. Anderson's claim that he has never made a BIASED hiring decision is undercut by the fact that his staff is composed exclusively of white male Ivy League graduates.

bibelot *(BEE-buh-low), noun*

A beautiful trinket.

The rest of the family dismissed the contents of Grandma's jewelry box as junk, but I found a few BIBELOTS.

bibulous *(BIB-yuh-luss), adjective*

Ah, a fancy word for one of humankind's favorite activities: drinking! *Bibulous* is related to drinking or to drunkenness.

You may think you're "fine," but your BIBULOUS activities will put you in the poorhouse or in jail one of these days!

biennial *(bye-EN-ee-yul), adjective*

Happening every second year.

Ms. Webster argues that the summer Olympics, which now occur every four years, should become a BIENNIAL event.

bifurcate *(BI-fur-kait), verb*

To divide one thing into two.

The group seemed unified at first, but it soon BIFURCATED into two very disagreeable factions.

bigamy *(BIG-uh-mee), noun*

The crime of taking marriage vows while still legally married to someone else. *Bigamy* is an offense involving illicit marriage, but it also describes other ecclesiastical violations of religious law regarding marital status.

By marrying June before her divorce was finalized, Stanley was technically guilty of BIGAMY.

bilateral *(bye-LAT-er-uhl), adjective*
Involving or pertaining to both sides of something. A *bilateral* agreement is one that affects and is binding upon both parties.

> *It is useless to try to settle such issues in our legislature; only a BILATERAL trade agreement will resolve our disputes with that nation.*

bildungsroman *(BILL-dungs-roh-man), noun*
Impress your friends with this German word for a coming-of-age novel, such as *The Catcher in the Rye* or *Bastard Out of Carolina.*

> *I enjoyed Professor Graham's class, but I wish he hadn't limited us to studies of BILDUNGSROMANS.*

bilge *(bilj), noun*
The lowest portion of a ship's hull.

> *The sailors ventured to the bowels of the ship to find that the BILGE had sprung a leak.*

bilious *(BILL-yes), adjective*
This word relates to bile, a bitter substance that helps in digestion. Thus, *bilious* has come to describe people who are irritable or peevish, as though afflicted by severe indigestion.

> *Benny's BILIOUS behavior does not endear him to strangers.*

bilk *(bilk), verb*
To swindle or cheat. Someone who defrauds a person or institution of funds or goods *bilks* the victim.

> *The accountant, investigators learned, had been BILKING the company of nearly a quarter of a million dollars a year.*

billet-doux *(bill-ay-DOO), noun*
A love letter. (Plural: *billets-doux.*)

> *The young couple exchanged BILLETS-DOUX almost every day the summer they were apart.*

binary *(BYE-nair-ee), adjective*
Constructed of two elements; of or pertaining to two. A *binary* number system is one with two digits; zero and one.

> *The decimal number 2 would be written as 10 in BINARY notation, since one times two to the first power plus zero times two to the zero power equals two.*

biogenesis *(bye-oh-JEN-ih-siss), noun*
The process of life arising from other living things. *Biogenesis,* a scientific word, was coined by T.H. Huxley in 1870.

> *BIOGENESIS involves an unending regenerative cycle of life and death.*

biopic *(BI-opp-ick OR BI-oh-pick), noun*
People disagree how this word, short for "biographical motion picture," should be pronounced. No matter how you say the word, a *biopic* is a film based on the lives of real, rather than fictional, people.

I was really impressed with the latest BIOPIC until I found out that much of the film's storyline was factually inaccurate.

biopsy *(BIE-op-see), noun*
An instance of taking samples of tissue, cells, or fluids from a living body and analyzing these samples.

Dr. Smith thought the lump was probably a benign cyst, not a tumor, but he scheduled a BIOPSY just to be sure.

bipolar *(bye-POE-luhr), adjective*
Possessing two sides or poles; marked by diametrically opposed extremes. A *bipolar* relationship is one between two opposites or counterparts.

Frank's behavior on the job was generally unremarkable, but we later learned that his severe mood swings were symptoms of a BIPOLAR personality disorder.

bisque *(bisk), noun*
A thick and creamy soup made from meat, fish, or shellfish.

Mom didn't care what else was on the menu, as long as the restaurant offered lobster BISQUE.

bizarre *(bih-ZAR), adjective*
Strange; incomprehensible; deviating from what is expected or in the rational order of things. (See, for comparison, the entry for *bazaar*.)

As the drug began to take effect, Bill began to make BIZARRE remarks about large insects and dancing toasters.

blacklist *(BLAK-list), verb*
To place on a list of disapproved or rejected persons and organizations.

Many prominent entertainment figures were BLACKLISTED in Hollywood for alleged ties with Communism.

blandish *(BLAN-dish), verb*
To coax someone to do something for you through the use of flattery. You might also hear the noun form of this word, which is *blandishment.*

Your attempts to BLANDISH me into giving in to your point of view will not work.

blasé *(blah-ZAY), adjective*

Unimpressed; bored. Someone who has seen too much of something to become excited about it can be said to be *blasé*.

> *I told Jim that he stood a very good chance of being fired this week, but to tell you the truth he seemed rather BLASÉ about the whole thing.*

blather *(BLATH-er), verb*

To gabble or talk ridiculously. Someone who *blathers* is prone to talk nonsense or discuss meaningless issues for extended periods.

> *We tried to leave the party, but Mark insisted on BLATHERING endlessly to the hostess about his new car.*

blazon *(BLAY-zuhn), verb*

A *blazon* is a coat of arms, which proclaims one's family's illustrious pedigree. Thus, to *blazon* is to proclaim something widely.

> *When the president died unexpectedly, the news was quickly BLAZONED by every media outlet.*

blithe *(blithe), adjective*

Cheerful or merry in disposition; carefree or indifferent. A person who is *blithe* is unconcerned with petty cares or problems.

> *Rod dismissed the accountant's objections with a BLITHE wave of the hand.*

bloc *(BLOK), noun*

A group of persons or nations with various political beliefs united for a common cause.

> *Former Eastern BLOC countries include Poland and Hungary.*

bloviate *(BLOW-vee-ate), verb*

A blowhard *bloviates* because the word means to speak pompously and at great length.

> *Don't get Doug near alcohol because once he's had a few he'll BLOVIATE until the cows come home.*

bludgeon *(BLUD-jun), verb and noun*

To beat. As a noun, a bludgeon is a short, heavy stick. To *bludgeon* someone is to beat or strike him with a similar instrument.

> *The detectives concluded that the victim had been BLUDGEONED repeatedly with a metal pipe.*

bluejacket *(BLOO-jak-eht), noun*

A person enlisted in the United States or British Navy.

> *Because San Diego is a big Navy town, many of its nightclubs cater to BLUEJACKETS and attract few civilians.*

bluster *(BLUS-ter), verb*
To threaten swaggeringly or issue extravagant threats. *Bluster* is related to the same old word from which blow (as in "the wind blows") is derived.
> *He seems fierce at first, but you must remember that he depends largely on BLUSTERING to get his way.*

bogey *(BOE-gie), verb and noun*
In golf, to post a score of one stroke over par on a hole; an instance of such a score.
> *Jeff BOGEYED on the fourteenth hole.*

bogus *(BOE-guss), adjective*
Fake; counterfeit.
> *Earnest-looking teens with obviously BOGUS IDs were nothing new to the area's liquor store owners; a six-year-old with a revolver demanding two quarts of Thunderbird was something else again.*

bohemian *(bo-HEE-mee-un), adjective*
Unconventional; reminiscent of a lifestyle free of the restraints and concerns of mainstream society. To say someone is *bohemian* is to say he is a free thinker and lives without much concern for the inhibitions associated with the workaday world.
> *Jane loved Carl, but was unprepared to share in his BOHEMIAN way of life.*

boisterous *(BOY-struhss), adjective*
Characterized by being very noisy and out of control.
> *The bar's BOISTEROUS crowd made it difficult to carry on a conversation.*

bolster *(BOWL-ster), verb*
To strengthen, support, or prop up.
> *Since Rhonda is a news junkie, she's always able to BOLSTER with facts her opinions about world events.*

bombarded *(bom-BARD-ud), verb*
Under attack; also, peppered with queries, problems, accusations, etc.
> *During the final class before the midterm exam, Professor Strang was BOMBARDED with questions from her panicky students.*

bombast *(BOM-bast), noun*
Haughty, overblown or pompous talk or writing. Someone who engages in *bombast* indulges a taste for an exaggerated rhetorical style.
> *We expected a compelling argument from our attorney, but he came to court offering little more than BOMBAST.*

bon mot *(bon moe), noun*

A clever or witty comment.

> *The secretary of state's well-timed BON MOT about the shortcomings of American beer helped to put everyone at ease at a tense moment of the summit meeting.*

bon vivant *(bon vih-VAHNT), noun*

A person who enjoys living well.

> *In Paris with her rich aunt, Janice lived the life of a BON VIVANT, shopping and dining out to her heart's content.*

bonhomie *(bohn-uh-MEE), noun*

A pleasant disposition.

> *Bill's attempts at BONHOMIE were usually futile, limited to a curt and forced "hello" for each staff member as the day began.*

boondoggle *(BOON-dahg-uhl), noun*

Useless activity designed to make one look busy.

> *In an effort to appear efficient, Sally filed and re-filed paperwork, but her boss caught on to her BOONDOGGLE.*

boorish *(BOO-rish), adjective*

Offensive; lacking manners, civility, or consideration. A *boorish* person is one completely unfamiliar with social graces.

> *Everett's BOORISH behavior at the party was completely out of character for him.*

born *(born), verb*

Carried to term in childbirth; given birth. (See, for comparison, the entry for *borne*.)

> *My son David was BORN at about four in the afternoon.*

borne *(born), verb*

Supported; carried; brought forth or produced.

> *"BORNE" is the past participle of the verb "to bear" in all senses that do not involve childbirth.*

bosky *(BOS-kee), adjective*

thick with underbrush; wooded.

> *Straying from the marked trail, the hikers soon found themselves lost in the BOSKY, uncharted wilderness.*

botanical *(buh-TAN-ih-kull), adjective*

Of or pertaining to plant life. A *botanical* garden is one that features a wide variety of plant life. The word comes from the Greek botanikos, meaning "herb."

> *Martin's BOTANICAL survey of rainforest plants required a series of trips to Borneo.*

bough *(bow), noun*
A branch of a tree. (See, for comparison, the entry for *bow.*)
> *The BOUGHS of the apple tree hung heavy with fruit.*

bouillabaisse *(BOO-yuh-base), noun*
A stew made from various kinds of fish, usually shellfish.
> *After Uncle Charlie helped us clean the fish and clams we'd caught, Aunt Pattie showed us how to make her famous BOUILLABAISSE.*

bourgeois *(BOO-zhwah), adjective or noun*
In its noun form, this French word was adopted by Karl Marx to describe members of the middle class who want to maintain the status quo. In both is adjective and noun form, *bourgeois* denotes a member of the middle class, and it often is used negatively.
> *Dave is so BOURGEOIS he goes to a liquor store across town so his neighbors won't know he drinks.*

bout *(BOWT), noun*
A contest or fight. Also, something that lasts a short time.
> *I quickly got over that BOUT of fever I picked up during my cruise.*

bovine *(BO-vine), noun*
Of or resembling a cow or ox; dull.
> *The hardest part of teaching high school for me has been getting used to the look of BOVINE submissiveness on most of my students' faces.*

bow *(bow), verb*
To bend low; to yield. (See, for comparison, the entry for *bough.*)
> *The Japanese ambassador BOWED in the direction of the prime minister.*

bowdlerize *(BOWD-lur-ize), verb*
To cleanse or modify a work of literature (or art) by removing parts considered offensive or otherwise altering content and style.
> *Producers of Gone with the Wind refused to BOWDLERIZE Margaret Mitchell's famous line, "Frankly, my dear, I don't give a damn."*

braggadocio *(brag-uh-DOCE-ee-oo), noun*
Bragging or meaningless boasting. *Braggadocio* can refer both to actual boasting or to a person who engages in it.
> *It appears that the dire warnings we received some weeks back were nothing more than BRAGGADOCIO.*

brake *(brake), verb*

To control or stop. (See, for comparison, the entry for *break.*)

The car's BRAKING ability was truly remarkable; it felt as though I could stop on a dime.

brandish *(BRAN-dish), verb*

To fluorish or shake menacingly or ostentatiously. Something can be *brandished* either out of defiance, as a warning of potential future harm, or out of pride, as a sign of status.

He BRANDISHED a revolver; the room suddenly fell silent.

brash *(brash), adjective*

Impudent; hasty. Something done impetuously and quickly is *brash*. *Brash* can also refer to a certain zesty or irreverent quality that may be seen as refreshing.

The action you have taken is brash; you will regret your recklessness.

brassy *(BRASS-ee), adjective*

Brazen; cheap or showy. *Brassy* can also refer to a bold, outgoing nature.

The promotional campaign struck a BRASSY, daring tone that instantly won consumer attention.

bravado *(bruh-VA-do), noun*

An open show of bravery. That which is characterized by a display of boldness shows *bravado*.

The mayor's swaggering attitude of BRAVADO was of little help when the town was finally attacked.

bravura *(bruh-VOOR-uh), adjective and noun*

An amazing or daring display of style, technique, or expertise; also, as a noun, a particularly difficult and showy passage in a piece of music requiring both technical proficiency and great energy on the part of the performer.

Ron Liebman's portrayal of attorney Roy Cohn was a BRAVURA performance, the kind that makes critics sit back in awe.

brazen *(BRAY-zun), adjective*

Bold or shameless in display; unconcerned with the reactions of others.

None of us understood how Julia and Ted, each of whom is married, could have been so BRAZEN about their romance.

brazier *(BRAY-zhur), noun*

A metal container for holding burning coals.

Sitting side by side in the cozy farm kitchen, we sipped hot cider and toasted muffins over the BRAZIER.

breadth *(bredth), noun*

The side-to-side extent of something; width; expanse. (See, for comparison, the entry for *breath*.)

The alley was so narrow that my car had a clearance of perhaps two inches beyond its BREADTH on either side.

breath *(breth), noun*

The process or act of breathing; an inhalation or exhalation. (See, for comparison, the entry for *breadth*.)

Take a deep BREATH; I'm about to give you some bad news.

brevity *(BREV-ih-tee), noun*

Shortness. Someone who writes with *brevity* writes in a way that is terse and to the point.

Paine's argument was stated with such BREVITY and passion that within one short month of its publication it seemed every colonist was in favor or independence from Britain.

brigand *(BRIG-und), noun*

One who lives as a bandit, plundering riches.

The BRIGANDS held up the stagecoach and terrified the passengers.

broach *(broach), verb*

To bring up or put forth as a topic for discussion.

The evening with Dan was pleasant enough, probably because none of us had the courage to BROACH the subject of his impending indictment.

brogue *(BROAG), noun*

An Irish accent in spoken English.

Although Mrs. O'Leary left Ireland when she was a young girl you can still detect a slight BROGUE in her speech.

bromidic *(bro-MID-ick), adjective*

Trite and commonplace.

The marketing executive groaned as one BROMIDIC ad campaign after another crossed her desk.

brooch *(broach or brooch), noun*

An ornamental pin, usually large.

Christmas just wouldn't be Christmas without Aunt Gertrude in her green-flowered dress and ruby BROOCH.

B

brouhaha *(BROO-ha-ha), noun*

An event that involves or invokes excitement, turmoil, or conflict.

> *The BROUHAHA in the hotel lobby was the result of a rock star making his way from his limousine to the elevator.*

brummagem *(BRUHM-uh-juhm), noun or adjective*

Describes something that looks great but performs poorly, or *brummagem* can be used as the name for such a thing.

> *I would have been better off getting an old heap with a good engine than buying this snazzy-looking BRUMMAGEM.*

brunt *(brunt), noun*

The primary impact of a blow. The *brunt* of an attack is the point of its main force.

> *If there is a war, rest assured that it is our country that will be asked to bear the BRUNT of it.*

brusque *(brush), adjective*

Short; abrupt or curt in manner. A person who discusses things impatiently or with shortness is said to be *brusque*.

> *Her BRUSQUE exterior put Tom off at first, but he later discussed many imprtant issues with Ann in depth.*

bucolic *(byoo-KOL-ik), adjective*

Pastoral; rural or rustic in nature.

> *Deana's farm, with its blooming apple trees and peaceful brooks, was just the kind of BUCOLIC scene we had been hoping to photograph for our article.*

buffalo *(BUFF-uh-low), verb*

When used as a verb, this familiar animal means to baffle thoroughly.

> *I was completely BUFFALOED by Karen's angry response to my courteous greeting.*

bugaboo *(BUG-uh-boo), noun*

An object of fear. Something that causes worry or dismay is a *bugaboo*.

> *I hope you're not going to be swayed by the old BUGABOO that changing a package design is a sure way to kill a product.*

bulbous *(BULL-buss), adjective*

Shaped like a bulb, or bloated.

> *One look at my BULBOUS shape in the three-way mirror convinced me to join a gym right away.*

bulimia *(buh-LEE-mee-uh), noun*
An eating disorder in which sufferers alternately binge, then purge, forcing
themselves to vomit.

> *The faculty health center featured a nurse with special training in dealing with
> BULIMIA and other eating disorders.*

bull *(BULL), noun and verb*
In addition to the animal, this word has a number of meanings. As a noun, a
"bull" is someone who buys stocks expecting a price rise. It also denotes a formal
proclamation by the Pope. As an adjective, "bull" means to act with force or to
engage in idle, boastful talk.

> *The bouncer BULLED his way through the crowd to remove the man who was
> causing a disturbance.*

bulwark *(BULL-wurk), noun*
A wall made of earthen materials built as a defense mechanism; any extensive
protective measure taken against external danger.

> *The money set aside in the emergency fund was regarded as a BULWARK against
> future disasters, to ensure that we would be prepared the next time.*

bumptious *(BUMP-shuss), adjective*
Overbearing or crudely assertive. Someone who is *bumptious* is overly pushy or
impertinent.

> *We had difficulty crossing the border because Nan got into a squabble with a
> BUMPTIOUS border guard.*

bureaucracy *(byoo-ROK-ruh-see), noun*
The concentration of power and authority in administrative bodies. Also: an
administrative body. *Bureaucracy* is often characterized by adherence to routine
and lack of innovation.

> *As the company grew, the entrenched BUREAUCRACIES in the accounting and
> finance departments gained more and more influence.*

burgeon *(BURR-jin), verb*
To sprout, to grow, to blossom and flourish.

> *The BURGEONING "green" movement may change the way people live their
> everyday lives.*

burlesque *(burr-LESK), adjective*

This French word concerns literary works or plays that mock conventions by grotesquely caricaturing them.

> *The play was intentionally BURLESQUE because the dramatist was trying to point out the absurdity of racial hatred.*

burqa *(BURR-kuh), noun*

A completely enveloping outer garment worn by women in some Islamic traditions.

> *Even though she is becoming thoroughly Americanized, Ameena continues faithfully to wear her BURQA.*

burnish *(BURR-nish), verb*

To make shiny or lustrous due to rubbing or polishing.

> *Every day, Sam lovingly BURNISHES his Lexus's custom purple paint job.*

burnout *(BURN-out), noun*

A condition of fatigue, low morale, or frustration resulting from excessive stress or overwork.

> *Although Leland's family feared he would suffer BURNOUT if he continued to work fourteen hours a day, seven days a week, he seemed to be happier than anyone could remember seeing him.*

bursar *(BUR-ser), noun*

The treasurer of a college.

> *At the beginning of each semester the students receiving financial aid would line up outside the BURSAR's office to sign their student loan papers.*

butte *(BYOOT), noun*

A solitary hill on a large plain.

> *The mission was situated atop a lonely-looking BUTTE outside of town.*

bygone *(BYE-gone), adjective and noun*

Something gone by. A *bygone* occurrence is one that took place in the past. Used as a noun, a *bygone* refers to an event that took place long enough ago to be seen in the proper perspective, as in the phrase "Let *bygones* be *bygones*."

> *The inn calls to mind a BYGONE era of Southern hospitality.*

Byzantine *(BIZ-un-teen), noun*

Of or referring to the ornate, detailed architectural style developed in Byzantium during the fifth century a.d.; also, devious; also, exceptionally complex or minutely laid out.

> *The company's BYZANTINE organizational scheme sometimes left newcomers feeling that they reported to everyone in general and no one in particular.*

doctrinaire
abstemious
levity hubris panacea
veracity cerebellum
labyrinth
criterion
nonagenarian
meticulous zither

C

erbiage
quondam
colloquial
vok palpable pagination
incipient salutary
evity redact fervent
beleaguered yawnful
elixir beneficent
amoose pragmatism

cabal *(kuh-BALL), noun*
A group that meets secretly and plots to overthrow a government, religion, community, etc.

> *To call that sorry splinter group of the neighborhood improvement association a CABAL is to give its members way too much credit.*

cache *(kash), noun*
A place where things of value are hidden; also, the things stored there.

> *Elwood, a shrewd swindler, kept a CACHE of stock certificates, Swiss bank account numbers, and jewels just in case he had to leave the country in short order.*

cachet *(kah-SHAY), noun*
A mark of distinction or originality.

> *Walter thought that the velvet smoking jacket lent him a certain CACHET that was in keeping with his image as a man of leisure.*

cacophony *(kuh-KAHF-uh-knee), noun*
Harsh, unpleasant sounds that can create a disturbing feeling. Poets sometimes will use *cacophony* on purpose, for effect, in their works.

> *The CACOPHONY of the nearby construction site made it almost impossible for me to get any work done.*

cadaverous *(kuh-DAH-vuh-russ), adjective*
A cadaver is a dead body, so someone or something that is *cadaverous* is painfully thin and suggests death.

> *Images of the CADAVEROUS survivors of Nazi concentration camps continue to haunt the world's consciousness.*

cadence *(KAY-dence), noun*
The rhythm or flow of a series of words or sounds; often, the harmonious rhythm or flow of the spoken word.

> *The poem's CADENCE echoed the lazy summer days of the poet's youth.*

cadre *(KAH-dray), noun*
This French word refers to the backbone or framework of a group, typically a government or military agency.

> *Even after the war ended, a number of officers were left to form a CADRE in order to quell future unrest in the region.*

cajole *(kuh-JOLE), verb*
To coax; to persuade by using flattery; to wheedle.

> *My brother's efforts to CAJOLE me out of my allowance, by reminding me that I would be a rich superstar in big-league baseball someday, were in vain.*

calamitous *(kuh-LAMM-ih-tuss), adjective*
Having extremely dire consequences that point toward a calamity.
> *The stock market's CALAMITOUS crash gave rise to a nationwide panic.*

callous *(KAL-uss), adjective*
Unfeeling; insensitive; hardened. (See, for comparison, the entry for *callus*.)
> *The chauffeur couldn't understand how Mr. Jensen could be so CALLOUS as to ride by the crowd of homeless people every day without taking the least notice of them.*

callow *(KAL-oh), adjective*
Lacking experience; immature.
> *Ellis, a CALLOW youth accompanying Madame Hempstead, seemed not to understand that his joke about the Ambassador's choice of underwear was inappropriate for a state dinner.*

callus *(KAL-us), noun*
A hardened patch of skin. (See, for comparison, the entry for *callous*.)
> *George had developed a CALLUS on his forefinger from his constant guitar playing.*

calumny *(KAL-um-nee), noun*
A slanderous statement made with the intent of hurting another's reputation; a malicious rumor.
> *The columnist apparently thought that the CALUMNY she directed at Senator Martin would cause him to lose only the election, not his wife and family as well.*

calvary *(CAL-vuh-ree), noun*
A scene of intense anguish (named for the hill on which Jesus Christ was crucified, *Calvary*). Calvary is frequently confused with *cavalry* but their meanings are entirely different.
> *Herbert faced his own private CALVARY after his wife told him she wanted a divorce.*

calzone *(kal-ZONE), noun*
An Italian food roll resembling a turnover made by wrapping meat, cheese, or vegetables in dough.
> *We asked Aunt Joan if she would bring her famous steak and cheese CALZONE to the party.*

cambric *(KAM-brik), noun*
A variety of fine linen.
> *My grandmother gave us a beautiful CAMBRIC tablecloth as a wedding present.*

canapé *(KAN-uh-pay), noun*
An appetizer made by spreading meat, fish, or cheese on a small piece of toasted bread.

> *While the guests waited for the bridal party, waiters strolled through the reception area with trays of champagne and CANAPÉS.*

canard *(kuh-NARD), noun*
A fabrication or unfounded story. Someone who spreads a rumor he knows to be false and harmful would be guilty of circulating a *canard*.

> *The claim that the president of the company is likely to resign soon has been throughly discredited, but you will still hear some members of the opposition spreading the CANARD.*

candor *(KAN-duhr), noun*
Openness or honesty. Someone who speaks directly or openly, without equivocation or doubletalk, can be said to speak with *candor*.

> *Let me say with all CANDOR that I did not look forward to coming here today.*

cannon *(KAH-nun), noun*
A weapon used to fire large metal projectiles. (See, for comparison, the entry for *canon*.)

> *The thunderous sound of CANNONS being fired resonated across the valley.*

canon *(KAH-nun), noun*
A principle governing political or religious groups; a law or set of laws.

> *Early in the play, Hamlet expresses his wish that God "had not fix'd his CANON 'gainst self-slaughter."*

canonical *(kuh-NON-ih-kuhl), adjective*
In accordance with or conforming to established (church) law. *Also:* accepted as belonging within a body of work (especially the Bible). Orthodox behavior can be said to be *canonical*.

> *The CANONICAL requirements of the sect were stringent and difficult to obey.*

cantankerous (kan-TANG-ker-us), *adjective*
Ill-tempered; grumpy.

> *"You kids stay off my lawn!" our CANTANKEROUS old neighbor barked.*

canvas *(KAN-vus), noun*
A type of coarse cloth. (See, for comparison, the entry for *canvass*.)

> *Many of Van Gogh's works were destroyed and sold as scrap CANVAS.*

canvass *(KAN-vus), verb*

To solicit (support, opinions, votes, etc.). (See, for comparison, the entry for *canvas*.)

Virgil and I spent all Sunday walking around the city CANVASSING for our candidate.

capacious *(kuh-PAY-shus), adjective*

Capable of holding a great deal of something. Something that is spacious or capable of encompassing a large quantity of an item can be said to be *capacious*.

Don't let his show of ignorance fool you; he has a CAPACIOUS memory and a strong eye for detail.

capital *(KAP-ih-tul), noun*

A city designated as a seat of government. Also: economic resources. Also: excellent. (See, for comparison, the entry for *capitol*.)

In Washington D.C., our nation's CAPITAL, the three branches of government make their formal headquarters.

capitalize *(KAH-pih-tuh-lize), verb*

To draw an advantage from. Also, in business terms, *capitalize* can mean funding a business or converting a business's value to personal income.

By CAPITALIZING on the candidate's mistake, her opponent managed to win the election.

capitol *(KAP-ih-tul), noun*

The building in which a legislature meets. (See, for comparison, the entry for *capital*.)

One of the highlights of our trip to Washington was our visit to the CAPITOL building.

capitulate *(kuh-PIT-yoo-late), verb*

To accede to a demand for surrender. Someone who yields a point under dispute can be said to *capitulate* to the other party.

The ambassador had been instructed to show flexibility on cultural exchanges, but not to CAPITULATE when it came to trade issues.

capricious *(kuh-PREE-shuss), adjective*

Characterized by a whimsical attitude. A person who acts impulsively or unpredictably can be said to be *capricious*.

Given his CAPRICIOUS approach to life, it is not surprising that Andrew never settled into one field of employment.

capstone *(CAP-stone), noun*

Originally used to describe the protective stone at the top of an arch, which keeps the arch stable, *capstone* has come to have the broader meaning of "a crowning achievement" or "a finishing touch."

> *When she won the Pulitzer Prize for her last novel, it was the CAPSTONE to a long and distinguished literary career.*

captious *(KAP-shuss), adjective*

Extremely critical; likely to find fault. A person who makes many criticisms about petty matters can be said to be *captious*.

> *Myra had shown great tolerance throughout her stay, but when Mr. Clements subjected her to a CAPTIOUS interrogation about her academic career, she decided to leave.*

carafe *(kuh-RAFF), noun*

A wide-mouthed bottle for holding liquid.

> *I would have been happy with a single glass of the house wine, but Billy, who was in a generous mood, insisted we order a CARAFE of the expensive Chardonnay.*

carbuncle *(KAR-bunk-uhl), noun*

A painful inflammation of the skin similar to, but more serious than, a boil.

> *Jimmy's inventive excuses for his absences reached a new level when he told his teacher he had been unable to attend Spanish class because of a CARBUNCLE.*

carcinogen *(kar-SIN-uh-gen), noun*

An agent that causes cancer.

> *When experimenting with CARCINOGENS in the lab, the technicians would always wear protective masks.*

cardiac *(KAR-dee-ack), adjective*

Relating to the heart.

> *When their son's pediatrician detected a heart murmur, the Simpsons insisted on having him examined by the best CARDIAC team in the city.*

cardinal *(KAR-dih-nul), adjective*

Primarily important; vital; prominent. A *cardinal* sin is one of great seriousness. As a noun, *cardinal* can refer to a number of things or people regarded as primary or important, including a kind of high official in the Roman Catholic church.

> *Whatever you do, remember the CARDINAL rule we have in this house about avoiding the subject of religion.*

careen *(kuh-REEN), verb*
To lurch while moving; to swerve.
> *Suddenly we hit a patch of oil, and our car CAREENED into the guardrail.*

caricature *(KARE-ihk-uh-choor), noun*
A grotesquely or absurdly exaggerated representation. Political cartoons are the most common examples of *caricature*.
> *The paintings of Toulouse-Lautrec are often rooted in CARICATURE, out they are more than mere cartoons.*

carnivorous *(kar-NIV-uh-russ), adjective*
Flesh-eating.
> *Mel and his photographer set off for three months in the Serengeti in search of the CARNIVOROUS wildlife of the region.*

carouse *(kuh-ROWZ), verb*
To engage in boisterous social activity or to drink to excess.
> *During his twenty-fifth high school reunion, Dave CAROUSED more in twenty-four hours than he had in the last ten years combined.*

carp *(KARP), verb*
It's not just a fish! To *carp* is to raise picky, trivial objections.
> *All the CARPING at the staff meeting kept anything substantive from being done.*

carpe diem *(KAR-pay DEE-uhm) noun*
Relish the present and take joy now in the pleasure of life, rather than focusing on the future. *Carpe diem* is Latin for "seize the day."
> *His final admonition was to live life to the fullest—a CARPE DIEM he seemed to have heeded rarely himself.*

carte blanche *(kart blonsh), noun*
Unrestricted power, access, or privilege; permission to act entirely as one wishes. *Carte blanche* is from the French for "blank document"; the essential meaning is that one is free to "write one's own ticket."
> *Jean had CARTE BLANCHE during her first month or so as office manager, but the vice-president eventually came to supervise her much more closely.*

cartel *(kar-TELL), noun*
A group assembled with the objective of establishing mutual control over prices, production, and marketing of goods by the members. While a *cartel* is usually a group of representatives from independent business organizations, the term can also refer to a coalition of political figures united for a particular cause.
> *The oil CARTEL had succeeded in driving world energy prices up significantly.*

C

Casanova *(kaz-uh-NO-vuh), noun*

Giacomo Casanova was an eighteenth-century Italian adventurer who wrote at great length about his sexual exploits. His name has come to be synonymous with a man noted for his amorous—and probably unscrupulous—activities.

Phil likes to think of himself as a CASANOVA, but most women just think he's pathetic.

caste *(kast), noun*

A social class marked by strong hereditary and cultural ties. *Caste* also refers to the strict set of social boundaries and customs determined by birth within Hindu society.

When Roland married the daughter of a shopkeeper, he was accused by some of having betrayed his CASTE.

castigate *(KASS-tuh-gate), verb*

To criticize or rebuke severely, usually with the intention of correcting wrongdoing.

The committee CASTIGATED the college's administration for unethical recruiting practices.

cataclysmic *(kat-uh-KLIZZ-mick), adjective*

Very destructive and causing great upheaval.

The assassination of the prime minister was a CATACLYSMIC event that led to a lengthy civil war.

catacomb *(KAT-uh-kome), noun*

A chamber below the ground with openings for graves.

During times of religious persecution, early Christians often had to worship alongside the dead in the CATACOMBS.

catalyst *(KAT-uh-list), noun*

That which initiates a process or event and is itself unaffected. *Catalyst* has a technical meaning in chemistry, but in general usage it refers to a person or thing that sets off a new sequence of events while remaining uninvolved in those events.

The film served as a CATALYST for Peter; he began keeping a journal regularly soon after he saw it.

catapult *(KAT-uh-pult), noun*

To hurl or shoot (as from a sling); to provide or exhibit sudden upward movement. As a noun: an ancient military weapon designed to hurl arrows, stones, and other missiles.

When he heard the approaching sirens, Michael CATAPULTED out of bed.

catarrh *(kuh-TARR), noun*

An inflammation of the mucous membrane, especially one affecting the throat or nose.

> *Dr. Alonzo promised us that his special elixir would relieve any and all illnesses, including influenza, CATARRH, and snakebite.*

catch-22 *(KATCH-twen-tee-too), noun*

An impossible situation in which one is presented with logically contradictory options. A demand that one call the phone repair service from the very telephone that is out of order, for instance, could be regarded as a *catch-22*. (The phrase is drawn from Joseph Heller's novel of the same name.)

> *Mr. Brown's lighthearted memo issued a playful CATCH-22: he was only to be scheduled for meetings taking place during those days he planned to be out of town.*

catharsis *(kuh-THAR-siss), noun*

To purify and rejuvenate the body and spirit by purging them of whatever is causing problems; to release tensions and achieve renewal by an outpouring of emotion.

> *Jimmy's therapist suggested that the young boy take up painting as a means of achieving a CATHARSIS after his father's death.*

catheter *(KATH-uh-tur), noun*

A slim, flexible tube inserted in a bodily channel to maintain an opening to another internal opening.

> *The endless months in my hospital room took their toll on my spirits; one morning I contemplated tearing the CATHETER from my arm, grabbing a bathrobe, and simply stalking out of the place.*

caustic *(KOSS-tick), adjective*

Corrosive or capable of burning. Something is *caustic* if it can eat away at something else. A person is *caustic* if he speaks sharply and maliciously.

> *The CAUSTIC nature of Jane's speech caused all the members to reexamine their support of her candidacy.*

cavalcade *(KAV-uhl-kade), noun*

A procession, especially one involving people on horses or in vehicles. A *cavalcade* can refer to a parade or to anything that is to be displayed with great pageantry.

> *The president served as host to a CAVALCADE of visiting dignitaries.*

C

cavalier *(KAV-uh-leer), adjective*
Unconcerned with what is considered important; nonchalantly unengaged, especially with regard to serious matters. A reckless or inattentive person charged with responsibility in affairs of importance can be said to be *cavalier*.

> *His CAVALIER attitude toward financial management may be his company's undoing.*

cavalry *(CAV-ul-ree), noun*
A group of soldiers on horseback. *Cavalry* is frequently confused with *calvary* (See *calvary* above), but their meanings are entirely different.

> *After three days of delay, the CAVALRY finally came to the rescue.*

caveat emptor *(KAH-vee-ott EMP-tore), noun*
"Let the buyer beware." *Caveat emptor* is a Latin phrase warning that swindles and misrepresentation are common in the world of commerce. (A caveat is a warning.) The term can also mean that goods are sold without warranty.

> *Fran bought the goods at her own peril and regretted her act: CAVEAT EMPTOR!*

cavil *(KAV-ihl), verb*
To find fault in trivial matters or raise petty objections. As a noun, *cavil* can mean a trivial objection.

> *Susan CAVILLED for some time about the lateness of the milk delivery, but since it was only a matter of minutes, she eventually gave in and paid the bill.*

cavort **(kuh-VORT),**
to caper about; to prance.

> *Elwood and Riley were so happy to be released from the kennel that they spent half an hour CAVORTING wildly about on our lawn.*

cede *(seed) verb*
To give up, as by treaty.

> *In 1819, Spain CEDED to the United States the territory we now know as the state of Florida.*

celerity *(suh-LAIR-ih-tee), noun*
Speed; swiftness of action or motion. *Celerity* comes from the same Latin root as accelerate.

> *I will carry out your orders with CELERITY, sir.*

celestial *(suh-LESS-chul), noun*
Relating to the skies or the heavens.

> *At first Sam thought that the CELESTIAL body he had picked up on his telescope was a spaceship, but it turned out to be a meteor.*

celibacy *(SELL-ih-bus-see), noun*
The quality of being chaste; the act of abstaining from sexual activity. For instance, someone who remains unmarried in order to follow a religious calling is said to commit to a lifestyle of *celibacy*.

> *Although he took Holy Orders, David eventually found that he could not live a life of CELIBACY and left the priesthood.*

censer *(SEN-sur), noun*
A vessel for burning incense.

> *Father Riley looked in vain for the altar boy, then placed the CENSER on the altar himself.*

censor *(SEN-sur), noun*
One who reviews for offensive or objectionable material, deleting that which is found to fall into such categories. (See, for comparison, the entry for *censer*.)

> *W.C. Fields was constantly at odds with Hays Commission CENSORS, who found fault with many of his references to alcohol and women.*

censorious *(sen-SOR-ee-us), adjective*
Critical; easily finding fault.

> *When it came to grading term papers, Mrs. Edwards was seen by many as overly CENSORIOUS, even taking off points for using a paper clip instead of a staple.*

censure *(SEN-sher), noun*
A show of disapproval or blame. *Censure* is formal rebuke or stern reproof.

> *You could not have acted as you did without expecting CENSURE from this organization.*

cerebellum *(sare-uh-BELL-um), noun*
A region of the brain located the back of the cerebrum and the brain stem; the portion of the brain concerned with muscle coordination and bodily equilibrium.

> *Mary's frequent dizziness after the car accident led doctors to believe that there might have been an injury to her CEREBELLUM.*

cerebral *(suh-REEB-rul), adjective*
Appealing to or involving the human mind; characteristic of intellectual pursuits; also, pertaining to the brain.

> *Bill's lofty observations on the nature of existence are a little too CEREBRAL for a party like this; you'd be better off inviting Charlie, who tells such funny stories.*

cerulean *(suh-RUE-lee-un), adjective*

The color of the sky.

> *The brochure told me to expect perfectly CERULEAN skies, but it rained so much during my vacation that I never saw them.*

cessation *(sess-SAY-shun), noun*

The act of drawing to a close. *Cessation* is the process of ceasing or reaching a point of abatement.

> *Continued diplomatic effort may well bring about a CESSATION of hostilities.*

chafe *(chayf), verb*

To rub or irritate. (See, for comparison, the entry for *chaff*)

> *The new shoes CHAFED my heels the first day and left me with two prize-winning blisters.*

chaff *(chaff), noun*

Worthless stuff; material to be cast away.

> *I usually write for an hour straight in my journal, knowing full well that much of what comes out will be drivel, and allowing myself to go back later and separate the wheat from the CHAFF.*

chagrin *(shuh-GRIN), noun*

The emotion of humiliation or embarrassment arising from disheartening experience. To show *chagrin* is to give evidence of disappointment and disquiet with oneself.

> *Much to my CHAGRIN, my application was rejected instantly.*

chalet *(sha-LAY), noun*

A small country house, named after a type of Swiss cottage with overhanging eaves.

> *We rented a CHALET on the edge of the mountain, and had immediate access to the ski slopes.*

chameleon *(kuh-MEE-lee-un), noun*

A lizard (*chameleontidae* and similar animals) with the ability to change the color of its skin for the purpose of camouflage; also, a person who shifts outlooks, opinions, or identities frequently or easily.

> *I'm afraid we haven't been able to get Ian to give us his final opinion on the merger plans; he's been something of a CHAMELEON on the issue.*

chanteuse *(shan-TEUZ), noun*
A female singer, usually one who performs in nightclubs.
> *Although he claimed to like the decor and the atmosphere of the club, we suspected that Elaine, the CHANTEUSE who performed there, was the real reason Jimmy kept going back.*

chantey *(SHAN-tee), noun*
A song sung by sailors in rhythm to their labors.
> *As they hauled up anchor, the ship's crew would join together in "What Shall We Do with a Drunken Sailor" and other CHANTEYS.*

charismatic *(kare-ihz-MAT-ik), adjective*
Possessing a special quality associated with leadership, authority, confidence, and overall personal appeal. While we generally use *charismatic* in reference to a person, the word also refers to certain Christian sects and ideas that emphasize demonstrative or ecstatic worship.
> *The CHARISMATIC salesman seemed to sell himself as much as his product.*

charlatan *(SHAR-luh-tun), noun*
A fake or humbug. A *charlatan* falsely claims to possess a given level of status, skills, or knowledge.
> *The defendant, it has been claimed, is a CHARLATAN and a liar—but where is the evidence for this?*

chary *(TCHAIR-ee), adjective*
Describes someone who is very cautious or wary.
> *I was CHARY of Lillian's new business scheme because her "great" ideas always result in spectacular disasters.*

chasm *(KAZ-um), noun*
A deep gorge; a deep hole in the earth's surface.
> *Dawn stood peering across the seemingly bottomless CHASM, meditating on the mysteries of nature.*

chastise *(TCHAH-stize), verb*
To punish or scold severely in hopes that by so doing, new behavior will result.
> *The teacher CHASTISED the student for being constantly disruptive.*

chateau *(sha-TOE), noun*
A large country house; a French manor house or castle.
> *Eva liked to spend her summers at the family's CHATEAU, strolling through the gardens and riding horseback over the expansive grounds.*

chemotherapy *(kee-mo-THARE-uh-pee), noun*
The treatment of disease by means of administering chemicals that have a toxic effect on the microorganisms that cause the disease, or that can destroy a body's cancerous cells.

The doctors warned Amelia that the CHEMOTHERAPY she was about to undergo would not be without side effects.

chiaroscuro *(kee-are-uh-SCURE-oh), noun*
This Italian word means a pattern of light and dark (or light and shadow) in a painting or literary work.

The power of the painting comes from its CHIAROSCURO, which seems to indicate looming disaster.

chic *(SHEEK), adjective or noun*
From the French meaning "skill," "chic" means stylishness and elegance in dress or manner.

Without spending very much, Lydia always seems able to look incredibly CHIC.

chicanery *(shih-KAIN-uh-ree), noun*
Cheating or deception, especially through the use of language.

The way the candidate consistently quibbled about the precise meaning of his statements made me feel he was guilty of CHICANERY.

chide *(chide), verb*
To scold or lecture; to reprove.

My brother CHIDED me for neglecting to visit our grandparents during my trip to California.

chimera *(KI-mer-uh), noun*
In Greek mythology, a *chimera* is a terrifying monster, a cross between a lion, a goat, and a dragon. In modern times the word has come to mean an illusion of the mind or a dream that can't possibly be realized.

Leon's painful shyness has become a CHIMERA that keeps him from realizing his goal of finding true love.

chimerical *(kih-MARE-ih-kull), adjective*
Fanciful, imaginary, or unreal. A *chimerical* event is one that seems dreamlike or surrealistic.

A CHIMERICAL landscape greeted those brave enough to emerge from the ship.

chintzy *(CHINT-see), adjective*
Considered cheap, tacky, or of low quality.

> *Angela insisted on wearing a CHINTZY leopard-skin jumpsuit and high heels to the company Christmas party.*

chivalrous *(SHIV-uhl-russ), adjective*
Honorable; in keeping with a code of behavior reminiscent of that followed by medieval knights. *Chivalrous* applies especially to courteousness and/or consideration toward women, the poor, or the vanquished.

> *Those who expected a barbarian were surprised to find the renegade leader both even-tempered and CHIVALROUS in bearing.*

chloroform *(KLORE-uh-form), noun*
A colorless, toxic liquid chemical possessing a strong ether smell, and sometimes used as an anesthetic.

> *Police found a CHLOROFORM soaked-rag on the floor of the study and surmised that the kidnappers had used it to knock Mr. Robinson out.*

choleric *(KAHL-er-ick), adjective*
Characterized by becoming quickly angry.

> *No one would work for Mr. Sanchez because his CHOLERIC temper drove many to tears.*

chord *(kord), noun*
A combination of musical tones. (See, for comparison, the entry for *cord*.)

> *The major CHORDS in the key of C are the easiest for the beginning piano student to learn.*

churlish *(CHUR-lish), adjective*
Ill-bred; boorish.

> *When he started drinking soup noisily straight from the bowl, Beverly decided she had seen enough of her blind date's CHURLISH behavior.*

cinematic *(sin-uh-MAT-ik), adjective*
Reminiscent of or pertaining to the cinema; similar in imagery or approach to the visual styles employed in motion pictures.

> *The use of a large rotating disk on the stage allows the director to stage scenes in such a way that scenery and actors pass steadily across the stage as action proceeds, lending a CINEMATIC feel to the performance.*

C

cinephile *(SIN-uh-file), noun*
One who loves movies and is extremely knowledgeable about them. The word usually contains the suggestion that the movie-lover prefers obscure cult or foreign films rather than Hollywood blockbusters.

> *Elaine is such a CINEPHILE that she won't even go to see a film without subtitles.*

cipher *(SIE-fur), noun*
A person or thing without meaning or value; a mystery; literally, the mathematical symbol for zero.

> *Despite the best efforts of the intelligence community to gather evidence against him, Doctor Lysenko remained a CIPHER.*

circa *(SUR-ka), noun*
An estimated historical time period.

> *Based on the diary's condition, as well as the handwriting style and vocabulary choices of its author, Professor Evans set the date at CIRCA 1910.*

circuitous *(sir-CUE-uh-tuss), adjective*
Extremely twisty and windy; indirect.

> *Tameeka called it a shortcut, but her CIRCUITOUS directions added thirty minutes to the trip.*

circumflex *(SUR-kum-flex), noun*
An accent mark (^) placed over a letter to indicate a certain pronunciation.

> *Much to the dismay of the European journalists in town to cover the road race, the American typewriters in their hotels had no keys for CIRCUMFLEXES or other accent marks.*

circumlocution *(sir-kum-lo-CUE-shun), noun*
Overwordy and indirect language. Language that is overblown and tedious is considered *circumlocution*.

> *The student's use of CIRCUMLOCUTION lengthened his report, but lowered his grade.*

circumspect *(SUR-kum-spekt), adjective*
Wary of consequences.

> *Having been stung once, Ferdinand was CIRCUMSPECT about where he sat, and always checked for bees.*

circumvent *(SIR-kum-vent), verb*

To evade by means of artful contrivance. Someone who *circumvents* a regulation has not broken it in the strict sense, but found a gray area or loophole within which to operate. Similarly, to *circumvent* someone's authority is to maneuver around him.

> *In CIRCUMVENTING the will of the board of directors, the CEO knew he was taking a risk.*

cistern *(SIS-tern), noun*

A large container or tank used for holding water, particularly rainwater.

> *Mary watered her garden with rainwater collected in a CISTERN behind the garage.*

citadel *(SIT-uh-del), noun*

A stronghold; literally, a strategically positioned fortress in control of a town or city. Something that is forfeited against attack or adversity may be referred to metaphorically as a *citadel*.

> *Gentlemen, this business is our CITADEL, and we must be prepared to defend it as such.*

cite *(site), verb*

To quote or refer to. (See, for comparison, the entry for *site*.)

> *I've CITED your brilliant paper several times in my upcoming book, Dr. Wilson.*

citify *(SIT-uh-fie), verb*

To cause to become city-like.

> *I'm afraid it will take more than a week in Chicago to CITIFY old Uncle Parker.*

clairvoyance *(klare-VOY-uhnce), noun*

Supernatural perceptive skills. *Clairvoyance* (from the French for "clear sight") refers to the ability to perceive things normally out of the range of human intuition.

> *Michael claimed to have CLAIRVOYANCE, and even held a few playful "seances," but no one took his claims seriously.*

clamorous *(KIAM-uhr-uss), adjective*

Loud; expressively vehement. A *clamorous* crowd is noisy and demanding; a *clamor* is a loud outcry.

> *The throngs in the street roared with CLAMOROUS applause.*

C

clandestine *(klan-DESS-tin), adjective*
Kept hidden; secreted away from authorities or public observance. A *clandestine* object is one that is concealed for a purpose hidden from general view.

> *The message reached the resistance movement by means of a coded broadcast heard in hundreds of CLANDESTINE radios around the country.*

clangor *(KLAYN-gurr), noun*
A loud, repeating noise that can be unnerving.

> *The CLANGOR of the parade actually frightened my daughter, rather than exciting her.*

claque *(KLAK), noun*
A group of people hired to applaud at an entertainment event.

> *The first comedian was absolutely terrible; if it hadn't been for the CLAQUE the management had assembled at the last minute, there wouldn't have been any applause at all.*

clarion *(KLAR-ee-uhn), adjective*
From the Latin meaning "trumpet," *clarion* describes something, such as a sound, that is clear and shrill.

> *On the first day back to school, Robby groaned at the CLARION call of his morning alarm.*

clemency *(KLEM-uhn-see), noun*
Forbearance or mercy toward a wrongdoer or opponent. To show *clemency* is to be lenient in cases where circumstances warrant.

> *The governor's show of CLEMENCY for Callahan may come back to haunt him at election time.*

climacteric *(klih-MACK-ter-ick), adjective or noun*
In ancient Greece, the climacterics were considered important years in a person's life, times when great changes occurred. Today, one meaning of *climacteric* is "menopause," but it also means any pivotal time in a person's life.

> *After Gwen graduated from college and moved across the country, her life was filled with CLIMACTERIC events.*

climactic *(klie-MAK-tik), adjective*
Of or pertaining to a climax. (See, for comparison, the entry for climatic.)

> *The CLIMACTIC moment of the play comes when Hamlet finally kills Claudius.*

climatic *(klie-MAT-ik), adjective*

Of or pertaining to climate. (See, for comparison, the entry for climactic)

> *The CLIMATIC conditions in northern Alberta during the winter really don't agree with me.*

clinch *(klinch), verb*

To settle a matter decisively or definitely. Also, as a noun: a passionate embrace.

> *Even Coach Jones admitted that his team had slacked off after they CLINCHED first place in their division.*

clique *(KLICK), noun*

From the French meaning "latch," a clique is a small, exclusive group, one that often looks down on those who do not belong to it.

> *Shelly was pleased to find that her sorority was not riddled with in-fighting CLIQUES.*

cloistered *(KLOI-sturd), adjective*

Secluded; isolated; removed or hidden.

> *Shocked by the news of the shooting on our street, we remained CLOISTERED in our house for days afterward.*

clout *(KLOWT), noun*

"Clout" has two common meanings. It either means someone who has a lot of influence, or it means to strike someone.

> *I was afraid we wouldn't get into the exclusive club, but Reggie's business connections give him a lot of CLOUT. We got in with no problem.*

coagulate *(ko-AG-yoo-late), adjective*

To change from a liquid to a solid-like mass.

> *As someone who claims to be qualified to teach high school biology, you should certainly be able to answer a question on what makes blood COAGULATE.*

coalesce *(ko-uh-LESS), verb*

To unite or grow into a single whole. Disparate groups that *coalesce* for a single cause (thus forming a coalition) put aside their differences or separate goals to present a united front.

> *No amount of pleading from Jones could convince the two unions to COALESCE.*

coarse *(KOARSS), adjective*

Clumsy and crude, lacking in social graces. Also, describes fabric that is rough to the touch.

> *Ron's COARSE manner is sure to get him caught in a sexual harassment suit.*

cocksure *(KAHK-SURE), adjective*
Extremely, swaggeringly confident . . . probably overconfident.
> *Steve always acts like the COCKSURE man-about-town just because his uncle is the mayor.*

coda *(KO-duh), noun*
In music, the final passage of a movement or piece; also, the final part of anything, especially an artistic work.
> *As the "experimental" orchestral piece finally reached its CODA, I saw the percussionist yawn and look at his watch.*

codger *(KOD-jur), noun*
A peculiar or eccentric man, generally of advanced years.
> *Our next-door neighbor was Mr. Pottman, a likeable CODGER who used to wash his car every afternoon, even if it had rained in the morning.*

codify *(KOD-ih-fy), verb*
To reduce to the form of a code. To *codify* a series of positions is to systematize them, setting them down into distinct rules and guidelines.
> *It is high time we CODIFIED the existing maze of tax regulations.*

coeval *(koh-EE-vuhl), adjective or noun*
Of the same period, having the same duration, or being of the same age.
> *It's interesting to think that the squeaky clean Cleavers of Leave It to Beaver and the polite society-shunning members of the Beat Generation were COEVALS.*

coffers *(KAH-furs OR KAW-furs), noun*
A treasury, a place in which money is kept or stored.
> *When the minister suddenly bought a brand new sports car, his flock began carefully checking the church's COFFERS.*

cogent *(KOE-junt), adjective*
Compelling or convincing. Something that appeals effectively to the intellect or reason is said to be *cogent*.
> *I must admit that my counterpart has put forward a COGENT argument in defense of his client.*

cogitate *(KOJ-ih-tate), verb*
To think about or ponder seriously.
> *The president, never one to be pressured into a decision, closed the discussion by saying he needed another week to COGITATE on the matter.*

cognition *(kog-NISH-un), noun*

Perception; the process of knowing. *Cognition* can also mean "knowledge."

> *The process of COGNITION develops with amazing rapidity over the first two years of life.*

cognizant *(KOG-nuh-zunt), adjective*

Aware or well informed.

> *The attorney angrily denied the charges that his client had been COGNIZANT of the scheme to defraud consumers.*

cognomen *(kog-NO-muhn), noun*

A nickname.

> *He doesn't mind being called "Leopold," but he prefers his COGNOMEN, "Lee."*

cognoscente *(kon-yuh-SHEN-tee), noun*

A connoisseur; an expert. (Plural: cognoscenti.)

> *When it comes to wine-tasting, Arthur is well respected as a COGNOSCENTE.*

cohabitate *(KOH-HAB-ih-tait), verb*

To live together as man and wife, or to live together as though one were man and wife.

> *I don't know why Jim and Liza don't go ahead and get married. They've been COHABITATING for six years now!*

cohort *(KO-hort), noun*

An associate or companion with whom one is united through common experience. *Cohort* originally referred to one of the ten divisions of a Roman legion, consisting of men who had developed strong ties of comradeship.

> *Because Mark and his COHORTS had grown up together in the town, leaving for different colleges was quite difficult.*

coiffure *(kwa-FYOOR), noun*

A hairdo; the style of one's hair.

> *When you're as rich and powerful as Don King. I imagine you can get away with wearing any COIFFURE you like.*

coitus *(KO-uh-tus), noun*

Sexual intercourse.

> *Professor Wells sternly informed me that he would prefer that I use the term "COITUS" in describing the activities of the test couples, rather than the less formal "making whoopee."*

collate *(KOE-late), verb*
To arrange (usually paper) in proper or logical order.

> *Chef LeBlanc's assistant was responsible for writing down the recipes and COLLATING them for inclusion in the restaurant's internal cookbook.*

collateral *(kuh-LAT-uh-rul), noun*
Something pledged as security or insurance for the fulfillment of an obligation or payment. (Also, as an adjective: secondary or accompanying.)

> *Sheila offered her house as COLLATERAL in order to obtain the loan she needed to start her business.*

collegiality *(kuh-LEEG-ee-al-ih-tee), noun*
An effective working relationship among colleagues.

> *The COLLEGIALITY of the office is one reason there's very little turnover there.*

colloquial *(kuh-LO-kwee-ul), adjective*
In common conversational use. *Colloquial* is used to describe breezy, informal communication, either written or spoken. A *colloquialism* is a common phrase or expression of a conversational or informal nature.

> *You cannot expect a college president to take seriously a letter so COLLOQUIAL in tone.*

collusion *(kuh-LOO-zhun), noun*
A conspiratorial or secret understanding entered into for an illicit or fraudulent end. To enter into *collusion* with someone is to join with him in a secret plot or strategy.

> *The leaders were arraigned on price COLLUSION in violation of anti-trust laws.*

combustible *(kum-BUS-tih-bul), adjective*
Susceptible to catching fire; able to be burned.

> *The local consumer group tried to help make neighborhood homes as safe as possible by publishing lists of products found to be poisonous, COMBUSTIBLE, or potentially hazardous to small children.*

comely *(KUM-lee), adjective*
Pleasing or attractive. Also; appropriate. A *comely* appearance is one that is fetching or inviting.

> *Jane is COMELY, but her mother fears that the men she attracts will not make her happy.*

---

comity *(KOM-ih-tee), noun*
Courtesy; mutual civility.

> *The police were kind enough to grant me the COMITY of a private telephone call once I promised to stop removing pieces of clothing and flinging them at the sergeant.*

comme ci, comme ça *(kum SEE kum SA), adverb*
Middling; neither extraordinarily good nor extraordinarily poor. French for "like this, like that."

> *"COMME CI, COMME ÇA," shrugged Wells when I asked him how he was doing.*

commemorate *(kum-MEM-uh-rate), verb*
To serve as a memorial for; to mark or celebrate as a significant event.

> *Arthur, a Korean War veteran, would COMMEMORATE Memorial Day by visiting the cemetery and placing flags on the graves of friends who had fallen in battle.*

commensurate *(kuh-MEN-sir-it), adjective*
Having an equal measure; of equivalent duration or extent. Something that is *commensurate* with something else is of a proper scope or size by comparison.

> *Michael received a raise COMMENSURATE with his performance.*

commiserate *(kuh-MIZ-uh-rate), verb*
To share in another's sorrow or disappointment. *Commiserate* comes from the Latin roots for "with" and "pitiable."

> *Jane and Anita COMMISERATED with Frank over the failure of the business.*

commodious *(kuh-MODE-ee-uss), adjective*
Very spacious, large, and roomy.

> *The COMMODIOUS suite at the hotel was worth all we paid for it and more.*

compendious *(kum-PEN-dee-us), adjective*
Comprised of all necessary or essential components, yet concise. Something that is *compendious* (usually a piece of writing) deals with all important matters in a tight, succinct format.

> *The new desk encyclopedia is COMPENDIOUS but typographically unattractive.*

compensate *(KOM-pun-sate), verb*
Something given in return for or to make up for services performed, or for something lost; something given in exchange.

> *Although management COMPENSATED George for crossing the picket line during the strike by giving him a promotion and a big raise, he had lost several friends as a result of his decision and regretted it bitterly.*

C

compile *(kum-PILE), verb*
To gather or put together in one place or form.
> *The disc jockey asked Janet and Peter to COMPILE a list of the songs they would most like to hear at their wedding.*

complacent *(kum-PLAY-sent), adjective*
Satisfied with oneself; smug; content.
> *Brian was so COMPLACENT during the practice scrimmages before the big game that his coach considered benching him and playing the backup quarterback instead.*

complaisant *(kum-PLAY-zunt), adjective*
Eager to please; agreeable. *Complaisant* is frequently confused with the similar-sounding "complacent," which means "self-satisfied."
> *After months of personality problems with Trish, Fran suddenly found her quite COMPLAISANT.*

complement *(KOM-pluh-munt), noun*
To accompany in a pleasing or harmonious style. Also, as a noun: something that completes or brings to perfection. (See, for comparison, the entry for *compliment.*)
> *That scarf you're wearing certainly COMPLEMENTS your blouse.*

complementary *(kom-pluh-MEN-tuh-ree), adjective*
Serving to complete or to accompany in a harmonious fashion. (See, for comparison, the entry for *complimentary.*)
> *The trick is to pick a living room style COMPLEMENTARY to the one we've already established in the kitchen.*

compliant *(kum-PLY-ant), adverb*
Submissive; yielding.
> *After we phoned the police a few times, our noisy neighbor found it in his heart to be more COMPLIANT when we asked him to keep down the racket.*

complicity *(kum-PLIS-ity), verb*
To be involved in or be associated with, or to participate in or have previous knowledge of, an instance of wrongdoing.
> *Although he did not receive money for throwing the 1919 World Series, Buck Weaver was nevertheless suspended from baseball for life, because his failure to expose the scheme was seen as COMPLICITY in his teammates' plans.*

compliment *(KOM-pluh-munt), verb*
To praise or flatter. (See, for comparison, the entry for *complement.*)
> *The waiter COMPLIMENTED Harry on his choice of wine.*

complimentary *(kom-pluh-MEN-tuh-ree), adjective*
Expressing praise or admiration; also, extended without charge. (See, for comparison, the entry for *complementary.*)

> *The play was uneven and only mildly interesting, but I couldn't complain too much, as the tickets had been COMPLIMENTARY.*

comport *(kum-PORT), verb*
To behave in a particular fashion. Also: to stand in harmonious relation. This second sense of *comport* is usually followed by "with."

> *That does not COMPORT with the facts, counselor.*

compose *(kum-POZE), verb*
To be the constituent components of; to make up. (See, for comparison, the entry for *comprise.*)

> *Teamwork COMPOSES the essence of success in business.*

compote *(KOM-poat), noun*
A stewed fruit and sugar dessert.

> *In addition to an unidentifiable brownish meat in a dark, concealing sauce, many of the TV dinners I ate as a child included a rather leaden strawberry COMPOTE.*

comprise *(kum-PRIZE), verb*
To include or contain; to consist of. (See, for comparison, the entry for *compose.*)

> *The new complex COMPRISES several floors of student residences, a cafeteria, and a recreation area.*

compunction *(kum-PUNK-shun), noun*
Unrest or self-dissatisfaction arising out of a feeling of guiltiness. A *compunction* is a sensation of remorse or uncertainty about a decision or course of action.

> *I will sign her dismissal notice myself without COMPUNCTION; she is easily the most incompetent salesperson I have ever worked with.*

concave *(kahn-CAVE), adjective*
Curving inward, as the inside of a sphere. (See, for comparison, the entry for *convex.*)

> *After Bill threw it in anger, the baseball left a CONCAVE impression in the wall.*

concerted *(kun-SUR-tid), adjective*
Mutually devised or planned. A *concerted* effort is one that features mutual effort toward an established goal.

> *The two made a CONCERTED effort to get Vivian to change her mind, but she was resolute.*

conciliatory *(kun-SILL-ee-uh-tore-ee), adjective*
Describes someone willing to compromise or to make concessions in order to preserve peaceful relations.

> *After Lou lost his temper with Margery, he was excessively CONCILIATORY to her for weeks afterward.*

concord *(KAHN-cord), noun*
A state of agreement and harmony.

> *While most siblings fight, the CONCORD among the Lewis triplets is nothing short of phenomenal.*

concise *(kun-SICE), adjective*
Clear and to the point; brief; expressing much with few words.

> *Rather than detail the grievances he had with his supervisor, Randy handed in a CONCISE resignation letter outlining his desire to move on to something new.*

conclave *(KON-klave), noun*
A secret meeting; also, the room in which this meeting is held.

> *Fearing he might crack under pressure, the rebels did not include Eli in the CONCLAVE in which they gathered to plan their attack strategy.*

concoct *(kun-KOKT), verb*
To combine in the process of preparation.

> *How on earth did Myra manage to CONCOCT a story like that for her mother on such short notice?*

concourse *(KON-korse), noun*
An assembly of a large number of people. A *concourse* can also be a large open area meant to accommodate public gatherings.

> *He looked all around the CONCOURSE, but could not see Robin.*

concur *(kun-KUR), verb*
To agree; to share the same opinion.

> *The prosecutor felt that Jim's crime deserved the maximum penalty, but the judge did not CONCUR.*

concurrence *(kun-KER-runce), noun*
The condition of being in agreement. To concur is to agree, so a *concurrence* is in effect when two or more people have "signed on" to a given idea, plan, or judgment.

> *I will proceed with the acquisition; as president, I do not require anyone else's CONCURRENCE.*

concupiscent *(kahn-KYU-puh-cent), adjective*
Marked by strong desire, especially strong sexual desire.

> *Connie's CONCUPISCENT manner makes some people question her virtue.*

condensed *(kun-DENSED), adjective*
Shortened; decreased in size; compressed, made more concise.

> *Cindy thought she could get through the class by reading only the CONDENSED versions of the novels that had been assigned, but she ended up failing both the midterm and the final.*

conduit *(KAHN-dew-it), noun*
A means by which something is transmitted.

> *A traveler from Malaysia turned out to be the CONDUIT for the deadly epidemic.*

confabulate *(kun-FAB-yoo-late), verb*
To chat or talk informally. *Confabulate* derives from the Latin for "to have a conversation with." (*Confabulation* also has a technical meaning in psychiatry: the process by which people invent and believe stories to fill mental gaps due to memory loss. *Confabulation* is sometimes used in this sense in general discourse to describe extravagant storytelling.)

> *"I have no time to CONFABULATE," the actor exclaimed melodramatically before leaving.*

confiscate *(KON-fiss-kate), verb*
To deprive of (one's property), especially as part of an official or governmental body.

> *The news that his boat had been CONFISCATED by the IRS to satisfy his back tax debt hit Michael like a body blow.*

conflagration *(kahn-fluh-GRAY-shun), noun*
In general, a *conflagration* is a fire, but the word typically denotes a massive, uncontrollable, and very destructive fire.

> *The CONFLAGRATION caused when the separate wildfires united led to evacuations up and down the coast.*

conflate *(kuhn-FLATE), verb*
Depending on the context, *conflate* means either a fusion—a coming together of disparate elements—or it means to confuse.

> *I am completely CONFLATED by molecular physics.*

confluence *(KON-flu-ence), noun*

A point of meeting or flowing together. Literally, a *confluence* is the point at which two rivers join. The word has been expanded significantly through metaphorical use.

> *It is on the issue of human spiritual growth that the two philosophies find their CONFLUENCE.*

conform *(kun-FORM), verb*

To go along with what is popular; to follow the actions of others. Also: not to be in violation of (a rule, principle, ideal, or edict).

> *As though eager to prove she had no intention of CONFORMING to her parents' idea of the perfect daughter, Bridget left home at eighteen to become a truck driver.*

confraternity *(kahn-fruh-TURN-ih-tee), noun*

An association of people united for a common cause.

> *Eager to improve the condition of our neighborhood playgrounds, Carol and I joined a town CONFRATERNITY that had formed for that purpose.*

congeal *(kuhn-JEEL), verb*

When discussing inanimate objects, something congeals when it thickens or gels. When discussing people's attitudes, "congeal" means to become hard-headed and rigid.

> *Over time, the delusions that caused my father-in-law to launch a multitude of harebrained schemes CONGEALED until it was impossible to talk sense to him.*

congenial *(kun-JEEN-ee-ul), adjective*

Having similar habits or tastes; temperamentally suitable. *Congenial* surroundings are those that yield a sense of being pleasant and inviting. (*Congenial* is sometimes confused with congenital, see below.)

> *He found Jane a CONGENIAL hostess: easy to engage in conversation and knowledgeable on topics of interest to others.*

congenital *(kun-JEN-it-ul), adjective*

Present or existing from birth. A *congenital* disease or condition can be inherited, or can result from environmental influences (usually influences on growth within the womb).

> *The young child suffered from a CONGENITAL heart defect.*

conjecture *(kun-JEK-shur), noun*

Speculation based on inconclusive data or on evidence that is not complete. A *conjecture* can be considered a "best guess" unsupported by fact or observation.

> *The item that appeared in your column of December 16th is based totally on CONJECTURE, and is extremely misleading.*

conjoin *(kuhn-JOIN), verb*

To join together or unite. The word often is used to mean "to wed."

> *After the battling factions CONJOINED, they were able to accomplish peacefully most of their separate goals.*

conjugate *(KAHN-juh-gut OR KAHN-juh-gate), verb*

To join together, especially in a pair or in pairs.

> *As soon as the music started, men and women began to CONJUGATE on the dance floor.*

conjure *(KON-jur), verb*

To summon or bring about (as if by supernatural means). Someone who *conjures* up an image of something brings it to mind in a vivid way.

> *I cannot simply CONJURE up the figures you are looking for; the project will take some time.*

connoisseur *(KAHN-uh-sue-er), noun*

This French word refers to someone who is an expert in a field, especially in one of the fine arts.

> *Jake is a CONNOISSEUR of rare blues 78s.*

connotation *(kon-uh-TAY-shun), noun*

An implication beyond literal meaning; an unspoken suggestion. To connote is to suggest something implicitly; accordingly, a *connotation* is a secondary meaning discernable "beneath the surface."

> *His article on race relations uses several phrases that carry unfortunate CONNOTATIONS.*

connote *(kuh-NOTE), verb*

To imply, suggest, or hint at another meaning in addition to a primary one.

> *To many people the term "frontier" CONNOTES a rough and primitive lifestyle, but most pioneer families maintained household living standards that equaled those of the eastern relatives they'd left behind.*

connubial *(kuh-NUBE-ee-uhl), adjective*

Of, or related to, the state of being married.

> *My parents will celebrate fifty years of CONNUBIAL bliss this year.*

C

conoidal *(kuh-NOYD-uhl), adjective*
Shaped like, or nearly like, a cone.

My son's paintings of CONOIDAL shapes are all the rage in his preschool.

consanguineous *(con-san-GWIN-ee-us), adjective*
Related by blood; of common lineage. Two people or entities that are
consanguineous are commonly descended. The word derives from the Latin roots
for "with" and "blood."

*The two brothers learned of their CONSANGUINEOUS relationship after a series of
blood tests.*

consecrate *(KON-si-krate), verb*
To proclaim as sacred; to set aside or declare to be holy. By extension, to *consecrate*
oneself to a given goal is to commit to it with a conviction in keeping with strong
faith.

*Lincoln's words, more than any other action after the carnage, served to
CONSECRATE the battlefield at Gettysburg.*

consensus *(kun-SEN-sus), noun*
Collective agreement.

*There was a strong consensus around town was that Mayor Bergeron was doing a
poor job—a CONSENSUS that extended to both of his children, his uncles, and his
barber.*

consortium *(kon-SOR-tee-um), noun*
A union, partnership, or alliance, especially one among financial or business
entities. *Consortium* also has a legal meaning related to the rights of married
persons, but use in this sense is rare.

Mr. Sparks represented a CONSORTIUM of firms.

conspicuous *(kun-SPIK-yoo-uss), adjective*
Strikingly noticeable; obvious.

*The present Supreme Court term has been marked by a CONSPICUOUS absence of
controversial cases.*

conspiracy *(kun-SPEER-uh-see), noun*
A treacherous plan involving two or more persons.

*Your contention that Lyndon Johnson was part of a CONSPIRACY to assassinate
President Kennedy amounts to what, in an earlier day, would have been called
seditious libel, Mr. Oliver.*

constant dollars *(KON-stuhnt DOLL-urz), noun*

In economics, a measure of monetary value in which the factors of inflation and deflation are accounted for; a base year's currency value used to determine what costs would presumably have been in other years.

> *The figures on our division's growth were extremely misleading because they had not been converted to CONSTANT DOLLARS.*

consternation *(kahn-ster-NAY-shun), noun*

A sense of alarm, confusion, or amazement.

> *The repeated arguments with my wife over the same issues filled me with CONSTERNATION.*

construe *(kun-STROO), verb*

To interpret or guess the meaning of.

> *Ann's constant tardiness was CONSTRUED by her supervisor as an inability to balance the demands of her job and her family.*

consummate *(KON-sum-mate), verb*

To complete or finalize; to bring to a point of finality or a desired end. To *consummate* something is to bring it to its point of fulfillment. When we speak or a marriage's *consummation*, we refer to the married couple's establishment of a sexual relationship. Business agreements and contracts are also *consummated*.

> *The real estate agent CONSUMMATING the deal realized a substantial commission.*

contemptuous *(kun-TEMP-choo-us), adjective*

Feeling disdain or scorn. A *contemptuous* act is one that flies in the face of established procedures or traditions.

> *The defendant's CONTEMPTUOUS behavior on the stand was, amazingly, overlooked by the judge.*

contentious *(kuhn-TEN-chuss), adjective*

Argumentative, characterized by being prone to disputes and controversy.

> *I walked away when the discussion heated up and got too CONTENTIOUS.*

contiguous *(kun-TIG-yoo-uss), adjective*

Joining physically; touching.

> *The prize offer is limited to residents of the forty-eight CONTIGUOUS states.*

contingent *(kuhn-TIN-jent), adjective or noun*

As a noun, "contingent" refers to people who are considered representative of a larger group. As an adjective, something contingent is either accidental or dependent upon something else in order to occur.

> *Getting to the concert on time is CONTINGENT on you getting to my house by 7:30.*

C

contraband *(KAHN-truh-band), noun*
Illegal or prohibited goods.

> *Jean tried to smuggle a tape recorder into the concert, but her CONTRABAND was quickly discovered and taken from her.*

contravene *(kon-truh-VEEN), verb*
To go against or deny. A person who opposes something by action or argument can be said to *contravene* that thing.

> *The orders I left were to be CONTRAVENED by no one but the colonel.*

contravention *(kon-truh-VEN-shun), noun*
An instance of contradiction or opposition; also, the condition of being overruled or disobeyed.

> *Your appearance here without the full report is in blatant CONTRAVENTION of the instructions laid out in my memo.*

contretemps *(KAHN-truh-tah), noun*
This French word means an embarrassing and inopportune occurrence.

> *I really would have preferred to avoid that CONTRETEMPS with my wife while her parents were at our house.*

contrite *(kun-TRITE), adjective*
Inclined to express penitence or apology.

> *Myrtle's CONTRITE speech did little to mitigate her supervisor's frustration at the delay in the release of the Model X.*

contrition *(kun-TRISH-un), noun*
Sadness or remorse over past wrong actions. Technically, *contrition* is one of the conditions for absolution from sin for members of the Roman Catholic church. The word is also used in a broader secular sense.

> *He showed not the least CONTRITION for his acts, even when confronted by his victims.*

contrivance *(kun-TRY-vunce), noun*
A device or artful means of acquiring or performing something. *Contrivance* may refer to an actual mechanical object, or, more darkly, to a plot or scheme.

> *The false expense report totals—a rather obvious CONTRIVANCE—were discovered well before the embezzlement took place.*

controvert *(KON-truh-vert), verb*

To oppose with logical reasoning; to dispute or contradict.

> *No matter how many attempts the defense makes to CONTROVERT the details of this sequence of events, the fact remains that the defendant was seen leaving the building immediately after the murder.*

contumely *(kon-TYOO-muh-lee), noun*

A rude display in speech or deed; contemptuous behavior. *Contumely* can also mean humiliating derision.

> *No matter how long he had held the grudge against Aaron, his CONTUMELY at the wedding was uncalled for.*

conundrum *(kuh-NUN-drum), noun*

A riddle or puzzle.

> *"I don't understand anything," Stan said, in the months following graduation. "Now that I'm out on my own, my whole life is one big CONUNDRUM."*

convalescence *(kon-vuh-LESS-unce), noun*

The process of regaining one's health after an illness. *Convalescence* is derived from the Latin for "to grow stronger."

> *Her CONVALESCENCE was impeded by the primitive medical facilities on the island.*

convene *(kun-VEEN), verb*

To gather or assemble.

> *The legislature will not CONVENE this year until February 1.*

convex *(kon-VEX), adjective*

Curving outward, as the outside of a sphere. (See, for comparison, the entry for *concave.*)

> *Little Stephen laughed as he watched the tiny car plunge off the CONVEX surface of his large toy ball.*

conveyance *(kuhn-VAY-unts), noun*

In general, a *conveyance* is something that serves to transport something or someone. In real estate terms, a *conveyance* is the document that creates a property transfer.

> *Our visit to the "wild west" site was greatly enhanced by a ride on an authentic CONVEYANCE: a Conestoga wagon.*

convivial *(kuhn-VIV-ee-ull), adjective*
Describes someone who is fond of good times: drinking, feasting, hanging out with good friends.
> *Kevin is so CONVIVIAL that he's always the life of the party.*

convocation *(kon-vo-KAY-shun), noun*
An assembly of people gathered in response to a summons. *Convocation* also has a technical meaning within the Episcopal church: a gathering of laity requested by church officials.
> *The address Mr. Freling gave at the CONVOCATION challenged all graduates to excel.*

convoke *(kuhn-VOKE), verb*
To call together for a meeting; to summon. You might also see the noun form of this word, which is "convocation."
> *An announcement went out over the intercom to CONVOKE seminar participants.*

convoluted *(kon-vuh-LOO-tid), adjective*
Complicated and twisted; intermingled or intimately folded together. *Convoluted* means, literally, folded into a coil or spiral; it is more commonly used to express an extreme state of complication and/or interdependency.
> *His argument, though perhaps sound to an expert in the field, seemed extremely CONVOLUTED to me.*

copious *(KO-pee-us), adjective*
Abundant; large or generous in extent. That which is broad in scope or abundant is *copious*.
> *The winter's COPIOUS rainfall was welcomed by area farmers.*

coquettish *(ko-KET-ish), adjective*
Given to flirting. *Coquettish* is almost always used to describe women rather than men.
> *Little Amy's COQUETTISH display was noted with amusement by all.*

cord *(kord), noun*
A thin piece of rope, plastic, etc. (See, for comparison, the entry for *chord*.)
> *Today's rock artists are used to performing with microphones that do not require CORDS.*

cordial *(KORD-jull), adjective*
Pleasant; marked by warmth or kindness.
> *The Fords extended a CORDIAL welcome to us as we arrived for the party.*

cornucopia *(korn-yuh-COE-pee-uh), noun*
This Latin word means "horn of plenty," and a *cornucopia* has become a familiar symbol of Thanksgiving: a horn-like container overflowing with nature's bounty. In general, a *cornucopia* is an overabundance, a seemingly inexhaustible supply of something.

> *Jenny returned from the beach with a CORNUCOPIA of beach junk: T-shirts, coffee mugs, and liquefied bags of saltwater taffy.*

corollary *(KORE-uh-lare-ee), noun*
Accompanying element; consequence; thing brought about as a result (of some factor).

> *The natural COROLLARY of your theory that Hawkins murdered his mistress to silence her would appear to be that she had told him she was about to go public with details of their affair.*

corporal *(KOR-puh-rul), adjective*
Related to the body. Also: a military rank. (See, for comparison, the entry for *corporeal*.)

> *The school has a strict policy forbidding CORPORAL punishment.*

corporeal *(kor-PORE-ee-ul), adjective*
Tangible; having material existence. (See, for comparison, the entry for *corporal*.)

> *The estate sold the late author's CORPOREAL assets, but it retained the copyright of all his intellectual properties, both published and unpublished.*

corpulent *(KORP-you-lunt), adjective*
Obese; fat; bulky.

> *A CORPULENT waiter, apparently meant to frighten us into sensible eating, waddled out to ask us whether we were interested in hearing about the restaurant's special low-calorie entrees.*

correlate *(KORE-uh-late), noun and adjective*
To relate logically or systematically; to link; as a noun (KORE-uh-lut), something correlated to something else.

> *I believe I can demonstrate convincingly that the increased cancer rate in the town is directly CORRELATED to the dumping practices of your firm over the past twenty.*

corrigendum *(kor-ih-JEHN-dum), noun*
An error to be corrected in a manuscript. (Plural: corrigenda.)

> *The proofreader handed the manuscript back to Bill, who was horrified to find that it still contained hundreds of CORRIGENDA.*

C

corroborate *(kuh-ROB-uh-reyt) verb*

To make more certain; to confirm.

> *The witness was able to CORROBORATE the defendant's testimony.*

cosmic *(KOZ-mik), adjective*

Of or pertaining to the universe as a whole; also, far-reaching or pervasive.

> *It is my hope that the council will use our report as a blueprint for COSMIC, rather than cosmetic, changes in city government.*

cosmopolitan *(kahz-muh-PAUL-uh-ton), adjective*

Describes someone who is worldly and sophisticated.

> *You would never think someone so COSMOPOLITAN was raised in a small town two hundred miles from the nearest city.*

costive *(KAH-stiv), adjective*

Specifically, *costive* refers to constipation or something that causes constipation. More generally, the word describes slow and sluggish people or things.

> *I took my car to a mechanic because of my car's increasingly COSTIVE performance.*

coterie *(KOH-tuh-ree), noun*

From the French meaning "an association of tenant farmers," a *coterie* is an exclusive group of people, often meeting with a specific goal in mind.

> *Those in favor of the proposal formed a COTERIE that quickly became a very vocal minority.*

council *(KOWN-sul), noun*

An assembly gathered together for deliberation or consultation.

> *The neighborhood COUNCIL meets every Tuesday night to discuss issues of interest to our community.*

counsel *(KOWN-sul), noun*

A discussion of ideas or opinions.

> *Katrina's advisor was always available to COUNSEL her about work-related issues.*

countenance *(KOUNT-nunce), verb*

The familiar noun form of this word means "appearance." As a verb, *countenance* is to indicate approval, to sanction something.

> *I'm afraid I can't COUNTENANCE your dangerous exploits, so please take me home.*

counterculture *(KOUNT-er-kuhl-chuhr), noun*

A group of people—typically young people—whose actions and values oppose those of the larger society.

> *Whether the nation is at war or at peace, it always spawns a COUNTERCULTURE.*

counterintuitive *(kount-er-in-TOO-ih-tiv), adjective*
An assertion or belief that does not seem logical but which, in practice, turns out to be true and accurate.

> *Since people have so much more control over local politics, it seems COUNTERINTUITIVE that people are more likely to vote for president of the United States than for city council members.*

countermand *(KOUNT-er-mand), verb*
To cancel officially, especially to cancel a previous order.

> *Once Harold began smoking again, he COUNTERMANDED the no-smoking policy he'd recently adopted for his business.*

countervail *(kown-tur-VAIL), verb*
To use equal force against; to compensate.

> *The challenger hit the champion with two quick left jabs and a right uppercut, but the champion COUNTERVAILED with a left hook.*

coup de grace *(koo duh GRAHCE), noun*
A decisive act or event that brings a situation to a close; the finishing blow.

> *The COUP DE GRACE came when Paul threw his bowl of oatmeal at Mona's feet, leading her to reevaluate their relationship.*

couplet *(KUP-lut), noun*
In poetry, two related lines, similar in rhyme or rhythm.

> *The use of the rhymed COUPLET at the end of a scene is a stock technique employed by Elizabethan playwrights to alert the audience to an upcoming shift in the action.*

covenant *(KUH-vuh-nent), noun*
A binding agreement entered into by two or more. According to the Bible, a *covenant* was made between the ancient Israelites and Jehovah.

> *To James the arrangement was an informal understanding, but to Michael it was a holy COVENANT.*

covert *(KO-vert), adjective*
Secret; covered over. Something that is *covert* is concealed or surreptitious.

> *The COVERT operation was a success, but only a few people would ever know its significance.*

covetous *(KUHV-ih-tuss), adjective*
Greedy and willing to go to shameless lengths to earn wealth.

> *"The COVETOUS behavior of the average game show contestant makes me feel sick to my stomach," Helen said.*

cow (COW), verb

As a verb, "cow" means to intimidate, to frighten with a show of strength.

Even after the Blitz's repeated bombings, England was not COWED by Hitler's Nazis.

crag (KRAGG), noun

A steep rock formation rising higher than its surrounding rocks.

Because this was my first rock-climbing experience, I regarded the huge CRAG we were approaching with some nervousness.

crapulous (KRAP-yuh-luss), adjective

From the Latin meaning "sick with gluttony," *crapulous* describes someone who eats and drinks too much, or it describes the effects of eating and drinking too much. In other words . . . it's a great way to describe a hangover.

Jim spent the day after the party in a CRAPULOUS state.

crass (KRASS), adjective

Describes those who are coarse and crude in their actions and manner—and often—the language such people use.

Will you please remember that you're over fifty and stop being so CRASS?

credence (KREE-dence), noun

Acceptance as factual; legitimacy. *Credence* is belief or plausibility.

His pacifist arguments lost CREDENCE when he admitted that he had worked for a defense contractor for some years.

credible (KRED-ih-bul), adjective

Worthy of belief; plausible. (See, for comparison, the entry for *creditable*.)

The prosecution's witnesses seemed forthright and CREDIBLE, while those of the defense weren't quite as believable.

creditable (KRED-ih-tuh-bull), adjective

Worthy of praise. (See, for comparison, the entry for *credible*.)

You've done a CREDITABLE job on this project, Farnsworth; remind me to give you a raise.

credulous (KREJ-uh-luss), adjective

Given to acceptance or belief. A *credulous* person is one who accepts even outlandish assertions easily.

The swindler found a ready market for his wares in the CREDULOUS townsfolk.

crepitate *(KREPP-uh-tate), verb*
To crack, crinkle, or pop. *Crepitate* has come to be a "polite" word for flatulence because flatulence often makes a cracking or popping sound.

> *Joe jumped up and sat down several times, as if to prove that his chair—and not he—was CREPITATING.*

crepuscular *(krih-PUSS-kya-lerr), adjective*
Having to do with twilight or things—like certain bugs—that are active at twilight. In addition, *crepuscular* means "dim."

> *There's nothing like the CREPUSCULAR cast of the sky just before full dark falls.*

crescendo *(kruh-SHEN-doe), noun*
A gradual increase in volume or intensity to a certain point (used especially in relation to musical works).

> *As the orchestra reached a thundering CRESCENDO, my six-year-old son continued to sleep peacefully by my side.*

crestfallen *(KREST-fall-uhn), adjective*
In low spirits; extremely depressed.

> *When I heard that Mapa would have to work late that evening, I was CRESTFALLEN.*

criterion *(krie-TEER-ee-un), noun*
Standards; qualities or preconditions that must be met. Plural: criteria.

> *Stan met all of the college's CRITERIA for admission, but he put off applying because he simply didn't believe he was smart enough to survive there.*

croissant *(kruh-SONT or kwa-SON), noun*
A crescent-shaped roll or pastry, sometimes prepared with a sweet or savory filling.

> *For Ellen, the CROISSANTS and fresh-squeezed orange juice were about the only things that made the company's breakfast meetings bearable.*

cryptic *(KRIP-tik), adjective*
Secret; coded; concealed from open understanding.

> *After making a few CRYPTIC comments on the impermanence of all artistic effort, Melody slunk into her room; we learned in the morning that she had burned every page of her manuscript.*

crystalline *(KRISS-tuh-lean), adjective*
Extremely clear or clear-cut, resembling crystal.

> *The docent's CRYSTALLINE description of a springhouse was easily understood by the children.*

cubism *(KYOO-biz-um), noun*

A school of sculpture and painting that came to prominence in the early twentieth century in which forms are rendered as geometric structures.

> *Although Picasso is the first painter most people think of when asked to name a pioneer of CUBISM, his friend George Braque was equally important in the development of the movement.*

cubit *(KYOO-bit), noun*

An archaic unit of measure, roughly equivalent to twenty inches.

> *Most editions of the Book of Genesis give the measurements of Noah's Ark in CUBITS, although some editors have converted such passages to modern terms of measurement.*

culinary *(KYOO-lih-nar-ee), adjective*

Relating to cooking or the preparation of food.

> *My CULINARY efforts these days are much humbler than my library of cookbooks would lead you to believe.*

cull *(kull), verb*

To assemble or collect bit by bit; to select.

> *Having CULLED the most impressive poems from her early work, Ariel felt she was ready to submit the collection for publication.*

culminate *(KUL-mih-nate), verb*

To climax or reach a high point. Something that *culminates* concludes or reaches its fulfillment.

> *The seemingly endless series of Union victories CULMINATE in Lee's surrender at Appomatox.*

culpable *(KUL-puh-bull), adjective*

Blameworthy; accountable for error or wrongdoing. Someone who is *culpable* is responsible for misdeed.

> *After Ryan was found CULPABLE for the financial mismanagement at his firm, he was forced to resign.*

cumbersome *(KUM-ber-sum), adjective*

Hard to manage; awkward in handling due to bulk, weight, or extent. Something that is troublesome and unwieldy is *cumbersome.*

> *The six-volume set is exhaustive, but rather CUMBERSOME; I prefer the abridged version.*

cupidity *(kyoo-PID-ih-tee), noun*
Greed; extreme desire for wealth. One who is obsessed with acquiring money shows *cupidity*.

> *Paul's CUPIDITY led to much unhappiness and sorrow in later life, though his wealth was not to be denied.*

curing *(KYOO-ring), verb*
Serving to provide a remedy. *Curative* refers to the ability to provide alleviation of an ailment.

> *The CURATIVE measures were slow but effective; Joseph eventually recovered completely.*

curriculum *(KUH-rik-yuh-lum), noun*
The courses of study, educational plan, or study path of a learning institution.

> *The history department here offers a solid, challenging CURRICULUM equal to that of the more prestigious Ivy League schools—and at a fraction of the cost.*

cursory *(KUR-suh-ree), adjective*
Performed with haste and without care.

> *Mrs. Wallace avoided giving tests on the Friday before a vacation, as she knew her students' efforts would be CURSORY at best.*

curtail *(ker-TALE), verb*
To abridge or truncate; to lessen, usually by taking or cutting away from.

> *His new office's 8:00 a.m. meetings meant Dwight would have to CURTAIL his late-night television watching.*

curvaceous *(kurr-VAY-shuss), adjective*
Having shapely and voluptuous curves.

> *In the five years since I last saw her, Brenda had blossomed from a beanpole tomboy into a CURVACEOUS young beauty.*

cusp *(kusp), noun*
A point formed by the intersection of two curves.

> *Just above the CUSP of the arch was a hook meant to hold a hanging plant.*

cygnet *(SIG-nit), noun*
A young swan.

> *The proud mother swan led her brood of CYGNETS toward the north end of the pond.*

C

cynical *(SIN-uh-kuhl), adjective*
The cynics were a group of ancient Greek philosophers who rejected all conventions and conventional behavior. In modern times, a *cynical* person is one who thinks the worst of human nature, often in a smug and self-superior way.

> *You don't have to be so CYNICAL just because your favorite casino stopped offering bottled beer for a dollar!*

cynosure *(SIN-uh-sure), noun*
Derived from the Latin word denoting the North Star, a *cynosure* is a center of attention or attraction.

> *Even with all the games and the colorful parade, the fireworks were the obvious CYNOSURE of the Independence Day festivities.*

D

dabble *(DAB-uhl), verb*

To work in something or concern oneself with something in an offhand manner.

I always just thought I DABBLED in watercolors until the mayor saw one of my paintings and offered me a thousand dollars for it.

daedal *(DEE-duhl), adjective*

Daedalus was a genius of ancient Greece who invented the dreaded, nearly-escape-proof Cretan labyrinth. As a result, *daedal* means either something extremely intricate (like Daedalus's labyrinth) or something/someone very skillful and artistic (like Daedalus himself).

I thought I could repair my computer until I got a look at the machine's DAEDAL circuitry.

dalliance *(DAL-ee-unce), noun*

A lighthearted undertaking; carefree spending of time. A *dalliance* is an inconsequential event. (The word often refers to an amorous flirtation or distraction).

Jean made a show of being jealous, but the truth was she understood Brian's past DALLIANCES.

dandle *(DAN-dull), verb*

To bounce (a child) on one's knees or in one's arms.

To calm the baby down, Aunt Irene DANDLED her on her knee and sang nursery rhymes.

dank *(dank), adjective*

Damp and chilly. That which is unpleasantly cold and moist is *dank*.

Inside the cold, DANK recesses of the cave, Fred felt suddenly and terrifyingly isolated.

daub *(dawb), verb*

To smear with a sticky substance; to paint a surface in a hurried fashion.

I can see you've DAUBED a little black grease paint under your nose, Frank, but I'm afraid a good Groucho costume will require more than that.

dauntless *(DAWNT-luss), adjective*

Unable to be intimidated or put down; brave; fearless.

Although Jan had told Michael she would never marry him, he was a DAUNTLESS suitor, sending flowers and candy on a daily basis.

dawdle *(DAW-dull), verb*

To waste time; to loiter or loaf.

"If you don't stop DAWDLING," Mrs. Adams scolded her husband, "we'll be late for the opera."

de facto *(dih FAK-toe), noun*
In fact; actual.

> *The death of the prime minister left Jones, for the moment, the DE FACTO leader of the nation.*

de rigueur *(deuh rih-GER), adjective*
Required by etiquette; in good taste or form.

> *Since black tie and tails were DE RIGUEUR for the social events his new wife attended regularly, Julian found himself buying a tuxedo for the first time in his life.*

deadlock *(DED-lok), noun*
An impasse resulting from two opposing and resistant forces.

> *With one member absent due to illness, the council found itself facing a four-to-four DEADLOCK after nearly two days of debate on the measure.*

dearth *(DURRTH), noun*
An inadequate supply, especially one that leads to a catastrophic event.

> *The DEARTH of rice worldwide has sparked fears of a global famine.*

debacle *(dih-BA-kull), noun*
Utter collapse or rout. A *debacle* is a complete (often ludicrous) failure. The word originally referred to collapsing sheets or river ice.

> *The initiative seemed promising enough, but turned out to be another of George's DEBACLES.*

debase *(dih-BASE), verb*
To lower in value.

> *Once I lost its back bumper and crunched in its rear quarterpanel, my car was so DEBASED I practically had to give it away.*

debauchery *(dih-BOCH-er-ee), noun*
Licentiousness; overindulgent sexual expression. To accuse someone of *debauchery* is to say that person is intemperate and immoral with regard to indulgence in physical pleasures.

> *DeSade's critics claimed they had only to consult his writings for evidence of his own DEBAUCHERY.*

debilitate *(dih-BIIL-ih-tate), verb*
To enfeeble or weaken. Something that *debilitates* a person devitalizes him and depletes his strength.

> *Fran's DEBILITATING illness slowly sapped her will to live.*

D

debonair *(deb-uh-NAIR), adjective*
Suave: sophisticated and charming. *Debonair* derives from the French for "of good lineage."

> *Paul's DEBONAIR manner never abandoned him, even at the most difficult moments.*

debug *(dee-BUG), verb*
To remove errors from (a computer program).

> *Although the initial programming work was complete, Aaron anticipated that the DEBUGGING process would be long and arduous.*

debutante *(DEB-yoo-tont), noun*
A young woman making her debut into society; any unmarried young woman perceived to move in high social circles.

> *Amanda and her friends scanned the newspaper's society column for a review of their DEBUTANTE ball.*

decadence *(dek-uh-dunce), noun*
Characterized by declining moral standards. *Decadence* can refer to the declining standards of a nation, a period of time, or an individual.

> *After six months on the prairie. Clyde found it difficult to return to what he saw as the DECADENCE of city life.*

decalogue *(DEK-uh-log), noun*
The Ten Commandments. *Decalogue* refers to the commandments given to Moses on Mount Sinai as recounted in the Bible.

> *Mr. Collins, we are dealing here with a series of administrative guidelines we may administer as we see fit—not with a DECALOGUE.*

decanter *(dih-CAN-ter), noun*
A fancy glass bottle used for serving wine, brandy, etc.

> *As teenagers, Austin and Billy would sometimes steal wine from the DECANTER in the den, replacing it with fruit juice.*

decapitate *(dee-KAP-ih-tate), verb*
To remove the head of.

> *Although the guillotine was initially proposed as a humane method of execution, the idea of using a machine to DECAPITATE criminals now strikes most people as barbaric.*

decasyllabic *(dek-uh-sil-LAB-ik), noun*
In verse, having ten syllables in one line.

> *The epic poem followed a DECASYLLABIC form.*

deciduous *(dih-SID-you-us), adjective*
Describes something that falls off or sheds seasonally during development.

> *Every autumn people travel here from miles around to watch the multihued pageant of DECIDUOUS trees.*

decimate *(DESS-ih-mate), verb*
Technically, something is *decimated* if it is reduced one-tenth. But the term has been generalized to mean greatly reducing something, to the point of wiping it out.

> *Logging has DECIMATED North America's Northern Spotted Owl population.*

decipher *(dih-CIE-fur), verb*
To figure out or make sense of; to get the meaning of (particularly with relation to ancient or difficult writing).

> *"If we can DECIPHER the symbols on these scrolls," said the archaeologist, "I believe we'll know exactly where to look for the tomb."*

déclassé *(day-klass-AY), adjective*
This French word describes someone whose social position has fallen or labels someone or something as being of inferior status.

> *Jean thought her imitation designer bag looked like the real thing, but the other girls in her exclusive private school ridiculed Jean—and her bag—for being DÉCLASSÉ.*

decorous *(DECK-er-us), adjective*
Marked by good taste, dignity, and propriety.

> *Marshall's DECOROUS demeanor will serve him well as an ambassador.*

decorum *(di-COR-um), noun*
Social propriety; dignified conduct. *Decorum* can also refer to a harmonious union of elements in a piece of art or literature.

> *Though the delegates were extremely frustrated at the chairman's move, they betrayed no emotion, and strict DECORUM was observed in the meeting hall.*

decree *(dih-KREE), noun*
An official order or announcement, especially from the government or another recognized authority, that settles a matter with finality; also, to issue such an order.

> *The DECREE mandating integration of public schools set off one of the most bitterly divisive conflicts in the town's history.*

decrepit *(di-KREP-it), adjective*
Enfeebled, as by old age. *Decrepit* can refer to a weakened person, or to an object or idea that is past its prime.

> *The car's DECREPIT appearance was deceiving; Colin found it capable of 75 mph on the highway, and it got very good mileage.*

D

decry *(dih-CRY), verb*
To condemn, ridicule, or denounce as harmful.

> *It is unconscionable to DECRY due process just because the system is sometimes abused.*

deduce *(di-DOOSE), verb*
To infer; to derive from evidence or assumption. *Deduce* can also mean to trace down, but the logical sense is much more widespread.

> *Holmes looked around the garden and somehow DEDUCED that the killer was a man of middle age with thinning brown hair, approximately six feet tall.*

deem *(deem), verb*
To judge; to regard or assess.

> *For reasons the writer could not fathom, his boardroom scene, which contained no nudity or violence and only the mildest language, was DEEMED unsuitable for network broadcast.*

deescalate *(dee-ES-kuh-late), verb*
To diminish in size, intensity, or extent. *Deescalate* is the opposite of escalate.

> *The president's decision to DEESCALATE the war won him considerable support on the nation's college campuses.*

deface *(dih-FACE), verb*
To disfigure or damage.

> *It breaks my heart to see the old stone bridge, my one unchanging companion from boyhood, DEFACED with the spray painted grumblings of drunken teenagers.*

defalcate *(dih-FAL-kate), verb*
To embezzle.

> *No one knew for certain how the corrupt banker had made his fortune, but it was rumored that he had DEFALCATED funds from a bogus charitable organization.*

defamation *(def-uh-MAY-shun), noun*
False, baseless attack on a person's or group's reputation. To *defame* is to disgrace; defamation is the act of defaming.

> *After the last of the Journal's articles on her, Virginia decided she had put up with enough DEFAMATION and decided to sue.*

defeatist *(dih-FEET-ist), adjective*
Accepting defeat as an unavoidable consequence of life; pessimistic.

> *Sheldon's DEFEATIST attitude led Monica, his supervisor, to wonder whether he would ever complete the project he was working on.*

defer *(dih-FUR), verb*

To delay or put off until another time; also, to yield with respect.

> *With regard to the scheduling of our announcement, I DEFER to my friend the chairman.*

deference *(DEF-er-ence), noun*

Due respect or submission to the ideas and/or judgment of another. *Deference* is the courtesy of yielding to a (presumably higher, senior, or more authoritative) entity.

> *In DEFERENCE to my family's wishes, I am not discussing this issue with the media.*

deficient *(dih-FISH-unt), adjective*

Lacking.

> *As a result of a diet DEFICIENT in calcium, Cathy's fingernails were very thin and easily broken.*

defile *(dih-FILE), verb*

To pollute; to corrupt or make unclean.

> *The river that only a few years ago ran clean and clear is now DEFILED with a witches' brew of chemicals, thanks to the new tanning plant.*

deft *(DEFT), adjective*

Skillful and quick in one's movements or actions.

> *The magician's DEFT fingers seemed to make all manner of objects disappear and reappear.*

defunct *(dih-FUNKT), adjective*

Related to something that—or someone who—has ceased to exist.

> *Once a staple of the American landscape, so-called five-and-dime stores are now all but DEFUNCT in the United States.*

degenerate *(di-JEN-er-it), adjective and noun*

Having regressed or descended to a lower state. As a noun, *degenerate* means a person who has declined to a point of immorality or low refinement.

> *What began as an intellectually rigorous debate concluded as a DEGENERATE shouting match.*

deify *(DAY-ih-fy), verb*

To elevate to the level of divinity. When something is *deified*, it is exalted or revered as godlike.

> *To promote a celebrity is one thing, to DEIFY him quite another.*

deign *(dane), verb*
To condescend; to lower oneself to a position or role considered unsuitable.
> *Since Walter won that writing prize, he hasn't DEIGNED to return my phone calls.*

deja vu *(day-zhuh VOO), noun*
The experience of seeming to have seen or experienced a present event at some time in the past. *Deja vu* is French for "already seen."
> *Those who remember the format of last year's test may feel a sense of DEJA VU upon reviewing this year's.*

delectable *(de-LEK-tuh-bull), adjective*
Highly pleasing; enjoyable (especially of a food). *Delectable* is derived from the Latin root for "delightful."
> *The Thanksgiving table was crammed with DELECTABLE dishes, but they would not be eaten that night; the news from abroad had diminished everyone's appetite.*

delete *(duh-LEET), verb*
To leave out or omit.
> *After a brief discussion with the principal, the members of the booster club decided to DELETE the section of their cheer that questioned the ancestry of the coach of the Brentwater football team.*

deleterious *(del-i-TEER-ee-us), adjective*
Harmful or injurious. *Deleterious* is a word used primarily in legal circles to give a sense of formality to the assessment of harm.
> *My client was regularly subjected to high radiation levels, hazardous compounds, and many other DELETERIOUS environmental conditions.*

delft *(delft), noun*
A kind of glazed earthenware featuring blue and white patterns.
> *My mother's gift of DELFT cookware complemented our blue and white kitchen beautifully.*

delineate *(di-LIN-ee-ate), verb*
To outline; to describe the primary features of. One can *delineate* by sketching, or by using words or concepts to describe the principle points of something.
> *The rules, which had been quite vague, were now DELINEATED clearly.*

delinquent *(dih-LINK-went), adjective*
Describes someone who—or some group that—offends due to the violation of laws. Also, *delinquent* describes a payment that is overdue.
> *Carl's drawer full of unpaid parking tickets has caused the local police to label him a DELINQUENT.*

dell *(dell), noun*

A small wooded valley; a glen.

> *I emerged from the tent in the wee hours of the morning to find a sand-colored doe peering at me from the edge of the DELL.*

delphic *(DELL-fick), adjective*

Delphi is the site of an ancient Greek oracle, or shrine to a prophetic god. Oracles's prophecies often were obscure and had to be interpreted by experts. As a result, *Delphic* describes something that is obscurely prophetic.

> *For years, other economists, reporters, and just plain folks scrambled to interpret Federal Reserve chairman Alan Greenspan's DELPHIC comments about the strength or weakness of the economy.*

deluge *(DELL-yoodje), noun*

A great flood or heavy rain; an overwhelming inundation of anything.

> *As the newest member of the accounting firm, Fred was unprepared for the DELUGE of tax returns that landed on his desk two weeks before the April 15 deadline.*

delusion *(de-LOO-zhun), noun*

An accepted (but undetected) falsehood. To delude is to deceive or mislead; a *delusion* is an instance of that act.

> *His DELUSIONS increased to such a point that rational discussion was impossible.*

demagogue *(DEM-uh-gog), noun*

An individual (usually a politician or other leader) who gains power by appealing to the emotions and passions of the people, especially by means of inflamed speech. *Demagogues* often address complicated issues by suggesting simplistic measures that appeal to public prejudice or misconception.

> *The senator's aides honestly believed that they had agreed to go to work for a statesman, but saw now that they were furthering the ambitions of a DEMAGOGUE.*

demarcate *(de-MAR-kate), verb*

To establish the limits of. *Demarcating* is the process of setting down boundaries.

> *The idea of a new house had been abstract, but once Joan and Peter DEMARCATED the land, their undertaking felt suddenly real.*

dementia *(duh-MEN-chuh), noun*

A mental illness characterized by loss of reason. *Dementia* is caused by neuron damage or loss within the brain.

> *Owing to the deceased's DEMENTIA at the time the will was signed, there was considerable legal wrangling over the estate.*

demerit *(dih-MARE-it), noun*

A mark resulting in a loss of privilege for an offender.

> *Max received five DEMERITS from Mrs. Collins for his constant tardiness.*

demimonde *(DEMM-ih-mond), noun*

This French word initially described prostitutes. The word still carries with it that connotation, but in general, it refers to women who are considered to have loose morals due to their indiscreet or promiscuous behavior.

> *Unless you're trying to get yourself labeled a DEMIMONDE, Sylvia, you need to stop hanging out with guys like Roger.*

demiurge *(DEM-ee-urj), noun*

From the Greek meaning "artisan," a *demiurge* is a powerful creative force or a creative personality.

> *After trying several different professions, Jake realized he was a marketing DEMIURGE.*

demographics *(dih-muh-GRAF-icks), noun*

The study of people's lifestyles, habits, spending, etc., typically for the purpose of targeting products for—or culling votes from—these different sub-groups.

> *The DEMOGRAPHICS suggested that the new flavor of juice would be a hit with young mothers.*

demur *(dih-MUR), verb*

To take exception; to object, particularly as a result of deeply held principles.

> *Mike suggested that we run an ad alluding to our opponent's supposed ties to organized crime, but Congressman Taylor DEMURRED.*

demure *(di-MYOOR), adjective*

Modest; affecting a reserved and shy appearance. Someone whose behavior is (outwardly, at least) sober, retiring, or sedate is *demure*.

> *Mr. Atkins found the Hallis twins DEMURE, and wondered at what they would say about him when he left.*

denigrate *(DEN-ih-grate), verb*

To defame or speak ill of; literally, to blacken (a reputation, for instance).

> *Reprinting, without permission, the cruder poems of the writer's formative years was one strategy the reviewer used to DENIGRATE her entire body of work.*

denizen *(DEN-ih-zun), noun*

An inhabitant or resident.

> *Michael regarded homeless people as DENIZENS of another world until a series of setbacks landed him unexpectedly on the street.*

denote *(de-NOTE), verb*
To indicate or make clear; to serve as sign or symbol for something else. To say that A *denotes* B is to say that A signifies or indicates B.

Her chills and discoloration, Dr. Smith observed, DENOTED severe hypothermia.

denouement *(day-new-MAH), noun*
This French word for "untying" is used in literary circles to describe the resolution of a plot following its climax. In general, a *denouement* is the "wrapping-up" of any complex series of events.

I was disappointed with the play because I felt its DENOUEMENT left too many loose ends.

denounce *(dih-NOWNTS), verb*
To criticize or speak out against someone or something.

Joan DENOUNCED Walter for his sexist opinions.

dentifrice *(DEN-ti-friss), noun*
Any substance used to clean the teeth.

Dr. Sanchez gave me a lecture on the proper use of DENTIFRICES, and recommended several brands I could purchase in any supermarket.

denunciation *(de-nun-see-AY-shun), noun*
The act or example of denouncing. *Denunciation* is the act of accusing another (usually in a public forum) of some misdeed.

Paul's angry DENUNCIATION of his former company shocked even his friends.

deplete *(dih-PLEET), verb*
To use up completely; to exhaust.

Once the coal deposits in the valley had been DEPLETED, the town of Harlenville, which had thrived for thirty years, virtually ceased to exist.

deplorable *(de-PLORE-uh-bull), adjective*
Extremely reproachful; worthy of censure. Something that is *deplorable* is wretched or grievous.

Bill's spelling was DEPLORABLE; all his friends told him it was hopeless to pursue a career as a proofreader.

depose *(dih-POZE), verb*
To oust or remove from office or a position of power and authority; also, to take testimony from someone under oath.

After the dictator was DEPOSED, the country set about healing the wounds of a long civil war.

depraved *(duh-PRAVED), adjective*
Describes someone whose conduct or actions deviate considerably from what most believe is acceptable or morally right.

> *I knew I needed to stop dating Jared immediately when I saw that all the books on his shelves concerned the lives of DEPRAVED murderers.*

depravity *(dih-PRAV-ih-tee), noun*
Corruption, moral reprehensibility. Someone who corrupts something or introduces wickedness to it commits *depravity.*

> *The DEPRAVITY of those years is still summoned up with reverence by some of our more naive writers.*

deprecate *(DEP-ri-kate), verb*
To belittle or make known one's disapproval of. To *deprecate* someone is to "cut him down" verbally.

> *Jean insisted that her report contained not a single DEPRECATING word, but it was easy enough to read between the lines.*

depreciation *(dih-pree-shee-AY-shun), noun*
A decrease in value, quality, or power, particularly due to wear or age.

> *Thanks to five years of DEPRECIATION, I couldn't get more than $2,000 for that car if I took it back to the dealer now.*

deracinate *(dee-RASS-ih-nate), verb*
To uproot or to remove by force.

> *The hurricane DERACINATED populations all over the island.*

dereliction *(dare-uh-LIK-shun), noun*
Willful neglect; shirking of responsibility. *Dereliction* is the knowing failure to perform one's duty.

> *The sergeant's inaction that night led to troubling accusations of DERELICTION of duty.*

deride *(dih-RIDE), verb*
To ridicule with cruelty; to laugh at and make fun of.

> *His classmates DERIDED Joe for wearing argyle socks to the prom.*

derision *(de-RIZH-un), noun*
Ridicule. *Derision* is formed from the verb "deride," meaning "to belittle or make light of something or someone."

> *War seems imminent; our suggestions on finding a peaceful solution to this crisis have been met with DERISION from the other side.*

derivation *(dare-ih-VAY-shun), noun*
Source. Also: the act or process of deriving. A thing's *derivation* is its origin or path of descent.

> *The phrase's DERIVATION is unclear, but it may have its roots in an obscure tribal dialect of Borneo.*

derogatory *(dih-ROG-uh-tore-ee), adjective*
Tending to lessen or impair someone or something; disparaging and negative.

> *Butch's DEROGATORY remarks about my girlfriend were meant to goad me into a fight, but I was determined to keep my cool.*

derring-do *(DARE-ing-DOO), noun*
Heroic deeds; acts of bravery.

> *Luke Skywalker's challenges and feats of DERRING-DO are perhaps the most memorable elements of the Star Wars trilogy.*

descant *(DESS-kant), verb*
A *descant* is an improvised or composed harmonic melody sung above the main melody in a piece of music. As a verb, one *descants* if one talks or writes about a subject at great length.

> *The way Jay DESCANTS about obscure sports stars just tends to bore me to tears.*

descry *(dih-SKRIE), verb*
To spot as a result of attentive observation; to discover or find.

> *With mingled relief and dread the crew learned that the lookout had DESCRIED the white whale Ahab had been hunting.*

desecrate *(DESS-ih-krate), verb*
To abuse the sacred character of a thing. Those who write lewd sayings on a church wall, for instance, *desecrate* the church.

> *Such profane language from our organization's current leader serves only to DESECRATE the memory of the founder.*

desiccate *(DESS-ih-late), verb*
To cause to dry out.

> *The food preparation process for the items to be taken on the astronauts' voyage involved elaborate DESICCATING and sanitation procedures.*

desideratum *(di-sid-uh-RAH-tum), noun*
A thing to be desired. *Desideratum* finds its plural in *desiderata*, which is also the name of a popular short writing that outlines worthy spiritual objectives.

> *He eventually accepted that her love was a fleeting DESIDERATUM, one he could learn in time to do without.*

D

designate *(DEZ-ig-nate), verb*
To indicate; to point out or specify.
> *The Walker sisters DESIGNATED the last Thursday of each month as their evening to leave their husbands at home and go out to dinner together.*

despondency *(di-SPON-dun-see), noun*
Dejection; depression. *Despondency* is marked by a feeling that all hope is in vain.
> *It took Cloris several weeks to emerge from the DESPONDENCY that accompanied her breakup.*

despotism *(DESS-po-tiz-um), noun*
Authoritarian rule. *Despotism* is a system where one dominant figure exercises complete power.
> *It was not until some years after the revolution began that the General's DESPOTISM passed into history.*

destitute *(DESS-tih-tyoot), adjective*
Lacking something necessary; often refers to extreme poverty.
> *The DESTITUTE family still managed to put something into the collection plate every Sunday.*

desuetude *(DEHZ-wih-tyood), noun*
From the French meaning "to become unaccustomed," *desuetude* means disuse or discontinuance.
> *Telephones plugged into walls are one of many once-ubiquitous items that have fallen into DESUETUDE.*

desultory *(de-SUL-to-ree), adjective*
Aimless. A person or thing lacking guidance or progressing randomly can be said to be *desultory*.
> *Unable to believe it was his last day on the job, Bill wandered through the building, DESULTORY.*

detain *(dih-TANE), verb*
To delay; to keep from going on; to confine.
> *The border police DETAINED the pair for two hours while they searched every inch of their vehicle for narcotics.*

détente *(DAY-tahnt), noun*
From the French meaning "to slacken," a *détente* is the loosening of strained relations.
> *After Graham and Heather stopped yelling at and started listening to each other, the DÉTENTE between them began.*

determinism *(dih-TUR-mun-iz-um), noun*
The belief that a person's course of action is not free but predetermined by external circumstances.

> *A true disciple of DETERMINISM, Jerry felt he should not be held accountable for having married three women—since, as he argued, each of the relationships had been "meant to be."*

deterrent *(dih-TURR-ent), noun*
Something that prevents something from happening.

> *My mom and dad's presence at the condo acted as a DETERRENT to any hanky panky between me and my new girlfriend.*

detrimental *(det-rih-MEN-tul), adjective*
Damaging or harmful in effect.

> *Your husband's cruel words to the children will prove DETRIMENTAL to his cause during the custody hearing.*

detritus *(dih-TRITE-us), noun*
Loose material worn away from rocks or, generally, debris of any kind.

> *The DETRITUS left by the beachgoers made it clear why our oceans are polluted.*

deviate *(DEE-vee-ate), verb*
To turn away from or go off course; change course or direction. As a noun (DEE-vee-ut), a person who departs from the standard or norm.

> *My daughter's choice to wear cowboy boots with her wedding gown certainly DEVIATED from my standards of propriety, but there was no changing her mind.*

devoid *(dih-VOID), adjective*
Lacking utterly; without.

> *"No matter how skilled a surgeon you become," Dr. Smith told the intern, "you'll fail as a doctor if you continue to be DEVOID of compassion and sympathy for patients."*

dexterity *(dek-STARE-ih-tee), noun*
Adroitness; the quality of being skilled in using one's hands and body.

> *I couldn't hit a jump-shot to save my life, but my speed, DEXTERITY, and passing ability made me a valuable member of the varsity basketball team.*

dexterous *(DEK-ster-uss), adjective*
Skillful. *Dexterous* has its roots in the Latin for "right"—since that is the hand with which the majority of people are most skillful.

> *Byron proved a DEXTEROUS carpenter, making few errors even in his earliest days as an apprentice.*

diabolical *(die-uh-BOL-ih-kul), adjective*
Devilish, evil. Something *diabolical* is considered to be wicked or cruel.
> *The terrorists, the papers claimed, had a DIABOLICAL agenda.*

diadem *(DIE-uh-dem), noun*
A royal crown.
> *The princess arrived at the state banquet wearing a DIADEM of emeralds and diamonds.*

diagnostic *(die-ug-NOSS-tik), adjective*
Of or pertaining to diagnosis. Something used in evaluating a person's or thing's condition can be said to be *diagnostic* in nature.
> *The mechanic ran a DIAGNOSTIC computer test on the car.*

dialect *(DIE-uh-lekt), noun*
The aspects of a language (grammar, pronunciation, and vocabulary, for instance) particular to a geographic region.
> *Armed with four years of high school Spanish, I set out confidently on my vacation to Madrid—only to find myself adrift in a sea of incomprehensible DIALECTS on my arrival.*

dialectic *(die-uh-LEK-tic), adjective and noun*
Having to do with logical arguments. (Also: *dialectical.*) As a noun, *dialectic* means the practice of arriving nearer to the truth by means of logical examination.
> *The DIALECTIC thoroughness with which Paul could destroy an opponent's argument was legendary.*

diaphanous *(die-APH-uh-nuss), adjective*
So fine and sheer as to allow light to pass through. Also, describes something insubstantial or vague.
> *Your DIAPHANOUS logic might impress some people, but I can always tell when you're just shooting bull.*

diatribe *(DIE-uh-tribe), noun*
Bitter denunciation. A *diatribe* is a pointed and abusive critique.
> *The professor had scrawled a scathing DIATRIBE in red on the unfortunate boy's paper.*

dicey *(DIE-see), adjective*
Characterized by being risky, chancy, and of uncertain outcome.
> *Jordan was filled with confidence about hiking the unexplored terrain, but I found the prospect pretty DICEY myself.*

dichotomy *(die-KOT-uh-me), noun*
Division into two (contrasting) halves, pairs, or sets. A *dichotomy* is the division of mutually exclusive ideas or groups.
> *"There is public interest and there is private interest," said the Senator. "And reconciling that DICHOTOMY can be a difficult job."*

didactic *(die-DAK-tik), adjective*
Made or framed for the purpose of moral or ethical betterment. To say a work of art is *didactic* is to say that it forwards a clear vision of what is right and wrong, a vision the artist would like to pass on to his audience.
> *Simpson's early writings let the reader draw his own conclusions, but his later work is extremely DIDACTIC.*

diffident *(DIFF-ih-dunt), adjective*
Unassertive and lacking a sense of self-worth. A shy, retiring person can be said to be *diffident*.
> *Cheryl was perhaps too DIFFIDENT to work comfortably in such an outgoing office environment.*

diffuse *(diff-YOOZ), verb*
To spread out and circulate through air, water, etc. As an adjective, the word is pronounced "diff-USE" and describes something that is scattered.
> *Serious allergies and colds were traced to mold DIFFUSED by the faulty air conditioning system.*

digress *(die-GRESS), verb*
To wander off the point of a discourse or conversation; to turn away from a course.
> *The topic of the speech was interesting enough, but Bill had an unfortunate habit of DIGRESSING from his text with irrelevant off-the-cuff stories.*

dilapidated *(di-LAP-ih-date), adjective*
To fall into disrepair. To *dilapidate* is to decay or break down.
> *The DILAPIDATED barn swayed, heaved, and finally collapsed before Caitlyn's eyes.*

dilate *(DIE-late), verb*
To expand.
> *The rock star's DILATED pupils led some to believe that he had been experimenting again with narcotics, and quite recently.*

dilatory *(DIL-uh-tore-ee), adjective*
Likely to cause delay. That which proceeds at an unsatisfactorily slow rate is *dilatory*.
> *The workers' DILATORY attitude lost them a large contract.*

dilettante *(DIL-uh-tont), noun*

Someone with only an amateurish or aimless interest in a subject or discipline. A man who cultivates a superficial knowledge of modern art solely to impress others, for instance, might be called a *dilettante*.

> *The cafe was once a meeting-place for struggling artists and poets of genuine talent, but by 1970 it was nothing more than a swamp of DILETTANTES.*

dilute *(die-LOOT), verb*

To make the strength of something, such as a mixture, weaker by adding additional objects, ingredients, compounds, etc. to it.

> *Frederica never DILUTES her words. She'll tell you exactly how she feels.*

diminish *(dih-MIN-ish), verb*

To cause to be smaller; to decrease in size or importance.

> *In pointing out these problems, I don't mean for a moment to DIMINISH the achievements of your department this year.*

diminution *(dim-ih-NOO-shen), noun*

Reduction or decrease due to outside influence. In music, *diminution* is the repetition of a theme in notes of briefer duration than the original passage.

> *The stock fell in value by 75% in just over three hours; few issues can fully recover from such DIMINUTION.*

diminutive *(dih-MIN-yuh-tiv), adjective*

Describes someone or something of small stature.

> *Marcia's forceful personality overcomes her DIMINUTIVE stature.*

din *(DIN), noun or verb*

As a verb, "din" means to instill by constant repetition. As a noun, "din" is a noisy disturbance.

> *I could barely hear the waiter above the DIN in the popular restaurant.*

Dionysian *(die-uh-NIH-shun), adjective*

Relating to Dionysius, a Greek god of revelry; reminiscent of or pertaining to frenzied, uninhibited, or hedonistic behavior.

> *The fraternity's DIONYSIAN exploits were fun for a while, but when they resulted in his failing two classes, Emmett decided to go back to the quiet life.*

diorama *(di-uh-RA-mah), noun*

A small model of a scene featuring painted figures and backgrounds.

> *Using a cardboard box, paint, and plaster of Paris, Frank helped his son construct a working DIORAMA of a corner store for a school art project.*

diplomacy *(dih-PLO-muh-see), noun*

The conduct of relations among nations. *Diplomacy* can also refer to a tact among individuals that calls to mind the great discretion and sensitivity required of diplomats.

> *When DIPLOMACY fails, it is too often the young who pay the price of death on the battlefield.*

dipsomaniacal *(dip-so-muh-NIE-ih-kul), adjective*

Dipsomania is an uncontrolled craving for alcohol, so someone who suffers from this craving is considered *dipsomaniacal*.

> *The private detective summed up his latest client, a booze-loving gold digger, as the "DIPSOMANIACAL dame."*

diphthong *(DIF-thawng), noun*

A sound made by smoothly pronouncing two vowel sounds within one syllable.

> *English is full of DIPHTHONGS, examples of which can be found in such words as boil, house, and smile.*

dirge *(durj), noun*

A funeral song; a song of mourning.

> *The DIRGE from Cymbeline, according to Professor Alpert, is the only worthwhile passage to be found in that seldom-produced Shakespeare play.*

disabuse *(diss-uh-BYOOZ), verb*

To free oneself or someone else from an incorrect assumption or belief.

> *The bestselling work of history caused many to DISABUSE themselves of the notion that President Franklin Roosevelt was an entirely benevolent leader.*

disburse *(dis-BURSE), verb*

To pay out; to expend.

> *After meeting with the president, our comptroller was finally authorized to DISBURSE the funds.*

discerning *(Dis-SURN-ing), adjective*

Insightful; sound in evaluation or judgment.

> *Although Jamie is excellent at acquiring reference works, she is not the most DISCERNING editor when it comes to evaluating children's book proposals.*

discombobulate *(diss-kum-BOB-yoo-late), verb*

To confuse or throw into an awkward predicament. To say that someone is *discombobulated* is to say that he is utterly disconcerted.

> *The frenzied pace of eight hours on the trading floor had left me utterly DISCOMBOBULATED.*

D

discomfit *(diss-KUM-fit), verb*
To cause to come into disorder. *Discomfit* can also mean "to frustrate (someone)."
> *Fern's household was DISCOMFITED by the sudden, unannounced arrival of her relatives.*

disconcerting *(diss-kun-SERT-ing), adjective*
Ruffled; upset. That which upsets harmony or balance is *disconcerting*.
> *Michelle's escapades were quite DISCONCERTING to her parents.*

disconsolate *(dis-KON-suh-lut), adjective*
Beyond consolation; unable to be comforted; deep in grief or sorrow.
> *Jamie was DISCONSOLATE after missing what should have been the game-winning field goal.*

discordant *(dis-KOR-dunt), adjective*
Conflicting; lacking in harmony.
> *I find that composer's DISCORDANT style difficult to listen to.*

discreet *(dis-KREET), adjective*
Displaying or possessing tact and restraint in behavior and speech.
> *Mel felt his mother had been less than DISCREET in marrying Claude so soon after her first husband's funeral, and that she could easily have waited six months or so rather than three weeks.*

discrepancy *(dis-KREP-un-see), noun*
Inconsistency; an instance of disagreement or difference.
> *John was the only one to notice the DISCREPANCY between the cash register receipts and the amount of money in the drawer.*

discretion *(dis-KRESH-un), noun*
The ability or right to make decisions independently; also, the ability to be tactful and act with decorum.
> *Tim's use of profanity at the dinner party showed a startling lack of DISCRETION.*

discursive *(dis-KUR-siv), adjective*
Rambling; not to the point.
> *Unfortunately, the study group tended toward long, DISCURSIVE examinations of the day's social events rather than preparation for our term papers.*

disdain *(diss-DANE), verb*
To treat with contempt; to dismiss haughtily. To *disdain* is to reject due to unworthiness.
> *Mark DISDAINS Janet's company; he cannot forgive her lapse at last September's party.*

disenfranchise *(diss-in-FRAN-chize), verb*

To take away someone's right to vote or to deprive someone of legal rights or privileges.

> *By changing the bylaws, the city council effectively DISENFRANCHISED residents who lived near the city's urban core.*

disgruntle *(diss-GRUN-tull), verb*

To cause to become cross or discontented. To *disgruntle* is also to cause to feel cheated.

> *After years of mistreatment, the DISGRUNTLED employees finally decided to strike.*

dishabille *(dis-uh-BEE-uhl), noun*

From the French meaning "to undress," this word refers to someone who is dressed very casually or to someone with a careless manner.

> *"The only problem with working near the beach," said Jack, "is seeing all those elderly folks in various states of DISHABILLE."*

dishevel *(dih-SHEV-ul), verb*

To put (hair or clothing) into disarray.

> *Although Adam answered the interview questions intelligently, his DISHEVELED appearance led the interviewer to doubt his professionalism.*

disingenuous *(diss-in-JEN-yoo-uss), adjective*

Not inclined toward open dealing; less than truthful; other than appearances would suggest.

> *The Mayor's carefully worded denials never explicitly touched on her involvement in her campaign's alleged effort to buy votes, leading many to conclude that she was being DISINGENUOUS.*

disparage *(diss-PARE-udge), verb*

To speak or write debasingly of. To *disparage* is to communicate in such a way as to diminish another's reputation.

> *His disparaging remarks damaged both her character and her pride.*

disparate *(DISS-puh-rut), adjective*

Utterly dissimilar. Two things entirely or fundamentally different can be said to be *disparate*.

> *After inviting his mother to live on the East Coast with him, Clark wondered at how they would reconcile their DISPARATE lifestyles.*

disparity *(diss-PARE-ih-tee), noun*
The condition of being inequivalent or unequal. *Disparity* is inequality in age, measure, or extent.

> *The DISPARITY between the two horses was obvious: one was a swaybacked old nag, the other a stunning thoroughbred.*

dispel *(dis-PELL), verb*
To disperse; to drive away.

> *After the rioters had been DISPELLED and the fires put out, an eerie quiet fell over the smoldering city streets.*

disperse *(dis-PURSE), verb*
To cause to scatter or to break up.

> *With a few angry words, the candidate DISPERSED the meeting and stormed off.*

disport *(dih-SPORT), verb*
To play or frolic. To find a diversion is to *disport* oneself.

> *Jean and Michael DISPORTED themselves at the amusement park for the better part of the morning.*

disputation *(dis-pyoo-TA-shun), noun*
A debate, especially, a formal debate.

> *The two candidates for student body president gave surprisingly mature and well-reasoned DISPUTATIONS about important school issues.*

disquisition *(diss-kwuh-ZISH-un), noun*
A formal written or spoken exploration of a particular subject.

> *I was fascinated by the author's DISQUISITION concerning the history of the remote control.*

dissemble *(diss-SEM-bul), verb*
to act with an insincere or disguised motive.

> *Although many on the committee were convinced that the undersecretary was DISSEMBLING about how much he knew of rebel activities, there was no hard proof to support this view.*

disseminate *(diss-SEM-ih-nate), verb*
To scatter across a broad spectrum; to spread far and wide. To *disseminate* is to promulgate (a message, for instance).

> *In DISSEMINATING this information, Mr. Powers placed innumerable foreign operatives at grave risk.*

dissidence *(DISS-uh-dents), noun or adjective*
Strong disagreement, especially with a government. You might also see the adjective form of this word, which is *dissident*. Recently, the word *dissident* has become a noun, describing someone who expresses dissidence.

> *The newly-formed government decided to crack down on DISSIDENCE by jailing anyone who disagreed with governmental policies.*

dissimulate *(diss-IHM-you-late), verb*
To hide one's feelings from another, often by using untruths.

> *Feeling extremely guilty about his affair, Jake would DISSIMULATE behind a wall of anger whenever Tricia asked him pointed questions.*

dissipate *(DISS-ih-pate), verb*
To dispel by means of dispersal. To *dissipate* is also to vanish or cease.

> *The rain DISSIPATED and the flood waters receded.*

dissolution *(diss-so-LOO-shun), noun*
The act of dissolving into fragments or parts. *Dissolution* is the disintegration of that which comprises something.

> *The union's DISSOLUTION seemed imminent, but a change of leadership forestalled that crisis.*

dissonance *(DISS-uh-nunce), noun*
A harsh or inharmonious combination, especially of sounds. Elements of a logical argument that are in conflict can also be said to be in *dissonance*.

> *I could have no peace; the city's DISSONANCE poured unceasingly into my apartment.*

dissuade *(diss-SWADE), noun*
To convince to take alternate action. Someone who *dissuades* someone from doing something persuades that person to pursue another course.

> *Marge DISSUADED her brother from joining the army.*

distraught *(dih-STRAWT), adjective*
Deeply hurt emotionally.

> *Phyllis was DISTRAUGHT after her favorite cat died.*

diuretic *(die-er-ET-ik), noun*
Tending to increase urination; a drug that causes this increase.

> *After being admitted to the clinic for anorexia, Danielle told the doctors how she had used amphetamines and DIURETICS to speed her weight loss.*

diurnal *(dye-UHR-nul), adjective*
Occurring during the daytime. That which is not nocturnal and occurs only while the sun is out is *diurnal*.

> *Unlike other members of this species, the one we are studying is DIURNAL.*

divergence *(di-VER-gence), noun*
The act or process of departing from a given course or pattern. That which extends in separate directions from a single point experiences a *divergence*.

> *The DIVERGENCE in our opinions begins with the question of whether there can ever be a just war.*

divulge *(dih-VULJ), verb*
To make public something that once was secret.

> *Most information about John F. Kennedy's extramarital inclinations was not DIVULGED until after the president's death.*

DNA *(dee enn ay), noun*
A molecule that carries genetic information in all life forms. The workings of *DNA* are central concerns of biology and genetics.

> *The fantasy film E.T. led us to believe that space aliens, like humans, possess DNA, but it is safe to say that scientists are fairly skeptical about the whole subject.*

docile *(DOSS-ul), adjective*
Easily taught. In addition, someone is *docile* if he is submissive and easily led.

> *Susan was DOCILE in her younger days, but shows a real independent streak now.*

doctrinaire *(dok-trin-AIR), noun*
Favoring doctrines without concern for their practicability.

> *The resident is not well served by such DOCTRINAIRE advisers as Hawkins.*

dogged *(DAW-gid), adjective*
Stubbornly obstinate in pursuit of a particular goal.

> *Janice's DOGGED determination to get to the truth of every story makes her an excellent reporter.*

dogmatic *(dog-MAT-ik), adjective*
Adhering rigidly to a principle or belief. Someone who takes a *dogmatic* approach to an issue stays within ideological bounds at all times, even when circumstances might seem to dictate another course.

> *The most DOGMATIC of the king's advisors proved to be of little help during the crisis.*

doldrums *(DOLE-drums), noun*
A spell of low feeling; an instance of sadness or stagnation. Also: a specific belt
of calms and light winds in the Atlantic and Pacific oceans, difficult to navigate
by sail.

> *Kyle is in the DOLDRUMS because he doesn't have enough money to go to the concert
> with his buddies.*

doleful *(DOLE-full), adjective*
Causing or expressing grief or affliction.

> *I decided to rescue Rex from the animal shelter because I was entranced by his
> DOLEFUL expression.*

domain *(do-MANE), noun*
An area over which one rules; a field within which one has power, influence or
authority; a sphere of influence.

> *The local hockey rink was truly Jon's DOMAIN; when he stepped onto the ice, every
> other player stopped for a moment to watch him with mingled fear and respect.*

domesticate *(do-MESS-ti-kate), verb*
To make accustomed to home life. To *domesticate* often carries the sense of
refining another's "uncivilized" instincts.

> *Though she had done her best to DOMESTICATE Charles, Prudence had to admit
> that he was still a difficult marriage partner.*

domicile *(DOM-ih-sile), noun*
A residence. A *domicile* is one's legal, permanent home.

> *The defendant at that time had no DOMICILE, your honor; she was a homeless
> person.*

donnybrook *(dahn-EE-brook), noun*
A free-for-all, knock-down, drag-out fight.

> *Police expected a DONNYBROOK at the protest march, but both those for and those
> against the issue were peaceful and courteous.*

dossier *(DOSS-ee-ay), noun*
A collection of documents offering detailed information on a particular individual
or topic. Keeping or referring to a *dossier* on someone often carries sinister
overtones of that person's espionage or subversion.

> *Marie finally obtained her DOSSIER by means of an appeal under the Freedom of
> Information Act.*

D

double-entendre *(DUH-bul on-TON-druh), noun*
A statement in which one or many of the words may be interpreted in several ways, resulting in ambiguity; an expression that can be taken two ways, one of which often has sexual or threatening undertones.

Although Japanese adult comic books must abide by some very stringent codes forbidding profanity and the overt depiction of sexual activity, they often feature a barrage of steamy DOUBLE-ENTENDRES.

dour *(dowr), adjective*
Grim, stern, or sullen.

Nelson, the McKays' DOUR old butler, always made me feel as though I had transgressed some grave social precept in coming to visit Marjorie.

douse *(dowce), verb*
To cover with a liquid thoroughly; to drench or soak. (See, for comparison, the entry for *dowse.*)

Even after DOUSING the charcoal with lighter fluid, Uncle Al couldn't seem to get the grill fired up.

dowdy *(DOW-dee), adjective*
Lacking stylishness, most likely because one is dressed in a prim, out-of-date manner.

After my grandmother retired, she dropped her DOWDY pantsuits and began to wear skirts and shoulder-exposing blouses.

downside *(DOWN-side), noun*
A negative aspect attending a proposal or option; particularly, the potential hazard accompanying a business proposition.

The advantage of accepting your proposal, of course, is that it allows us to get the planes back in the air; the DOWNSIDE is that we must accept the decision of the arbitrator as final even if it goes against the interests of our stockholders.

dowse *(dowze), verb*
To search for water with a divining rod.

A skeptical man by nature, my father refused to believe that we had succeeded in locating the right spot for our well by DOWSING.

doxology *(doks-AH-lo-jee), noun*
A hymn praising God.

This morning's ceremony will conclude with the DOXOLOGY found on page 312 of your hymnals.

dregs *(dreGGS), noun*
Literally, the (sediment-bearing) contents of the bottom of a nearly empty container of wine, coffee, or the like; also, something or someone perceived as worthless or as the last and least appealing in a series of choices.

> *Though many in her town looked on ex-convicts as the DREGS of society, it was Debbie's job as a social worker to try to rehabilitate everyone who came through her door, regardless of past history.*

droll *(drole), adjective*
Wryly amusing. Something that is strikingly odd and humorous is *droll*.

> *The little volume was filled with DROLL illustrations that further undermined any attempt at authoritativeness.*

dromedary *(DROM-uh-dare-ee), noun*
A camel of North Africa and Arabia possessing only one hump.

> *For a small zoo such as ours to have a pair of DROMEDARIES is, I think, something of a coup.*

dross *(dross), noun*
Useless material; trash.

> *The young poet was scarred for life when her father described her poems as "DROSS" and told her to throw them away.*

dubious *(DOO-bee-uss), adjective*
Tending to cause skepticism, uncertainty, or doubt. *Dubious* can also mean "reluctant to accept a particular version or account (of something.)"

> *His claim of direct descent from Richard II was regarded as DUBIOUS at best.*

dun *(DUNN), verb*
To torment, especially to torment someone because he or she has not paid a bill.

> *Alan declared bankruptcy to stop being DUNNED by numerous creditors.*

dupe *(doop), verb and noun*
To fool, trick, or deceive. As a noun: a person so deceived.

> *Cliff's attempts to DUPE me into finishing his homework for him were about what I expected from an older brother used to getting his own way.*

duplicity *(doo-PLISS-ih-tee), verb*
Trickery; two-facedness; purposeful deceptiveness.

> *Officer Wilkins began to suspect his informant of DUPLICITY, and wondered whether she was leading him into a trap.*

duress *(dur-ESS), noun*

Compulsion resulting from the threat of force; coercion. Also: physical restraint or imprisonment.

>*The prisoner's confession, which had clearly been obtained under DURESS, was instantly ruled inadmissible by the judge.*

dwindle (DWIN-dul),

To become smaller; to shrink or waste away; to decrease.

>*I had planned to run away forever, but my DWINDLING supply of cookies and pennies forced me to return home by nightfall.*

dysfunctional *(diss-FUNK-shun-uhl), adjective*

Characterized by not working properly.

>*Charlie always blames his rotten behavior on being the product of a DYSFUNCTIONAL family.*

dyslexia *(dis-LEKS-ee-uh), noun*

Unusual trouble with spelling or reading caused by a brain condition. *Dyslexia* is rooted in an impairment in interpreting spatial relationships.

>*Judith's DYSLEXIA frequently caused her to transpose letters in words.*

dyspeptic *(diss-PEP-tick), adjective*

Dyspepsia is indigestion, so *dyspeptic* can describe something—such as certain foods—that causes dyspepsia, or it describes someone who is irritable as though suffering from dyspepsia.

>*No wonder Fred can't get a girlfriend. His DYSPEPTIC temperament drives all potential mates away.*

dystopia *(diss-TOPE-ee-uh), noun*

A utopia is a perfect world. A *dystopia* is the complete opposite, a world that has gone terribly wrong. A good example is Oceania, the setting for George Orwell's novel, *Nineteen Eighty-Four.*

>*With the rising price of gas and food, some are starting to wonder if the United States has become a DYSTOPIA.*

E

e.g. *(ee jee), abbreviation, adverb*
An abbreviation for the Latin term *exempli gratia,* "or example."

> *Many of the luxury cars so popular twenty years ago, e.g., Cadillacs and Lincoln Continentals, have been forced to develop smaller models to compete with today's popular compact vehicles.*

earthy *(EARTH-ee), adjective*
Be careful with this word. It CAN suggest someone who is down-to-earth and practical, but it also can be used as an insult, to suggest that someone is crude and tasteless.

> *Immediately after the accident, Jody forgot her usually impeccable manners and let loose a string of EARTHY accusations directed at the other driver.*

ebonite *(EBB-ah-nite), noun*
Hard black rubber; vulcanite.

> *The sturdy EBONITE hoses, flimsy and prone to breakdown in last year's model, were just one of the improvements the company made in its product line.*

ebullience *(ih-BOLL-yunce), noun*
The quality of being optimistic in speech or writing; vivaciousness. *Ebullience* is the expression of feelings or notions in a lively, upbeat manner.

> *Sharon's EBULLIENCE in delivering the presentation really set her apart from the others on the team.*

ebullition *(ebb-uh-LISH-un), noun*
The tiny bubbles of a sparkling liquid; also, a sudden outpouring of strong emotion.

> *The champagne's delicate EBULLITION tickled my nose.*

eccentric *(ek-SEN-trik), adjective*
Unpredictable; erratic or marked by unconventional behavior. Someone who is given to odd behavior can be considered *eccentric.*

> *Lionel's ECCENTRIC behavior eventually led to problems with his father.*

echelon *(ESH-uh-lon), noun*
A level of command. Literally, *echelon* pertains to military organizational structure.

> *Tom's proposal eventually won the approval of the company's upper ECHELON.*

éclat *(ay-KLAH), noun*
This French word suggests great public acclaim . . . or notoriety.

> *The ÉCLAT that greeted the reclusive author's last book seemed to cause him dismay rather than joy.*

eclectic *(ek-LEK-tic), adjective*

Choosing from a variety of sources or origins. Something that offers a diverse selection of items, styles, or approaches is said to be *eclectic*.

Ryan's anthology offers selections from authors from around the world, resulting in a rather ECLETCIC volume.

ecology *(ee-KAHL-uh-jee), noun*

The study of how organisms interact with each other and with their environment. You might also hear the adjective form of this word, which is "ecological."

The study of ECOLOGY led scientists to discover global warming.

ecosystem *(EE-ko-sis-tuhm), noun*

The interaction of all living organisms within a particular environment.

Carl has created an interesting new ECOSYSTEM in his room, since his domain includes everything from uneaten slices of pizza to filthy sweatsocks.

ecstatic *(eck-STAT-ick), adjective*

Describes a feeling of great delight, even rapture.

June was ECSTATIC when she learned she had gotten the job.

ecumenical *(ek-yoo-MEN-ih-kul), adjective*

Universal. *Ecumenical* is often used to refer to the beliefs, movements, and actions common to the various branches of Christianity worldwide.

This is not a Protestant question or a Catholic question, but a matter of ECUMENICAL significance.

eczema *(EG-zuh-muh), noun*

An inflammatory skin condition, characterized by red, itching skin that erupts into lesions that later become scaly, hard, and crusty.

The skin cleanser Noxzema was named after its supposed ability to "knock ECZEMA."

eddy *(EDD-ee), noun*

A small current of air or water that flows against the main current; a small whirlpool or whirlwind.

Because it had a strong undertow and a multitude of unpredictable EDDIES, the sound was considered dangerous for even the strongest and most experienced swimmers.

edification *(ed-ih-fih-KAY-shun), noun*

Enlightenment. To edify someone is to instruct him or share important insights with him; *edification* is the process by which this is done.

Although the author includes several supplements on ancient Egyptian construction methods for the EDIFICATION of his readers, these are not directly connected with the book's central idea.

E

edifice *(ED-ih-fiss), noun*

A building, particularly one that is large and imposing.

> *Jacob, who had worked for twelve years in a small family-owned firm, was unprepared for the prospect of working at the Webster corporate headquarters, a massive EDIFICE of brick and glass located in midtown Manhattan.*

educe *(ee-DYOOCE), verb*

To draw out. *Educe* also means to reason out or establish from given facts.

> *Myron's attempts to EDUCE his sister's whereabouts were futile.*

efface *(ih-FACE), verb*

To rub away.

> *Although the letter had been filed and held and folded so many times that the embossed seal pressed into it by the county clerk was nearly EFFACED, it was genuine.*

effect *(ih-FECT), noun*

A thing taking place as the result of a cause. Also, as a verb (often pronounced ee-FEKT), to cause or influence (a change); to bring about a hoped-for outcome. (See, for comparison, the entry for *affect*)

> *The entrepreneur's entry into the race had the EFFECT of splitting the Republican vote.*

effeminate *(eh-FEM-uh-nit), adjective*

More reminiscent of women than men. *Effeminate* was once a positive description of female refinement; today, it is more common as a derogatory word used to question a male's masculinity. (Contrast this word with *effete*, below.)

> *Dean, a quiet, thoughtful boy, was sometimes labeled as EFFEMINATE by his crueler classmates.*

effervescent *(eff-ur-VESS-unt), adjective*

Bubbly; sparkling; lively.

> *Myra's EFFERVESCENT personality makes her a favorite guest at our parties.*

effete *(uh-FEET), adjective*

Lacking robust vitality; sterile; without force. *Effete* originally meant exhausted from the labors of childbirth, but is rarely if ever used in that context today.

> *Thomas was labeled an EFFETE snob by some, but Jane had seen him work miracles in the office through pure concentration of effort and solid teamwork.*

efficacious *(eff-ih-KAY-shuss), adjective*

Producing the desired outcome; effective.

> *Tom's lawyer tried a battery of shrewd negotiating techniques during the meeting, but only outright threats to walk away from the deal proved EFFICACIOUS.*

efflorescent *(ef-flore-RES-sunt), adjective*
Blossoming. *Efflorescent* is a biological term used to describe the final development of something, but it is used by metaphor in other contexts, as well.
> *The poet's middle years were marked by some remarkable—and EFFLORESCENT— work of unparallelled quality.*

effluent *(EF-loo-unt), noun*
In general, something that flows out, but more specifically, an *effluent* is a fluid discharged as waste.
> *EFFLUENT from the factory polluted the river for decades.*

effrontery *(ih-FRON-ter-ee), noun*
Impudent boldness. *Effrontery* is shameless audacity.
> *She had the EFFRONTERY to ask for a raise after three months of dreadful performance.*

effulgent *(ih-FULJ-unt), adjective*
Radiant; brilliantly shining. Something that is *effulgent* shines forth resplendently.
> *The explosion, devastating though it was, left the night sky so effulgent that Belva could not help but marvel at the display.*

effusion (ih-FYOO-zhun),
An outpouring; also, an unrehearsed flow of speech or writing that is emotional in nature.
> *Reviewing the old love letters he had written to Susan, Brian found it hard to believe that the EFFUSIONS of lovestruck prose he found on every page had actually come from his pen.*

egalitarian *(ih-gal-uh-TARE-ee-un) adjective*
Arising from a belief in the equality of all persons. Something is *egalitarian* if it is scrupulously fair toward all parties.
> *I must admit that Miles took an EGALITARIAN approach to assigning office space.*

egocentric *(ee-go-SEN-trik), adjective*
Selfish; tending toward the belief that one's own existence is all-important. An *egocentric* person places his interests above those of all others.
> *His was a strange and EGOCENTRIC way of life that had no place for a mate.*

egregious *(ih-GREE-juss), adjective*
Flagrantly incorrect or bad. An *egregious* error is one that stands out dramatically and therefore should not have been made.
> *Tim, an EGREGIOUS liar, is the last person I would go to for reliable information.*

egress *(EE-gress), noun*

Exit.

> *The stewardess's earnest request that we try to make an orderly EGRESS from the burning plane had little effect.*

eidetic *(EYE-dett-ick), adjective*

Describes a memory or mental image recalled with perfect clarity.

> *I'd studied the travel brochures so much that I had a perfectly EIDETIC vision of what to expect on the cruise ship.*

eke *(eek), verb*

To supplement through adversity. Also: to survive or subsist by means of hard labor or strenuous effort. *Eke* (usually used with "out") is derived from the Greek for "augment."

> *Roger managed to EKE out an existence by working two jobs.*

élan *(AY-lahn), noun*

From the French meaning "to hurl," *élan* is high-spirited morale that results from extreme confidence.

> *The ÉLAN with which my son attacked the obstacle course filled me with pride.*

elapse *(ee-LAPS), verb*

To pass or go by (said of time).

> *Two hours ELAPSED at the dentist's office before my name was finally called.*

eldritch *(ELL-dritch), adjective*

Describes something (or possibly someone) eerie, spooky, supernatural, or unearthly.

> *I was terrified by the ELDRITCH screeches until I realized they merely emanated from a cat in heat.*

eleemosynary *(eh-lee-MAHSS-uh-nair-ee), adjective*

Having to do with charity or charitable activity.

> *Our boss is always reminding us that we're a for-profit business, not an ELEEMOSYNARY organization.*

elegy *(ELL-uh-jee), noun*

A poem of mourning; a poem reflecting on and praising the deceased.

> *At the funeral, Mitch read a touching ELEGY for his grandmother, reminding all present of the life of kindness and sacrifice she had led.*

elephantine *(ELL-uh-fun-tine), adjective*
An elephant is an extremely large animal, so the adjective derived from the animal describes anything that is huge in size or scope.

I figured out that the ELEPHANTINE present had to be a new refrigerator.

elicit *(ih-LISS-it), verb*
To bring out. To *elicit* is to evoke or stimulate so as to yield a response. *Elicit* is occasionally confused with illicit, which means "improper or illegal."

Of the many responses our broadcast ELICITED, I like Mrs. Miller's the best.

elision *(ih-LEE-zhun), noun*
A deliberate act of omission or the omission of one or more syllables in a word, such as when a poet writes "ne'er" for "never."

Keeping some of the details of the accident from the children seemed like a reasonable ELISION.

elitism *(ih-LEE-tiz-um), noun*
Adherence to the belief that leadership is best managed by an elite (a group considered to be the highest or best class). *Elitism* often carries negative overtones of snobbery.

We have not worked so long for democracy to see it exchanged halfheartedly for ELITISM.

elixir *(e-LIX-ur), noun*
A solution meant to be used for medicinal purposes; in medieval times, a supposedly curative drink made from mixing alcohol and drugs in water.

Dr. Callahan's ELIXIR of Life, a patent medicine popular in Kansas in the late 1880s, may have owed part of its popularity to the coca leaves used in its preparation.

elliptical *(ih-LIP-tuh-kuhl), adjective*
In addition to meaning "shaped like an ellipse," "elliptical" describes writing or speech that is intentionally obscure.

I could not follow the professor's ELLIPTICAL arguments, so I dropped his course.

elocution *(el-oh-KYOO-shun), noun*
An individual's style of public speech. Unlike eloquence (see eloquent below), which has to do with the content of a person's speech, *elocution* refers to the manner in which speech is delivered.

The cast's ELOCUTION left a great deal to be desired.

E

eloquent *(EL-oh-kwent), adjective*
Fluent and persuasive in speech or expression. *Eloquent* people are convincing and pleasant to listen to.

> *Lincoln and Douglas, both ELOQUENT debaters, knew that much more was at stake in their public meetings than a Senate seat.*

elucidate *(ee-LOO-si-date), verb*
To make clear; to explain or provide key information leading to a full understanding. Someone who *elucidates* an issue or problem throws light on it and clarifies it.

> *What is behind Frank's bizarre work habits is something only he can ELUCIDATE.*

elusive *(ee-LOO-siv), adjective*
Difficult to perceive, comprehend, or describe. An *elusive* issue or point is one that would require real work to grasp completely.

> *Our goals are easily understood; the nature of the obstacles we face is somewhat more ELUSIVE.*

emaciated *(ee-MAY-shee-ay-tud), adjective*
Dangerously thin.

> *Winston knew that not everyone would be willing to watch the footage he had shot of the EMACIATED bodies of the famine victims.*

emanate *(EM-uh-nate), verb*
To issue forth as from a source. To *emanate* is to flow from a point.

> *The sounds EMANATING from the room next door were not comforting.*

emancipate *(ee-MAN-si-pate), verb*
To liberate. That which *emancipates* frees from restraint or oppression.

> *Lincoln's decision to EMANCIPATE the slaves is considered by many to be the most significant event of the period.*

emasculate *(ee-MASS-kyoo-late), verb*
To castrate; also, to deprive of strength or essential elements.

> *In the editor's view my book had been subject to "deft pruning of occasional offensive passages"; in mine, it had been utterly EMASCULATED.*

embellish *(em-BELL-ish), verb*
To ornament and beautify. To *embellish* is to improve in appearance by adornment; an embellishment, then, can be a fanciful addition (or, by extension, even a convenient exaggeration of the facts).

> *Marie's gown was EMBELLISHED with tiny pearls.*

embezzle *(im-BEZ-ul), verb*
To appropriate funds for oneself that were placed in one's care for another party.
> *Bill had always seemed to be a model employee, so the news that he had been EMBEZZLING money from the company for some years came as a complete shock to us all.*

embodiment *(em-BOD-ee-ment), noun*
The incarnation (of a given thing or idea); the condition of being embodied. To be the *embodiment* of something is to be so imbued with it as to be its physical representation.
> *Jane was usually the EMBODIMENT of tact; her slip at the party was most uncharacteristic.*

embroil *(im-BROIL), verb*
To force someone into a situation or to cause someone to become involved in a situation.
> *Even though I was apathetic about the argument at first, I soon found myself EMBROILED in it.*

embryo *(EMM-bree-oh), noun*
Something that is undeveloped or that is just beginning.
> *Walt's home-based business was the EMBRYO that launched his industrial empire.*

emend *(ee-MEND), verb*
To change by means of editing; to correct (a text or reading).
> *Many of Shakespeare's most famous lines, such as "A rose by any other name would smell as sweet," are the result of a critic's choice to EMEND a troublesome source text.*

emeritus *(ih-MARE-ih-tuss), adjective*
Emeritus describes the position of one who has retired but who still holds an honorary title corresponding to the position held prior to retirement.
> *Watkins has been awarded the position of Professor EMERITUS.*

emigrant *(EM-ih-grunt), noun*
One who leaves a country or region for the purpose of settling in another.
> *The Irish potato famine of the 1840s turned many relatively prosperous citizens into penniless EMIGRANTS bound for the United States.*

eminence *(EM-ih-nunce), noun*
Superiority or outstanding notability. An *eminent* person is one of great achievements or high rank. Eminence may be used as part of a formal form of address.
> *His EMINENCE Cardinal Powers has asked me to respond to your letter.*

eminent *(EM-ih-nunt), adjective*
Prominent or noted; of high esteem; outstanding and distinguished.

> *I found the prospect of studying physics under an EMINENT professor like Dr. Maxwell who had just won a Nobel prize, daunting to say the least.*

emissary *(EM-ih-sare-ee), noun*
An agent acting in the interests of another party. An *emissary* is one sent to undertake a mission or task as a representative.

> *The president's EMISSARY left on a special plane from Washington; his time of return was unknown.*

empathize *(EM-puh-thize), verb*
To share another's emotions. To *empathize* with someone is to understand and identify with his situation and feelings.

> *Although I can EMPATHIZE with your plight, there is very little I can do to help.*

emphatic *(em-FA-tik), adjective*
Highlighted; extremely expressive. Something that is delivered with forceful or undeniable emphasis is *emphatic*.

> *Beth was EMPHATIC about collecting the overdue invoice.*

empirical *(imm-PEER-ih-kuhl), adjective*
Describes knowledge that is based on direct observation or practical experience.

> *Phyllis failed her science class because her experiment was based on EMPIRICAL evidence rather than on scientific verification.*

emulate *(EM-yoo-late), verb*
To strive to match or better by means of imitation. Someone who *emulates* another uses that person's actions as a model for future success or mastery.

> *David always felt that the key to his success was his decision to EMULATE his father in his professional and home life.*

emulsify *(ih-MULL-sih-fie), verb*
The process of breaking up something into small pieces.

> *Over several hours, your digestive system EMULSIFIES your meal into nutrients small enough for your body to absorb and use.*

en masse *(on MASS), adverb*
Together; in one body or group. *En masse* is a French term that translates loosely as "in the form of a crowd."

> *The mob moved EN MASSE toward the Capitol.*

enceinte *(en-SAYNT), adjective*

French, by way of Latin, for "enclosed area," *enceinte* describes a woman who is pregnant.

> *After two years of trying to get pregnant, Lena was overjoyed the day she learned she was ENCEINTE.*

enclave *(ON-klayv), noun*

A small territory surrounded by a larger (and usually foreign) one; also, any secluded area.

> *The garden, filled with fragrant flowers and a small, babbling fountain, was an ENCLAVE of serenity in the midst of the busy city.*

encomium *(en-KOME-ee-um), noun*

A formal (and often, a spoken) expression of extreme praise.

> *The evening, featuring warm ENCOMIUMS for basketball great Larry Bird from coaches, former opponents, and family members, concluded when his jersey was raised to the rafters and his number retired.*

encore *(ON-kore), noun*

Sustained applause, cheers and the like meant to encourage a performer or performers to appear again after the formal conclusion of a performance.

> *It didn't seem possible that the maestro could ignore the our emphatic demands for an ENCORE, but when the houselights went up we all began to file slowly out of the auditorium.*

encumber *(in-KUHM-ber), verb*

In legal terms, encumber means to place a lien on something. Generally, encumber means to load something—or someone—down with burdens.

> *No wonder you can't lift your backpack. It's encumbered with all sorts of stuff you don't need!*

endeavor *(in-DEV-ur), verb*

To strive for or attempt; to try to reach.

> *For the better part of a decade, Michael had ENDEAVORED to turn his novel into something that would touch the souls of everyone who read it.*

endemic *(en-DEM-ik), adjective*

Indigenous; characteristic of a certain place, region, or populace. When something is widespread within an area—to the extent that it helps to characterize that area—we often say the thing is *endemic* to the area.

> *Poverty in the mountain region was ENDEMIC; education was almost nonexistent.*

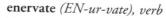

E

enervate *(EN-ur-vate), verb*

To weaken. To *enervate* is to deprive of vitality, strength, or endurance.

> *The vacation's whirlwind pace actually served to ENERVATE Madge.*

enfilade *(EN-fuh-layd), noun*

From the French meaning "to thread a needle," *enfilade* is a troop that is in a formation allowing it to be subject to sweeping gunfire, or it is the name for the sweeping gunfire itself. By extension, *enfilade* can refer to a barrage of any kind.

> *The attorney's ENFILADE of harsh questions quickly caused the accused murderer to admit to his guilt.*

engender *(en-JEN-dur), verb*

To beget; to cause to exist.

> *My decision to move east has ENGENDERED a good deal of hostility on my brother's part.*

engross *(in-GROSS), verb*

To completely consume one's attention.

> *I was so ENGROSSED in the novel that I didn't hear Melinda calling my name at first.*

enigmatic *(en-ig-MA-tick), adjective*

Reminiscent of an enigma; puzzling or perplexing. *Enigmatic* refers to the quality of being inexplicable or ambiguous.

> *An ENIGMATIC scrawl across the title sheet was the only clue to the work's authorship.*

enjoin *(in-JOIN), verb*

To forbid someone from doing something. Also, to use authority to instruct someone to do something.

> *The moviegoers were ENJOINED by the manager to stop talking during the film.*

enmesh *(en-MESH), verb*

To involve, entangle, or implicate. Literally, *enmesh* means to catch with a mesh net; the word has acquired a broader metaphorical sense as well.

> *The judge suddenly found himself ENMESHED in the ins and outs of local politics.*

enmity *(EN-mi-tee), noun*

Mutual antagonism or hatred. To show *enmity* toward a person is to harbor animosity or bitterness toward him.

> *The ENMITY between the feuding families only increased with the passage of time.*

ennoble *(in-OH-bull), verb*

To elevate or confer dignity upon someone or something.

> *Historians ENNOBLED that rotting shack on the edge of town after they determined that the home was once an important stop on the Underground Railroad.*

ennui *(on-noo-EE), noun*

Listlessness, dissatisfaction, or boredom. *Ennui* is French for "boredom."

> *A sense of ENNUI pervaded the office during the long offseason period.*

enrapture *(in-RAP-chur), verb*

To delight; to thrill or give pleasure to.

> *The music of the symphony seemed to ENRAPTURE Olivia, who sat breathless and wide-eyed throughout the performance.*

ensemble *(on-SOMB-ul), noun*

A group of individuals performing together as, for example, a cast of actors or musicians; also, an outfit composed of complementary clothing and accessories.

> *Mort's time with the jazz ENSEMBLE was humbling after his long career as a solo star, but it was the best musical experience he'd ever had.*

enshrine *(en-SHRINE), verb*

To cherish as though sacred; to preserve as if held within a shrine. To *enshrine* something is to memorialize it with the special reverence associated with religious ceremonies.

> *There is a movement to ENSHRINE Shoeless Joe Jackson in the Baseball Hall of Fame, but I do not think him a suitable candidate.*

ensue *(in-SOO), verb*

To come afterward; to follow; to happen as a result.

> *When a tractor-trailer skidded out of control and spilled its load of lumber across Route 128 yesterday afternoon, a huge rush-hour backup ENSUED.*

enthrall *(en-THRALL), verb*

To hold spellbound. To *enthrall* is to captivate or mesmerize.

> *Garbo's performance was simply ENTHRALLING.*

entice *(in-TICE), verb*

To tempt in a pleasing fashion; to attract or lure.

> *The delicious aroma emanating from the bakeshop often ENTICES me to stop in and pick up a doughnut or muffin on my way to work.*

E

entity *(EN-tuh-tee), noun*
Something that exists separately. *Entity* can also refer more broadly to existence or being.

> *The accounting department operated as a separate ENTITY.*

entomology *(en-tuh-MOL-uh-jee), noun*
The study of insects.

> *Judy's little boy so loved to collect bugs from the garden that we wondered if he might grow up to study ENTOMOLOGY.*

entourage *(ON-too-rahj), noun*
A group of associates; people who commonly surround, protect, and attend to someone of importance.

> *Melanie had hoped to score a front-page story by interviewing the reclusive movie star, but she never made it past his ENTOURAGE.*

entrepreneurial *(on-truh-pruh-NOOR-ee-uhl), adjective*
Entrepreneurs start their own businesses . . . usually a risky venture. Therefore, someone who is entrepreneurial is willing to take risks, especially in order to turn a profit.

> *As Elaine sold more and more of her handmade jewelry, she tapped into her hitherto unknown ENTREPRENEURIAL spirit.*

enunciate *(ee-NUN-see-ate), verb*
To articulate or pronounce. To *enunciate* something is to set it forth systematically and lucidly.

> *The ideas he ENUNCIATED were simple, implementable, and accepted by all.*

environmentalist *(in-VI-run-men-tull-ist), noun*
Someone who places a high value on the environment and works to protect or conserve it.

> *My daughter became an amateur ENVIRONMENTALIST after her first nature hike.*

envisage *(en-VIZ-uj), verb*
To picture or conceive of. To *envisage* is also to consider or project mentally.

> *The group of developers ENVISAGED an apartment complex on the waterfront property.*

eon *(EE-on), noun*
A very long, indefinite period of time; seemingly forever; a span of time beyond comprehension. (In the disciplines of geometry and astronomy, however, eons have specific durations.)

> *After what felt like several EONS, the tow truck finally arrived and we were able to haul our car back to the campground.*

epaulet *(EP-uh-let), noun*
An ornamental shoulder piece worn on a military uniform.

Ernie tried his best to sew the EPAULET back on his uniform before morning inspection.

ephemeral *(ih-FEMM-uh-rul), adjective*
Lasting only a short while.

Our school's joy at winning the state basketball championship turned out to be EPHEMERAL, as the title was suspended when officials learned of the presence of an ineligible player on the team's roster.

epic *(EP-ik), adjective*
Of major proportions; extraordinary.

Rosa Park's refusal to go to the back of the bus would take on legendary status in the EPIC struggle for civil rights.

epicenter *(EPP-ih-cent-uhr), noun*
This is the spot on the surface of the Earth directly above the site where an earthquake occurs, but—more generally—an *epicenter* is the focal point or origin of an activity, event, fad, etc.

I wonder when it was that Seattle became the EPICENTER of gourmet coffee?

epicure *(EP-ih-kyoor), noun*
A connoisseur; one who cultivates refined tastes, especially in reference to food and drink. *Epicure* is derived from the name of the Roman philosopher Epicurus, who lived between 341 and 279 B.C.

Matt, who never seemed at all interested in gourmet dining, has suddenly become something of an EPICURE.

epigram *(EP-ih-gram), noun*
A short, witty saying or poem.

Alexander Pope was famous for EPIGRAMS, but his body of work features much more profound efforts, as well.

epigraph *(EF-ih-graff), noun*
An inscription written on a stone, monument or building; also, a short quotation coming at the beginning of a book or chapter.

The EPIGRAPH carved above the entrance to the college library, "That they may have life and have it abundantly," confused some and inspired others.

E

epilepsy *(EP-ih-lep-see), noun*
A condition characterized by seizures and tremblings resulting from abnormal rhythmic impulses in the brain.

> *Researchers believe that many of the "demonic possessions" recounted in the Bible were actually instances of EPILEPSY.*

episodic *(ep-ih-SOD-ik), adjective*
Made up of episodes; consisting of a group of separate but only externally related anecdotes; tending to digress.

> *Although the novels of Dickens and Twain still enthrall modern readers, many are puzzled by their EPISODIC structures.*

epistemology *(uh-PIST-uh-mall-uh-jee), noun*
The study of the nature of knowledge and understanding. The adjective form, which you might see, is *epistemological*.

> *An interest in people's purchasing habits led Martina to begin studying EPISTEMOLOGY.*

epistle *(uh-PISS-uhl), noun*
An *epistle* is a formal letter. Christians and biblical scholars are familiar with the epistles of the Apostle Paul.

> *As the popularity of text messaging rises, the EPISTLE is becoming a dying art form.*

epithet *(EP-ih-thet), noun*
A word, description or expression (often disparaging) meant to characterize a person.

> *The EPITHETS used by members of the Nixon administration to describe their political enemies were often unsuitable for publication in family newspapers.*

epitome *(ee-PIT-uh-mee), noun*
The highest or supreme example.

> *Many people consider "The Mary Tyler Moore Show" to be the EPITOME of 1970s situation comedy.*

epoch *(EP-uk), noun*
A particular time or era notable or significant in history.

> *The first Apollo lunar landing marked the beginning of a new EPOCH for space travel.*

eponymous *(ih-PAHN-ih-muss), adjective*
An eponym is the name of a real or fictional person that has been adopted to name something else. *Eponymous* is the adjective form of the word.

> *Burt has created a website about EPONYMOUS American cities like Lincoln, Nebraska and Buffalo, New York.*

equable *(EK-wuh-bull), adjective*
Without variation.

> *The island boasted a pleasant and EQUABLE climate, with temperatures in the low seventies virtually every day.*

equanimity *(ee-kwa-NIM-ih-tee), noun*
Even-temperedness; calmness. Someone who possesses *equanimity* keeps his composure even in a difficult situation.

> *He rebutted each of the charges against him convincingly and with EQUANIMITY.*

equidistant *(ee-kwih-DIS-tunt), adjective*
Describes two objects, places, people, etc. that are exactly the same distance from one vantage point.

> *Even though the homes of my parents and my in-laws are EQUIDISTANT from us, it takes longer to reach my folks because they live on the other side of mountainous two-lane roads.*

equilibrium *(ee-kwuh-LIB-ree-um), noun*
Mental or emotional balance.

> *Brenda's EQUILIBRIUM went off-kilter when she dropped and broke all her groceries, the climax of a frustrating day.*

equinox *(EK-wih-nox), noun*
The point in time when the sun crosses the equator, causing night and day to be of roughly equal length everywhere on earth.

> *The vernal (or spring) EQUINOX generally occurs around March 21; the autumnal equinox, around September 22.*

equitable *(EK-wih-tuh-bull), adjective*
Free from bias; just to all involved. (See, for comparison, the entry for *equable*.)

> *The parties have reached what both sides believe to be an EQUITABLE settlement.*

equity *(ECK-wuh-tee), noun*
The state of not showing bias or favoritism.

> *Mr. Harris always manages to exhibit EQUITY toward all of his students.*

equivocal *(ee-KWIV-uh-kul), adjective*
Capable of varying interpretation. Also: dubious, uncertain, or suspect. To say a statement is *equivocal* is usually to cast doubt on the sincerity or truthfulness of the person making it.

> *The EQUIVOCAL nature of Paul's replies caused many to wonder about his suitability for the post.*

E

eradicate *(ee-RAD-ih-cate), verb*
To do away with utterly. To eradicate *something is to wipe it out and leave no sign of it.*
> *"Until we have ERADICATED poverty," the priest vowed, "our struggle will continue."*

eroticize *(ih-ROT-uh-size), verb*
To take something "tame" and sexualize it.
> *There's no need to EROTICIZE Shakespeare because his works are already filled with bawdy—sometimes downright filthy—puns.*

errant *(AIR-unt), adjective*
Describes someone who likes to travel or something that/someone who wanders about aimlessly.
> *The buzzing of ERRANT flies practically wrecked the contentment I had been feeling while sitting on the dock.*

erratic *(ih-RAT-ik), adjective*
Inconsistent; lacking a set course. Something that wanders or fluctuates unpredictably can be considered *erratic.*
> *Elaine's ERRATIC uniting style irritated her superiors, who had no time to puzzle over an indecipherable and meandering memo.*

erroneous *(ih-RONE-ee-us), adjective*
Wrong.
> *Your suggestion that I spent the summer on the coast of California avoiding writing my book is completely ERRONEOUS.*

ersatz *(AIR-sats), noun*
An unconvincing substitute. That which is not "the real thing" is *ersatz.*
> *If you think you can pass off that ERSATZ diamond as the real thing, you're in for a surprise.*

erstwhile *(URST-hwile), adjective*
Former; of or pertaining to a long-past time.
> *Boston Red Sox fans can only dream of what might have been had their ERSTWHILE star Babe Ruth not been sold to their archrivals, the New York Yankees.*

eructation *(ih-ruhk-TAY-shun), noun*
A fancy word for "belch." The verb form is *"eructate."*
> *Miss Smithers hid her dainty ERUCTATIONS behind a charming cloth napkin.*

erudite *(AIR-yoo-dite), adjective*
Possessing extensive knowledge on a given subject; learned. An *erudite* person has received a thorough and well-rounded education.
> *Borges is nothing if not ERUDITE; it is clear from his short stories that he is a man of immense learning.*

eschew *(ess-CHOO), verb*
To shun; to stay away from, especially as a result of moral or ethical concerns.
> *Chuck ESCHEWED his coworkers' nights out on the town, knowing they almost always concluded with a visit to a strip club.*

esoteric *(ess-oh-TARE-ik), adjective*
Comprehensible only to a particular, restricted category of people. To say something is *esoteric* is to say it lacks broad appeal.
> *The novel is likely to be enthralling to those familiar with the Revolutionary War period; others may find it ESOTERIC.*

esplanade *(ESS-pluh-nahd), noun*
An open, level strip of ground, usually near a body of water.
> *While strolling along the ESPLANADE, we watched the rowing teams train for the upcoming regatta.*

espouse *(ih-SPOWZ), verb*
To advocate as though one's own. *Espouse* can also mean to take in marriage.
> *Do you have any idea how complicated it would be to implement the plans you are ESPOUSING?*

espresso *(es-PRESS-oh), noun*
A potent, dark coffee brewed by means of forced steam.
> *The ESPRESSO machine had to be one of the most useless birthday presents I'd ever received, given my caffeine intolerance.*

estrange *(ih-strange), verb*
To alienate or remove from a position or relationship. A family member who is *estranged* by others in the family is no longer regarded as part of the group.
> *Her ESTRANGED brother made many attempts to visit, but Michelle would have no part of any such plan.*

estuary *(ESS-choo-ayre-ee), noun*
The point of a water passage where a river empties into a tidal area.
> *Dr. Green argued against allowing the plant to be built so near the river, on the grounds that it would threaten several important species living in the ESTUARY.*

et al *(et al), abbreviation, adverb*
The abbreviation for the Latin term *et alia,* meaning "and others."

> *Members of Congress, the justices of the Supreme Court, the Joint Chiefs of Staff, ET AL waited for President Clinton to enter and give his first State of the Union address.*

etching *(ETCH-ing), noun*
An impression on metal or glass made by means of corrosive acid; a picture or design produced by using this process to impart a design on a plate with acid.

> *The ornate images on our paper currency are the result of intricate ETCHINGS meant to foil counterfeiters.*

ethereal *(uh-THEER-ee-ul), adjective*
Airy; light; more heavenly than earthly.

> *Norman's paintings had an ETHEREAL quality that gave Lynne an instant sense of peace.*

ethnocentricity *(eth-no-sen-TRISS-ih-tee), noun*
The belief that cultures different from one's own are inherently inferior.

> *The Nazis displayed a monstrous ETHNOCENTRICTTY, to be sure, but they were also pragmatic enough to know when an alliance with the Japanese served their interests.*

ethos *(EE-THoass), noun*
From the Greek meaning "custom" or "habit," an ethos is the underpinning philosophy that guides a person, community, nation, group, etc.

> *I can't support any group that seems to have divisiveness as its guiding ETHOS.*

etiolate *(EE-tee-uh-late), verb*
To cause to become weak and sickly-appearing.

> *Over time, Brad's poor health choices increasingly ETIOLATED his once-handsome appearance.*

etymology *(et-ih-MOLL-uh-gee), noun*
The study of the development and history of words. A word's *etymology* is its lineage or descent.

> *I took a little Greek in school, so I think I can make an educated guess at this word's ETYMOLOGY.*

eulogy *(YOO-luh-gee), noun*
Speech or writing in praise of a person, typically used for a person who has recently died. Keep in mind that, unlike a *eulogy*, an ELEGY denotes a mournful poem, one not necessarily written for a particular person.

> *Diane delivered a EULOGY for her uncle that managed to be simultaneously sad and heartwarming.*

euphemism *(YOU-fuh-miz-um), noun*

A word or expression used as a substitute for one that may be considered offensive or distasteful.

> *My Aunt Polly's quaint EUPHEMISM for "toilet" was "freshening-up room."*

euphonious *(you-PHONE-ee-uss), adjective*

Pleasing to the ear.

> *The low, EUPHONIOUS thrumming of the crickets outside my window those summer nights always put me to sleep quickly.*

euphony *(YOO-fuh-nee), noun*

Harmonious language or sounds. One instance of *euphony* is pleasant-sounding, musical phrasing employed in speech or writing.

> *There came a point when what mattered was not so much what the poet said, but the EUPHONY of his language.*

euphoria *(yoo-FOR-ee-uh), noun*

A state of happiness and well-being that could be perceived by others as manic. The adjective form is "euphoric."

> *As the home team sank the three-pointer in the final seconds and won the game, EUPHORIC erupted in the bar.*

evade *(ee-VADE), verb*

To sidestep or dodge; to flee from (a pursuer). (See, for comparison, the entry for *avoid.*)

> *The fugitives EVADED the authorities for three months, but were finally apprehended near Scottsdale, Arizona.*

evanesce *(ev-uh-NESS), verb*

To vanish or fade away gradually. The adjective form is "evanescent."

> *As twilight filled the valley, all signs of civilization began to EVANESCE.*

evasive *(ee-VAY-siv), adjective*

Prone to hiding. Also: deliberately ambiguous in speech or response. An *evasive* answer is one that is meant to yield as little meaningful information to the questioner as possible.

> *The defense attorney found the witness hostile and EVASIVE on the stand.*

evince *(ee-VINCE), verb*

To prove conclusively or demonstrate. To *evince* something is to show it clearly.

> *You have not EVINCED a single one of the claims you put forward.*

eviscerate *(ee-VIS-uh-rate), verb*
To disembowel; to remove the entrails of. *Eviscerate* is often used metaphorically to describe the process of cutting down or reducing something almost to nothing.
> *Having EVISCERATED the novel's key chapter, the censor was content to let the earlier exposition stand.*

evocative *(ih-VOCK-uh-tive), adjective*
Describes something that tends to draw forth—or evoke—feelings, thoughts, responses, etc.
> *Lydia's perfume was EVOCATIVE of a spring day in the woods.*

evoke *(ee-VOKE), verb*
To call forth or summon. To *evoke* is also to bring back to life through appeal to memory.
> *The sight of the old mansion EVOKED many bittersweet memories for Charles.*

ex officio *(ECKS uh-FISH-ee-oh), noun*
This Latin expression denotes someone who holds a title by virtue of his or her office.
> *The president of the United States is the EX OFFICIO commander in chief of the United States's armed forces.*

exacerbate *(ig-ZASS-ur-bate), verb*
To worsen or aggravate. To *exacerbate* something is to make it even more unpleasant or severe.
> *You have only EXACERBATED the situation by lying about your activities that night.*

exalted *(ig-ZALT), adjective*
Glorified or praised; held up high in honor.
> *Colvin's album earned the kind of EXALTED commendations usually reserved for major new works of literature.*

excelsior *(ik-SEL-see-ur), noun*
Wood shavings used as a packing agent.
> *The fragile china was shipped in sturdy wooden crates filled with EXCELSIOR.*

except *(ek-SEPT), verb*
To exclude; also, to express opposition or disagreement to by means of argument. (See, for comparison, the listing for *accept*.)
> *I want everyone we know to come to the dinner party, my old boyfriend EXCEPTED.*

excerpt *(EK-surpt), noun*
To quote or reproduce a portion of a book, play, poem, etc.
>*Although it may not have been his intention, the rock singer was helping to educate his young audience by using EXCERPTS from the sonnets of Shakespeare in his lyrics.*

excise *(ECK-size), verb*
To cut a passage from a text or, in general, to cut something out or off. As a noun, an *excise* denotes a tax placed on the manufacture and sale of certain items—like liquor or cigarettes—that are produced within a country.
>*I went to the dermatologist and had that mole EXCISED.*

excogitate *(ecks-CAHJ-ih-tate), verb*
To study something carefully in order to understand it as fully as possible.
>*Dad spent so much time EXCOGITATING over the map that we missed our flight.*

excommunicate *(eks-kuh-MVOO-nih-kate), verb*
To banish; to revoke formally one's status as member of a group. *Excommunicate* is used primarily with regard to members of the Catholic church who are excluded from that church due to misconduct or doctrinal conflict.
>*The priest knew that he faced EXCOMMUNICATION if he refused to resign from the legislature.*

excoriate *(ik-SORE-ee-ate), verb*
To denounce emphatically. Literally, *excoriate* means to remove the exterior (skin) of something.
>*To be EXCORIATED in this way is bad enough; to endure such remarks on the floor of the Senate is a sad commentary on our times.*

exculpate *(EK-skul-pate), verb*
To remove responsibility or guilt from. To *exculpate* someone is to clear his name.
>*The fact that I was convicted is immaterial; I have been fully EXCULPATED.*

execrable *(ig-ZEK-ruh-bul), adjective*
Disgusting; detestable; vulgar.
>*Collectors of unauthorized Beatles records must be prepared to pay high prices for the illegal discs, which often feature tracks of EXECRABLE recording quality.*

exemplar *(ig-ZEHM-plur), noun*
The original, to which all future examples are compared.
>*For many, Abraham Lincoln is the EXEMPLAR of a war-time president.*

exemplify *(egg-ZEMP-lih-fie), verb*

To illustrate with an example or to serve as an example of something.

Beethoven's music EXEMPLIFIES both the heights of joy and the depths of despair.

exert *(ig-ZURT), verb*

To expend effort.

"Please don't EXERT yourself," Alice sneered sarcastically to her husband Fred as he lay on the couch while she vacuumed.

exfoliate *(ecks-FOAL-ee-ate), verb*

To remove the surface of something—such as skin—in flakes or scales.

Andrea's skin is always perfect because she EXFOLIATES twice a day.

exhilarated *(ig-ZILL-uh-rate-ud), verb*

To make lively; to excite or energize.

Those evening runs in the cool air of the spring were always EXHILARATING, especially after a day spent cooped up in a stuffy office.

exhort *(ig-ZORT), verb*

To urge or entreat; to plead with (usually in an attempt to warn or advise).

The hostages EXHORTED their captors to give up, arguing that the authorities would deal more leniently with them if no one were hurt.

exhume *(egg-ZYOOM), verb*

The primary meaning of "exhume" is to dig something up, such as a body or buried treasure. In addition, one can exhume anything by rescuing it from obscurity.

The film's soundtrack managed to EXHUME the career of the songwriter, who hadn't had a hit in more than three decades.

exigency *(EK-si-jen-see), noun*

Something requiring immediate action or attention; an emergency. An *exigency* is an unexpected development of some urgency.

The printer's failure to meet the deadline presented us with an EXIGENCY we were ill-equipped to face.

exiguous *(ex-IG-you-uss), adjective*

Meager; small; scanty.

Dinner turned out to be an EXIGUOUS offering of two thin slices of chicken, three green beans, and a potato-albeit quite artistically arranged.

existential *(eggs-ih-STENCH-uhl), adjective*
Existentialism is a twentieth-century philosophy characterized by a belief in individuals making their own choices and finding their own meaning of life, while shunning faith in a higher being. The adjective derived from the philosophy describes periods when individuals question their choices, especially choices related to the meaning of life.

> *While going through another horrible day at her boring office job, Phyllis had an EXISTENTIAL moment and decided—right then and there—to quit her job and move to a new town.*

exodus *(EX-uh-duss), noun*
A going out; a departure, particularly of a large group of people.

> *After the film reel jammed for the third time, there was a mass EXODUS of angry patrons.*

exonerate *(ig-ZON-uh-rate), verb*
To clear or free from blame or guilt; to restore (one's reputation).

> *After the charges were thrown out and Brian was completely EXONERATED, he was free to continue his work in the securities industry.*

exorbitant *(egg-ZORE-bih-tunt), adjective*
Beyond what is reasonable; extreme or excessive.

> *Christopher had thought he needed a laptop computer to make his business trips easier, but after seeing the EXORBITANT prices, he decided he could go without for another year.*

expatiate *(ick-SPAY-she-ate), verb*
To speak or write at length. The word typically suggests that you are speaking or writing at TOO MUCH length.

> *I just tuned out Tyrone as he began to EXPATIATE again on his troubled relationship with Mavis.*

expatriate *(ecks-PAY-tree-it), noun*
Someone who chooses to leave his or her home country and to resettle in another. The word gained currency in the early twentieth century, when many American writers, musicians, and artists chose to leave America and settle in Europe.

> *Even though she had lived in France for many years, Trudy never considered herself a true EXPATRIATE because her love for America remained so strong.*

expedite *(EKS-puh-dite), verb*

To speed up (a process or action); to complete promptly.

> *My father's friend at the Registry of Motor Vehicles was able to EXPEDITE my driver's license application, and I was spared the standard six-week wait.*

expeditious *(ek-spuh-DISH-uss), adjective*

Speedy and efficient. That which is conducted in a brisk manner is *expeditious*.

> *Ryan came upon an EXPEDITIOUS means of solving the problem that had vexed the firm for so long.*

expiate *(ECK-spee-ate), verb*

To make amends or to atone for one's actions.

> *After a lifetime of working for a company known for polluting local waterways, Dean EXPIATED his guilt by donating hundreds of acres of his property to various land conservancies.*

expletive *(EK-splih-tive)*

An exclamation, interjection, or profane oath. An *expletive* is also a "filler" word that holds a grammatical position but has no independent meaning, such as the word "it" in "It is imperative that you read this."

> *A shower of EXPLETIVES descended on the umpire from the stands.*

explicit *(ik-SPLISS-it), adjective*

Detailed; revealing in full expression; emphatically stated.

> *I felt that certain EXPLICIT scenes in Last Tango in Paris were not quite right for five-year-olds, and urged the twins to select a Barney videocassette instead.*

exploitation *(eck-sploy-TAY-shun), noun*

The use of something for profit, especially if the profit-making does not benefit the person or thing being used.

> *Paying uneducated workers less than educated ones for the exact same work is an example of EXPLOITATION, Mr. Crowthers.*

expostulate *(ick-SPAHSS-chew-late), verb*

To use reason and logic in an effort to talk someone out of doing something he or she intends to do.

> *I EXPOSTULATED with Nora about the mistake I believed she was about to make, but she paid me no attention.*

expressionism *(ex-PRESH-un-iz-um), noun*

An art movement with roots in the late nineteenth and early twentieth centuries in which external forms of reality are distorted as a means of communicating an interior vision of the artist.

> *For Edvard Munch, whose painting The Scream is perhaps the single most recognizable image of EXPRESSIONISM, the themes of isolation and anxiety were of paramount importance.*

expunge *(iks-PUNGE), verb*

To obliterate, remove, or mark for deletion.

> *In exchange for her testimony against her former lover, the charges against Carrie were dropped and her record EXPUNGED of any connection to his crimes.*

expurgate *(EX-pur-gate), verb*

To remove or delete something unacceptable or objectionable, (particularly, passages in a text).

> *Fearing a public backlash, the publisher promised that all offensive material would be EXPURGATED from future editions of the book.*

extant *(ik-STANT), adjective*

Existing; in existence.

> *The EXTANT laws on the subject did not make adequate provisions for issues of sexual harassment, Maria argued, and would have to be updated.*

extempore *(iks-TEM-puh-ray), adjective*

Without forethought or preparation; spontaneous, impromptu.

> *As he watched the note cards to his speech fly away in the breeze, Griswold stood before the crowd and wished, once again and more fervently than ever before, that he had the ability to deliver a magnificent speech EXTEMPORE.*

extenuate *(ik-STEN-yoo-ate), verb*

To reduce in seriousness, external aspect, or extent. To *extenuate* is to make a fault or error less grave.

> *The trip was delayed, not because we dawdled, but because of EXTENUATING circumstances.*

extol *(ex-TOLE), verb*

To praise highly.

> *The principal EXTOLLED the hard work of the members of the honor society, detailing their many academic achievements for the assembly.*

extradition *(eks-tra-DISH-un), noun*
The handing over of an alleged fugitive from one country, state, etc., to another.
> *Because there was no formal EXTRADITION agreement between the two countries, the trial of the accused did not begin until two years after the warrant for his arrest had been issued.*

extraneous *(ex-TRAY-nee-uss), adjective*
Coming from the outside; not innate; foreign.
> *Miles was a resourceful debater who deflected attacks from his opponents by raising EXTRANEOUS but inflammatory issues.*

extrapolate *(ik-STRAP-uh-late), verb*
To arrive at an estimate by examining unknown values. To *extrapolate* is to make a supposition or model based on shifting or tenuous information.
> *While there were no eyewitnesses, we can EXTRAPOLATE the victim's movements that night based on his past activities.*

extricate *(EKS-trih-kate), verb*
To remove from an entanglement.
> *Having gotten us into an impossible dilemma, Warren appeared to have no idea how we should go about EXTRICATING ourselves from it.*

extrinsic *(iks-TRINZ-ik), adjective*
Not part of the true nature of something.
> *The revolution was less of a spontaneous eruption of anger against capitalism as a system, and more of a reaction to EXTRINSIC forces like the constant oil shortages that came about because of international sanctions.*

exuberant *(ig-ZOO-burr-uhnt), adjective*
Extremely enthusiastic.
> *I was EXUBERANT about my unexpected holiday bonus.*

exult *(ig-ZULT), verb*
To celebrate or rejoice heartily.
> *There was no EXULTING among the families of the victims, who greeted the verdict with a sense of solemn resolution.*

exurb *(ECK-surb), noun*
A mostly self-contained community that lies well beyond a city's suburbs and which is often inhabited by the wealthy or upper-middle class.
> *I could track my family's fortunes by our addresses. The lean years were spent in the city's urban core. Then came a move to the suburbs. Finally, we hit the big time and relocated to an EXURB.*

F

F

fabricate *(FAB-rih-kait), verb*

To create something. Often, this word is used negatively, to suggest that one is lying, or "creating" false information.

> *Mom shook her head because she could tell I was just FABRICATING my explanations.*

fabulist *(FAB-yuh-list), noun*

A liar. Someone who tells outrageously untrue stories is a *fabulist*.

> *Sir Gerald, a notorious FABULIST, was not consulted for an authoritative account of the crime.*

facade *(fuh-SOD), noun*

The ornamental front of a building; also, a false or misleading appearance; a contrived surface meant to deceive.

> *Not many took the time to look beyond the FACADE of the burly, rough-hewn pig farmer to see the kind-hearted, gentle soul that resided deep inside Big Jim.*

facet *(FASS-it), noun*

A component or aspect. A *facet* is also the flat smooth surface of a polished gem. To say something is multifaceted is to say it has many dimensions or components.

> *I am afraid I am unfamiliar with this FACET of the case.*

facetious *(fuh-SEE-shuss), adjective*

Meant to evoke laughter or enjoyment; not intended seriously.

> *My suggestion that we pack the children off to live with their grandparents for a few decades was FACETIOUS.*

facile *(FASS-ill), adjective*

Describes something accomplished easily.

> *The teacher said the work would be difficult, but most students found it rather FACILE.*

facilitate *(fuh-SILL-uh-tate), verb*

To help, to ease the way.

> *My knowledge of Moroccan customs FACILITATED our team's negotiations in that country.*

facsimile *(fak-SIM-uh-lee), noun*

An exact copy, imitation, or reproduction.

> *The centerpiece of Victor's library was a FACSIMILE of the First Folio of the collected plays of Shakespeare.*

faction *(FAK-shun), noun*
A group of persons united within an organization for a common purpose.

> *The meetings of the board of directors were marked by perpetual squabbling between its two bitterly antagonistic FACTIONS.*

factitious *(fack-TISH-us), adjective*
Lacking spontaneity; contrived.

> *The news network's FACTITIOUS commentary seemed to be mere talking points for the current presidential administration.*

fainéant *(FAY-knee-unt), adjective or noun*
Someone who is lazy and idle or the description of such a person. From a French contraction meaning "he does nothing."

> *I spent my vacation in such a FAINÉANT state that I found it hard to focus on work once I returned to my "real life."*

fait accompli *(FATE uh-com-PLEE), noun*
Something undertaken and already concluded. A *fait accompli* (from the French for "accomplished fact") is an act or event presented as beyond challenge or attempted reversal.

> *Clive simply signed the contract without consulting his superior and presented the agreement as a FAIT ACCOMPLI.*

fajita *(fuh-HEE-tuh), noun*
A soft flat tortilla shell filled with chicken, beef (or both) and assorted vegetables; Spanish in origin.

> *This restaurant is famous for its FAJITAS, but I prefer the chimichangas myself.*

falafel *(fuh-LOFF-ul), noun*
Fried food balls or patties consisting of spicy ground vegetables, such as fava beans or chick peas, originating in the Middle East.

> *Moody's in Central Square offers a delicious Middle Eastern dinner special featuring FALAFEL and lentil soup, for under $5.00.*

fallacious *(fuh-LAY-shuss), adjective*
False; containing a logical error or serious misapprehension. *Fallacious* is derived from fallacy, which means a false notion.

> *As it turned out, McCarthy's accusations against the Army were totally FALLACIOUS.*

fallacy *(FALL-uh-see), noun*

A misconception; an erroneous perception; a deceit.

> *For some childhood is a time of innocence; but it's a FALLACY to say it is like this for all children.*

fallow *(FAL-low), adjective*

Describing land: uncultivated; plowed but not seeded for a season or more in order to improve the soil. Also: not active or in use.

> *Brenda's creative forces have lain FALLOW since she completed that third novel of hers.*

falsetto *(fal-SET-oh), noun*

A male singing voice higher than the normal range for that voice. Also: a person who sings falsetto.

> *Our soprano is home with the flu, so poor old Mike is going to have to sing FALSETTO.*

falter *(FALL-tur), verb*

To hesitate, stumble, or waver; to move uncertainly.

> *Stan had FALTERED so many times in his attempts to ask Julie for a date that his friends began to wonder whether he had ever contemplated simply giving up and becoming a monk.*

fantasia *(fan-TAY-zhuh), noun*

Originally used to signify a musical piece with an irregular form, *fantasia* has come to denote anything considered unreal, weird, or grotesque.

> *I emerged from the darkened subway entrance and shaded my eyes from the FANTASIA of headlights and neon signs.*

farce *(farce), noun*

A comedy in which situation, satire and preposterous coincidence are predominant over character; also, a ridiculous, empty display not worth serious consideration; a mockery.

> *Although the proceedings were presented to the outside world as a fair trial, Roland knew that he was watching a FARCE in which all the principal witnesses had been bribed to help convict the defendant.*

farouche *(fuh-ROOSH), adjective*

From the French meaning "belonging outside," *farouche* describes someone who is unsociable, cranky, and withdrawn.

> *Your FAROUCHE behavior will not win you any friends. In fact, it will simply alienate you from everyone.*

farrago *(fuh-ROG-oh), noun*
A careless mixture; mish-mash.

> *My four-year-old, who picked out his own outfit for the first time this morning, walked into the kitchen sporting a FARRAGO of mismatched clothing.*

fascist *(FASH-ist), adjective*
Fascism is a governmental system run with an iron grip by a dictator. The adjective form, *fascist*, has come to describe any person, system, group, etc. that is run as though by dictatorial control.

> *As his supervisor got increasingly bossy and meddlesome, Paul began to describe him as FASCIST.*

fastidious *(fuh-STID-ee-uss), adjective*
Attentive to detail or issues of propriety; hard to please. A *fastidious* person is meticulous, exacting, and sensitive to procedure.

> *Carl, a FASTIDIOUS ledger-keeper, seemed destined to do well in the accounting department.*

fastuous *(FASS-chew-us), adjective*
Haughty and arrogant.

> *Despite her beauty, Jenny rarely got asked out, due to her FASTUOUS behavior.*

fatuous *(FAT-yoo-uss), adjective*
Stupid or foolish. That which is complacently idiotic is *fatuous*.

> *She made so many FATUOUS remarks at the party that I became disgusted and stopped apologizing for her.*

fauna *(FAW-nuh), noun*
The animal population of a particular region or time period. (A plural noun.)

> *According to this article, the FAUNA of Australia include more marsupials than are found on any other continent.*

Faustian *(FOUS-tee-un), adjective*
Faust is the anti-hero of a German legend who sold his soul to the devil in order to gain great knowledge. Thus, *Faustian* describes the sacrificing of moral or spiritual values in order to gain knowledge, fame, money, etc.

> *When she stopped being a public defender and became a corporate lawyer, Tia couldn't help thinking she'd made a FAUSTIAN bargain.*

faux *(foe), adjective*
Fake or counterfeit in nature.

> *Jill made such commotion over the FAUX pearls I gave her that I began to suspect she thought they were real.*

F

faux pas *(foe PAW), noun*
A social error. *Faux pas* is French for "false step."

> *I'm afraid that by publicly refusing to shake hands with your opponent you've done more than commit a FAUX PAS; you may well have lost the election.*

faze *(faze), verb*
To bother; to disturb or annoy.

> *We thought Seth would be angry when he found out Phillip was dating his old girlfriend, but the news didn't seem to FAZE him a bit.*

fealty *(FEE-ul-tee), noun*
Loyalty. Literally, *fealty* describes the historical obligation of a vassal (a person granted use of land) to a lord.

> *I don't think you have any right to keep me from looking for another job; I never took an oath of FEALTY here, sir.*

febrile *(FEE-brul), adjective*
Feverish. That which is marked by elevated body temperature is *febrile*.

> *Due to Mother's current FEBRILE condition, we are uneasy about her accompanying us on the trip.*

feckless *(FEK-liss), adjective*
Ineffective or feeble. A person who lacks initiative or ability in a given area could be said to be *feckless* in that area.

> *We had hoped for a well-trained and motivated consulting firm; what showed up was a pack of FECKLESS hangers-on.*

fecund *(FEE-kund), noun and adjective*
Fruitful or fertile; prolific.

> *Although he certainly had a FECUND imagination, the screenwriter's most successful efforts had been adaptations of the works of others.*

feign *(FANE), verb*
To fake or counterfeit; to pretend.

> *Instinctively I knew the man was going to grab for my purse, but I thwarted his efforts by FEIGNING a heart attack, attracting the crowd's attention.*

feint *(faint), noun*
A false advance or attack intended to catch an opponent off guard.

> *Jim FEINTED several times with his left before decking his opponent with a fierce right cross.*

felicitous *(fih-LISS-ih-tuss), adjective*
Appropriate and well-suited for a particular occasion.
> *The prince's decision to go to the costume party dressed as a Nazi was not a FELICITOUS one.*

felicity *(fih-LISS-ih-tee), noun*
Bliss; extreme happiness. *Felicity* can also refer to something that gives rise to sublime contentment.
> *Her FELICITY at the news that her brother had been located knew no bounds.*

felonious *(fuh-LONE-ee-uss), adjective*
Criminal; villainous; reminiscent of or relating to a felony crime.
> *Although no court in the land would consider it FELONIOUS, my brother's attempt to blackmail me over that little dent I put in my parent's car was, in my mind, worthy of a long jail sentence.*

femme fatale *(femme fuh-TAL), noun*
A seductive woman who uses her charms to trick men into compromising or dangerous situations; a woman who uses her feminine wiles for gain.
> *Although the movie industry makes much of its supposed progressiveness, feminists note with disdain that most leading roles for women still lean heavily on stereotype: the ingenue, the FEMME FATALE, the devoted mother battling for her children against all odds.*

femur *(FEE-mur),*
The bone between the pelvis and the knee; the thighbone.
> *The force of the tackle caused a hairline fracture that extended along the entire length of Eli's right FEMUR.*

feral *(FEER-uhl), adjective*
Wild and uncontrolled (said especially of animals who were once domesticated). *Feral* can also mean "natural."
> *The islands of Hawaii suffer from a severe infestation of FERAL pigs not native to the area.*

ferment *(furr-MENT), verb*
To cause agitation or excitement, typically in order to incite drastic change.
> *High oil prices began to FERMENT efforts to find alternative fuel sources.*

ferret *(FARE-ut), verb*
To drive or force out; to discover by forcing out.
> *Colonel Gonzalez declared that he would take any measure necessary to FERRET the rebels out of the hillsides.*

ferrous *(FAIR-us), adjective*

Relating to iron; of or pertaining to a substance that contains iron.

> *To counteract the loss of iron during menstruation, many doctors suggest that their female patients take a FERROUS vitamin supplement every day.*

ferule *(FER-uhl), noun or verb*

A stick used to punish children, or the act of hitting with a ferule. More generally, the word is equivalent to "punish" or "punishment."

> *Since my distracted state had led to the accident, I stood patiently as the other driver FERULED me with harsh words.*

fervent *(FER-vunt), adjective*

Ardent and enthusiastic. Literally, *fervent* means extremely hot. A fervent desire, then, is one that is strongly held.

> *Russell's speech was characterized by FERVENT emotion*

festoon *(feh-STOON), verb*

A *festoon* is a garland strung between two points, so "to festoon" means to decorate as with garlands.

> *Balloons and banners FESTOONED the room, in preparation for my son's birthday party.*

fetid *(FET-id), adjective*

Smelly. That which has an unpleasant odor is *fetid*.

> *The FETID contents of the abandoned apartment's refrigerator are best left undescribed.*

fetish *(FETT-ish), noun*

Any object, idea, leader, etc. inspiring unquestioned awe and reverence. Often, this word is used negatively.

> *"It sickens me," Nora said, "how so many colleges have made a FETISH of high grades on standardized tests."*

fetters *(FET-urz), noun*

Literally, shackles or handcuffs; a restraint. Also, as a verb *(FET-ur)*, to restrain or restrict movement.

> *The prisoners were led to the bowels of the ship, where narrow wooden benches, FETTERS, and a thin scattering of straw awaited them.*

fiasco *(fee-ASS-koe), noun*

An utter and pathetic failure. *Fiasco* derives from an Italian verb meaning "to fail."

> *The failure of the Administration to get the housing bill through Congress is only the latest in a series of legislative FIASCOS.*

fiat *(FEE-at), noun*

An arbitrary pronouncement or decree. To rule by *fiat* is to constantly issue orders on one's own authority, without any check or consultation.

> *The king issued a FIAT on the question of religious worship, but the citizenry ignored it.*

fibrous *(FIE-bruss), adjective*

made up of fibers; sinewy; of or pertaining to something that can be separated into fibers.

> *With horror I realized that the FIBROUS mass the dog was dragging through the rose bushes was my cashmere sweater—or what was left of it.*

fibula *(FIB-you-luh), noun*

The large outer bone of the lower portion of the leg.

> *The little brat kicked me so hard I thought for a moment that she might have broken my FIBULA.*

fidelity *(fih-DEL-ih-tee), noun*

Faithfulness to duties; observance of responsibilities. One maintains *fidelity* in marriage by honoring a vow of sexual faithfulness.

> *The published book's FIDELITY to the author's original text is suspect.*

fiduciary *(fih-DOO-she-air-ee), adjective*

Regarding trust and confidence in public affairs.

> *The government has a FIDUCIARY responsibility to do the most good for the most people.*

fiefdom *(FEEF-dum), noun*

The domain over which a feudal lord rules; an area over which one has control or domain.

> *Mr. Duncan treated his wife and children as if they were his subjects, the lucky few privileged to occupy his FIEFDOM.*

filch *(FILCH), verb*

To steal, especially to steal petty amounts or inexpensive goods.

> *Brian is proud of how many motel towels he's FILCHED over the years.*

filial *(FILL-ee-ull), adjective*

That which is due from or befitting a son or daughter; pertaining to a son a daughter.

> *Mother considered it my FILIAL responsibility to take over the family business when I graduated, but I wanted to pursue a career of my own.*

filibuster *(FILL-ih-buss-ter), noun*
A legislative tactic by which a member prevents or delays the passage of a law, typically by focusing on irrelevant issues during a long speech to prevent a vote from taking place; any similar technique that monopolizes the floor of legislature by means of parliamentary maneuvers.

> *Even an epic FILIBUSTER staged by Southern legislators could not stop President Johnson from guiding the Civil Rights Act through Congress.*

filigree *(FIL-uh-gree), noun or adjective*
Delicate decorative work made of twisted wire.

> *The crown was adorned with beautiful jewels and intricate gold FILIGREE.*

fillip *(FILL-up), verb*
To strike or tap energetically. Also, to excite or stimulate, as though one were tapped.

> *Unemployment FILLIPED my efforts to finish and publish my novel.*

fin de siecle *(fahn-day-say-ECK-luh), adjective*
This French expression meaning "end of the century" typically refers to the fashions, art, ideas, etc. associated with the end of the nineteenth century, but in general use, the expression describes ideas, art, fashions, etc. considered modern and up-to-date.

> *Martin prides himself on always being aware of FIN DE SIECLE philosophies, especially those that come from Europe.*

finagle *(fih-NAY-gul), verb*
To wangle; to use clever, often underhanded methods to achieve one's desires.

> *Justin FINAGLED his way into the press conference by borrowing a pass from another reporter.*

finesse *(fih-NESS), verb*
Using subtle charm and style to resolve a problem; smooth, skillful maneuvering.

> *David's legendary ability to FINESSE his way out of any situation was taxed to the extreme when his wife returned early from a business trip and found him in the hot tub with his secretary.*

finis *(fih-NEE), noun*
The end or conclusion; also, as an adjective: finished.

> *Many people considered Mr. Clinton's presidential campaign FINIS in the weeks before the New Hampshire primary.*

First Amendment *(first uh-MEND-munt), noun*

An article of the United States Constitution guaranteeing citizens the right to freedom of speech and the free exercise of religion.

> *A court order suppressing this story would be a blatant violation of our newspaper's FIRST AMENDMENT rights.*

fissure *(FISH-er), noun or verb*

A narrow opening produced by a crack or other form of accidental or purposeful separation. As a verb, "fissure" describes the act of splitting.

> *The explosion was traced to a small FISSURE that had developed on the bottom of the fuel tank.*

fitful *(FIT-fuhl), adjective*

Occurring irregularly or intermittently.

> *I felt rotten in the morning, after a night of FITFUL sleep.*

fixate *(FICK-sate), verb*

To focus one's attention on, often to an alarming degree.

> *Roy is getting to old to FIXATE on partying and casual relationships.*

fjord *(fyord), noun*

A thin strip of sea flowing between cliffs or hills.

> *Prison officials were able to determine that the two escapees had managed to escape the island fortress by drugging the guards, crawling through a secret tunnel, and swimming out to the small motorboat accomplices had hidden in the FJORD.*

flaccid *(FLASS-id), adjective*

Lacking firmness, stiffness, vigor.

> *After sitting out on the deli counter all day long, the celery stalks and leaves of lettuce looked FLACCID and unappealing.*

flagellate *(FLADGE-uh-late), verb*

To whip.

> *My daughter, a lifelong animal lover, refused to go on the stage coach ride at the amusement park because of the way the driver FLAGELLATED the horses.*

flagitious *(fluh-JISH-us), adjective*

Describes someone shamefully wicked or describes particularly heinous events.

> *For many years, apartheid was the FLAGITIOUS wound around which South Africa was built.*

flagrant *(FLAY-grunt), adjective*
Obvious and very noticeable in a notorious or scandalous way.

> *The fact that the referees let only one team get away with a series of FLAGRANT fouls caused many in the crowd to believe the game was fixed.*

flak *(flak), noun*
The bursting shell fired from antiaircraft guns, or an antiaircraft gun itself; also, impediments, arguments, or opposition (to a course of action or situation).

> *"If you give me any more FLAK about the time I set for your curfew," my mom promised, "you won't be going out at all."*

flambé *(flom-BAY), verb*
To serve in flaming liquor (usually brandy).

> *Although the dinner was only so-so, the raspberry custard FLAMBÉ, which the waiter ignited at our table, was both dramatic and delicious.*

flashback *(FLASH-back), noun*
To interject a scene containing events from the past into a chronological series of present-day events; an instance of such a scene.

> *Casablanca's FLASHBACK scenes of the two lovers during their time in Paris give us a sense of the love they shared—and the magnitude of Rick's loss.*

flashpoint *(FLASH-point), noun*
Denotes either the site at which significant—typically violent—action has occurred or a place or situation that is likely to erupt in violence.

> *The murder of the prime minister was a FLASHPOINT for global warfare.*

flaunt *(flont), verb*
To display (oneself or a possession) in an ostentatious way. *Flaunt* is often confused with flout (see flout below), but the words have completely different meanings.

> *Mr. Miller's habit of wearing many jewelled rings is one of the many ways he has found to FLAUNT his wealth.*

flaxen *(FLAK-sun), adjective*
A pale yellow color.

> *I'm not sure Mel would have admired Renee's FLAXEN hair quite so much if he'd known it was the result of a recent visit to the hair salon.*

fledgling *(FLEJ-ling), adjective and noun*
Young or inexperienced. Literally, a *fledgling* is a young bird that has only recently gained the power of flight.

> *The FLEDGLING reporter had little respect around the newsroom.*

flibbertigibbet *(FLIB-er-tee-jibb-it), noun*

A chatty, scatterbrained person.

> *Estelle liked Phil at first, but she quickly realized he was a FLIBBERTIGIBBET and not worth her time.*

flim-flam *(FLIM-flam), noun and adjective*

A swindle. A *flim-flam* operation is a scam or confidence game.

> *Vern may call himself an entrepreneur; he appears to me to he's nothing more than a FLIM-FLAM artist.*

flimsy *(FLIM-zee), adjective*

Lightweight; cheap; unsturdy; of poor quality.

> *The department store circular advertised an amazing sale on bureaus, desks, and other furniture, but when we got to the store we found that all the items we were interested in were constructed from FLIMSY particleboard, not pine or oak.*

flippant *(FLIP-unt), adjective*

Disrespectful or harsh in tone; shallow or frivolous.

> *Mario, still upset about the previous night's quarrel greeted his wife's cheery "Good morning" with a FLIPPANT "Who says it is?"*

floe *(FLOW), noun*

A large chunk or sheet of floating ice.

> *The penguins would amuse themselves for hours jumping and sliding off the broad, flat FLOES and careening into the water.*

florid *(FLOOR-id), adjective*

Describes something or someone with a reddish, rosy tint. In addition, *florid* can be used to describe writing or speech one considers too showy and ornate.

> *Critics praised her, but I found the pundit's FLORID prose a real turnoff and got through only the first twenty pages of her book.*

flotilla *(floe-TILL-uh), noun*

A fleet of ships, usually military vessels; also, any large group of moving objects.

> *On the appointed evening, a massive FLOTILLA of Allied warships—the largest assembly of naval battle vessels in human history—steamed toward Normandy.*

flotsam *(FLOT-sum), noun*

The debris from a shipwreck that floats on water or is washed ashore.

> *When they collected and examined the FLOTSAM from the Intrepid, investigators found minute traces of dynamite that proved once and for all that the ship's explosion was not the result of a faulty fuel line.*

flounce *(FLOWNTS), verb*

To move about with exaggerated motion or in a spasmodic manner.

> *The actress flounced about as she entered the premiere with her entourage.*

flounder *(FLOWN-dur), verb*

To struggle clumsily. (See, for comparison, the entry for *founder*.) Also: a fish.

> *My FLOUNDERING efforts to open the door while holding five packages were the object of some amusement to my roommate, but he did not offer to relieve me of any of them.*

flout *(flowt), verb*

To brazenly or openly break a law, regulation, or tradition. *Flout* is often confused with flaunt (see flaunt above), but the words have completely different meanings.

> *To begin the baseball game without singing the national anthem would be to FLOUT a tradition of more than a century.*

fluctuate *(FLUK-choo-ate), verb*

To waver between one thing and another; to change or shift back and forth constantly.

> *The dietitian said we should not worry if our weight FLUCTUATED between two and five pounds in either direction of our goal as long as we were able to maintain a weight in that range.*

flue *(floo), noun*

A duct or tube used for the passage of smoke.

> *David vowed to spend Christmas Eve staring up the FLUE so he could alert the family the moment Santa arrived, but he fell asleep after only a short time at his post.*

fluency *(FLOO-un-see), noun*

Ready and unhindered expression.

> *Alice's FLUENCY in Spanish proved a real advantage during our trip to Mexico.*

flummox *(FLUHM-ucks), verb*

To completely bewilder or confuse.

> *No matter how much I study, mathematics continues to FLUMMOX me.*

flux *(fluks), noun*

Ongoing flow. *Flux* can also refer to unceasing change.

> *The organization's plans were in a state of constant FLUX.*

fob *(FOB), verb*

To get rid of (usually by unscrupulous means).

> *Don't let him fool you; those "courtside" tickets he's trying to FOB off on you at such a bargain price are counterfeit.*

foible *(FOI-bull), noun*
Fault or character flaw. To say a person has a *foible* is to say he exhibits a flaw or failing that is comparatively insignificant.

> *The tendency to remember only the pleasant occurrences in our past is a common human FOIBLE.*

foist *(foist), verb*
To pawn off (something undesirable). To *foist* something on someone is to assign it or pass it along to him despite his wishes.

> *This project was FOISTED on us because everyone believed it was impossible, and because we were considered the worst department in the organization.*

folderol *(FALL-duh-rahl), noun*
Foolishness, a trifle, something nonsensical and unimportant.

> *The commentator called all of the political wrangling nothing but FOLDEROL that kept anything substantive from being done to solve the problem.*

foliage *(FOLE-ee-udge), noun*
A group of leaves, branches, and flowers.

> *The best time to view the fall FOLIAGE in New England is at generally early October, when the reds, oranges, and golden yellows are at their most brilliant.*

foliate *(FOAL-ee-ate), verb or adjective*
To bring forth leaves, to decorate with leaves or leafy patterns, or to shape something into thin sheets. As an adjective, the word is pronounced "FOAL-ee-uht," and describes something covered with leaves or shaped like a leaf.

> *Once Jill found the right combination of water and food, the dying plant began to FOLIATE with abandon.*

foment *(fo-MENT), verb*
To aid, nourish, feed, or encourage.

> *Some in the university argued that our group's purpose was to FOMENT a revolution, not work for reform, and they demanded that we dissolve.*

foofaraw *(FOO-fuh-raw), noun*
A lot of fuss about a lot of nothing, or an excessive amount of decoration on oneself, in a room, etc.

> *Whether or not the celebrity had removed a mole became a FOOFARAW debated for days by the entertainment press.*

foolhardy *(FOOL-har-dee), adjective*

Rash; hasty; unthinking.

> *Mack's FOOLHARDLY decision to leave his job and visit Trinidad and Tobago for two years was apparently the result of a chance encounter with a palm reader he met in a Greyhound station in West Covina, California.*

fop *(fop), noun*

A dandy. An extravagant (male) person who is uncommonly vain or pretentious is a *fop*.

> *I was cornered by Charles, the biggest FOP on campus, who subjected me to a lecture about how wonderfully he was dressed.*

forage *(FOR-uj), verb*

To search or hunt for food and provisions.

> *I awoke just in time to find the dog FORAGING in our picnic basket.*

foray *(FORE-ay), noun*

An initial try. Originally, a *foray* was a sudden military advance.

> *Elizabeth's FORAY into the world of publishing was not without disheartening moments.*

forcible *(FORCE-ih-bul), adjective*

Powerful; using force to achieve a goal.

> *The editors of the campus paper were shocked at the campus police's FORCIBLE entry into their offices.*

forebear *(FORE-bare), noun*

An ancestor; forefather.

> *Kate's illustrious FOREBEAR was a preeminent figure in the abolitionist movement.*

foreclosure *(fore-CLOZH-er), noun*

The act of repossessing a mortgaged property due to a default on payments, resulting in the mortgagee losing all rights to the property.

> *Neither Mrs. Walker nor her estranged husband could keep up the mortgage payments on the condo during their divorce proceedings, and the bank FORECLOSED on the property.*

forefend *(for-FEND), verb*

To protect, defend, secure, etc.

> *After he bought a television with a fifty-five inch screen, Keith bought an alarm system to FOREFEND it.*

foreordained *(fore-or-DANED), verb*

To ordain or appoint in advance; predestined.

> *Although Milton viewed his promotion to management as FOREORDAINED, his wife had her doubts.*

forestall *(for-STALL), verb*

To anticipate an action and thus work to prevent it from happening.

> *Alice saw that the driver was going to run the red light, so she paused at the intersection, FORESTALLING an accident.*

forge *(forj), verb*

To form and mold metals or other materials by using intense heat; to expend effort for the purpose of creating something; to fuse or join two formerly disparate elements.

> *By the end of the rigorous Outward Bound weekend, the friends had FORGED a bond that would last a lifetime.*

formidable *(FOR-mih-duh-bull), adjective*

Capable of inspiring fear or respect. Something that is *formidable* is challenging or difficult to overcome.

> *Alfred faced a FORMIDABLE opponent; he knew he had to plan carefully.*

formulaic *(form-you-LAY-ick), adjective*

Made according to a formula, usually used in a negative way.

> *John stopped watching television because he was fed up with the FORMULAIC junk networks palmed off as "entertainment."*

forsake *(for-SAKE), verb*

To abandon.

> *Emily has FORSAKEN California for an island in the Indian Ocean.*

forte *(fort), noun*

One's niche or strong point; that at which one excels.

> *Interior decorating was Frank's FORTE, but he resisted making a career of it for fear of what "the guys" would say.*

fortuitous *(fore-TOO-ih-tuss), adjective*

Accidental; lucky or fortunate. A *fortuitous* event is one that comes as a pleasant surprise.

> *After years of trial and error, Dr. Powers made a FORTUITOUS discovery when he mistakenly combined two chemical compounds.*

forum *(FOR-um), noun*

A gathering, meeting, or program held for the purpose of discussing matters of public or common concern.

> *"Although I am sure your neighbor's constantly barking dog is irritating, Mrs. Wakefield," the chairman intoned, "the purpose of this FORUM is to discuss the proposed waste site."*

founder *(FOUN-dur), adjective*

To sink; to fail in an undertaking. (See, for comparison, the entry for *flounder*.)

> *The new firm FOUNDERED because the promised investment capital never materialized.*

four-flusher *(FOR-flush-ur), noun*

In poker, a player who bluffs.

> *Our Friday-night poker games aren't played with the highest degree of honesty; everyone involved is a well-known FOUR-FLUSHER.*

foyer *(FOY-ur), noun*

Hall; vestibule; entryway; a lobby (as in a theater or hotel).

> *"If the FOYER is any indication of what I'll find on the upper floors," I thought to myself, "my new office is going to be a real dump."*

fracas *(FRAK-us), noun*

Commotion; a noisy disagreement.

> *The nightly FRACAS between the couple next door is always loud enough to wake me out of a sound sleep.*

fractious *(FRAK-shuss), adjective*

Unruly; likely to cause disturbance or trouble. A *fractious* person is quarrelsome and difficult.

> *Michael's FRACTIOUS nature made him an unsuitable candidate for a career in customer service.*

frangible *(FRAN-juh-bull), adjective*

Easily breakable.

> *The FRANGIBLE vase did not survive the cross-country move.*

fratricide *(FRAT-rih-side), noun*

The act of killing a brother. *Fratricide* refers to the murder of a male sibling; the word for killing a sister is sororicide.

> *It is only when Hamlet is told of the king's FRATRICIDE that a tragic chain of events is initated.*

fraught *(frot), adjective*
Loaded or filled with; accompanied by; involving.
> *Buck accepted the task, although he knew it was FRAUGHT with peril.*

freebooter *(FREE-boo-ter), noun*
A pirate; one who takes his loot—or booty—without asking.
> *John quickly thought of Alan as a FREEBOOTER and not as a roommate splitting costs fifty-fifty.*

frenetic *(fruh-NET-ik), adjective*
Frantic; frenzied.
> *I tried to avoid the FRENETIC Christmas rush by buying presents over the summer.*

frenzy *(FREN-zee), noun*
A state of wild excitement; extreme emotional or mental agitation.
> *What with studying for the bar exam and planning her wedding, Sara had been in an almost constant FRENZY for nearly two months.*

freshet *(FRESH-it), noun*
Either a stream of freshwater that runs into the sea or a quick rise in a body of water due to rain or melting snow.
> *The quick spring thaw created FRESHETS throughout the county that threatened many homes.*

friable *(FRY-uh-bull), adjective*
Easily crumbled; brittle.
> *The FRIABLE pottery was packed in layers of bubble wrap to prevent breakage.*

fribble *(FRIB-uhl), verb or noun*
To waste one's in a foolish manner, or the term for someone who does this.
> *Tom knew he needed to focus on the project, but he couldn't keep himself from FRIBBLING away his time with video games.*

frisson *(free-SON), noun*
A brief shudder of excitement; a thrill.
> *Maria felt a FRISSON of joy at winning the drama award, but it was tempered by the fact that one of the people she had beaten out was her best friend.*

frivolity *(frih-VOL-ih-tee), noun*
Unworthy of serious note; insubstantial. To engage in *frivolity* is to behave in a lighthearted or even ludicrous way.
> *We have no time for FRIVOLITY; tomorrow morning, the manager is coming.*

froufrou *(FROO-froo), adjective*

Excessive or unnecessary decoration; especially, an elaborate adornment in women's fashion.

> *Angela had never seen so many ill-fitting tuxedoes and self-conscious frills and FROUFROUS than she beheld the night of the senior prom.*

frowzy *(FROW-zee), adjective*

Sloppy; unkept; stale.

> *One would never know that beneath those FROWZY, oversized dresses and grungy cowboy hats was a model who had recently appeared on the cover of Vogue.*

fructify *(FRUCK-tih-fie), verb*

To bear fruit or to make fruitful.

> *I believe the partnership of our firms will FRUCTIFY both our companies.*

fruition *(froo-ISH-un), noun*

That which has arisen from development, possession, use, or effort. The achievement of something desired or labored for is the *fruition* of that deed.

> *The novel was, in a sense, the FRUITION of a lifetime of work for Melville.*

fugacious *(fyoo-GAY-shuss), adjective*

Fleeting, transitory, short-lived.

> *The FUGACIOUS mid-summer cold snap was a welcome relief from the heat.*

fugue *(fyoog), noun*

A piece of music that builds up from a central theme.

> *Many music enthusiasts find Bach's FUGUES more hauntingly beautiful than his sonatas and cantatas.*

fulcrum *(FUL-krum), noun*

The point of support on which a lever turns.

> *To illustrate the function of a FULCRUM, Mr. Hess directed our attention to the window, where two children could be seen playing on a see-saw in the park.*

fulminate *(FUL-mih-nate), verb*

To explode. Also: to denounce loudly or forcefully. Someone who *fulminates* thunders forth or issues a dramatic attack.

> *He FULMINATED against the bill on the floor of the Senate, but he knew he did not have the votes to defeat it.*

fulsome *(FUL-sum), adjective*
Excessive and overdone, especially in a way inconsistent with good taste. Also: insincerely earnest in expression.

Although Marian greeted my work with FULSOME praise, it was clear to me within five minutes of our meeting that she hadn't read a page of it.

fumigate *(FYOO-mih-gate), verb*
To release fumes in order to get rid of insects or other pests.

We had the place FUMIGATED, used sound-waves, and set dozens of traps, but our house continued to be plagued by cockroaches.

funereal *(fyoo-NIR-ee-uhl), adjective*
Reminiscent of a funeral. That which is dark, brooding, and mournful is *funereal*.

The FUNEREAL tone of the meeting was not at all what we had in mind to raise morale.

fungible *(FUHN-jih-bull), adjective*
A fancy way to say "interchangeable."

I don't think a twelve-inch black and white television is FUNGIBLE for a forty-two inch color set.

funicular *(fyoo-NICK-you-ler), adjective*
A *funicular* railway contains cars that are toted up and down hillsides by means of a cord or cable. Thus, something *funicular* is related to ropes, cables, and cords as well as the tension on them.

We got to the site and couldn't go climbing because Jenny had left behind all the necessary FUNICULAR equipment.

furbelow *(FUR-buh-low), noun*
A showy ruffle.

Deborah's floor-length dress ended in a beautiful silk FURBELOW.

furlough *(FUR-low), noun*
A leave of absence, especially for a member of the armed forces; the act of granting this leave.

During his FURLOUGH Dan concentrated on finding a job in the private sector, as he was scheduled to be discharged from the Navy in three months.

furor *(FYOOR-ur), noun*
Widespread excitement or anger; fury or uproar among persons or institutions.

Governor White's indictment for embezzlement caused a FUROR in the state.

furrow *(FUR-oh), noun or verb*
A furrow is a narrow groove in the ground, such as one formed by a plow. Thus, one furrows when one creates grooves or wrinkles in something.

> *I could tell mom didn't believe my story as she began to FURROW her brow.*

furtive *(FUR-tiv), adjective*
Stealthy. That which is surreptitious or sly is *furtive.*

> *Marie's FURTIVE designs were soon detected and exposed.*

fusty *(FUHSS-tee), adjective*
Old-fashioned and out of date, or clinging to old-fashioned, conservative values.

> *My father-in-law's FUSTY opinions of "a woman's place" make me want to sock him every time I have to see him!*

futility *(fyoo-TILL-ih-tee), noun*
That which is characterized by uselessness. Something that is impractical or vainly undertaken shows *futility.*

> *The FUTILITY of attempting to reason with Paula could no longer be denied; Michael gave up trying.*

futurism *(FYOO-chur-ih-zim), noun*
An early 20th-century arts movement stressing the dynamics and movements of the industrial age.

> *Jones was fascinated by early industrial art; last semester he took a course on FUTURISM.*

futz *(futs), verb*
To pass the time idly or without purpose.

> *Kevin spent so much time this morning FUTZING around with his new espresso maker that he was late for work.*

doctrinaire
abstemious
levity hubris panacea
veracity cerebellum
labyrinth
criterion
nonagenarian
meticulous zither

G

erbiage quondam
colloquial
vokpalpable pagination
incipient salutary
evity redact fervent
beleaguered yawnful
elixir beneficent
amoose pragmatism

gadabout *(GAD-uh-bout), noun*
A person who wanders about aimlessly or restlessly, especially one in constant search of pleasure.
> *Though most everyone thought of her as a flighty GADABOUT, Karen certainly knew when to bear down and get serious about her schoolwork.*

gadfly *(GAD-fly), noun*
A fly that bites livestock; also, one who annoys, irritates or provokes.
> *With his constant grumbling and irritating habits, Morton has turned into the GADFLY of our department.*

gainsay *(GANE-say), verb*
To declare false. To *gainsay* is to oppose or contradict.
> *The principles of the Bill of Rights, Mr. Secretary, will admit no GAINSAYING.*

gallantry *(GAL-un-tree), noun*
Something displaying dashing bravery or chivalry. *Gallantry* pertains to an air of courage and nobility.
> *His GALLANTRY and sophistication will do little to solve this problem; what is needed is cold cash.*

galoot *(guh-LOOT), noun*
An eccentric or foolish person.
> *Mike's outdated clothes and hairstyle cause many to consider him a GALOOT.*

galore *(guh-LORE), adjective*
In abundance; plentiful.
> *Once Mom hit the lottery, she promised, it would be presents GALORE for all of us: new cars, clothes, jewelry, vacations, and just about anything else we wanted.*

galvanize *(GAL-vuh-nize), verb*
To stimulate into action; to motivate (as if with an electric shock).
> *After considerable national debate over the merits of entering into a "European war," the Japanese attack on Pearl Harbor GALVANIZED American public opinion as nothing else could.*

gambit *(GAM-but), noun*
In chess, an opening in which a piece is sacrificed with the hope of gaining strategic advantage; also, any maneuver or plan calculated to gain advantage.
> *Bill's plan to get the inside track on the new position by dating the boss's daughter was a risky and ill-conceived GAMBIT that ended in failure.*

gambol *(GAM-buhl), verb*
To skip or frolic about with delight.

> *The birds GAMBOLED outside my screened-in porch as I sat there with my morning coffee.*

gamesome *(GAIM-sum), adjective*
Merry; frolicsome.

> *It's sad to see that Sally has become such a stick-in-the mud; as a young woman, she was so GAMESOME and full of high spirits.*

gamine *(GAH-mean), adjective or noun*
A slight, diminutive girl who often is plucky or perky; or the description of such a girl.

> *As the actress grew older and put on weight, she was no longer able to play the GAMINE roles that had made her reputation.*

gamut *(GAM-ut), noun*
The full range or extent. *Gamut* also refers to the entire series of standard musical notes.

> *His house featured an entertainment center whose components ran the GAMUT of state-of-the-art equipment.*

gamy *(GAY-me), adjective*
Originally used to describe the tangy flavor and odor of wild game, the word *gamy* has branched out to have several meanings: lewd, spirited, and disgusting. It's all in the context!

> *After three hours of playing basketball, I feared my sweat-soaked gym clothes were more than a little GAMY.*

gargantuan *(gar-GAN-choo-un), adjective*
Enormous. *Gargantuan* derives from the name of a fictional king (Gargantua) famous for his massive appetite.

> *The GARGANTUAN scale of the budget deficit caught both Congress and the financial markets by surprise.*

garish *(GAIR-ish), adjective*
Showy in an excessive and over-the-top manner.

> *I'd always thought of Martha as refined, so I was surprised by the GARISH way she decorated her home.*

garner *(GAR-nur), verb*
To amass, gather, or accumulate. To *garner* something is to acquire it over a period.

> *William GARNERED much praise for his writing but little cash.*

garret *(GARE-ut), noun*

An attic room; also, a secluded, generally unfinished area near the top of a structure used as an observation post or as a place for privacy and refuge.

> *Although he had a computer and printer set up in his downstairs study, Christopher found that he did his best writing sitting up in the GARRET with a pad of paper and a pencil.*

garrulity *(guh-ROO-lih-tee), noun*

Talkativeness. *Garrulity* refers to one who is overly or habitually given to talking.

> *If Michael's insight only matched his GARRULITY, he would be quite popular.*

gastropod *(GAS-tro-pawd), noun*

A variety of mollusk having no shell or a single spiral shell and moving by means of a ventral disk or foot.

> *June retorted that she hadn't ever considered eating GASTROPODS in the United States, and saw no reason to do so in France no matter what they were called.*

gaudy *(GAHW-dee), adjective*

Showy; tasteless. Something that bespeaks tackiness or excessive ornamentation is *gaudy*.

> *For some reason, Cheryl always adorns herself with the GAUDIEST jewelry imaginable.*

gaunt *(gawnt), adjective*

Extremely thin; haggard, as by deprivation or worry.

> *The televised images of the hostages showed the world a series of GAUNT faces, worn by months of torture and captivity, reading words that had obviously been written for them.*

gauntlet *(GONT-let), noun*

A challenge. To "throw down the *gauntlet*" in medieval times, was to issue a challenge to a duel.

> *This deadline is not simply a goal for this department; it is a GAUNTLET that has been thrown before us.*

gazebo *(guh-ZEE-boe), noun*

A small outdoor structure, roofed but open on the sides, usually placed in a backyard or a park.

> *The GAZEBO in the church courtyard was freshened up with a new coat of white paint every spring in preparation for outdoor weddings.*

gazetteer *(gah-zih-TEER), noun*
A dictionary or index of geographical locations.

> *The Smiths' method of deciding where to go on their vacation is to open the GAZETTEER at random and stab the page with a finger; whatever they land on will become their summer destination.*

gelding *(GEL-ding), noun*
A castrated animal and, by extension, an emasculated man.

> *We called Al a GELDING, but he said he had no problem letting his wife, Mary, take charge of the couple's financial decisions.*

gemology *(jeh-MALL-uh-jee), noun*
The study of gems.

> *Despite a lifelong interest in GEMOLOGY, Lucas knew he was in no position to make a valid assessment of the stone's worth.*

gendarme *(zhon-DARM), noun*
An officer in a police force in any of several European countries, but particularly those of France.

> *After months of difficult undercover work, the Parisian GENDARME was able to recover the stolen artwork and return it to its rightful place in the Louvre.*

generic *(juh-NARE-ik), adjective*
Of or pertaining to all members of a group or category; also, unprotected by trademark; common and unremarkable.

> *Senator Smith used the press conference as an opportunity to deliver his GENERIC speech on the role of the media in the development of public policy.*

genial *(JEEN-yul), adjective*
Kindly or pleasant in disposition. A *genial* attitude is one of warmth and openness.

> *Although we expected to confront the enemy in full force, we encountered only GENIAL townsfolk.*

genocide *(JENN-uh-side), noun*
The deliberate, systematic destruction of a culture, people, nation, etc.

> *Attempts at tribal GENOCIDE have drawn attention to the African province of Darfur.*

genre *(ZHAWN-ruh), noun*
A particular style that characterizes a type of music, art, literature, film, etc.

> *Though their GENRE doesn't make for pleasant or easy reading, one has to admire muckrakers like Upton Sinclair, who aimed to bring about important social reforms with their novels.*

genteel *(jen-TEEL), adjective*
Refined; conveying a sense of high style and/or respectability. *Genteel* is often meant to imply a sense of social superiority, as well.

Tom's vulgar remarks were not appreciated by his GENTEEL dining companions.

gentrify *(JENN-truh-fie), verb*
To take something rundown, such as a neighborhood, and improve it. The noun form, with which you may be familiar, is *"gentrification."*

Attempts to GENTRIFY the historic neighborhood failed because of community apathy.

gentry *(JEN-tree), noun*
Those claiming high birth. In England, *gentry* refers to the class immediately below the nobility.

The fact that the GENTRY would benefit most from victory was taken by many of the soldiers to mean that they were fighting a rich man's war.

genuflect *(JENN-you-flect), verb*
To bow deeply on one knee. Often, the word is used negatively, to suggest that someone is acting in a servile or overly reverential way toward someone else.

"The way Harold GENUFLECTS to Mr. Thomas at staff meetings just makes me want to barf," Alice said.

germane *(jur-MAYN), adjective*
Pertinent; relevant; related to the matter at hand.

The defendant's exemplary qualities as a breadwinner are hardly GERMANE to the question of whether he shot his cousin, Your Honor.

germinate *(JUHR-muh-nate), verb*
To cause something, such as a concept, to come into existence.

The ideas we GERMINATED that day have led to numerous improvements in the area of global communication.

gerontocracy *(jare-un-TOCK-ruh-see), noun*
A group in which the order and rule is kept by a group of elders; government by the older members of a society.

One of the potential drawbacks of a GERONTOCRACY, of course, is that people entrusted with great political power may well become mentally infirm.

gerontology *(jare-un-TOL-uh-jee), noun*
The field of medicine concerned with illnesses, diseases, and problems specific to old age.

My decision to enter the field of GERONTOLOGY was greeted with skepticism by my father, who had hoped I would follow in his footsteps and become a general practitioner.

gerrymander *(JARE-ee-man-dur), verb*
To divide voting districts in such a way as to give unfair advantage to a particular party.

> *Senator Belger dismissed the charges of racist GERRYMANDERING that had been made against him as so much hogwash from opponents eager to draw the district maps to their own liking.*

gestation *(jes-TAY-shun), noun*
Inception and creation. The period of *gestation* among humans, for instance, would be the nine months spent within the womb. Concepts and ideas are also said to have gestation.

> *The ad campaign's GESTATION was fraught with conflict, but the end result was well worth all the quarrelling.*

gesticulate *(jes-TICK-yoo-late), verb*
To employ gestures, especially in place of speech. *Gesticulate* usually implies more animation and excitement than the simpler gesture.

> *Unable to speak French, Michael was forced to GESTICULATE to try to make himself understood.*

ghoulish *(GOO-lish), adjective*
Having a morbid fascination with subjects like death, disease, serial killers, etc.

> *I wouldn't call Jim GHOULISH, but his favorite activity is to tour local cemeteries and to take pictures of area funeral homes.*

gibber *(JIB-bur), verb*
To speak nervously and incomprehensibly; to speak in a fast, jumbled, inarticulate manner.

> *Zack may have been believable playing the part of a Casanova in the television show, but off-screen he could barely GIBBER his way through a conversation with a woman.*

gild *(gild), verb*
To cover thinly with gold; also, to make something appear more valuable or appealing than it actually is.

> *Ross attempted to GILD his offer by promising not to lay off current employees for at least two years, but the board's only question was whether he could match the $630 million figure put forth by the Stradbury group.*

G

gimcrackery *(JIM-crack-ur-ee), noun*
An object or objects that has no real value except for the purpose of show.
> *Paul's father used to tell him that all the academic honors he earned in college amounted to so much GIMCRACKERY if he couldn't put his intelligence to work for him in the "real" world.*

gingivitis *(jin-jih-VIE-tuss), noun*
A gum disease; the condition of having swollen gums.
> *The rinse promised lifetime protection against GINGIVITIS, a claim Fred viewed with some skepticism.*

girth *(GIRTH), noun*
The circumference of something. "Girth" often is used as a nice way to say "fat."
> *My mind was boggled as I tried to conceive of the GIRTH of the planet Jupiter.*

gist *(jist), noun*
The main point; the essential meaning, the core or heart of a message.
> *The GIST of the letter from the grievance committee is that the workers are tired of being unappreciated and underpaid.*

glaucoma *(glaw-KOE-muh), noun*
A disease of the eye caused by increasing pressure on the eyeball, creating damage to the optic disk that, if severe enough, can cause loss of vision.
> *The portion of my annual visit to the eye doctor that I like the least is the GLAUCOMA test, in which a blast of air is shot into each eye at close range.*

glean *(gleen), verb*
To collect; to gain bit by bit; to obtain one piece or morsel at a time.
> *Although Mr. Willis never came out and said as much, his secretary was able to GLEAN that he would soon be retiring.*

glib *(glib), adjective*
Articulate yet superficial; facile.
> *I asked for an analysis of the construction of Shakespeare's tragedies, but you have turned in a series of GLIB observations on the most famous speeches in the plays.*

glissade *(glih-SOD), noun*
In mountain climbing, a slide down a steep, snow-covered slope.
> *The instructor had made the GLISSADE look easy, but as I looked after him down the slope, I had a feeling my own trek down wouldn't be quite as smooth.*

glissando *(glih-SAHN-doe), adjective*
In music, a smooth transition between intervals, such as the sound a slide
trombone or pedal steel guitar makes in moving from one note to another.
> *Since there is no way to "bend" its notes, the piano cannot produce a true*
> *GLISSANDO.*

globular *(GLOB-yoo-lar), adjective*
Spherically shaped. *Globular* means, primarily, "in the shape of a globe." The best
word for "of worldwide interest or applicability" is global.
> *Several GLOBULAR lampheads illuminated the room.*

glom *(GLAHM), verb*
To look at with rapt attention or to steal something. "*Glom* onto" means to take
possession of something, such as someone else's ideas.
> *Once he realized it would get him votes, the candidate GLOMMED onto the plight of*
> *blue-collar workers and made the issue his campaign's emphasis.*

glower *(GLOU-ur), verb*
To give a brooding, annoyed, or angry look.
> *Mark hoped GLOWERING at our mother would convey that he didn't appreciate her*
> *telling his new girlfriend how difficult he had been to toilet train, but Mom didn't*
> *seem to notice.*

gnash *(nash), verb*
To grind or strike (usually the teeth) together.
> *Although she claimed not to be, I could tell that Elaine was angry by the way she*
> *GNASHED her teeth.*

gnocchi *(NYAW-kee), noun*
An Italian pasta dish; small round balls of pasta.
> *Dawn ordered GNOCCHI for Ellen, her five-year-old, but the little girl seemed to*
> *enjoy playing with the little things more than eating them.*

Gnostic *(NOSS-tik), adjective*
Pertaining to or reminiscent of certain early Christian sects (known as
Gnostics) who valued personal knowledge and inquiry as supreme religious
values transcending physical experience. (*Gnostic* also can mean "pertaining to
knowldedge," especially in the context of spirituality. It is not normally used as the
opposite of agnostic.
> *The ancient GNOSTIC gospels, while not part of my formal church teaching,*
> *nevertheless made for illuminating reading.*

G

goad *(goad), verb*
To stimulate, urge, or prod, especially toward a given action. Originally, a *goad* was a pointed stick used to prod animals.

> *Brian decided not to write his name on the wall, despite his friends' attempts to GOAD him into doing so.*

gormandize *(GORE-mun-dize), verb*
To eat in a greedy, ravenous manner. Someone who *gormandizes* eats to satisfy a voracious appetite. Someone who does this is known as a *gormand* (or *gourmand*); this is very different from gourmet, which describes someone who cultivates refined tastes for food of the finest quantity.

> *Tom's tendency to GORMANDIZE eventually made him an unwelcome dinner guest.*

gossamer *(GOSS-uh-mer), adjective*
A delicate, floating film of cobwebs; also: thin and light, and therefore reminiscent of *gossamer*.

> *Some mornings, the grass outside our house takes on a veil of GOSSAMERS.*

goulash *(GOO-losh), noun*
A stew made with beef, vegetables, and paprika.

> *The chef's famous GOULASH was an old family recipe that had been handed by from his Hungarian ancestors for generations.*

gourmand *(GOOR-mahnd), noun*
One who eats well and to excess.

> *A well-known GOURMAND, Uncle Abe was forced to change his eating habits after his heart attack.*

gradation *(gra-DAY-shun), noun*
A progression by state or degree. To progress in *gradation* is to move ahead in measured, distinct stages.

> *The portrait's haunting effect may be due to Singer's extremely subtle GRADATIONS of color.*

gradient *(GRAY-dee-unt), noun*
An incline or slope.

> *The hike was refreshing but not taxing because the trail had a gentle GRADIENT.*

grandeur *(GRAN-jur), noun*
The quality of being grand; extravagance in scale or appearance. *Grandeur* refers to magnificence.

> *The Emerald City's GRANDEUR exceeded anything Dorothy had ever seen.*

grandiloquence *(gran-DIL-uh-kwence), noun*
Pompous speech or expression; bombast. *Grandiloquence* refers to an attitude of haughtiness, especially in one's means of communication.

> *I may not always employ the GRANDILOQUENCE my opponent does, but I believe I have a commonsense solution to the problem he has just outlined.*

grandiose *(GRAN-dee-oce), adjective*
Pompous. Someone whose pretentions or ambitions exceed his abilities, sensitivities, or means could be considered *grandiose.*

> *His GRANDIOSE scheme for career advancement simply will not pan out.*

grapple *(GRAP-ul), verb*
To struggle (with an opponent or enemy); to attempt to pin down or throw to the ground.

> *Alert Secret Service agents GRAPPLED with the armed intruder and wrestled him to the ground before any shots were fired.*

gratis *(GRAT-iss), adjective*
Free of charge.

> *I liked visiting Renee when she was working at the ice cream parlor, but the sundaes and banana splits she always offered GRATIS were impossible to resist—and they weren't helping my diet much.*

gratuitous *(gruh-TOO-ih-tuss), adjective*
Unnecessary. Also: given or granted without recompense or charge. Something that is *gratuitous* is excessive, out of place, or unnecessary.

> *His GRATUITOUS attacks on the popular governor only weakened his standing among voters.*

gratuity *(gruh-TOO-ih-tee), noun*
A tip; extra money given for service beyond the amount required by the bill.

> *I make it a point never to leave a GRATUITY if the service has been truly horrible.*

graven *(GRAY-vuhn), adjective*
Deeply impressed or firmly fixed, such as ideas, concepts, beliefs, etc.

> *Although it is not necessarily common throughout the world, freedom of religion is a GRAVEN concept in the United States.*

gravid *(GRAV-id), adjective*
Large, due to pregnancy.

> *Jean's GRAVID condition made it difficult for her to climb stairs.*

gravitas *(GRAV-ih-tahss), noun*
From the Latin meaning "heavy," *gravitas* denotes seriousness and weightiness of thought.

> *Jim's boyish looks kept him from attaining the GRAVITAS he desired to convey.*

gravitate *(GRAV-ih-tate), verb*
To have a natural inclination toward or to be strongly attracted to something (or someone).

> *As soon as we entered the electronics store, my kids GRAVITATED toward the video games.*

greenhouse effect *(GREEN-HOUSE uh-fect), noun*
Many believe the greenhouse effect is the cause of global warming. A greenhouse traps heat because the short waves of solar radiation easily go through glass. Once the sun's light passes through the glass and hits something, it is converted to longer-waved heat radiation, which cannot pass back out of the greenhouse. On Earth, the burning of fossil fuels has created something akin to the panes of glass on a greenhouse. The sun's rays can pass into the planet's atmosphere, but then, once converted to heat radiation, they are trapped inside our atmosphere.

> *Al Gore's film, An Inconvenient Truth, brought attention to the perils of the GREENHOUSE EFFECT.*

gregarious *(gri-GARE-ee-uss), adjective*
Outgoing, cordial, or friendly. *Gregarious* people enjoy the company of others.

> *Many would have been put off by such a reception, but Bill was unusually GREGARIOUS; he made many friends that night.*

grenadine *(GREN-uh-deen), noun*
Reddish-orange in color; also, a pomegranate-flavored syrup used in preparing mixed drinks.

> *Ted had planned to make Tequila Sunrises for the party, but as he had no GRENADINE to add a hint of red, he called the drinks "Tequila Sunbursts."*

grievous *(GREE-vuss), adjective*
Grave; severe; causing or likely to cause grief.

> *Failing to get a tuneup before driving to the shore turned out to be a GRIEVOUS error: I broke down in the middle of nowhere and had to pay a small fortune for a tow truck.*

grifter *(GRIFF-ter), noun*
A person who engages in unseemly activities; a swindler, a dishonest gambler, etc.

> *The small-town bar was filled with reprobates, toothless legions, and GRIFTERS. I felt right at home.*

grimace *(GRIM-uss), noun*
A facial expression showing disgust or discomfort. A *grimace* is a sharp facial contortion indicating pain, dissatisfaction, or disgust.

> *Billy GRIMACED at the thought of eating his vegetables.*

grisly *(GRIZ-lee), adjective*
Gruesome.

> *The final confrontation with Brando's character, GRISLY though it is, effectively follows through on the themes of ritual sacrifice established earlier in the film.*

grope *(groap), verb*
To reach about blindly. *Grope* can also be used figuratively to describe someone who acts in uncertainty of purpose.

> *He GROPED for the right words, but could not manage to come up with an acceptable explanation.*

grouse *(GROUSS), verb*
This common bird becomes something entirely different when transformed into a verb. Then, to *grouse* is to complain and grumble.

> *We were just ten minutes late, but my in-laws GROUSED about our tardiness for the rest of the day.*

grovel *(GROV-ul), verb*
To lie prostrate, especially when done as a sign of humility. Another meaning of *grovel* is to give oneself over completely to subservience.

> *To see his sister reduced to GROVELING for approval in this way was almost too much for Ryan to take.*

gruel *(grool), noun*
A thin, soup-like dish made from cooked cereal or grain.

> *In one of the most memorable scenes Dickens ever wrote, young Oliver Twist loses a lottery among the workhouse boys and must ask for an unprecedented second helping of GRUEL.*

guerrilla *(guh-RILL-uh), noun and adjective*
A *guerilla* is a member of an informal group of fighters that attacks enemies with surprise raids, sabotage, booby traps, etc. When used as an adjective, the word *guerilla* describes these fighters or their actions.

> *The nation's army could not defeat the GUERRILLAS, who seemed to swoop down invisibly from the mountains, wreak havoc, then disappear.*

guffaw *(guh-FAW), noun*

An instance of full, unrestrained laughter.

> *From the howls and GUFFAWS I heard issuing from the auditorium, I gathered that the principal's speech introducing a new dress code for the school was not going well.*

guild *(gild), noun*

A group of people dedicated to common interests or goals; an association of like-minded individuals.

> *Although she knew it was only a first step, Andrea couldn't help feeling that joining the Screen Actors GUILD meant she was on her way to becoming a star.*

guile *(gile), noun*

Cunning; treacherous deceit. Someone who exercises *guile* is insidious and misleading.

> *In laying the groundwork for embezzlement on such a large scale, Donald showed considerable GUILE and no small amount of daring.*

guise *(guys), noun*

Semblance; outer appearance; manner of dress.

> *Having assumed the GUISE of a pirate for the costume ball, Tom looked dashing and dangerous for what may well have been the first time in his life.*

gullible *(GULL-ih-bull), adjective*

Easily cheated, tricked, or deceived.

> *I'm afraid Terry is a little too GULLIBLE to survive for long as an aspiring actor in a city like New York.*

guru *(GOO-roo), noun*

An inspiring spiritual or intellectual leader; a revered teacher.

> *Though I found the self-help seminar to be helpful enough, I wasn't as awed as some others in the course, who made the instructor out to be some kind of GURU.*

guttural *(GUTT-er-ul), adjective*

Harsh or raspy; reminiscent of deep sounds produced in the throat. Also: of or pertaining to the throat.

> *The dog let out a low, GUTTURAL growl that was likely to give pause to whomever was standing on the other side of the door.*

gyrate *(JIE-rate), verb*

To spin; to wind or coil.

> *"What you kids do today isn't dancing," said Grandma; "all you do is jump and GYRATE willy-nilly.*

H

habiliment *(huh-BIL-eh-ment), noun*
A piece of clothing; a garment.

> *Much to the puzzlement of his staid colleagues, Professor Herriot looked upon the hippies of the 1960s, with their unorthodox choices in lifestyle and HABILIMENT, as welcome additions to a stagnant social order.*

habitué *(huh-BICH-oo-ay), noun*
From the French meaning "to frequent," a *habitué* is someone who frequents or spends a lot of time in a place, especially places like bars, casinos, nightclubs, etc.

> *Ellen has become known as a HABITUÉ of the shadier coffeehouses.*

hacienda *(ha-see-EN-duh), noun*
A large estate or plantation.

> *After spending his junior year living on a HACIENDA while he studied Spanish in Madrid, Oscar had a tough time readjusting to his tiny dorm room.*

hackneyed *(HAK-need), adjective*
Rendered less significant by common use. Literally, a *hackney* is a horse suited for routine riding or driving (and not a prime racehorse).

> *The primitive construction and reliance on HACKNEYED expressions make it perfectly clear: this is not the work of Shakespeare.*

haggis *(HAG-iss), noun*
A dish originating in Scotland made by removing the heart, liver, and lungs of a sheep or cow, dicing these, adding onions, suet, oatmeal, and seasonings, and placing the mixture into the animal's stomach, and boiling it.

> *Ivan had been enjoying the HAGGIS Mrs. MacIntyre had prepared for him until he asked her how it was made.*

haggle *(HAG-ul), verb*
To bargain with; to dicker or negotiate on price or terms.

> *I think Tom enjoyed the process of HAGGLING at the flea market more than the items he bought.*

haiku *(HIE-koo), noun*
A Japanese form of poetry. A *haiku* has three lines of five, seven, and five syllables, and often evokes images from nature.

> *Dean even tried his hand at poetry, composing several pleasant HAIKUS for the newsletter.*

halcyon *(HAL-see-on), adjective and noun*
Tranquil. Also: prosperous, carefree. A *halcyon* is a mythical bird, identified with the Kingfisher, that could supposedly calm ocean storms.

> *The company's HALCYON years were behind it; all was in chaos now.*

hale *(hale), adjective*
Healthy and vigorous; disease-free.

> *Lydia had been assured by the surgeon that she'd be HALE and hearty again in two weeks.*

hallow *(HAL-low), verb*
To establish as holy. To *hallow* can also be to extend the highest possible honor toward something.

> *This ancient burial ground, which is HALLOWED ground to many Native Americans, attracts a few too many tourists for my tastes.*

hallucinogenic *(huh-loo-sih-noe-JEN-ik), adjective*
Reminiscent of or pertaining to a drug or other substance that causes imaginary visions or delusions.

> *It seems difficult to believe that any person would knowingly administer HALLUCINOGENIC drugs to a seven-year-old child, Your Honor, but such are the facts before us in this case.*

halyard *(HAL-yurd), noun*
A tackle or rope usually used on ships to help hoist and lower sails.

> *As the storm intensified, Mary told us to slacken the HALYARD while Billy tried to guide the boat back toward shore.*

haphazard *(hap-HAZ-urd), adjective*
Irregular; governed by chance. Something that is done in a *haphazard* manner is not guided by a system or regular method.

> *After a few HAPHAZARD guesses at the box's contents, Steve gave up.*

hapless *(HAP-liss), adjective*
Luckless, unfortunate. A *hapless* person is unlucky.

> *Oliver presented a rather HAPLESS figure during his first few days on the job, but he soon mastered his new responsibilities.*

harangue *(huh-RANG), verb*
Lecture; berate; also, an instance of such berating.

> *Professor Thomas kept me after class to HARANGUE me for handing in a handwritten term paper.*

harbinger *(HAR-bin-jur), noun*
Someone or something that announces the approach of another, or of a forthcoming event.

> *The artist's mediocre early work, while commercially unsuccessful, did serve as a HARBINGER of future triumphs that dealing with similar themes.*

hardscrabble *(HARD-scrabb-uhl), adjective*
Describes a task, activity, profession, etc. that is extremely arduous yet offers little reward in return.

My family comes from dirt farmers who barely survived their HARDSCRABBLE existence.

hardtack *(HARD-tak), noun*
A hard biscuit once common in the rations of sailors and soldiers. *Hardtack* did not spoil—a major logistical benefit.

By the end of the war, the Union soldiers were thoroughly sick of the HARDTACK and vegetable soup that had been the mainstay of their diet.

harlequin *(HAR-luh-kwin), noun*
A comic character from the Italian *commedia* tradition, usually masked and wearing a tight-fitting costume.

Instead of the standard joker, the ornamental deck of playing cards featured a HARLEQUIN in colorful attire.

harrowing *(HARE-roe-ing), adjective*
Extremely distressing; disturbing or frightening in the extreme.

After her HARROWING ride down a hill in a car with failed brakes, Monica vowed never to drive again.

harry *(HAR-ee), verb*
To harass and annoy to an excessive degree.

The bill collectors HARRIED Susan until she felt forced to declare bankruptcy.

haughty *(HAUT-ee), adjective*
Snobbishly proud.

I tried to apologize for bumping into the woman, but she only gave me a HAUGHTY glance and inspected her fur coat for damage.

haute couture *(OAT kyoo-CHOOR), noun*
High fashion. *Haute couture* is the most stylish and influential way of designing clothes at a given time. (*Haute couture* also refers to articles of clothing currently considered of the highest style.)

Unfamiliar with the ways of HAUTE COUTURE, Wendell decided to pass up the fashion show.

haute cuisine *(oat kwi-ZEEN), noun*
Gourmet preparation of food. *Haute cuisine* can also refer to the preparation of meals as an art form.

Glenn knows more than we do about HAUTE CUISINE; let's let him pick the restaurant tonight.

hedonist *(HEE-duh-nist), noun*

One whose life is devoted solely or primarily to the pursuit of pleasure and gratification.

> *I took offense at Jane's implication that a glass of white wine during dinner made some kind of HEDONIST.*

heed *(heed), verb*

To pay attention to; to take into consideration; as a noun, an instance of notice or attention.

> *Don't HEED my brother George; he always tries to make me look bad in front of my dates.*

hegemony *(he-JEM-uh-nee), noun*

Predominant influence, especially in reference to the affairs of nations. To say one nation practices *hegemony* over another is to suggest that it exercises undue influence over conduct, mores, or administration within that nation.

> *Our foe's HEGEMONY will not stop with his control of smaller nations; his aim is world domination.*

heinous *(HAY-nuss), adjective*

Evil; reprehensible. To say something is *heinous* is to say that it far exceeds the bounds of morality.

> *Because of the HEINOUS nature of this crime, I am forced to pass a stern sentence.*

heirloom *(AIR-loom), noun*

A possession of commercial or sentimental value handed down from generation to generation.

> *As the oldest child, I was given the most precious family HEIRLOOM, our old grandfather clock, when my mother passed away.*

heliocentric *(hee-lee-oh-SEN-trick), adjective*

Of or pertaining to the theory that the sun is the center of the solar system; having the sun at the center; also, seen as from the center of the sun.

> *At the time Copernicus published his theory that our solar system is HELIOCENTRIC, the orthodox teaching was that the sun and all other planets revolved around the earth.*

helter-skelter *(HEL-tur SKEL-tur), adjective*

Haphazard; lacking order or purpose; confused in manner or array.

> *While the children ran HELTER-SKELTER through the living room, Mrs. Moore tried to light the candles on her son's birthday cake and set out party bags.*

hemophilia *(hee-mo-FEE-lee-uh), noun*
A blood defect usually affecting males but transmitted by females in which the blood fails to clot normally, often leading to uncontrolled hemorrhaging.

> *Because so many HEMOPHILIA patients have contracted the AIDS virus from contaminated blood, many will only accept transfusions using blood that has been donated by family and friends.*

hemorrhoid, *noun*
A condition where the mass of tissues at the base of the anus becomes swollen as a result of dilated veins.

> *After enduring a thirty-hour labor and a severe case of post-partum HEMORRHOIDS, Meg doubted she'd ever have another child.*

herbicide *(URB-ih-syde), noun*
A chemical that kills plants. *Herbicide* refers especially to that which eradicates weeds.

> *Although originally described as a comparatively harmless HERBICIDE, Agent Orange was (as thousands of soldiers learned much later) anything but.*

Herculean *(hur-kyuh-LEE-un), adjective*
Strong and powerful; reminiscent of the god *Hercules* in vitality. In addition, herculean can mean daunting or formidable—so difficult as to require the strength of *Hercules*.

> *Robert made a HERCULEAN effort to complete the project before midnight.*

hereditary *(huh-RED-ih-tare-ee), adjective*
Passed through the genes from parents to their children.

> *Although the doctors of his time believed him to be suffering from a host of exotic contagious illnesses, experts now believe that George III's madness was caused by HEREDITARY factors.*

heresy *(HARE-uh-see), noun*
An instance of espousing religious beliefs contrary to a church doctrine.

> *After having been suppressed centuries ago as HERESY, the newly discovered Gospel of Thomas has given scholars and lay readers valuable insights on the teachings of Jesus.*

heretic *(HARE-uh-tic), noun*
A person who professes belief in a dogma or system of belief (especially a religion), but differs with a tenet of that system. *Heretic* is often used more loosely to describe a member of group or organization who airs opinions that conflict with established principles or routines.

> *His stand against the Agency's involvement in Guatemala led someto brand Clint a HERETIC.*

hermaphrodite *(hur-MAFF-ruh-dite), noun*
One who possesses both male and female reproductive organs.
> *Sheldon brought back miniature statues of the island's mythic hero, a HERMAPHRODITE warrior.*

heterodox *(HETT-uh-ruh-docks), adjective*
Holding unorthodox opinions, especially opinions concerned with religion.
> *I believe George will grow out of his HETERODOX beliefs as he gets older.*

heterogeneous *(het-er-uh-JEEN-ee-us), adjective*
Different. *Heterogeneous* means consisting of utterly dissimilar parts or styles.
> *Marie invited a HETEROGENEOUS group: poets, potters, mechanics, bureaucrats, and who knows who else.*

hiatus *(hie-AY-tuss), noun*
An interruption or break. A *hiatus* is an intermission or break in continuity.
> *After a long HIATUS from the stage, Peter auditioned for a role in A Midsummer Night's Dream.*

hibachi *(hih-BOCH-ee), noun*
A small, table-top charcoal grill.
> *The manager of the apartment complex would not allow her tenants to keep full-sized gas or charcoal grills on the balconies, but she did make occasional allowances for HIBACHIS.*

hidebound *(HIDE-bound), adjective*
Narrow and rigid in one's beliefs or opinions . . . a somewhat nicer way to call someone stubborn.
> *I wouldn't mind Mary's hidebound beliefs, if she just didn't share them so freely!*

hierarchy *(HIE-uh-rar-kee), noun*
A system (of people, concepts, groups, etc.) in which there is a ranking of entities one above another. A *hierarchy* often refers to a formal chain of command.
> *The famous psychologist Abraham Maslow has established a HIERARCHY of human needs.*

highbrow *(HIE-brow), adjective*
Intelligent and cultured; also, one who is pretentious or snobby about intelligence and culture.
> *Al liked going to gallery shows to see the work of new artists, but he found the HIGHBROW analysis of some of his fellow patrons almost unbearable.*

highfalutin *(hi-fuh-LOO-tin), adjective*
Pompous; pretentious; overblown and extravagant.

Al said he'd rather have root canal work than attend another one of Gina's HIGHFALUTIN dinner parties and suffer in humiliation for not using the proper utensils for each course.

hinterlands *(HIN-tur-lands), noun*
An area far away from the coastline; also, an area far removed from a city.

The blizzard dumped nearly three feet of snow on my relatives in the HINTERLANDS, while those of us in town had to deal with icy rain and flooding.

hippodrome *(HIP-uh-drome), noun*
Arena for events such as circuses and horse shows.

Once a year Dad would take us down to the HIPPODROME in Springville for the 4-H Club's exposition.

hirsute *(HUR-soot), adjective*
Hairy.

"Here you are, my HIRSUTE friend," Dr. Fredericks called out, "a nice juicy bone from the butcher."

histrionic *(hiss-tree-AHN-ick), adjective*
Describes the on-stage work of actors and actresses, but, more broadly, *histrionic* describes people who are given to acting theatrical, affected, and self-consciously emotional when NOT on a stage.

Melinda's HISTRIONIC behavior at the dinner party embarrassed everyone.

hoarfrost *(HORE-frost), noun*
White, frozen dew that coats surfaces on winter mornings.

A layer of HOARFROST had covered the drab garden in silver, and the children squealed that the frost fairies had come.

hoary *(HOHR-ee), adjective*
Gray or white with age. Also, describes someone or something that is old and venerable.

Those HOARY urban myths about madmen lurking along lovers lanes no longer have the power to scare teenagers.

hobgoblin *(HOB-gob-lin), noun*
A goblin purported to engage in mischievous behavior.

Ever since I read her those fairy stories the other night, my daughter has tried to convince me that a HOBGOBLIN is responsible for every piece of mischief she gets into.

holistic *(ho-LISS-tik), adjective*
Emphasizing wholeness and/or the cooperation of the constituent members of a thing. *Holistic* is often used to describe medical or healing practices that emphasize an organism's totality, rather than focusing exclusively on one symptom or illness.

> *Fenwick takes a HOLISTIC approach to problem-solving that has drawn much positive attention.*

hologram *(HOLL-uh-gram), noun*
A three-dimensional image created electronically and without a lens.

> *The HOLOGRAM was such a convincing illusion that the dog actually barked at the image of its owner, apparently expecting to be fed.*

homage *(HOM-ij), noun*
Display of special respect or honor. To pay *homage* to someone is to act in a way that shows high reverence or alleigance.

> *The family made the long auto trip primarily to pay HOMAGE to their dying uncle.*

homeopathy *(ho-mee-OP-uh-thee), noun*
A means of treating a disease by administering small doses of medicine that in large doses, would bring about effects similar to the disease being treated.

> *HOMEOPATHY relies on the body's ability to develop immune responses in warding off disease.*

homiletics *(hom-uh-LET-iks), noun*
The art of preaching.

> *Rather than risk being swayed by the HOMILETICS of its proponents and opponents, Grandpa made it a point to read the text of every ballot initiative in full before deciding how he would vote on it.*

homily *(HOM-uh-lee), noun*
A religious talk or speech, usually given to a congregation; a talk that expounds on religious themes.

> *Father Graham's HOMILY on the power of faith inspired Warren to go home and try to work through his problems with his wife.*

hominid *(HOM-ih-nid), noun*
A member of the animal family to which humans belong. *Hominids* are humans and their ancestors.

> *The first ten minutes of the film depict the first use of tools by a group of ancient African HOMINIDS.*

homogeneous *(ho-mo-JEE-nee-uss), adjective*
The same throughout; made up of like parts; not heterogeneous.
> *The island supported a small HOMOGENEOUS population of aboriginal tribes.*

homonym *(HOM-uh-nim), noun*
A word that sounds the same as another word. "To" and "two" are *homonyms.*
> *I think in this sentence you have confused the word "real" with its HOMONYM "reel."*

honorific *(on-uh-RIFF-ick), adjective*
Describes an official or unofficial title or honor given to someone in order to show him or her respect.
> *After he finally managed to land a marlin, we gave my father the HONORIFIC, "the old man," a reference to Ernest Hemingway's The Old Man and the Sea.*

hookah *(HOOK-uh),*
A large multistemmed smoking apparatus that cools smoke by passing it through water.
> *Terry brought back many artifacts from her trip to India, including incense, silk saris, and even an antique HOOKAH.*

horde *(hord), noun*
A large crowd; a swarm of people.
> *Outside the department store, HORDES of angry shoppers, having been told that the doors would swing open at eight o'clock sharp, began to press against the huge window.*

hormonal *(HOR-moan-uhl), adjective*
A hormone is a substance released by the body to affect physiological activity. Thus, *hormonal* describes someone who acts as though he or she is being affected by hormones.
> *The HORMONAL shouts of teenagers and preteens annoyed me so much that I left the concert before the encore.*

horrific *(hor-RIFF-ik), adjective*
Horrifying; scary; terrifying.
> *Mr. Benton insisted on reading the newspaper's account of the HORRIFIC train wreck out loud during lunch.*

hosanna *(ho-ZAN-uh), noun*
From the Hebrew for "save us"; now an expression of praise, exaltation, and adoration typically heard in religious ceremonies; also, an instance of excessive praise.
> *Mel's agent warned him not to take too seriously the HOSANNAS that came his way after he won the acting award.*

hotspur *(HOT-spur), noun*

A quick-tempered, impulsive person. *Hotspur* is the name of a fiery character in Shakespeare's play Henry IV, Part One.

> *Ed was a real HOTSPUR around the office; he was likely to dominate a meeting with rash decrees and sudden denudations of plans he did not like.*

house organ *(HOUS-or-gun), noun*

A magazine or newsletter published by an organization for distribution within the organization.

> *I read about Joanne's promotion to sales manager in the last issue of On the Line, our HOUSE ORGAN.*

hovel *(HUV-ul), noun*

A modest, humble home or hut; a rude or dirty dwelling-place.

> *In the storm scenes of King Lear, Edward is disguised as Poor Tom, a lunatic who has sought shelter in a HOVEL on the barren heath.*

hubbub *(HUB-ub), noun*

A commotion; an outburst.

> *The HUBBUB outside our window came as a surprise; the parade was not due for an hour, yet the streets were already thronged with people.*

hubris *(HYOO-briss), noun*

Excessive pride. *Hubris* can refer to the "fatal flaw" of ancient Greek drama, or (more generally) to any disproportionate pride or self-love.

> *Colin may have begun as a pleasant and unassuming clerk, but by the time he took over the company in 1987 he showed signs of the HUBRIS that would accompany his downfall.*

hybrid *(HIE-brid), adjective*

The result of a mixture or combination of two dissimilar things (as in two breeds of animals, or two types of flowers).

> *Raymond spent his free time in the greenhouse perfecting his beautiful HYBRID orchids.*

hydraulic *(hie-DROLL-ik), adjective*

Related to the study of water, its properties, and distribution; powered by water.

> *Senator Graham argued that harnessing the river could provide HYDRAULIC power to three counties.*

hyperbole *(hie-PUR-buh-lee), noun*

Extravagant overstatement. To exaggerate something for the purpose of effect is to use *hyperbole*.

> *I think you can safely regard his promise to eat his hat if proven wrong as HYPERBOLE.*

hyperopia *(hi-pe-ROH-pee-uh), noun*
Farsightedness. Those who see distant things more clearly than those that are near experience *hyperopia*.

> *Although Fran's HYPEROPIA could have been corrected easily, she insisted on reading without glasses or contact lenses.*

hypertension *(hi-pur-TEN-shun), noun*
High blood pressure; the condition that occurs as a result of high blood pressure.

> *Some over-the-counter cough, cold, and allergy medicines tend to cause elevated blood pressure, and include with a warning that they may be hazardous to those suffering from HYPERTENSION.*

hyperthermia *(hie-pur-THUR-mee-uh), noun*
Extreme increase of body heat. *Hyperthermia* derives from the Greek roots "hyper" and "thermia," meaning "above" and "heat," respectively. (Compare with hypothermia.)

> *The reading is 108 degrees; we are dealing not with a simple fever, but with severe HYPERTHERMIA.*

hypocrite *(HIP-uh-krit), noun*
A person pretending to be something he or she is not, or pretending, for the sake of appearance, to have high moral beliefs; a person who does not act according to espoused beliefs.

> *In Marilyn's view, a marriage counselor who advised others to live up to the ideal of fidelity but who cheated on his own wife was the worst kind of HYPOCRITE.*

hypodermic *(hi-puh-DUR-mik), noun*
Related to parts under the skin; made expressly for the purpose of introducing medications via injection.

> *For Greg the mere sight of a HYPODERMIC needle was enough to produce a panic attack.*

hypothermia *(hie-po-THER-mee-uh), noun*
Extreme loss of body heat. *Hypothermia* derives from the Greek roots "hypo" and "thermia," meaning "below" and "heat," respectively. (Compare with hyperthermia.)

> *After seven hours in the freezing water, the victims had already succumbed to the effects of HYPOTHERMIA.*

hypothesis *(hie-POTH-uh-suss), noun*
An educated guess; a proposition; an untested theory put forth to explain something.

> *Our task was to test the instructor's HYPOTHESIS that constant exposure to high-pitched sounds impedes the growth of plants.*

doctrinaire

abstemious

levity hubris panacea

veracity cerebellum

labyrinth

criterion

nonagenarian

meticulous zither

I

verbiage quondam

colloquial

wok palpable paginatio

incipient salutary

evity redact fervent

beleaguered yawnful

elixir beneficent

vamoose pragmatism

i.e. (*eye ee*), *abbreviation, adverb*
An abbreviation for the Latin expression *id est,* meaning "that is."

> *Please make sure your child comes to school on the first day with all the necessary supplies, I.E., pencils, erasers, and notebooks.*

ibid, (*ih-bid*), *abbreviation*
abbreviation for "ibidem," literally "in the place mentioned before." (The word is typically used in bibliographies and other reference materials to indicate that a quote from a previously referenced source is being repeated.)

> *Mark's overreliance on a single source was evident in the paper's bibliography, which consisted of one reference to Mill's On Liberty and seventy-six notations reading "IBID."*

iconoclast (*eye-KON-uh-klast*), *noun*
A person who supports the destruction of holy images, or, more broadly, someone who challenges the status quo.

> *The first-year student's repeated verbal attacks on the art department, the president of the university, and the capitalist structure of society earned him a reputation as an ICONOCLAST.*

idle (*EYE-dul*), *adjective*
Not put to use; inactive. Also: lacking in substance. (See, for comparison, the entry for *idol.*)

> *When the phone service went down, our customer service operators had to sit IDLE at their stations, which drove Mr. Brown to distraction.*

ideogram (*ID-ee-o-gram*), *noun*
A symbol representing an idea rather than a word.

> *For foreigners, the most difficult part of learning to write in Chinese is generally mastering its many IDEOGRAMS.*

idiosyncrasy (*ih-dee-oh-SINK-ruh-see*), *noun*
A behavioral quirk or eccentricity.

> *One of my coworkers likes to engage in a brief round of calisthenics at the top of every hour, a harmless-enough IDIOSYNCRASY.*

idol (*EYE-dul*), *noun*
A worshiped image; a figure of a god. Also, any personage who is the object of devotion. (See, for comparison, the entry for *idle.*)

> *That flamenco dancer she went to see last week is my sister Cassandra's latest IDOL.*

idolatry *(eye-DOLL-uh-tree), noun*
The worship of a physical object as though it were a god or idol; to display an unusual and worshipful attachment to an object.

> *Buddy's IDOLATRY of his shiny new Corvette led a couple of his friends to remark that he would take it to bed with him if he could.*

idyllic *(eye-DILL-ick), adjective*
Pleasing; peaceful; ideal.

> *Our IDYLLIC honeymoon in the tropics was interrupted by a tropical hurricane.*

ignoble *(ig-NO-bull), adjective*
Dishonorable in nature. In contrast with *ignominious* (see below), *ignoble* carries the sense of baseness or lowness.

> *Peter's IGNOBLE aims were well known to all in the room.*

ignominious *(ig-no-MIN-ee-uss), adjective*
Shameful or disgraceful. *Ignominious* is generally used to describe public humiliation or failure.

> *Tyrone's IGNOMINIOUS defeat in court persuaded him to settle his other lawsuits against the company.*

ignominy *(ig-NOM-uh-knee), noun*
Public contempt or disgrace.

> *After he accidentally burned down the writer's home, Wally was treated with IGNOMINY by the town.*

ilk *(ilk), noun*
Family, type, or category.

> *I have no use for such vapid writers as Crennenfield, or anyone of his ILK.*

illicit *(ih-LISS-it), adjective*
Illegal or morally unjustifiable. *Illicit* refers to something not sanctioned by custom or law.

> *We all know now that the money was acquired through ILLICIT means, don't we?*

illusory *(ih-LOO-suh-ree), adjective*
An illusion is something that appears real but is not. Thus, something *illusory* seems genuine but is probably fake or deceptive.

> *After she moved to the beach, Lorna expected to feel joy but instead found that joy ILLUSORY.*

I

imam *(ih-MAHM), noun*
The governing priest at a mosque.

> *I was wary of attending the mosque, but I quickly found the IMAM welcoming and pleasant.*

imbecility *(im-buh-SILL-ih-tee), noun*
Foolishness; simplemindedness.

> *Although he lamented the IMBECILITY of mainstream television, Arnie was not above an occasional viewing of American Gladiators or Geraldo.*

imbibe *(im-BIBE), verb*
To drink. *Imbibe* is generally used to describe the drinking of alcoholic beverages, though it can also carry the meaning "to take in (an idea)."

> *Donald once had a drinking problem, but now he no longer IMBIBES.*

imbroglio *(im-BROA-lee-o), noun*
An entanglement or complicated misunderstanding. *Imbroglio* refers to a delicate situation from which it is difficult to extricate oneself.

> *The recent IMBROGLIO over conflict-of-interest violations has not improved the Mayor's standing with voters.*

imbue *(im-BYOO), verb*
To saturate or flow throughout by absorption. *Imbue* is often used metaphorically to describe the transmission of an idea, feeling, or emotion.

> *Bert's philosophy was IMBUED with the ideas of John Stuart Mill.*

immaculate *(im-MAK-yoo-lut), adjective*
Spotless; utterly free from fault, blemish, or stain. Something that is *immaculate* is impeccably clean.

> *After the boys had finished the cleanup job, the garage looked IMMACULATE.*

immeasurable *(ih-MEZH-er-uh-bull), adjective*
Describes a quantity that cannot be measured because it seems to be limitless.

> *I was gladdened by the IMMEASURABLE love my daughter clearly felt for her fiancé.*

immerse *(im-MURCE), verb*
To plunge into or surround with liquid.

> *Radios, electric shavers, and other electrical appliances can deliver lethal electric shocks if IMMERSED in water while plugged in.*

imminent *(IM-uh-nunt), adjective*
Likely to happen at any time; impending.
> *With his plane's departure IMMINENT, Greg gave his little girl a hug for the last time, kissed her on the forehead, and headed toward the gate.*

immolate *(IM-uh-late), verb*
To kill as if as a sacrifice, especially by fire. *Immolate* derives from a Latin word that pertained to sacrificial meals.
> *The monk's dramatic act of self-IMMOLATION made headlines around the world.*

immure *(i-MYOOR), verb*
To imprison or enclose behind walls; to shut in or confine.
> *My compound fracture left me IMMURED in the hospital for weeks.*

immutable *(ih-MYOO-tih-bull), adjective*
Describes something that cannot be changed or something that is changeless.
> *Mountains seem so IMMUTABLE that it amazes me to realize they actually do shift and change over the course of millions of years.*

impale *(im-PALE), verb*
To pierce with a sharp object; to pin or hold down.
> *Carol, with her flair for the dramatic, urged her husband to fix the loose pickets on the fence before one of the neighborhood children was IMPALED.*

impalpable *(im-PAL-puh-bull), adjective*
Impossible to perceive through use of the sense of touch. *Impalpable* also refers to anything extremely difficult to perceive or interpret.
> *The prosecution has tried to connect my client with the murderer, but all the connections they have put forward have been IMPALPABLE ones.*

imparity *(im-PARE-uh-tee), noun*
Inequality; disparity. Things that are unequal in scope or extent possess *imparity*.
> *The treaty will rectify the serious IMPARITY that now exists in weapons systems.*

impasse *(IM-pass), noun*
A situation that seems to offer no solution or escape. To reach an *impasse* is to come to a point of stalemate. Literally, an impasse is a dead-end street or passage.
> *Torn realized that his relationship with Betty had come to an IMPASSE; divorce was now on her mind, and he knew it.*

impeccable *(im-PEK-uh-buhl), adjective*
Flawless; faultless.
> *James Bond wore IMPECCABLE evening dress, marred only but the bulge where his gun was concealed.*

impecunious *(im-pih-KYOO-nee-uss), adjective*
Lacking in money; having little or nothing in the way of funds.
> *When Greg and Cheryl first met, their IMPECUNIOUS circumstances led them to take a lot of long walks instead of going out to dinner or dancing.*

impede *(im-PEED), verb*
To obstruct progress; to block.
> *The fire regulations are quite clear on the question of storage in this hallway; nothing is allowed to IMPEDE access to the main exit.*

imperative *(im-PAIR-uh-tiv), adjective and noun*
Essential, obligatory, or mandatory. As a noun, an *imperative* is a command or an essential objective. Imperative also has a grammatical sense referring to verbs that command or exhort. (For instance, in the sentence "Sit, Rex!" the word sit is in the *imperative*.)
> *It is IMPERATIVE that the soldiers evacuate as soon as possible.*

imperceptible *(im-pur-SEP-tuh-bull), adjective*
So subtle as to be unnoticeable. *Imperceptible* refers to that which is so gradual or unnoticeable it is virtually impossible to perceive.
> *The distinctions you draw in this paragraph are IMPERCEPTIBLE to the average reader.*

imperiled *(im-PARE-uld), adjective*
Endangered.
> *Fred knew that if he stumbled on the final history test of the year, the B-plus average he had worked toward all semester long would be IMPERILED.*

imperious *(im-PEER-ee-us), adjective*
Haughty. Also: urgent. *Imperious* is usually meant to convey a sense of dictatorial arrogance.
> *Mrs. Banks rushed around the kitchen, issuing a series of IMPERIOUS commands to the cook.*

impertinent *(im-PURR-tih-nent), adjective*
Rude; brash. Something that is improper or beyond established bounds is *impertinent*.
> *What an IMPERTINENT thing to say!*

imperturbable *(im-per-TUHR-buh-bull), adjective*
Describes someone or something incapable of being agitated or disturbed.
> *During the air turbulence, I felt calmer due to my father's IMPERTURBABLE demeanor.*

impervious *(im-PURR-vee-us), adjective*
Impenetrable. Also: impossible to alter or affect. *Impervious* usually means incapable of being changed from a given course.
> *We tried to dissuade Millicent from sending the children to Montana, but she was IMPERVIOUS.*

impetuous *(im-PET-you-us), adjective*
Impulsive. That which is driven by sudden force or emotion is *impetuous*.
> *Dirk's IMPETUOUS remark may well cost him his job.*

impetus *(IHM-puh-tuss), noun*
The force that moves something or someone to action.
> *Losing his job became the IMPETUS for John to focus full-time on his writing career.*

implacable *(ihm-PLACK-uh-bull), adjective*
Describes someone who cannot be calmed or pacified. "Implacable" can also serve as a synonym for "stubborn."
> *No matter what I did to try to please my mother, she remained grim and IMPLACABLE.*

implicit *(im-PLISS-it), adjective*
Implied or understood, though not expressed directly. An *implicit* understanding is one that two parties abide by but do not set out in specific language.
> *There was an IMPLICIT agreement between the two not to bring up the subject of Michael's first wife.*

implore *(im-PLORE), verb*
To beseech or beg for fervently. To *implore* is to plead urgently.
> *She IMPLORED him to attend the party.*

impolitic *(im-PAWL-i-tick), adjective*
Not expedient; injudicious.
> *After a few drinks, Uncle Roland has an unfortunate habit of making IMPOLITIC remarks about my father's failed business ventures.*

importunate *(im-PORE-chuh-nit), adjective*
Demanding or impatient in issuing repeated requests. An *importunate* person makes many annoying entreaties.
> *Two-year-olds, though lovable, can be IMPORTUNATE; Wesley seemed unprepared for this.*

importune (im-por-TOON), verb

To request repeatedly so as to be a bother.

> *After months of IMPORTUNING his employer for a promotion that did not yet exist, Hank was asked to leave the company.*

imposition (im-puh-ZISH-un), noun

An instance of inconvenience or the laying on of obligation; the act of causing another to take on a burden.

> *I knew full well that our staying with Aunt Sadie for six months was an IMPOSITION, but while the house was being built we really had no other choice.*

imprecation (im-prih-KAY-shun), noun

An oath or curse. The verb form is "imprecate."

> *When the wide receiver fumbled the ball, the crowd attacked him with numerous colorful IMPRECATIONS.*

impregnable (im-PREG-nuh-bull), adjective

Stubbornly resistant. Something that is *impregnable* is unshakeable and/or unconquerable.

> *The town proved IMPREGNABLE, despite the army's repeated assaults.*

impresario (im-pruh-SAHR-ee-o), noun

A person who organizes or sponsors entertainment or cultural events (such as concerts and plays).

> *Quentin's career as an IMPRESARIO came to an abrupt halt when he lost all his investors' money on a musical version of Marx's Das Kapital.*

impressionism (im-PRESH-un-iz-im), noun

An art movement of the late nineteenth century dedicated to reproducing the effect of light on objects, typically by means of short brush strokes.

> *The painter and sculptor Edgar Degas was one of the foremost practitioners of IMPRESSIONISM.*

imprimatur (im-pruh-MAH-ter), noun

Approval granted, usually by the Roman Catholic Church, to publish a book.

> *After directing several revisions of the controversial book's text, the Church finally gave its IMPRIMATUR.*

impromptu (im-PRAHMP-too), adjective

Spontaneous; not planned or rehearsed; conceived on the spur of the moment.

> *Sonya's IMPROMPTU New Year's Eve dinner party ended up being more fun than any of the formal affairs our group of friends had attended for New Years past.*

impropriety *(im-pruh-PRY-ih-tee), noun*
Incorrectness. An *impropriety* is a misdeed or crossing of established social mores.
> *Beverly's minor IMPROPRIETY at the dinner table was overlooked; the conversation turned quickly to other topics.*

improvident *(ihm-PRAHV-ih-dent), adjective*
Describes someone who does not plan well for the future or one who acts without thinking.
> *It was cute when he was younger, but now Mike's IMPROVIDENT behavior just makes him look like a total loser.*

impugn *(im-PYOON), verb*
To brand as false in argument or discourse. *Impugn* usually implies an open attack or challenge upon another's honesty or motives.
> *Are you attempting to IMPUGN my husband's version of the attack?*

impunity *(im-PYOO-nih-tee), noun*
Freedom from punishment or penalty. *Impunity* is sometimes confused with impugn (above), especially in its spelling.
> *We cannot let such an act of naked aggression stand with IMPUNITY.*

inadvertent *(in-ud-VERT-unt), adjective*
Unintentional; not on purpose; accidentally.
> *I INADVERTENTLY called attention to Glenda's tardiness by asking the boss what time it was just as she walked in the door.*

inalienable *(in-AY-lee-un-a-buhl), adjective*
Incapable of being taken away.
> *Although I have always believed freedom of speech to be the INALIENABLE right of every American, I must admit that the diatribes of those who preach hate and violence against members of my race are awfully tough to stomach.*

inane *(in-ANE), adjective*
Pointless or lacking in substance. Something that is *inane* is vacuous.
> *Among other INANE suggestions, Jeff proposed painting the lunchroom in a polka-dot pattern.*

inanimate *(in-AN-ih-mutt), adjective*
Reminiscent of an object that is not alive or animated; lacking in movement.
> *Ben gazed at the wax figure as if he expected the INANIMATE figure to come to life.*

I

inauguration *(in-og-yuh-RAY-shun), noun*

The act of ushering into office with a formal ceremony; an instance of marking or acknowledging the beginning of something in a ceremonious fashion.

> *President Clinton's INAUGURATION featured a poem composed for the occasion by Maya Angelou and read by the poet.*

inauspicious *(in-oss-PISH-uss), adjective*

Accompanied by or predictive of ill luck; not favorable in portent.

> *Who could have predicted that from such INAUSPICIOUS beginnings Grant would rise to command great armies and, eventually, lead his nation?*

incandescent *(in-kan-DESS-unt), adjective*

Very bright and hot; brilliant, as light or fire. Also: masterly or dynamic, especially with regard to individual creativity.

> *An INCANDESCENT lamp is one that emits light as a result of the glowing of a heated material, such as a tungsten filament.*

incantation *(in-kan-TAY-shun), noun*

The repeated chanting of words or phrases believed to have magical powers.

> *I believe Tom's dismissal of the rosary as a primitive set of INCANTATIONS shows how small a role religious faith plays in his life.*

incapacitate *(in-kuh-PASS-ih-tate), verb*

To disable; to deprive of strength, ability, or skill.

> *Uncle Jimmy missed an entire month of work due to a bout of pneumonia that left him completely INCAPACITATED.*

incarcerate *(in-KAHR-suh-rate), verb*

To jail or imprison.

> *I never thought I'd be INCARCERATED just for failing to pay over one hundred parking tickets!*

incarnate *(in-KAR-nut), adjective*

Embodied. Something that takes the bodily or physical form (especially human form) of "X" is said to be "X *incarnate.*"

> *Sarah is not simply quiet; she is tranquility INCARNATE.*

incendiary *(in-SEN-dee-air-ee), adjective*

Flammable. Also, reminiscent of or pertaining to speech or action that is meant to inflame or arouse; deliberately provocative.

> *Adam's INCENDIARY remarks about my mother's parentage resulted in a bloody nose for him and a night in jail for me.*

inception *(in-SEP-shun), noun*

Beginning. *Inception* refers to the generation of an idea or organism, from its initial developmental stages onward.

> *The car was riddled with design flaws, most dating back to the auto's INCEPTION in 1972.*

incessant *(in-SESS-unt), adjective*

Continuous. *Incessant* derives from the Latin roots for "without end."

> *His INCESSANT questions can become quite annoying.*

inchoate *(in-KO-ate), adjective*

Incomplete. *Inchoate* refers to something still in early development.

> *The concept, which Glenn readily admitted was INCHOATE, showed promise despite its flaws.*

incipient *(in-SIP-ee-unt), adjective*

Early in development; at a beginning stage.

> *Attempting to stave off an INCIPIENT flu, Marsha consumed glass after glass of orange juice.*

incisive *(in-SYE-siv), adjective*

Penetrating or sharp in analysis, observation, etc. *Incisive* derives from the Latin root for "cutting."

> *An INCISIVE Times review of the play notes that the dialogue is similar in many places to passages from the works of Proust.*

inclement *(in-CLEM-unt), adjective*

Harsh. *Inclement* is often used to refer to the condition of the weather.

> *The unexpected INCLEMENT weather ruined our vacation.*

incognito *(in-cog-NEE-to), adjective*

Hidden or unknown. To intentionally change appearance in such a way as to make one's real identity unknown is to go *incognito*.

> *The novelist wore sunglasses in hopes of remaining INCOGNITO at restaurants, but he was still pesteread by autograph hounds.*

incoherent *(in-koh-HEER-unt), adjective*

Not capable of being understood due to a lack of logical meaning.

> *After he's had one too many, I can't help laughing at Bob's INCOHERENT speech.*

incongruous *(in-CON-groo-uss), adjective*
Not consistent-incompatible.

> *Much of the troupe's humor relies on an absurd grouping of INCONGRUOUS elements, a technique best exemplified by the dapper-looking, by-the-numbers bureaucrat who heads up the Ministry of Silly Walks.*

incontestable *(in-kuhn-TES-tuh-bull), adjective*
Cannot be argued with because it is unquestionable.

> *The fact that Lloyd thinks his talent for birdcalls will be found attractive by women is INCONTESTABLE proof that he will remain a lifelong bachelor.*

incontrovertible *(in-kahn-truh-VER-tuh-bull), adjective*
Not open to question; indisputable.

> *The prosecution won the case after introducing INCONTROVERTIBLE evidence.*

incorporeal *(in-core-PORE-ee-al), adjective*
Lacking form. *Incorporeal* derives from the Latin roots meaning "without the body."

> *The moanings and low rumblings in the old house suggested INCORPOREAL visitors to Kate.*

incorrigible *(in-KORE-ij-uh-bul), adjective*
(Apparently) incapable of being reformed. *Incorrigible* is often used in a lighthearted, ironic sense.

> *Young Pete was an INCORRIGIBLE boy, forever getting into scrapes and causing mischief.*

incredible *(in-KRED-ih-bull), adjective*
Unbelievable; so remarkable as to be hard or impossible to accept. (See, for comparison, the entry for *incredulous*.)

> *The charges I am making against Mr. White may seem INCREDIBLE, but the evidence will show that they are absolutely true.*

incredulous *(in-KRED-you-luss), adjective*
Skeptical; refusing or reluctant to believe. (See, for comparison, the entry for *incredible*.)

> *Dan was absolutely INCREDULOUS when I told him I was the sole winner of the $10 million lottery.*

increment *(IN-kruh-munt), noun*
One in a series of additions; an increase in size or number.

> *The letter informed Nina that she would receive checks from the estate in $50,000 INCREMENTS over the course of twenty years.*

inculcate *(IN-kul-kate), verb*

To instill (learning) by means of repetition or instruction. To *inculcate* is to impress an idea upon someone with urging or earnest example.

> *Rachel tried to INCULCATE the virtue of thrift in her daughter.*

inculpate *(in-KUL-pate), verb*

To incriminate. To blame for a wrongdoing is to *inculpate*.

> *Myra's frequent visits to the scene of the crime, in Sarah's view, INCULPATED her as the guilty party.*

incumbent *(in-KUHM-bent), adjective or noun*

As a noun, "incumbent" means the holder of an office. As an adjective, the word suggests responsibility, such as the responsibility with which an officeholder is entrusted.

> *I've got to stop procrastinating, Stewart thought. It's INCUMBENT upon me to finish this proposal by Friday!*

indefatigable *(in-di-FAT-ih-guh-bul), adjective*

Tireless. Someone who possesses unyielding stamina is *indefatigable*.

> *Betty, an INDEFATIGABLE runner, never seemed to slow her pace.*

indelible *(in-DELL-ih-bul), adjective*

Un-removable. An *indelible* mark is one that is not easily erased or cleansed away.

> *Carl leaves an INDELIBLE impression on those he meets.*

indemnify *(in-DEM-nih-fy), verb*

To protect from or provide compensation for damages. To *indemnify* is to shield against the loss, destruction, or damage of something.

> *This policy INDEMNIFIES my house against fire, flood, and burglary.*

indeterminate *(in-dee-TUHR-mih-nut), adjective*

Not having a specific length or extent.

> *The wait at the Department of Motor Vehicles was both INDETERMINATE and interminable.*

indict *(in-DITE), verb*

To charge formally with a crime or offense. (See, for comparison, the entry for *indite*.)

> *Rumors that Mr. Brown would soon be INDICTED for his part in the scandal swept the city.*

I

indigent (IN-dih-junt), *adjective*
Lacking the essentials of life; impoverished.

> *At the shelter, I came across many INDIGENT families who had fallen victim to the failing economy.*

indignant *(in-DIG-nunt), adjective*
Marked by indignation; offended by behavior perceived as unjust or immoral; angered.

> *Although I apologized for the better part of a week for showing up raving drunk at Simon's parent's house, he remained INDIGNANT.*

indiscreet *(in-dih-SKREET), adjective*
Lacking good judgment and prudence; apt to run one's mouth about things that others would like left private.

> *Don't get alcohol near Melanie. It makes her go from prudent to INDISCREET in less than sixty seconds!*

indiscriminate *(in-dih-SKRIM-uh-net), adjective*
Lacking clear judgment. Also describes someone or something haphazard and jumbled.

> *The INDISCRIMINATE placement of books made it almost impossible to do any successful browsing in the bookshop.*

indite *(in-DITE), verb*
To cause to come into being by means of artistic effort; to write or compose.

> *The dozens of letters that passed between the two contained a number of rather steamy poems INDITED under the influence of mutual passion.*

indoctrinate *(in-DOCK-truh-nate), verb*
To teach; to impart with the knowledge or views of a particular group, philosophy, or theory.

> *Max's earnest attempts to INDOCTRINATE me with the ideals of the Communist Party left me howling with laughter.*

indolent *(IN-duh-lnt), adjective*
Lazy, as a way of life. Someone who is *indolent* is inactive and unlikely to exert himself.

> *Peter, an INDOLENT young man, spent his young days gazing out the window daydreaming.*

indomitable *(in-DOM-ih-tuh-bull), adjective*
Describes someone who acts in the face of fear, someone with unconquerable will.

> *Nadia's courage was INDOMITABLE, even though she faced much larger opponents.*

indubitable *(in-DOO-bih-tuh-bull), adjective*
Absolutely unquestionable and completely beyond doubt.
> *Warren's been right so many times that his judgment is considered INDUBITABLE.*

induct *(in-DUCT), verb*
To install as a member with formal ceremony; to install in office.
> *Many baseball fans feel it's a shame that Pete Rose will probably never be INDUCTED into the Baseball Hall of Fame.*

inebriated *(in-EE-bree-ate-ud), adjective*
Intoxicated. Someone who is *inebriated* is drunk.
> *The two men at the bar became steadily more INEBRIATED as the night wore on.*

ineffable *(in-EFF-uh-bull), adjective*
Beyond the capacity of expression. Also: forbidden as a subject of conversation. Something that is *ineffable* is indescribable or unspeakable.
> *Carlton presented new acquaintances with a certain INEFFABLE charm that lingered long after one's first meeting with him.*

ineluctable *(in-ee-LUK-tuh-bull), adjective*
Unavoidable; impossible to overcome. Something that is inevitable is *ineluctable*.
> *Oedipus' fate, we must remember, is INELUCTABLE; no amount of struggling will free him from it.*

inept *(in-EPT), adjective*
Inappropriate. Someone who lacks judgment, discretion, or ability can be said to be *inept*.
> *Williams, an INEPT craftsman, soon found that his goods would never fetch top dollar.*

inequity *(in-ECK-wih-tee), noun*
A person who, or situation that, is unfair, biased, or demonstrates favoritism.
> *The INEQUITY of your proposal borders on being insulting.*

inert (in-URT),
Inactive; unmoving; extremely slow in moving or reacting.
> *We came home from the supermarket to find Dad lying INERT on the sofa and the lawn still not mowed.*

inertia *(in-UR-shuh), noun*
Sluggishness; the quality of being inert. In physics, *inertia* is the tendency of an object to resist change (acceleration or change in direction, for instance) unless acted on by an outside force.

It is not a lack of opportunity that has hampered you, Jackson, but simple INERTIA.

inexorable *(in-EK-sur-uh-bul), adjective*
Unyielding. Something that is stubborn or unwavering is *inexorable*.

"The INEXORABLE advance of our troops," the Union general said happily, "will complicate things for Mr. Davis."

inexplicable *(in-eks-PLIK-uh-bul), adjective*
Defying explanation or interpretation. That which is hard to communicate is *inexplicable*.

My opponent's failure to file income tax returns is INEXPLICABLE.

inextricable *(in-ick-STRICK-uh-bull), adjective*
Incapable of being disentangled. Also describes something that is hopelessly complex. The adverb form, which you may see, is *"inextricably."*

The INEXTRICABLE problem remained unsolved, even after the company's best minds spent three days attacking it.

infallible *(in-FAL-uh-bul), adjective*
Incapable of making a mistake. Something that is regarded as beyond error might be said to be *infallible*.

You have no need to worry about the security of this mission, gentlemen; the HAL 9000 computer is INFALLIBLE.

infer *(in-FUR), verb*
To gather by reasoning. To *infer* is not the same as to imply, which means "to leave the suggestion that."

I think we can INFER here that the author is using the character as a mouthpiece of sorts to air her own concerns.

infernal *(in-FER-nul), adjective*
Fiendish; devilish. *Infernal* means, literally, "of or pertaining to hell." It is often used as a mild expletive.

This INFERNAL copier keeps breaking down!

infidel *(IN-fih-del), noun*
A person who does not accede to a particular set of religious beliefs. An *infidel* is an unbeliever: the word is often used metaphorically to refer to those who are unpersuaded of the wisdom and/or righteousness of a position or principle.

> *Because he failed to express the proper enthusiasm for Riley's campaign proposal, Wilson was regarded as something of an INFIDEL.*

infidelity *(in-fi-DEL-ih-tee) noun*
The quality or act of having been untrue or inconsistent with an (often implied) standard. *Infidelity* is often used to describe extramarital affairs.

> *Although Gwen suspected her husband of INFIDELITY, she had not come across any tangible proof.*

infinitesimal *(in-fin-uh-TESS-ih-mull), adjective*
So small that it can't accurately be measured.

> *Which color lipstick to wear tonight is an INFINITESIMAL, not a major, issue, so let's get going already!*

infirmity *(in-FUR-mih-tee), noun*
A physical ailment. Sometimes the word is used to denote a mental weakness, such as being overly cautious.

> *Randall, get over yourself. An ingrown toenail is annoying. It's not an INFIRMITY. You cannot park in the handicapped spot!*

influenza *(in-floo-EN-zuh), noun*
A contagious respiratory virus characterized by inflammation of the mucous membrane, fever, prostration, aches, and pains.

> *David was still weak from his bout with INFLUENZA.*

infraction *(in-FRACK-shun), noun*
A violation or breach, as of rules.

> *One citizen stood up and demanded to ask questions of the city council, a direct INFRACTION of protocol.*

infrastructure *(IN-fruh-struk-chur), noun*
Foundation; underlying base. An *infrastructure* is the collection of essential primary components or a system, organization, or structure.

> *The architect guessed that the INFRASTRUCTURE had probably begun to erode at the turn of the century; the building was now beyond repair.*

infuse *(in-FYUZE), verb*

To fill; to penetrate as if by pouring or soaking.

> *The dynamic commissioner INFUSED a new sense of pride into the beleaguered department.*

ingénue *(AHN-zhuh-new), noun*

From the French meaning "naive," an *ingénue* is an actress who specializes in playing the part of an innocent or unworldly young woman. The word also refers to this type of role in a film or on stage.

> *Since she hit thirty, that INGÉNUE has disappeared from the screen.*

ingot *(ING-gut), noun*

A piece of cast metal, usually in the form of a bar.

> *Charlie's job at the refinery was to inspect the INGOTS coming off conveyor belt number seven.*

ingrate *(IN-grate), noun*

An ungrateful person. A person who does not show the proper respect or gratitude toward someone who has provided help might be called an *ingrate*.

> *He lived with us for six months, but that INGRATE Ralph hasn't even written in over two years.*

ingratiate *(in-GRAY-she-ate), verb*

To work very hard to gain someone's favor, most likely with an eye toward receiving something in return at a future date.

> *Paul tried hard to INGRATIATE himself with his fiancee's stern parents.*

inherent *(in-HARE-unt), adjective*

Intrinsic; necessary. An important or essential part of something can be said to be *inherent*.

> *Dwayne's INHERENT reluctance to entrust newcomers with tasks of any significance was a major problem for the company.*

inimical *(in-IM-ih-kul), adjective*

Harmful; injurious. Something that possesses a dangerous or hostile character can be said to be *inimical*.

> *I'm afraid this work environment is INIMICAL to creative thinking.*

iniquity *(ih-NIK-wih-tee), noun*

Injustice or immoral action. *Iniquity* derives from the Latin for "unfairness."

> *The many INIQUITIES suffered by American Indians at the hands of government authorities is only now being widely acknowledged.*

initiative *(ih-NISH-uh-tiv), noun*
Personal enterprise and responsibility.

> *If you were to show a little more INITIATIVE, you would not keep being passed over for a promotion.*

innate *(ih-NATE), adjective*
Possessed at birth. Something that is inborn or central to a person or thing can be said to be *innate*.

> *Sol's INNATE sense for what will make a good plan has served him well since he was a small boy.*

innocuous *(ih-NOK-yoo-us), adjective*
Harmless. Also: lacking conflict or drama. Something is *innocuous* if it shows minimal significance, interest, or prominence.

> *The editor rejected my first news story, which I found fascinating but he considered INNOCUOUS.*

innovate *(IN-uh-vate), verb*
To introduce something new or to make significant changes to something, such as an invention, that already exists. The familiar adjective form is "innovative."

> *The inventors spent their day, tinkering and INNOVATING, until they came up with the perfect mousetrap. The world quickly beat a path to their door.*

innuendo *(in-you-ENN-doe), noun*
A subtle intimation; an indirect insinuation.

> *Through hints and INNUENDO her opponent managed to plant seeds of doubt about Governor Williams's past.*

innumerable *(in-NOOM-ur-uh-bul),*
Too many to be numbered or counted (but often used simply to express the idea "very numerous").

> *Over the past three months, Michelle has put in INNUMERABLE hours of overtime on this project.*

inoculate *(ih-NOK-yoo-late), verb*
To facilitate the buildup of resistance to a disease by introducing a minuscule sample of its virus into the body. *Inoculate* derives from the Latin for "to graft onto."

> *Marie, normally frightened of injections, summoned up all her courage when it came time for the doctor to inoculate her against smallpox.*

inordinate *(in-OR-den-it), adjective*
Excessive; too much.

> *An INORDINATE number of students failed the last test, leading Professor Harris to believe he'd made it too difficult.*

inquiry *(IN-kwuh-ree), noun*
In general, an inquiry is a question, but the word suggests an investigation that seeks the answer to profound or perplexing questions.

> *The detective's INQUIRY netted significant evidence, which led to the crime's perpetrators.*

inroad *(IN-road), noun*
An opening or entry (said especially of a new idea, campaign, or undertaking). *Inroad* originally referred to a military maneuver during invasion.

> *The new brand of cookies was still unknown in the South, although it had made significant INROADS in the Midwest.*

inscrutable *(in-SKROO-tuh-bul), adjective*
Dense or difficult to fathom; resisting of scrutiny. Something that is hard to decipher could be called *inscrutable.*

> *Tom's INSCRUTABLE smile made many in the room uneasy.*

insensate *(in-SENS-ate), adjective*
Without human feeling, or lacking judgment and good sense.

> *Owen's INSENSATE behavior the morning after their tryst made Amy realize she'd made a mistake in asking him to stay the night.*

inseparable *(in-SEP-uh-ruh-bull), adjective*
Incapable of being separated or parted.

> *Jean and Michael have been INSEPARABLE since they met online.*

insidious *(in-SID-ee-uss), adjective*
Designed to entrap; happening or spreading harmfully but subtly; stealthily and seductively treacherous.

> *Mark's chess games were full of INSIDIOUS traps meant to lull his opponent into a sense of complacency.*

insinuate *(in-SIN-you-ate), verb*
To hint at darkly; to suggest (typically, with negative connotations).

> *I hope you don't mean to INSINUATE that my husband is seeing another woman.*

insipid *(in-SIP-d), adjective*

Lacking in vigor; dull. *Insipid* (usually applied to bland ideas, personalities, or works of art) derives from the Latin for "without taste."

> *In Frank's opinion, the novel's plot was INSIPID and left much to be desired.*

insolent *(IN-suh-lnt), adjective*

Rude and arrogant. That which is insulting or disrespectful (especially speech) could be considered *insolent*.

> *Her INSOLENT retorts to Joan's well-intentioned queries stunned the dinner party.*

insouciant *(in-SOO-see-unt), adjective*

Calm and carefree; indifferent.

> *Despite his dire surroundings, Herbert managed to remain INSOUCIANT and at ease.*

insubordinate *(in-suh-BOR-dn-it), adjective*

Failing to accept or obey proper authority. In the military, an enlisted man who insults an officer could be accused of an *insubordinate* act.

> *Frank, not eager to be branded INSUBORDINATE, did his best to carry out the colonel's strange orders.*

insular *(IN-suh-ler), adjective*

Like an island . . . detached, standing alone. Typically, *insular* is used negatively, to suggest that someone has narrow-minded or provincial attitudes about politics, religion, ideas, etc.

> *The candidate's INSULAR views on diplomacy caused him to lose the election.*

insuperable *(in-SOO-pur-uh-bul), adjective*

Impossible to overcome.

> *Faced with hostile rhetoric from members of his own party, mounting opposition in Congress, and a seemingly INSUPERABLE resistance to his policies on the part of the press, the president must sometimes have wondered why he ever selected this line of work.*

insurgence *(in-SUR-junce), noun*

Revolt or uprising. An *insurgence* is a revolt against the government or existing authority.

> *The INSURGENCE against the dictator's regime was welcomed enthusiastically by the country's farmers.*

I

insurrection *(in-sur-REK-shun), noun*
A rebellion against a government or ruling power.

> *Before the president could get the treaty through Congress, however, he would have to attend to an INSURRECTION of sorts that had arisen in the left flank of his own party.*

intangible *(in-TAN-juh-bul), adjective*
Incapable of being touched, felt, or calculated.

> *Friends berated me for breaking up with Matthew, but there was something INTANGIBLE missing from the relationship, something I couldn't do without.*

integral *(IN-tuh-grul), adjective*
Acting as a constituent and essential member of a whole. *Integral* also carries a number of technical and mathematical definitions not in common usage.

> *Jane played an INTEGRAL role in the production's success.*

integrated *(IN-tuh-gray-ted), adjective*
Describes the harmonious assemblage of various parts into a whole.

> *Even though both Mike and Carol had children from previous marriages, their new union quickly created an INTEGRATED family unit.*

intelligentsia *(in-tell-uh-JENT-see-uh), noun*
The intellectual class and its social, political, and cultural habits and ideas.

> *Daniel considers himself a member of the INTELLIGENTSIA. I just consider him a snob.*

intercede *(in-tur-SEED), verb*
To offer aid or action on another's behalf; to interrupt (a conflict or altercation) to help another.

> *Much to my amazement, my big brother, whose main goal in life had always seemed to be to torment me, INTERCEDED when the school bully tried to attack me.*

intercession *(in-ter-SESH-un), noun*
An instance of pleading in favor of another person or party. To intercede is to act or speak in someone's behalf; *intercession* is mediation in a conflict in behalf of another.

> *France's INTERCESSION is credited by many with brining the crisis to a peaceful conclusion.*

interim *(IN-ter-im), noun*
The meantime. An *interim* is the period of time between one event and another.

> *The INTERIM—which lasted over a month—was filled with work and planning in preparation for the second series of meetings.*

interlope *(IN-tur-lope), verb*
To intrude; to interfere, meddle, or infringe.

> *Eric resented his fraternity brothers' attempts to INTERLOPE on his romantic evening with Sheena.*

intermediary *(in-ter-MEE-dee-air-ee), noun or adjective*
As a noun, an intermediary is a go-between, a middleman. As an adjective, the word describes someone who is a middleman or go-between.

> *My brother acted as an INTERMEDIARY in the dispute between our mom and me.*

interminable *(in-TUHR-mih-nuh-bull), adjective*
Describes something unpleasant that is seemingly without end.

> *My wait in the doctor's waiting room seemed INTERMINABLE.*

intermittent *(in-tur-MIT-nt), adjective*
Characterized by a cycle of stopping and starting. An *intermittent* storm is one that comes and goes.

> *Frank was bothered by an INTERMITTENT pain in his ankle.*

interpolate *(in-TUHR-puh-late), verb*
To introduce something foreign between other parts, such as secretly adding one's own ideas into a text.

> *The speaker was interrupted by an audience member who felt the need to interpolate his views into the panel's discussion.*

intersperse *(in-tur-SPURSE), verb*
To scatter here and there; to distribute or place at intervals.

> *INTERSPERSED throughout the studio audience were "clappers" whose sole purpose was to motivate the rest of the crowd into laughing and applauding for the show*

interstellar *(in-tur-STEL-lur), adjective*
Occurring or situated between the stars.

> *Due to problems with the base's satellite transmitter, INTERSTELLAR communication with the space shuttle was extremely difficult.*

interstice *(in-TUR-stis), noun*
A space between objects; a crevice or crack.

> *Greg shimmied up the INTERSTICE between the two rocks.*

intractable *(in-TRACK-tuh-bull), adjective*
Unwilling to be led; stubborn.

> *Although Monty tried everything he could think of to help Elston overcome his habit of exploding at his coworkers, and proved quite INTRACTABLE and actually seemed to resent his efforts.*

I

intransigent *(in-TRAN-si-junt), adjective*
Uncompromising; determined to remain beyond appeal or negotiation. Someone unyielding to any change is *intransigent*.
> *The INTRANSIGENT union negotiator seemed fully prepared to see the talks collapse.*

intrepid *(in-TREP-id), adjective*
Brave. Those who are fearless and show great courage are *intrepid*.
> *The INTREPID climber made her way down the icy mountain alone.*

intrigue *(in-TREEG), adjective*
To arouse suspicion or curiosity; to engender a sense of mystery. As a noun: a plot.
> *Keith's plan INTRIGUED us, but we had a nagging suspicion it wouldn't work.*

intrinsic *(in-TRIN-zik), adjective*
In the essential nature of a thing. Something *intrinsic* is fundamental in character.
> *The INTRINSIC value of gold was one of the few common economic factors the nations could take advantage of.*

introspection *(in-tro-SPEK-shun), noun*
Self-examination; interior meditation. To think closely on one's feelings, thoughts, and inclinations is to spend time in *introspection*.
> *The weekend at the cabin provided Clive with an opportunity for some much-needed INTROSPECTION.*

inundate *(IN-un-date), verb*
To flood. To *inundate* is to engulf as in a torrent or flood.
> *The operator knew she would be INUNDATED with calls that day.*

inured *(in-YOORD), verb*
Accustomed to (hardship or trial).
> *After a few months, Melvin became INURED to the paper boy's habit of tossing the New York Times into the furthest reaches of the front lawn's tall hedges.*

invective *(in-VEK-tiv), noun*
Abusive language. *Invective* is denunciatory or overly harsh speech or writing.
> *Clark's stream of INVECTIVE near the end of the meeting was totally uncalled for.*

inveigh *(in-VAY), verb*
To protest strongly. *Inveigh* is usually followed by against.
> *The crowd INVEIGHED against the governor's decision to commute Davidson's sentence.*

inveigle *(in-VAY-gul), verb*

To tempt or persuade by using deception, artful talk, or flattery.

> *My daughter Sharon tried to INVEIGLE me into playing gin rummy by promising to clean up the kitchen for the next week, even though she know she'd be at summer camp.*

invert *(in-VURT), verb*

To reverse; to change to an opposite orientation or course.

> *After complaining of poor vision all morning, Kathy found out that her problem was an INVERTED left contact lens.*

inveterate *(in-VET-er-ut), adjective*

Deep-rooted. A persisting or long-established habit is an *inveterate* one.

> *Mike is an INVETERATE gambler; his marriage suffered greatly because of it.*

invidious *(in-VTD-ee-uss), adjective*

Likely to damage a reputation.

> *Brent's INVIDIOUS remarks to the president at the company picnic are probably the main reason he was passed over for promotion.*

inviolate *(in-VIE-uh-let), adjective*

Solid and strong, incapable of being violated or injured.

> *Even after five failed marriages, Jenny remained INVIOLATE in her belief that she would one day find true love.*

invocation *(in-vuh-KAY-shun), noun*

The process or act of invoking. An *invocation* is a call to a higher power (usually God) for help.

> *The priest offered a special INVOCATION at the beginning of the service.*

iota *(eye-O-tuh), noun*

A minute quantity; an extremely small amount.

> *The fact that the prisoner's reprieve omits his middle initial doesn't matter one IOTA, Warden Holloway.*

irascible *(ih-RASS-uh-bul), adjective*

Easily angered. Those who are prone to fits of temper are *irascible*.

> *Sebastian, an IRASCIBLE man, did his best to put on a show of conviviality when he visited his in-laws, most of whom irritated him.*

iridescent *(ear-ih-DESS-unt), adjective*

Possessing rainbowlike colors. *Iridescent* can also mean "altering in hue when viewed from different angles or moved."

> *The IRIDESCENT light of the prism flooded Newton's shuttered room.*

irrefutable *(ihr-ree-FYOO-tuh-bull), adjective*
Describes something that cannot be disproved or refuted.
> *The evidence is IRREFUTABLE. You're under arrest!*

irremediable *(ihr-ree-MEE-dee-uh-bull), adjective*
Describes something that cannot be repaired, cured, or remedied.
> *One too many arguments between Rose and Jim finally left their fragile relationship IRREMEDIABLE.*

irresolute *(ihr-REZ-uh-loot), adjective*
Doubtful, waffling, incapable of being firm and resolute.
> *The candidate won the election because he was able to create the perception that his opponent was IRRESOLUTE about matters of national security.*

irrevocable *(ih-REV-uh-kuh-bull), adjective*
Cannot be rescinded or revoked.
> *Once you walk out that door, Pete, your decision is IRREVOCABLE!*

isthmus *(ISS-mus), noun*
A narrow strip of land connecting two larger masses of land.
> *The geologic evidence suggests that, long ago, an ISTHMUS linked Siberia and Alaska.*

itinerant *(eye-TIN-er-unt), adjective*
Describes someone who, or something that, travels from place to place with a purpose.
> *While I was between jobs, I worked as an ITINERANT farmer.*

itinerary *(eye-TIN-uh-rare-ee), noun*
A list of things to be done and seen while on a trip; a summary of the arrivals, departures, and other particulars of one's projected travels.
> *I had hoped this vacation would give me a chance to relax, but after glancing at the ITINERARY, I feel I'm likely to come back more exhausted than before I left.*

its *(its), pronoun*
Belonging to it. (For comparison, see the entry for *it's*.)
> *This job of mine has ITS ups and downs.*

it's *(its), contraction*
It is. (For comparison, see the entry for *its*.)
> *IT'S certainly a lovely morning!*

doctrinaire
abstemious
levity hubris panacea
veracity cerebellum
labyrinth
criterion
nonagenarian
meticulous zither

J & K

verbiage
quondam
colloquial
wok palpable pagination
incipient salutary
evity redact fervent
beleaguered yawnful
elixir beneficent
amoose pragmatism

jackanapes *(JAK-uh-napes), noun*

An arrogant or impertinent person; especially, an impudent young man.

If that JACKANAPES tells you to put his photo on the book jacket one more time, it will be the last day he works here as an editor.

jaded *(JAY-dud), adjective*

Worn out; dulled or satiated due to overindulgence.

Her parents thought that providing Tracy with everything her heart desired as a child would make her a happy person, but she grew up to be a JADED and selfish woman.

jambalaya *(jam-buh-LIE-uh), noun*

A spicy Cajun dish featuring rice cooked with ham, sausage, chicken, shrimp, or oysters, and seasoned with herbs.

Anna had so much ham left over from Easter dinner that she decided to try to whip up a JAMBALAYA.

jargon *(JAR-gun), noun*

The specialized language or vocabulary of a particular profession, trade, or hobby.

Throughout, the book asks the reader to make sense of some rather sophisticated JARGON likely to be comprehensible only to those familiar with accounting procedures.

jaundice *(JON-diss), noun*

A yellowish tint to the body's skin, fluids, and tissues as a result of the buildup of excessive bile; also, a biased, hostile attitude.

The cosmetics saleswoman tried to convince her that the makeover had given her a tanned, glowing appearance, but Shawna worried that she just looked JAUNDICED.

je ne sais quoi (zheuh-neuh-say-KWAH), *noun*

From the French for "I don't know what"; a special, intangible quality.

"This ascot you lent me lends a certain . . . JE NE SAIS QUOI," said Edgar, turning to catch himself at a better angle in the mirror."

jejune *(ji-JOON), adjective*

Dull or lackluster. *Jejune* can also mean immature or lacking in insight.

Ralph's JEJUNE fantasies of stardom brought only laughs of derision from his friends.

jeopardize *(JEP-ur-dize), verb*

To put in danger of being harmed or adversely affected.

Only after he had narrowly avoided being arrested id Marcus realize that his behavior could JEOPARDIZE his future as a lawyer.

jetsam *(JET-sum), noun*
Material thrown overboard to lighten the load of a ship in danger.
> *As the ship filled with seawater, Madame Fontaine pleaded with the sailor not to throw her trunk of clothes overboard with the rest of the JETSAM sinking beneath the wild waves.*

jettison *(JET-ih-sun), verb*
To cast off or overboard. When a captain *jettisons* items from a boat, he is sacrificing their value for the advantage of decreased weight on the ship. Similarly, to jettison can be to abandon something once thought valuable that has become a burden.
> *The project seemed promising initially, but now, with the looming possibility they could be accused of conflict of interest, Ted and Jan decided to JETTISON their plans.*

jihad *(jee-HAD), noun*
An Islamic holy war; a bitter war or dispute entered over a matter of principle.
> *The terminology can be troublesome, Mr. Ambassador; to us it was a terrorist act, but to those sympathetic with the group that planted the bomb it was a holy act undertaken as part of a JIHAD.*

jilt *(jilt), verb*
To cast (a lover) aside, to discard or dismiss unfeelingly.
> *After being JILTED so abruptly by Michael, Jane found it hard to trust men enough to enter another relationship.*

jingoism *(JING-go-iz-um), noun*
Staunch, extreme patriotism or chauvinism; calculatedly overblown patriotic rhetoric used for political advantage.
> *This kind of JINGOISM has no place in national political discourse, sir!*

jingoistic *(jin-go-ISS-tik), adjective*
Aggressively and overbearingly patriotic. A *jingo* is a person whose patriotism is expressed in bellicose rhetoric (for instance, injunctions to prepare for war). Someone who is *jingoistic* is blindly and aggressively nationalistic.
> *Such JINGOISTIC babbling can hardly be said to pass for decent advice to a head of state.*

jitney *(JIT-nee), noun*
A small car or bus charging a low fare.
> *Grandpa told us stories of how he used to make his living driving a JITNEY around town.*

jocose *(joh-KOHSS), adjective*
Characterized by joking and good humor.

Everyone loves Bob because of his JOCOSE manner.

jocund *(JOK-und), adjective*
Given to merriment. Someone who possesses a cheery disposition is *jocund*.

Tim's JOCUND personality made him the life of the party.

jostle *(JOS-l), verb*
To bump or disrupt by means of incidental contact. To make one's way by elbowing or pushing (as through a crowd) is to *jostle.*

Mark JOSTLED through the crowd, but could not find Sharon.

jovial *(JOE-vee-ul), adjective*
Possessing a joyous, happy nature; good-hearted.

Holly's JOVIAL spirit in the face of such adversity was an inspiration to us all.

jubilation *(joo-bih-LAY-shun), noun*
Extreme joy; a mood of high celebration.

Fifteen years in the maternity ward had not dulled the feeling of JUBILATION Doctor Meade experienced every time she helped bring new life into the world.

judicature *(JOO-di-kuh-choor), noun*
The authority of jurisdiction of a court of law. The rank, function, or authority of a judge is referred to as the judge's *judicature.*

This case is in fact within my JUDICATURE, despite counsel's arguments to the contrary.

judicious *(joo-DISH-us), adjective*
Demonstrating good judgment, as well as the ability to be prudent and politic.

Darlene is JUDICIOUS in everything . . . except boyfriends!

juggernaut *(JUG-ur-not), noun*
An object or force so powerful that it flattens or destroys anything in its path.

The earthquake did some minor structural damage to the city, but the tornado that followed a week late was a JUGGERNAUT, destroying every home and building it touched.

jujitsu *(ju-JIT-soo), noun*
A Japanese art of unarmed self-defense, the strategy of which is to use an opponent's strength and weight against him or her.

Cornered by a pair of thugs in the alley, Justine was able to call upon her JUJITSU skills to fight her way to safety.

julienne *(joo-lee-EN):, adjective and noun*
In thin strips (of vegetables); also, the soup containing such vegetables.

Lisa knew JULIENNE vegetables would look more elegant on the plates of her dinner guests than those cut in the normal way, but she wasn't up for the hours of preparation it would take to slice up carrots and celery for a party of twenty.

juncture *(JUNK-chur), noun*
A point in time, especially an important one.

"Thank you for your optimism," said Senator Byron, "but I feel that celebrating my victory at this JUNCTURE would be premature."

junket *(JUNK-it), noun*
A recreational trip, outing, or excursion; often, a pleasure trip taken by public officials for the ostensible purpose of gathering facts.

The congressman's eight-week trip to Oahu, supposedly to survey the Hawaiian approach to health care, is only the latest of a long series of JUNKETS that call into question his ability to manage public resources with integrity.

junta *(HOON-tuh), noun*
A group that rules a country, unofficially, following a coup d'etat.

The JUNTA declared control of the country, but control was wrested away by former members of the ruling party.

jurisprudence *(joor-iss-PROO-dnce), noun*
The science of law. *Jurisprudence* is the philosophy behind legal practice.

Casey's study of JURISPRUDENCE lasted for three long years.

juvenilia *(joo-vuh-NILL-yuh), noun*
Early work by a creative artist, usually produced when the artist was young.

What's amazing is that even this poet's JUVENILIA have a distinctive, nuanced voice.

juxtapose *(juk-stuh-poz), verb*
Place side by side for purposes of comparison and contrast.

The commander in chief JUXTAPOSED the two courses of action for his generals.

kabala *(kuh-BALL-uh), noun*
This word, which has a variety of spellings, denotes a body of mystical, ancient Hebraic writings. For whatever reason, celebrities—including Madonna—have become fans of the *kabala*, thus causing it to gain popularity.

Jane's newest obsession is the KABALA. I wonder what it will be next month.

karma (KAR-muh), noun

In Hinduism and Buddhism, the law or force dictating that current circumstances result from one's past actions, decisions, or lifestyle; consequences of one's past. Also: the general principle of cause and effect underlying the operations of the universe.

> *Greg put his car trouble down to the "bad automotive KARMA" that he felt had accompanied him since he overcharged for the used Volkswagen he sold in 1968.*

keynote (KEE-note), adjective

A prime theme, subject, or underlying element. A *keynote* address is given on a topic of relevance to a specific audience.

> *The KEYNOTE speaker addressed the many problems related to productivity that faced our organization.*

kibbutz (ki-BUHTZ), noun

A communal farm in Israel.

> *For her senior year of college, Linda completed a specialized program by living and working on a KIBBUTZ.*

kibosh (KYE-bosh), noun

The act of halting or squelching. To put the *kibosh* on something is to stop it. Literally, a *kibosh* is a spell that brings about the doom of something.

> *We had wanted to go to the baseball game, but Ryan—who's bored by the sport—put the KIBOSH on that pretty quickly.*

kilter (KIL-tur), noun

Working condition; correct position; order.

> *Although I had used a level and ruler when hanging the painting, I could see that it was off-KILTER when I stepped back a few feet.*

kin (kin), noun

One's relatives.

> *Eric was not used to spending such a long period of time away from his KIN in Ohio.*

kinesiology (kih-nee-see-OL-uh-jee), noun

The study or physical movement and musculature. *Kinesiology* is the science concerned with the movement of muscles and related physical conditioning.

> *Only an expert in KINESIOLOGY could provide insight into Carl's illness.*

kinetic (kih-NET-ik), adjective

Pertaining to motion. *Kinetic* energy is the energy associated with the movement of a system or body.

> *The artist's KINETIC sculptures captured spectator interest by means of grand sweeps, sudden plunges of pendulums, and dropping globes.*

kiosk *(KEE-osk), noun*
A small vending booth.

> *Once out of the subway station, I picked up a copy of the New York Times at a newspaper KIOSK.*

kith *(kith), noun*
One's friends and acquaintances. (Generally used with "kin."')

> *Linda enjoyed her job in Los Angeles, but she was willing to give it up to return to her KITH and kin back in Massachusetts.*

kitsch *(KITCH), noun*
From the German meaning "gaudy" or "trash," *kitsch* refers to items that are overly sentimental and gaudy and which are thought indicative of bad taste.

> *The tourist trap's gift shop was filled with row after of souvenir KITSCH.*

knell *(nell), noun*
A sound emanating from a bell; the toll of a bell, particularly a bell rung as part of a funeral ceremony.

> *Though she couldn't bring herself to attend her uncle's funeral, Brenda stood on the hill above the graveyard and listened to the KNELL of the church bells.*

kow-tow *(KOW-tow), verb*
To show respect, deference, or servility.

> *For the sake of keeping peace in the family, Alice KOW-TOWED to her father, spending her evenings at home instead of joining her friends at the dance club.*

kudos *(KOO-dos), noun*
Honor or accolades. The word *kudos,* occasionally used with a singular verb, is more commonly construed as a plural noun.

> *The KUDOS he received for his first novel were nothing compared to the glowing reviews that greeted his second.*

kung fu *(kung FOO), noun*
An Oriental art of self-defense, the strategy of which is to strike quick, successive blows to an opponent's weak spots using fluid hand and leg moves.

> *The mugging shook Adam up so badly that he began taking KUNG FU lessons the next day, hoping to protect himself in the future.*

Kwanzaa *(KWAHN-zuh), noun*
This Swahili word denotes a harvest festival celebrated, from December 26 to January 1, by some African Americans.

> *Reggie's family began to celebrate KWANZAA last year.*

L

L

laborious *(luh-BORE-ee-us), adjective*
Requiring a great deal of hard work and perseverance.
> *Even though the years in school were LABORIOUS, they were worth the effort when I earned my Ph.D.*

labyrinth *(LAB-uh-rinth), noun*
An intricate or oversized maze; any place or situation in which getting one's bearings seems difficult or impossible.
> *As part of his experiment, Herman timed how long it took the various breeds of mice to make it through a LABYRINTH to a dish bearing a piece of cheese.*

lacerated *(LASS-uh-ray-tud), adjective*
Cut, torn, ripped, or mangled.
> *Because I LACERATED my finger with the scissors while I was on the job, I was eligible to file a workers' compensation claim.*

lachrymose *(LACK-rih-moce), adjective*
Causing tears or sadness.
> *While most men I know dismiss An Affair to Remember as a LACHRYMOSE melodrama, the women in my office consider it one of the best movie romances in history.*

lackadaisical *(lack-uh-DAZE-ih-kul), adjective*
Lacking spirit or energy; languid.
> *I was feeling rather LACKADAISICAL last Sunday, so I stayed in bed all day and watched football games instead of mowing the lawn.*

lackluster *(LACK-lus-tur), adjective*
Dull; not shiny or brilliant.
> *Wanda's LACKLUSTER performance as Hedda Gabler led one critic to remark that she probably had a long career ahead of her in the theater—as a stage weight.*

laconic *(luh-KON-ik), adjective*
Of few words. Speech that is concise or terse is *laconic*.
> *Cooper's performances are LACONIC, but all the more powerful for their terseness.*

laggard *(LAG-urd), noun*
One who lags behind or loiters. A *laggard* fails to keep up.
> *We have completed our part of the project, Mr. Miller; it is the LAGGARDS in the accounting.*

laity *(LAY-uh-tee), noun*
A group of religious worshipers differentiated from the clergy; members of the lay community.

> *Bishop Riley, ever mindful that his predecessor had been criticized for his inaccessibility, made a point of mingling with the LAITY as much as possible.*

lalapalooza *(la-luh-puh-LOO-zuh), noun*
Something outstanding or unusual.

> *The charity carnival concluded with a LALAPALOOZA of a parade, in which the mayor rode a unicycle and juggled grapefruits to the sound of wild applause.*

lambaste *(LAM-baste), verb*
To reprimand sharply or attack verbally. *Lambaste* originally meant "to beat harshly."

> *What a LAMBASTING he received from his mother for coming home late!*

lamentation *(lam-en-TAY-shun), noun*
An expression of mourning. Originally, a *lament* was a song or poem expressing grief; a *lamentation* is the act of expressing grief and sorrow.

> *Karl heard groans of LAMENTATION from his mother's room.*

lamina: **(LAM-ih-nuh),**
A thin coating or sheet.

> *The new window came wrapped in a clear plastic LAMINA to protect it.*

lampoon *(lam-POON), noun or verb*
As a noun, *lampoon* denotes a typically mean-spirited satire directed at a person, group, institution, etc. The verb form suggests the act of mocking someone.

> *Many felt Trina's imitation of Jessica's nervous tic was a cruel LAMPOON.*

languid *(LANG-gwid), adjective*
Listless; lacking vitality. That which lacks force or vigor is *languid*.

> *Robert's LANGUID demeanor was mistaken by some for a lack of intelligence.*

largess *(lar-ZHESS), noun*
Generosity, especially generosity with money. Largess (*sometimes spelled* largesse; *can also refer to a generous nature*).

> *Her father's LARGESS was the only thing standing between Barbara and bankruptcy.*

lascivious *(luh-SIV-ee-us), adjective*
Wanton or lustful. That which excites sexual desires is *lascivious*.

> *Grandmother Jones, upon being informed that the dancers at the club had done a can-can for us, denounced such LASCIVIOUS goings on.*

L

lassitude *(LASS-ih-tood), noun*
A condition of listlessness, exhaustion, or weakness; a feeling of indifference.

> *Mary's uncharacteristic LASSITUDE at work can, I think, be explained by the fact that her father, who is gravely ill, is now living with her.*

latent *(LAY-tunt), adjective*
Existing and having the power to become visible or manifest, but for the time being remaining unseen or unknown.

> *The virus remained LATENT in his system for some time, causing him unknowingly to infect those he came in close contact with.*

latke *(LOT-kuh), noun*
A Jewish potato pancake, often eaten during Hanukkah.

> *Mrs. Bloom always made her famous LATKES for the children during the holiday season.*

lattice *(LAT-us), noun*
A pattern of crossed wooden or metal strips; any framework or decoration done in this style.

> *The fence in the garden near the main hall was an attractive LATTICE arrangement, apparently broad and discreet, but in fact unforgivingly porous when it came to the intimate conversations of lovers.*

laudable *(LAWD-uh-bul), adjective*
Worthy or deserving of praise.

> *Dryly, Professor Helmut told me that my ambition to write the great American novel was LAUDABLE, but that unfortunately my manuscript was a few drafts away from meeting that goal.*

laudatory *(LAW-duh-tore-ee), adjective*
Giving praise. A *laudatory* speech is one that praises or glorifies.

> *John's LAUDATORY remarks really motivated the sales force.*

laureate *(LORE-ee-ut), adjective and noun*
Honored as a result of achievements. As a noun, *laureate* refers to a person who has been singled out for a particular high honor or award.

> *The group included a remarkable cross-section of accomplished scientists, some of whom were Nobel LAUREATES.*

lax *(LACKS), adjective*
Undisciplined, careless, or negligent.

> *I was surprised by the LAX security at the armory.*

lay *(lay), verb*

To set something down in a certain position; to place (an object) upon something. (See, for comparison, the entry for *lie*.)

> *Unlike the verb "to lie," the verb "to LAY" must take a direct object, as in "That script really laid an egg."*

lead (led), *noun or verb*

A metal. Also, as a verb (pronounced *leed*), to take charge or guide. (See, for comparison, the entry for *led*.)

> *Most service stations have stopped selling gasoline containing LEAD.*

led *(led), verb*

The past tense of the verb "to lead." (See, for comparison, the entry for *lead*.)

> *To our great relief, Vernon LED us out of the forest without a compass.*

leery *(LEER-ee), adjective*

Wary; cautious; suspicious.

> *I was LEERY of meeting my friends at the bar downtown: I'd have to travel there by myself on the subway, and there had been several attacks in stations recently.*

legato *(leg-AH-toe), adjective*

In music, possessing a smooth, even, unbroken sound.

> *The soothing LEGATO of the second movement always draws me into a quiet world of reflection.*

legerdemain *(lej-ur-duh-MANE), noun*

Illusions performed by a magician; sleight-of-hand.

> *With his remarkable ability to make everyday objects seem to disappear, the Amazing Mannini was a true master of LEGERDEMAIN.*

leitmotif *(LIGHT-moe-teef), noun*

This German word denotes a recurring theme in a musical or opera associated with a particular character, situation, setting, etc. In general, *leitmotif* can signify a dominant theme in fiction or even in someone's life.

> *Ian's LEITMOTIF is the smell of never-washed and often-worn clothing.*

leonine *(LEE-uh-nine), adjective*

Describes something or someone characteristic of a lion.

> *Ben's LEONINE mane of hair makes most of his girlfriends jealous.*

lesser *(LESS-ur), adjective*

Smaller; littler. (See, for comparison, the entry for *lessor*.)

> *Sometimes in life we must choose the LESSER of two evils.*

L

lessor *(LESS-or), noun*
A person or group granting a lease.
> *The LESSOR must sign the agreement here, Mr. Watkins.*

lethargic *(luh-THAR-jik), adjective*
Sluggish; inactive to such a degree as to resemble sleep or unconsciousness. A *lethargic* person is difficult to rouse to action.
> *After many long hours of work, Pat and Corey stared at each other, LETHARGIC but unable to accept the necessity of calling it a night.*

levitate *(LEV-ih-tayt), verb*
To float, hover, or rise in the air, particularly as a result of supernatural or magical powers.
> *The audience watched breathlessly as the magician seemed to make his assistant LEVITATE high above the stage.*

levity *(LEH-vih-tee), noun*
Lightness; insubstantiality. *Levity* often refers to inappropriately idle or humorous chatter.
> *Gentlemen, with all due respect, we face a crisis; this is no time for LEVITY.*

lexicography *(lex-ih-KOG-ruh-fee), noun*
The compiling, writing, and editing of dictionaries.
> *Though he had never intended to pursue a career in LEXICOGRAPHY, Jeremy spent twenty years with Merriam-Webster, working his way up from researcher to editor.*

lexicon *(LEK-sih-kon), noun*
A dictionary composed for a specific, narrowly defined (professional) audience. *Lexicon* can also mean the vocabulary associated with a specific discipline or group.
> *Arthur, though not a doctor, was well versed in the LEXICON of medicine.*

liaison *(lee-ay-ZON), noun*
A communication channel. Also: A person who acts as a go-between or formal representative. Also: a romantic affair. *Liaison* is often used to describe the meetings of lovers, but it applies equally to formal organizational or bureaucratic contact.
> *Captain Morse was met by an Air Force LIAISON within minutes of his arrival.*

libation *(li-BAY-shun), noun*
An alcoholic beverage offered or accepted in celebration. (The word is usually used facetiously, as if to exaggerate the supposed formality of an informal occasion.) Originally, a *libation* was a liquid offering at a formal religious rite.
> *Will you join us in a LIBATION, Charles?*

libel *(LIE-bull), noun*

A written, printed, or pictorial statement or assertion that is unjustly negative, defaming, or hurtful to one's character and reputation.

> *Several celebrities have sued the supermarket tabloid for LIBEL, but the parade of lurid and preposterous headlines has continued unabated.*

liberal *(LIB-uh-rul), adjective*

Generous in giving; tolerant of different ideas and people; in politics, favoring democratic reform; progressive.

> *According to the tourist guide, Mario's was famous for its LIBERAL portions of lasagna, ravioli, and garlic bread.*

libertine *(LIB-ur-teen), noun*

One who lives life unconcerned and unrestrained by popular convention or morality; a promiscuous person, especially a man.

> *Presumably because he is divorced, my elderly grandmother refers to my fiance Eric as "that LIBERTINE," but everyone else in my family thinks he's wonderful.*

libretto *(li-BRET-oh), noun*

The text of a musical work, such as a cantata or opera, often accompanied by a translation.

> *As she is fluent in Italian, Maria rarely needs to refer to the LIBRETTO when attending the opera.*

licentious *(lie-SENN-shuss), adjective*

Having little or no moral restraint, especially with regard to sex.

> *After months of watching Gary leave the nightclub with one woman after another, Paul finally decided to tell Maureen of her husband's LICENTIOUS behavior.*

lie *(lie), verb*

To recline; to rest. Also: to tell an untruth. Also: a falsehood. (See, for comparison, the entry for *lay*.)

> *"I'm just LYING here doing nothing," Rick LIED, pointing to the tiny microphone and motioning for Trudy to keep quiet.*

lieu *(loo), noun*

Place; stead.

> *This year, in LIEU of individual Christmas presents, the five of us took a family vacation to Hawaii.*

Lilliputian *(lill-ih-PYOO-shun), adjective*
Of extremely small stature. From a land of small people found in Jonathan Swift's *Gulliver's Travels.*
> *The massive mural on the walls of the museum made me feel positively LILLIPUTIAN.*

limpid *(LIM-pid), adjective*
Very clear; transparent.
> *Looking into a LIMPID stream of swift-flowing water, we saw that it was full of migrating salmon.*

linchpin *(LYNCH-pin), noun*
Specifically, a linchpin is a pin pushed through an axle to keep a wheel in place. In general, "linchpin" denotes someone or something essential to holding together a complicated situation, business, organization, etc.
> *Once Mr. Crane, the LINCHPIN of the organization, retired, the business fell apart due to squabbling and infighting.*

lineage *(LIN-ee-uj), noun*
Ancestry; line of descent.
> *A thoroughbred German shepherd from a championship line, my dog Khan probably had a more prestigious LINEAGE than anyone in our family.*

lionize *(LIE-uh-nize), verb*
To praise excessively; to idolize.
> *For years young baseball fans LIONIZED Babe Ruth, whose many indiscretions were usually overlooked by the press.*

lip-sync *(LIP-sink), verb*
To simulate a live singing performance by mouthing along to a record.
> *It is common these days for recording artists to LIP-SYNC for the bulk of a "live" concert.*

liqueur *(li-KER), noun*
An alcoholic beverage flavored with fruit, nuts, seeds, spices, herbs, or a combination of these ingredients.
> *After diner, the hostess gave us a choice of several exotic LIQUEURS; I chose Frangelico because I love the taste of hazelnuts.*

lissome *(LISS-um), adjective*
Supple. Something that is easily bent is *lissome.*
> *The LISSOME young gymnast's body seemed to defy the laws of physics.*

litany *(LIT-uh-nee), noun*
Something (especially a list or a single sentence) related incessantly in an unwavering manner. A *litany* is a responsive prayer service within the Catholic church marked by much repetition.

> *We listened to Greta recite the usual LITANY of problems in the marketing department.*

literal *(LIT-uh-rul), adjective*
Meaning exactly what is said or written; not open to interpretation.

> *Mr. Pickney's unyielding, LITERAL-minded interpretations of his supervisor's directives left him very little flexibility in handling unanticipated crises in his department.*

lithe *(lithe), adjective*
Graceful; supple.

> *LITHE dancers dressed in brilliant gold sprang across the stage to the sound of drums and cymbals.*

litigious *(lih-TIJ-us), adjective*
Overly inclined to engage in lawsuits. *Litigious* can also mean "of or pertaining to litigation."

> *Mr. Green, a LITIGIOUS businessman in our town, once had seven cases pending at the same time.*

liturgy *(LIH-tur-jee), noun*
Worshipful ritual, especially the formal Christian service of the Eucharist. *Liturgy* is the accepted public form of religious worship.

> *Pat's attempts to reformulate the LITURGY in her church were greeted with great skepticism by the more conservative worshipers.*

livid *(LIH-vid), adjective*
Extremely angry; infuriated. Literally, *livid* means discolored (as from a bruise). To say someone is livid in the sense of being angry is really to say his anger is so acute as to cause a change in his coloring.

> *Caroline was LIVID after she realized she had been swindled.*

loath *(loath), adjective*
Unwilling; reluctant. (See, for comparison, the entry for *loathe*.)

> *George wanted to go to the party, but his wife was LOATH to leave little Amy, who had the flu, with a sitter.*

loathe *(loathe)*, *verb*
To hate or detest. (See, for comparison, the entry for *loath*)
> *My wife has always LOATHED the Three Stooges, a cultural lapse on her part that I am perfectly willing to forgive.*

locomotion *(lo-kuh-MO-shun)*, *noun*
The act or ability of moving from place to place.
> *Children's lack of LOCOMOTION today is resulting in an obesity epidemic.*

locution *(loe-KYOO-shun)*, *noun*
Style of speaking. A *locution* is also a particular word, expression, or phrase.
> *Martin's British LOCUTION would be a real asset during the many media appearances he would make over the next few years.*

logistics *(loe-JIS-tiks)*, *noun*
The essential details of how something is to be accomplished. In military usage, *logistics* is the discipline addressing supply and procurement.
> *Jane knew the trip could not begin until the LOGISTICS were worked out.*

logy *(LOW-gee)*, *adjective*
Pronounced with a hard "g," as in "gate," *logy* describes someone or something lethargic or sluggish.
> *On really cold days, my already LOGY car absolutely refuses to start.*

lope *(lope)*, *verb*
A long, galloping stride. As a verb: to move using such a stride.
> *My horse was LOPING along at an easy pace until a car backfired suddenly, causing him to break into a terrified gallop.*

loquacious *(loe-KWAY-shuss)*, *adjective*
Extremely talkative. Someone prone to nervous chatter could be said to be *loquacious*.
> *Michael proved a LOQUACIOUS houseguest; Mrs. Stevens did the best she could to manage his one-sided conversational torrents.*

lothario *(lo-THAR-ee-oe)*, *noun*
A seducer. The word *Lothario* originated from the name of a character in The Fair Penitent, a play (1703) by Nicholas Rowe.
> *Ryan is friendly, I'll admit, but be is certainly no LOTHARIO.*

lout *(LOWT)*, *noun*
A clumsy, stupid, bumbling, moronic individual.
> *If you would stop acting like a LOUT, Walter, you'd get a date once in a while.*

lowbrow *(LOE-brow), adjective*
Uncultured; unsophisticated.

> *Earl's LOWBROW humor may have been fine for his fellow mechanics down at the garage, but his wife did not consider her bridge companions the proper audience for such remarks.*

lucid *(LOO-sid), adjective*
Intelligible. *Lucid* can also refer to a clear mental state.

> *Although he lost consciousness for a few minutes, Glenn was LUCID before the ambulance arrived.*

lucre *(LOO-kur), noun*
Profits; financial rewards; money.

> *After untold hours creating and developing the software program, Miles received only $2,000 for his efforts—a tiny fraction of the LUCRE that poured into company coffers from sales of the product.*

ludicrous *(LOO-dih-kruss), adjective*
Absurd to the point of being laughable. Something that is obviously implausible or impractical could be considered *ludicrous.*

> *Your proposal that I accept a 75 percent pay cut is LUDICROUS, Mr. Robinson.*

lugubrious *(loo-GOO-bree-us), adjective*
Mournful in the extreme. *Lugubrious* refers to something or someone mournful to an inappropriate degree.

> *You may consider Steven's poems "dark"; to me, they are simply LUGUBRIOUS.*

luminary *(LOO-mih-nay-ree), noun*
Something that emits light; also, a person widely renowned and respected in his or her area of expertise.

> *Among other LUMINARIES who attended the party was the author of this year's Pulitzer winner for drama.*

lummox *(LUM-ox), noun*
A dim-witted and awkward person; an oaf.

> *Sherman had a heart of gold, but when it came to social etiquette, he was something of a LUMMOX.*

lupine *(LOO-pine), adjective*
Describes someone who acts like a wolf in that he or she is savage and predatory.

> *Sid's LUPINE behavior makes you feel like you should go home and take a shower after you've been around him for a little while.*

L

lurid *(LOOR-id), adjective*
Gruesome or sensationalistic. Something likely to elicit horror, lust, shock, or disgust could be considered *lurid*.

The LURID illustrations made it clear to Pamela that this was no children's book she had bought.

lustrous *(LUS-truss), adjective*
Radiant; shining. *Lustrous* refers to that which possesses a sheen or glow. Lustrous can also mean "brilliant" in the sense of outstanding or exceptional.

Gina's LUSTROUS eyes shimmered in the candlelight.

lycanthrope *(LIE-kan-thrope), noun*
A werewolf.

The newest LYCANTHROPE flick was not as exciting as its advertisements.

lyrical *(LEER-ih-kull), adjective*
Musical; flowing; expressive.

The LYRICAL quality of Ash's poetry often masks a harsh, mournful world view.

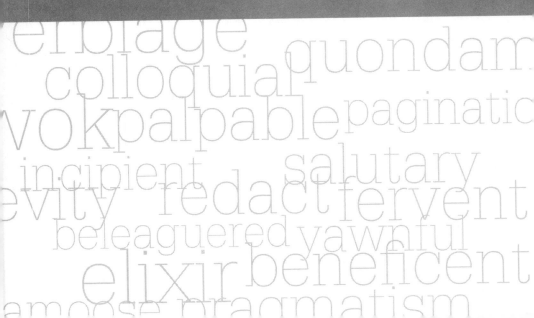

macabre *(mub-KAH-brub), adjective*
Horrifying; reminiscent of death. A *macabre* story is one that focuses on morbid, grisly subjects.
> *The old man's MACABRE tales frightened the children.*

machination *(mak-uh-NAY-shun), noun*
A conniving plot. A crafty scheme meant to achieve an illicit end is a *machination*.
> *Carrie was familiar with Desmond's MACHINATIONS when it came to winning raises.*

machiavellian (mok-ee-uh-VELL-ee-un), *adjective*
Relating to the qualities espoused by Machiavelli in *The Prince;* cunning and deceitful in the pursuit of power, particularly with regard to political matters.
> *Although Lyndon Johnson was certainly a ruthless politician, he was far from the MACHIAVELLIAN figure suggested by some of his biographers.*

macrobiotic *(mack-row-bi-AHT-ick), adjective*
Describes a diet rich in whole grains and beans, which some believe lengthens one's lifespan.
> *After she had a few health scares, Jean turned to a MACROBIOTIC diet.*

macrocosm *(MAK-ruh-koz-um), noun*
A representation on a large scale; the universe envisioned in its totality. In addition, a large system that reflects one of its component systems is a *macrocosm*.
> *Some early astronomers obviously believed the physical universe to be a a MACROCOSM of existing social and religious structures.*

maelstrom *(MAIL-strum), noun*
A situation marked by violence, turbulence, and uncertainty.
> *To outsiders, the MAELSTROM of Wall Street's trading floor looks frightening.*

magisterial *(madge-ih-STEER-ee-uhl), adjective*
Describes the authority, weight, and gravity of someone considered a master of a particular art, task, ability, etc.
> *With MAGISTERIAL grace, the conductor lifted her baton.*

magnate *(MAG-nayt), noun*
An industrial leader. A *magnate* is a powerful business figure.
> *Your Honor, I am no communications MAGNATE; I run a small town newspaper.*

maharajah *(mah-huh-RAH-zhuh), noun*
Formerly, an Indian ruling prince, especially one of a major state.
> *The MAHARAJAH and his entourage rode into the village on a procession of elephants.*

maladroit *(mal-uh-DROIT), adjective*
Clumsy; uncoordinated.

> *Having earned a reputation as the most MALADROIT member of the family, Ernie came in for a lot of teasing when he announced his plans to take up figure skating.*

malady *(MAL-uh-dee), noun*
An illness or unwholesome condition. A *malady* is a disorder or disease causing discomfort.

> *Jason's MALADY, if it had gone undiagnosed, could have taken his life.*

malaise *(muh-LAZE), noun*
A vague feeling of illness, uneasiness, or sadness.

> *"Sheer idiocy," commented the professor at the end of my paper, in which I argued that Shakespeare's King Lear suffered only a passing MALAISE, not madness.*

malapropism (MAL-a-prop-ism), *noun*
The ridiculous misuse of similar-sounding words.

> *Bert's reference to the accounting department's "physical prudence" was only one of the morning's many MALAPROPISMS.*

malcontent *(mal-kuhn-TENT), adjective or noun*
Someone unhappy with his or her circumstances or with his or her government, job, lifestyle, etc. As an adjective, *malcontent* describes such a person.

> *Harvey is such a MALCONTENT that he'll argue with you if you tell him it's a nice day!*

maleficence *(muh-LEF-ih-sence), noun*
The undertaking of evil or harmful acts. That which is mischievous or rooted in ill will could be said to possess *maleficence.*

> *The long-ignored MALEFICENCE of the county's corrupt prison system was finally exposed by a rookie Globe reporter.*

malevolent *(muh-LEV-uh-lent), adjective*
Malicious. Someone who is unrepentantly and viciously ill-willed is *malevolent.*

> *Glen cast a MALEVOLENT glance at his opponent.*

malfeasance *(mal-FEE-zunce), noun*
An instance of breaking the law or otherwise engaging in wrongdoing, particularly with regard to the acts of a public official.

> *The D.A.'s much-publicized MALFEASANCE during the Cooper case—concealing evidence and manipulating testimony—ended up ruining his political career.*

malice *(MAL-iss), noun*

The desire to commit harmful or unfair acts. Someone who intends to commit an act known to be immoral, unlawful, or likely to cause harm shows *malice*.

> *The defendant clearly showed MALICE in stating that he intended to kill Mrs. Powers.*

malicious *(muh-LISH-uss), adjective*

Spitefully mean; evil; bad in intent.

> *Fred said his comments were all intended as constructive criticism, but I detected a MALICIOUS note in some of his suggestions.*

malign *(muh-LINE), verb*

To defame; to besmirch (the reputation of).

> *The much-MALIGNED team owner's decision to trade his star quarterback turned out to be one of the best moves he ever made.*

malignant *(muh-LIG-nunt)t adjective*

Posing a serious threat or harm. A *malignant* tumor can cause death.

> *They bad feared the growth would be found MALIGNANT, but it turned out to be benign.*

malinger *(muh-LING-ger), verb*

To avoid work by making up excuses. Someone who pretends to be ill or injured in order to avoid effort or duty can be said to *malinger*.

> *"There will be no MALINGERING in this office," the new supervisor said sternly.*

malleable *(MAL-ee-uh-bull), adjective*

Shapeable; capable of being molded, changed, or influenced.

> *Senator Green was of the opinion that public opinion was fairly MALLEABLE, and that any scandal, if handled properly, could be overcome.*

manatee *(MAN-uh-tee), noun*

A large mammal reminiscent of a seal found in shallow waters off the coast of Florida.

> *Unfortunately, the MANATEE has joined the ever-growing list of animals in danger of extinction.*

mandate *(MAN-date), noun*

Authoritative command, endorsement, or instruction. A *mandate* is also an order issued by one court of law to another, lower court.

> *Having received only 40 percent of the vote nationwide, President Lincoln could hardly claim a national MANDATE for his policies.*

mandolin *(man-duh-LINN), noun*

An eight-stringed fretted instrument similar to a lute.

Patrick called the MANDOLIN player over to serenade the table while he asked Jeannie for her hand in marriage.

maniacal *(muh-NYE-uh-kull), adjective*

Insane. Also: overly emphatic or nervous. *Maniacal* is often used ironically to describe a person's near-fanatical devotion to a certain pursuit.

Chuck's obsession with baseball statistics bordered on the MANIACAL.

manifesto *(man-ih-FESS-toe), noun*

A public declaration of one's intentions or motives, typically of a political nature.

Instead of galvanizing the crowd to action, the poet's MANIFESTO collapsed the audience in laughter.

mar *(mar), verb*

To spoil, damage, or tarnish.

Alissa's birthday party was MARRED by a loud altercation between two motorists on the street outside our house.

maraud *(muh-ROD), verb*

To wander in search of booty. To loot or invade for treasure is to *maraud*.

The ship was waylaid by MARAUDING pirates on the fourteenth of May.

marrow *(MARE-oh), noun*

The essential part; literally, a vital material that fills the inside of bone cavities.

The doctor assured Ellen that, once an appropriate donor was found, her bone MARROW transplant would take place immediately.

martial *(MAR-shull), adjective*

Appropriate to wartime. *Martial* law is the imposition of military control over a civilian population. (We describe disciplines such as judo and karate—which focus on hand-to-hand combat-as martial arts.)

After capturing Richmond, the commander issued an order placing it under MARTIAL law.

martyrdom *(MAR-ter-dum), noun*

The condition of having suffered death as a martyr. A person who has attained *martyrdom* has died or been killed for a principle or cause, and has come to be regarded with reverence by others as a result.

Many say that John Brown's MARTYRDOM served his cause more effectively than anything he did at Harper's Ferry.

marzipan *(MAR-zuh-pan), noun*

A popular candy made from almonds, egg whites and sugar, often molded into the shapes of animals.

> *In Europe it is quite common to decorate a Christmas tree with edible decorations, including gingerbread men, MARZIPAN animals, and miniature fruitcakes.*

masticate *(MASS-tih-kate), verb*

To chew. To *masticate* is to knead and grind with the teeth.

> *Grandpa, always an extravagant speaker, referred to his dentures as his "MASTICATING companions."*

material *(muh-TEER-ee-ul), noun*

Physical substance; essence; something from which things are or can be constituted. (See, for comparison, the entry for *materiel.*)

> *With the right MATERIALS, Dave, we could build a treehouse out back.*

materiel *(muh-teer-ee-EL), noun*

Military equipment and weapons.

> *We have solid evidence that enemy MATERIEL has been making it past the embargo, Mr. President.*

matriarch *(MAY-tree-ark), noun*

A woman who presides over a family or group. A woman who holds the dominant position in an organization or family can be said to be the group's *matriarch.*

> *Millicent Bryant, MATRIARCH of the large Bryant family, made her customary speech at the reunion.*

matriarchy *(MAY-tree-ark-ee), noun*

A society that traces descent and inheritance through the female line.

> *If we lived in a MATRIARCHY, the husband and children would probably take the wife's last name.*

matrix *(MAY-trix), noun*

A place, situation, or object that acts as the point of origin or development for something else; a mold.

> *The art department was the MATRIX of all of the company's great creative works.*

maudlin *(MAUD-lin), adjective*

Gushingly or tearfully sentimental.

> *I would have liked to believe Kent when he swore I was his dearest friend in the world, but I had a feeling it was all the MAUDLIN babbling of a man who had had a little too much fun at a party.*

maunder *(MAWN-dur), verb*

To speak or act in an aimless, incoherent fashion.

> *In spite of—or perhaps because of—his father's tendency to be an overachiever, William MAUNDERED through life without the slightest ambition.*

maverick *(MAV-er-ik), noun*

Free and independent of outside association or contact. A *maverick* is an independent-minded person who resists the influence of a group. (The word referred originally to a horse or steer that escapes from a herd and runs alone.)

> *Although Ryan portrayed himself as a MAVERICK politician, he owed favors to the same special interest groups his opponent did.*

mawkish *(MAW-kish), adjective*

Overly sentimental. Something that is emotional or maudlin is *mawkish*.

> *Daytime soap operas irritated Melanie; she found them mawkish and unbelievable.*

mea culpa *(me-uh KULP-uh), noun*

From the Latin meaning "I am to blame," a *mea culpa* is acknowledgement, usually public acknowledgment, of a blunder or mistake.

> *After the politician made racially-tinged comments, he spent the better part of a month offering MEA CULPAS on national television.*

mean *(meen), noun*

In mathematics, an intermediate value or average of a series of figures. (See, for comparison, the entry for *median*.)

> *The MEAN of the series (0, 3, 6, 7, 9) is five.*

meander *(mee-AN-der), verb*

To follow a turning and winding path. To *meander* is to wander idly without a set goal.

> *Jack, lost without his shopping list, MEANDERED helplessly through the aisles of the supermarket.*

median *(MEE-DEE-UN), noun*

In mathematics, a middle number in a series of numbers. (See, for comparison, the entry for *mean*.)

> *The MEDIAN of the series (0, 3, 6, 7, 9) is six.*

medley *(MED-lee), noun*

A group of varying elements; a mixture; in music, a series of songs or melodies connected as one.

> *Dinner at the club that night was especially tasty: chicken piccata, wild rice, and a MEDLEY of winter vegetables.*

megalomania *(meg-uh-lo-MAY-nee-uh), noun*
Delusions of wealth and/or power. Literally, *megalomania* is a psychopathological condition in which a person is obsessed with fantasies of riches or authority. The word is also used to describe people whose ambitions and sense of self-importance are overblown.

> *Some have interpreted the tycoon's purchase of the old castle as an uncharacteristically bad real estate deal; I see it as pure MEGALOMANIA.*

melanin *(MEL-uh-nin), noun*
A dark pigment found in skin, eyes, and hair.

> *Albino organisms lack MELANIN, and many have white hair, pale skin, and pale, sensitive eyes.*

melee *(MAY-lay), noun*
From the French meaning "meddle," a *melee* is a confused struggle involving many people.

> *After the batter was struck by the pitcher's ball, players from both teams ran out onto the field, and a MELEE ensued.*

mellifluous *(muh-LIF-loo-us), adjective*
Flowing sweetly and smoothly. *Mellifluous* describes a smooth, sweet sensation.

> *Jane's MELLIFLUOUS cello playing was the envy of the other musicians.*

melodious *(muh-LOW-dee-us), adjective*
Pleasant or agreeable to the ear. *Melodious* refers to that which features a pleasing succession of sounds.

> *The MELODIOUS tones of his mother's voice always reminded Wayne of his childhood.*

melodrama *(MELL-uh-drah-muh), noun*
A performance or script that exaggerates dramatic situations, making such situations laughable and unbelievable. The adjective form, which you may see, is "melodramatic."

> *Unless you want to endure constant MELODRMA, Dave, don't get involved with Shirley.*

memento *(muh-MEN-toe), noun*
A souvenir.

> *I took home a variety of sea shells as MEMENTOS of my beach vacation.*

memoir *(MEM-wahr), noun*

A series of written reminiscences about people, places, and events composed by and from the point of view of someone with intimate knowledge of the details.

> *The pretense extended even to the former president's MEMOIRS, in which he repeated his assertion that he had no knowledge of how or why the crucial minutes were erased from the tape.*

menagerie *(muh-NAZH-uh-ree), noun*

A group of wild animals collected for exhibition; any exotic grouping of people or elements.

> *Wilma thought of her eccentric staff not so much as a group of artists, but as a strange MENAGERIE of very creative people who had to be approached with deference.*

mendacious *(men-DAY-shuss), adjective*

Lying or false. Someone who tells falsehoods could be said to be *mendacious.*

> *Clark's MENDACIOUS habits will catch up with him; one of these days his lies will be exposed.*

mendicant *(MEN-dih-kunt), noun*

Beggar.

> *There, among the castoffs of society, the lepers, MENDICANTS, and prostitutes of the city, he decided to begin his ministry.*

menorah *(muh-NORE-uh), noun*

A nine-branched candelabrum used during the Jewish festival of Hanukkah.

> *In our office we display both a Christmas tree and a brass MENORAH during the holiday season.*

mentor *(MEN-tor), noun*

A counselor or teacher. In contemporary use, *mentor* usually refers to a senior figure (in business or politics, for instance) who aids the progress of a junior figure's career.

> *Bart respected and revered his MENTOR, but he knew the time had come to move on to another company.*

mephitic *(muh-FIT-ick), adjective*

Describes something poisonous or something with an offensive odor.

> *After Mark burned dinner, the house was coated with a MEPHITIC odor that took hours to dissipate.*

mercurial *(mur-KYOOR-ee-ul), adjective*
Quickly changing; unpredictable.

> *Helen's MERCURIAL temperament often mystified her subordinates, who might find themselves showered with gifts one moment and subjected to verbal abuse the next.*

meretricious *(mare-uh-TRISH-uss), adjective*
Attracting attention by vulgar, trashy means; false or insincere.

> *Many critics claim that Madonna's success is more the result of her MERETRICIOUS self-promotion talents than her musical talent.*

meritocracy *(mare-ih-TOK-ruh-see), noun*
A system in which those perceived as talented or intelligent are granted positions of preeminence.

> *Dara, who felt popularity rather than quality of work was the main factor in getting a promotion in her department, snorted when I alluded to a MERITOCRACY.*

meritorious *(mare-uh-TORE-ee-uss), adjective*
Worthy of praise, laudable.

> *Earl's work at the homeless shelter was MERITORIOUS, but it left him little time for his family and friends.*

mesmerize *(MEZ-mur-ize), verb*
To hypnotize. *Mesmerize* is derived from the name of a nineteenth-century physician, Franz Mesmer, whose early work in the field we know call hypnotism won him acclaim in Austria and throughout Europe.

> *It is said that Huey Long MESMERIZED his audiences more with his style of speaking than with the substance of his speeches.*

messianic *(mess-ee-AN-ick), adjective*
With a capital letter, a Messiah is the expected deliverer of the Jewish people. A lower-case "messiah" is someone expected to deliver a situation or organization from ruin. The adjective form, *"messianic,"* often is used negatively, to describe someone with a mercenary or inflated view of his or her importance.

> *I'm sickened by the MESSIANIC zeal with which Irene tackles her duties as head of the neighborhood association.*

metamorphosis *(met-uh-MORE-fuh-siss), noun*
A transformation, as by magic or other supernatural influence. Someone or something undergoing a change in form can be said to undergo a *metamorphosis*.

> *Darryl's friends viewed his entry into reactionary politics with some concern; because of his past history, they feared his METAMORPHOSIS into a militant.*

mete *(meet), verb*

To measure out; to distribute in proportion.

> *Roland pressed ahead with the case, confident that right would prevail and that justice would eventually be METED out.*

meteor *(MEE-tee-or), noun*

Glowing matter from space, typically stone or metal, that passes through and lights up the sky; a shooting star.

> *Apparently, the vast majority of reported UFOs turn out to be METEORS.*

meticulous *(muh-TICK-you-luss), adjective*

Precise and thorough, to the point of fussiness.

> *James is so METICULOUS he can tell if you've moved anything on his dresser as little as a quarter of an inch!*

métier *(MAY-tee-yay), noun*

From the French meaning "minister," one's *métier* is one's occupation, profession, or field of work.

> *If you need some proofreading done, go see Albert. Editing is his MÉTIER.*

metonymy *(mih-TAHN-uh-mee), noun*

A figure of speech that uses a part of something to describe the whole thing, such as when a country singer says, "The bottle let me down." "The bottle" stands for alcohol.

> *Sam says her favorite example of METONYMY is, "Now hiring smiling faces."*

miasma *(my-AS-muh), noun*

An atmosphere that is dangerous and foreboding.

> *The unexpressed anger and disagreement between Rhonda and Scott made a MIASMA of their once-happy home.*

microcosm *(MY-kro-koz-um), noun*

A model that reflects a larger thing. A *microcosm* is a small system roughly comparable to a larger system.

> *A MICROCOSM of society is represented on board the Pequod in Herman Melville's novel Moby Dick.*

microfiche *(MEYE-kroh-feesh), noun*

Microfilm that has been converted to small sheets so that it can be read from a special viewing machine.

> *Seven straight hours at the MICROFICHE machine perusing old newspaper articles on World War II left Elaine blurry-eyed, but with a firm historical sense of the setting of her new novel.*

M

midriff *(MID-riff), noun*

On the human body, the middle area of the torso; the diaphragm.

> *Allison wondered if the outfit she had selected was appropriate for meeting her fiancé's parents; the shirt barely covered her MIDRIFF.*

mien *(meen), noun*

Demeanor; appearance; overall impression.

> *A punctual man with an attentive, organized MIEN, Tony seemed the ideal candidate for the job.*

migraine *(MIE-grane), noun*

An excruciating headache, caused by expanding capillaries, that occurs on one (usually the left) side of the head, and causes the sufferer nausea, vomiting, and extreme sensitivity to light.

> *As a treatment for my MIGRAINES, the doctor gave me a new prescription, suggesting I take two tablets and lie down in a very dark room whenever I felt one coming on.*

mildew *(MIL-doo), noun*

A pungent, fungus-like coating forming on paint, cloth, carpet, etc., as a result of excessive exposure to moisture.

> *I remembered too late that I had left my favorite sweater in the washer; after a week of sitting damp in the machine, it stank of MILDEW.*

milieu *(mill-YOU), noun*

From the French meaning "in the middle," *milieu* describes one's cultural and social surroundings.

> *When I walked into the skateboard store, I knew immediately that I was out of my MILIEU.*

millenium *(muh-LEN-ee-um), noun*

A period of one thousand years. In Christian theology, the *millenium* is a thousand-year span during which Christ is to rule human affairs.

> *The members of the small church prayed for the early arrival of the MILLENIUM.*

milquetoast *(MILK-toast), adjective*

Describes an unassertive person who is easily intimidated. The word was adopted from Caspar Milquetoast, a character in a comic strip, who exemplifies such a timid person.

> *Unless you just want to be a pencil-pusher all your life, you've got to stop being so MILQUETOAST, Arthur!*

mimic *(MIM-ik), verb*

To imitate (mannerisms or speech), usually in a playful or mocking way.

> *Jerome, who could MIMIC Mr. Harris's squeaky voice with great precision, never missed an opportunity to display his talents to the class when the instructor left the room.*

mince *(mince), verb*

To chop into small pieces; figuratively, to use evasive or indirect language. Also: to walk affectedly, taking short steps.

> *"Don't MINCE words with me, Henry," my boss growled; "if you aren't going to meet the deadline, tell me so."*

minion *(MIN-yuhn), noun*

Someone with a slavish devotion to a person in power.

> *Sheila ducked into the ladies room when she saw Sandra and all her MINIONS heading down the office halls.*

minotaur *(MIN-uh-tore), noun*

In mythology, a creature that is part human, part bull.

> *Half-human, half-Animal creatures such as the MINOTAUR, the centaur, and Medusa were pervasive in ancient Greek mythology.*

minuscule *(MIN-uss-kyool), adjective*

Extremely small.

> *Sometimes, trying to decipher the MINUSCULE names, numbers, and signs on a map only makes me feel more lost.*

minutiae *(mih-NOO-shuh), noun*

From the Latin meaning "smallness," *minutiae* are all the small, trifling matters that one encounters on an average day.

> *By the time I've taken care of all the day's MINUTIAE—paying bills, getting the kids to school—I barely have any time left to work!*

mire *(mire), noun*

Waterlogged ground; swampland. Also: any corrupt or unpleasing environment from which it is difficult to extricate oneself. As a verb: to cause to be stuck in mire.

> *In the early going, the administration found itself MIRED in issues far from its stated goal of improving the economy.*

misanthrope *(MISS-un-thrope), noun*
One who hates mankind or people; a person who expects only the worst in his dealings with others.

> *In the course of a single night, Scrooge undergoes a remarkable transformation from MISANTHROPE to enlightened benefactor.*

misanthropy *(miss-ANN-thruh-pee), noun*
Hatred of mankind. *Misanthropy* refers to contempt for the human race.

> *Scrooge's MISANTHROPY was to end that Christmas Eve.*

miscegenation *(mih-sej-uh-NAY-shun), noun*
Interbreeding between members of different racial groups. *Miscegenation* was once a crime in parts of the United States.

> *The musical Show Boat was daring for its time; certainly no previous show on Broadway had dared to examine an issue as sensitive as MISCEGENATION.*

miscellany *(MISS-uh-lay-nee), noun*
A grouping or collection of various elements.

> *The volume, which featured a hodgepodge of essays, poems, and interviews relating to the Beats, was an intriguing MISCELLANY of writings from the bohemian world of the fifties.*

misconstrue *(mis-kun-STROO), verb*
To get the wrong idea; to misunderstand or misinterpret.

> *Tom MISCONSTRUED Linda's friendliness as flirting—until he met her boyfriend.*

mise en scene *(mee-zahn-SENN), noun*
From the French meaning "putting on stage," *mise en scene* denotes the setting and placing of actors and scenery on a stage or in a film. In general, the term has become synonymous with one's surroundings and environment.

> *Most people either love or hate the MISE EN SCENE of Elvis Presley's Graceland and especially its infamous "jungle room."*

misnomer *(miss-NO-mur), noun*
An incorrect or inappropriate name.

> *Vlad the Impaler, the historical antecedent for the Dracula character, was a man apparently intent on demonstrating to the world that his name was no MISNOMER.*

misogamy *(mih-SOG-uh-mee) noun*
Hatred of marriage. Someone who holds only contempt for the institution of marriage and refuses to take a husband or wife could be said to practice *misogamy*.

> *After his divorce, Brent's mistrust of marriage bordered on MISOGAMY.*

misogyny *(my-SOJ-uh-nee), noun*

Hatred of women. Someone who holds a bitter contempt for all women practices *misogyny*.

> *Rousseau's prejudices against women frequently cross the line and harden into outright MISOGYNY.*

mitigate *(MIH-tih-gate), verb*

To moderate. To *mitigate* is to lessen in impact or degree, or to cause to become less intense or severe.

> *The international situation had seemed tense until a number of MITIGATING factors—notably the overthrow of General Sanchez—came into play.*

mnemonic *(ni-MON-ik), adjective and noun*

Meant to aid in memory. As a noun, a *mnemonic* is a device (a rhyme, for instance) meant to make memorizing easier.

> *The flashcards serve only as MNEMONIC devices; they cannot, by themselves, instill any understanding of mathematical processes.*

modicum *(MOD-ih-kuhm), noun*

A moderate or token amount.

> *Paul always complains about actors who have transformed a MODICUM of talent into successful careers.*

modulate *(MOJ-uh-late), verb*

To vary. In music, to *modulate* is to change from one key to another.

> *The radio announcer began MODULATING his voice in order to counter criticisms that be spoke in a monotone.*

modus operandi *(MO-duss op-uh-RAN-deye), noun*

The mode of operation or style of doing something; from the Latin for "method of operating."

> *When Jason confessed, the police thought they had their killer, but after careful questioning it became apparent he didn't know anything about the strange MODUS OPERANDI linking the murders, or about the silver cuff link always dropped at the scene of the crime.*

modus vivendi *(MO-duss vih-VEN-dee), noun*

Lifestyle; a way of living.

> *While most envied his rich and seemingly carefree existence, Glen often found his extravagant MODUS VIVENDI rather empty and lonely.*

M

mohair *(MO-hair), noun*
The hair of the angora goat; fabric or clothing made from this hair.
> *Rudy loved the MOHAIR sweater I knitted for his birthday, but it gave him a rash.*

moil *(MOYL), noun or verb*
Hard, grinding work or to engage in such work.
> *The MOIL of paperwork made Sheila long for early retirement.*

mollify *(MOL-uh-fy), verb*
To allay (a person's) anger. *Mollify* can also mean "to lessen the impact of."
> *The umpire's attempts to MOLLIFY the two screaming managers with some risque humor were to no avail.*

mon ami *(mone-ah-MEE), noun*
My friend.
> *Deadlines come and deadlines go, MON AMI, but you and I remain.*

monarchy *(MON-ark-ee), noun*
Government by a single ruler claiming a hereditary right to sovereignty; an example or instance of perceived royal lineage.
> *King George III's troubled reign, highlighting the disadvantages of MONARCHY as a form of government, was characterized by civil unrest in the colonies, mental incapacity in the sovereign, and the usual pack of useless hangers-on at court.*

moniker *(MON-ih-kur), noun*
Name; nickname.
> *The rock star Sting has revealed in interviews that even his parents and children refer to him by his famous MONIKER.*

monochromatic *(mon-owe-kru-MAT-ik), adjective*
Of a single color. Something that features varying shades of only one hue in addition to the background hue (usually white) is *monochromatic.*
> *The sweep and power of Adams's MONOCHROMATIC photography proves how much can be accomplished with a roll of black-and-white film.*

monogamy *(muh-NOG-uh-mee), noun*
The practice of being faithful to a single married partner. The opposite of *monogamy* is *polygamy.*
> *The priest reminded the couple that they should not get married without thoroughly examining their feelings toward maintaining a life of MONOGAMY.*

monograph *(MON-uh-grqff), noun*

A scholarly article or essay on a certain topic. A *monograph* is usually intended for an academic audience and not for the general public.

> *Peterson's MONOGRAPH on theoretical physics was well received in the scientific community, although it certainly makes for tough reading for the layman.*

monophonic *(mon-uh-FON-ik), adjective*

Of or pertaining to sound reproduction using a single signal channel.

> *Although the group's recordings were released for MONOPHONIC systems, the new compact disc features stereo remixes of their most famous songs.*

monosyllabic *(mah-no-sih-LAB-ik), adjective*

Having only one syllable.

> *We tried to engage Kathleen in conversation but couldn't get more than MONOSYLLABIC grunts for our pains.*

monolithic *(mon-uh-LITH-ik), adjective*

Unwieldy or cumbersome; huge. A *monolith* is a massive block of stone or other marker (such as a sculpture) that shows solidity and uniformity; something that is monolithic calls to mind the imposing nature of a *monolith*.

> *The MONOLITHIC presence of IBM in the computer field is sobering enough to make any competitor think twice before introducing a new product.*

mononucleosis *(mon-oh-noo-klee-OH-siss), noun*

An infectious illness caused by an increase of mononuclear leukocytes in the blood, and characterized by extremely swollen glands, a sore throat, and exhaustion.

> *Erika's MONONUCLEOSIS caused her to miss nearly two months of school.*

monotonous *(muh-NOT-uh-nuss), adjective*

Failing to excite interest; boring, tedious, repetitive and dull; literally, possessing only one tone or note.

> *Mike admitted that screwing the caps on soda bottles on an assembly line was MONOTONOUS work, but he claimed it paid surprisingly well.*

montage *(mon-TAZH), noun*

From the French meaning "a mounting," a *montage* is a variety of visuals—photographs, film clips, etc.—brought together to present an idea. In essence, a montage is a video collage.

> *The documentary's excellent use of MONTAGE really brought to life the triumphs and heartbreaks of World War II.*

morass *(muh-RASS), noun*
A quagmire; a difficult or bewildering situation.

> *By 1973 the military was more eager than ever before to extricate itself from the MORASS in Southeast Asia.*

moratorium *(more-uh-TORE-ee-um), noun*
An authorized period of delay.

> *The city council voted to place a six-month MORATORIUM on new commercial development.*

mordant *(MOR-duhnt), adjective*
Bitingly sarcastic; cynical.

> *Thelma had a MORDANT wit that could stop the most arrogant swaggerer in his tracks.*

moribund *(MORE-uh-bund), adjective*
About to die. *Moribund* means, literally, "bound toward death."

> *The Confederacy lay in ruins, its currency worthless, its capital desecrated, its once proud fighting force MORIBUND.*

morose *(muh-ROCE), adjective*
Frightening or gloomy. *Morose* refers to that which is melancholy or sullen in spirit.

> *Carl knew his company was headed for bankruptcy; he spent several long MOROSE nights alone staring silently at the accounting ledger.*

morphology *(more-FALL-uh-jee), noun*
The study of something's form or structure.

> *We spent a surprisingly interesting few minutes discussing the MORPHOLOGY of the duck-billed platypus.*

mortify *(MORE-tih-fy), verb*
To humiliate. To *mortify* is also to discipline (one's body) through austerity or self-denial.

> *Mrs. Jones's mother was MORIFIED at the thought of her daughter attending the dance unescorted.*

mossback *(MAWSS-back), noun*
A person with outdated values and beliefs, especially someone who tries to foist those beliefs and values onto others.

> *Far from being a MOSSBACK, my grandfather remains committed to new ideas.*

motley *(MOT-lee), adjective*
Of diverse composition. Something that shows many colors or facets could be said to be *motley*. (The word has come to carry negative overtones of raggedness or lack of union.)

> *It was Frederick's job to mold the MOTLEY assemblage he had been given into a powerful fighting force.*

mountebank *(MOUNT-uh-bank), noun*
A charlatan; one who sells worthless medicines, potions, and the like; a fake.

> *The line between visionary romantic and common MOUNTEBANK, for my father, was often a thin one.*

mulct *(MUHLKT), verb*
To get something from someone else by swindling him or her.

> *The grifter MULCTED ten bucks from the unsuspecting couple.*

mulish *(MYOO-lish), adjective*
Describes someone who acts like a mule: stubborn, intractable, etc.

> *If you were any more MULISH about making compromises, Trevor, you'd grow long ears!*

mullah *(MYOO-luh), noun*
An Islamic title of respect for one who teaches or is learned in sacred law.

> *The MULLAH came to my son's school and discussed the fundamentals of the Islamic faith.*

multifaceted *(mul-tee-FASS-ih-tid), adjective*
Possessing many facets or dimensions. Someone who has many talents is *multifaceted*.

> *Joan, a MULTIFACETED writer, had published poems, essays, and novels.*

multifarious *(mul-tih-FARE-ee-uss), adjective*
Made of many components. Something that has a large number of parts is *multifarious*.

> *From the air, New York's MULTIFARIOUS skyline sparkled—as if beckoning to Mary to try her hand there.*

mundane *(mun-DANE), adjective*
Ordinary or everyday. That which is common or pertains to the concerns of the workaday world is *mundane*.

> *Everett's concerns were MUNDANE enough: keep a roof over his head, track down the occasional meal.*

munificent *(myoo-NIF-ih-sent), adjective*
Generous. Someone who has liberal habits of giving could be said to be *munificent*.
> *The MUNIFICENT old widow gave abundantly to charity.*

munitions *(myoo-NISH-unz), noun*
The materials of war; weapons or ammunition.
> *Neil felt his training with the army's MUNITIONS unit put him in good standing for a position with the police department's bomb squad.*

murky *(MURR-key), adjective*
Unclear, obscure, and unsettling.
> *I was afraid of what creatures might be hiding just below the surface of the MURKY river.*

muse *(MYOOZ), verb*
To meditate (about a topic). To *muse* over something is to consider it closely.
> *Phyllis MUSED over the advertising campaign for some days before finally approving it.*

mutable *(MYOO-tuh-bull), adjective*
Unstable and likely to change at a moment's notice.
> *Barb's fashion sense is completely MUTABLE. One day she's in polka dots, the next in stripes, the next in imitation zebra skin.*

myopia *(mye-OH-pee-uh), noun*
Inability to see close things clearly. Figuratively, to suffer from *myopia* is to lack foresight.
> *My feeling is that by turning down that project, Fenster showed once again that he suffers from MYOPIA when it comes to marketing new consumer products.*

myopic *(my-AHP-ick), adjective*
This technical term for nearsightedness has come to mean, more broadly, narrow-mindedness or short-sightedness in one's views.
> *Your MYOPIC views will win you few votes during the election, senator.*

myriad *(MEER-ee-ud), adjective*
Innumerable. To say there are *myriad* reasons to do something is to say there are too many to list.
> *Edward's responsibilities were MYRIAD, but his authority was almost nonexistent.*

N

nabob *(NAY-bob), noun*
A wealthy person who is accustomed to luxury. Originally, a *nabob* was a person who returned to Europe from India with great riches.
> *All the city's NABOBS, potentates, and intellectual stars showed up for Iris's party.*

nadir *(NAY-dur), noun*
The lowest point.
> *The NADIR of my writing career was probably that spell in Omaha when I wrote obituaries for the local newspaper.*

nanosecond *(nan-o-sek-und), noun*
One billionth of a second; an extremely short period of time.
> *It seemed the phone was on the hook for only a NANOSECOND before it rang again.*

napalm *(NAY-pom), noun*
A type of burning plastic used as a weapon in military conflicts. *Napalm* is disfiguring and excruciatingly painful.
> *The United States used NAPALM extensively during the Vietnam war.*

narcissistic *(nar-sis-SIS-tik), adjective*
Possessed by self-love. Someone whose egotism replaces (or seems to replace) attention to others can be said to be narcissistic.
> *Self-promotion is one thing; the NARCISSISTIC zeal with which Gerald asserts himself is quite another.*

narcolepsy *(NAR-ko-lep-see), noun*
The disorder of suddenly and unpredictably falling asleep. Someone who has *narcolepsy* is prone to unexpectedly succumb to the urge to sleep.
> *After learning he suffered from NARCOLEPSY, Brian realized how dangerous it would be for him to drive, and voluntarily returned his license to the Registry.*

narcoma *(nar-KO-muh), noun*
A hazy state between sleep and wakefulness reminiscent of or signalling use of narcotics. To be in a *narcoma* is to be in a partially concious state associated with drug use.
> *Because she had worked in a city emergency room for four years, Ellen knew that the boy had slipped into NARCOMA.*

narcotic *(nahr-KAH-tick), noun*
Something that produces a soothing—especially a mind-numbing—effect.
> *Her incessant bragging acted on me like a NARCOTIC.*

nascent *(NAY-sunt), adjective*
Emerging. *Nascent* refers to something's early stages of coming into existence.
> *The NASCENT republic had few if any established democratic traditions.*

natatorium *(nay-tuh-TOR-ee-um), noun*
An indoor swimming pool.
> *Although he had swum in hundreds of venues, Melvin still had a dream of competing in the world's largest NATATORIUM.*

natter *(NA-tuhr), verb*
To talk mindlessly and at length.
> *The old guy started NATTERING so much that I wished I hadn't stopped and asked him for directions.*

nautical *(NAW-tih-kul), adjective*
Of the sea, ships, or sailors.
> *Mr. Petty's den is decorated in a NAUTICAL motif featuring wallpaper with anchors, paintings of colonial ships, and an authentic ship's wheel hanging on the wall.*

ne plus ultra *(nay plooce OOL-truh), noun*
The highest possible embodiment (of something). *Ne plus ultra* is Latin for "Do not go beyond this point."
> *Many consider Oedipus Rex the drama's NE PLUS ULTRA.*

neanderthal *(knee-AND-er-thall), adjective or noun*
Capitalized, *Neanderthal* denotes an early human species, whose remains were first discovered in Germany's Neanderthal valley. As an adjective and with a lower-case "n," *neanderthal* is used negatively to describe someone with backward, outdated, old-fashioned attitudes and beliefs. The lower-case version also can serve as a noun.
> *Of course she was scared away by your NEANDERTHAL impulses, Stephen!*

nebulous *(NEB-yuh-luss), adjective*
Cloudy; vague.
> *Every time Claudia tried to ask Philip about his intentions or the future of their relationship, he gave a NEBULOUS reply and changed the subject.*

necessitate *(nuh-SESS-ih-tate), verb*
To make necessary, to obligate.
> *Spilling coffee on my shirt just before the interview NECESSITATED a quick run home to change clothes.*

necrology *(nek-ROL-uh-jee), noun*
A list of people who have recently died. A *necrology* can also be an obituary.
> *Benjamin scoured the long necrology for the name of his father, but it was not there.*

necromancy *(NEK-ruh-man-see), noun*
The supposed practice of gaining insight by means of communication with the dead. *Necromancy* can also mean "witchcraft."
> *NECROMANCY is still a part of many tribal rituals on the island.*

nefarious *(nih-FARE-ee-uss), adjective*
Openly evil; wicked.
> *The NEFARIOUS Darth Vader serves as the unforgettable villain of George Lucas's Star Wars.*

negate *(nih-GATE), verb*
To cause to be ineffectual; to deny.
> *I imagine that double hot fudge sundae I ate completely NEGATED the effects of my morning exercises.*

nelson (NEL-sun),
In wrestling, a kind of hold in which one places one's arm under the opponent's arm and applies pressure to the back of the opponent's neck.
> *When I got Frank in a full NELSON, I knew I would win the match.*

nemesis *(NEM-i-sis), noun*
An opponent motivated by revenge. A person's *nemesis* is one who will stop at nothing to "settle a score."
> *Things looked bleak: Harold's NEMESIS, Mike, was in charge of all hiring decisions.*

neolithic *(nee-oh-LITH-ik), adjective*
Of or pertaining to the latter part of the Stone Age, when ground stone weapons and tools first came into use. To dismiss something as *neolithic* is to say it is so unsophisticated as to belong to a much earlier era.
> *In these days of computers and word processors, many consider the old-fashioned manual typewriter positively NEOLITHIC.*

neologism *(nee-OL-uh-jiz-um), noun*
A newly coined term or word.
> *The computer revolution has spawned not only new technologies but a wealth of NEOLOGISMS, such as "download" and "system crash," that have quickly become part of our workday vocabulary.*

neophyte *(NEE-uh-fite), noun*

A recent convert. *Neophyte* often refers to someone whose newfound zeal is not balanced by experience.

> *Jane, a relative NEOPHYTE, found little warmth in her discussions with the other, more knowledgeable members of the group.*

nepotism *(NEP-uh-tiz-um), noun*

The practice of favoring relatives.

> *The company practiced shameless NEPOTISM, regularly passing up qualified applicants and hiring the underqualified sons, daughters, and cousins of board members.*

n'est-ce pas *(ness PAH), adverb*

From the French "Is it not so?"; "Correct?"

> *"Well, class," our French teacher said, "since you all spent the weekend studying, this test should be a breeze, N'EST-CE PAS?"*

nether *(NETH-ur), adjective*

Lower; removed. The *nether* regions of something are the parts that lie beneath or beyond the main part.

> *Dante takes the reader on a journey to the NETHER regions of hell.*

nettle *(NET-uhl), verb*

A nettle is a plant covered with stinging hairs. Thus, when used as a verb, *nettle* means to provoke, irritate, or annoy.

> *Lynn's irksome comments never fail to NETTLE me.*

neurology *(noo-ROL-uh-gee), noun*

The study of the nervous system and its diseases. A neurologist is a doctor whose specialty is *neurology*.

> *The Man Who Mistook His Wife for a Hat is a fascinating account of NEUROLOGICAL disorders written for the layman.*

nexus *(NEK-sus), noun*

A linkage or connection. A *nexus* can also be the means by which two or more things are connected

> *The stars in the cluster formed a NEXUS one could trace across the sky.*

niggardly *(NIG-urd-lee), adjective*

Stingy. *Niggardly* refers to an unwillingness to give, share, or spend.

> *The NIGGARDLY merchant turned the begging man away with an impatient wave of the hand.*

niggling *(NIG-ling), adjective*
Petty; annoying.
> *I could usually deal with my roommate's NIGGLING complaints about hairs in the sink and my forgetting to take out the trash, but I was in no mood for it today.*

nihilism *(NIE-uh-liz-im), noun*
The belief that life is meaningless.
> *A profound NIHILISM seems to have fallen over the poet during the last six months she spent in London; her letters to her mother indicate a severe depression.*

nimbus *(NIM-bus), noun*
A halo-like source of light above the head of a saint or spiritual figure.
> *The mosaic depicts Christ and his disciples with bright NIMBUSES.*

nirvana *(nir-VAW-nuh), noun*
A point or state of spiritual perfection. *Nirvana* has a number of theological definitions, but is usually understood to mean "a transcendent state beyond the concerns of existence."
> *Some of the monks had meditated and maintained complete silence for years in an attempt to achieve NIRVANA.*

nitid *(NIT-id), adjective*
Bright and lustrous.
> *After I changed back to more expensive dog food, my dog regained her NITID coat.*

noblesse oblige *(no-BLESS oh-BLEEZH), noun*
Benevolence befitting a person's dignity and/or possession of high birth. *Noblesse oblige* is from the French for "nobility obliges." The phrase usually refers to charitable actions or disposition toward those in classes perceived as low.
> *A sense of NOBLESSE OBLIGE, not desire for headlines, motivates the Beal family's admirable tradition of giving and volunteerism.*

nocturnal *(nok-TUR-nal), adjective*
Pertaining to night. Activities that occur only at night are *nocturnal*.
> *Owls are perhaps the best known species of NOCTURNAL birds.*

noggin *(NOG-in), noun*
A small drinking vessel; a mug.
> *Dinner at our favorite seaport restaurant always began with a generous helping of clam chowder served in old-fashioned ceramic NOGGINS.*

noisome (NOY-sum),
Ill-smelling and offensive; also, harmful.

> That NOISOME gang of unwashed hooligans you call your friends will bring you to nothing but trouble, Steve.

nolo contendere *(NO-lo kun-TEND-er-ee), noun*
In law, a plea that admits no guilt, but subjects the defendant to penalty. (Literally, "I am unwilling to contend.")

> Charged with income tax evasion, Vice-President Spiro Agnew pleaded NOLO CONTENDERE, to the perfect satisfaction of the Internal Revenue Service.

nom de guerre *(nom dub GARE), noun*
A name taken or bestowed during wartime. *Nom de guerre* is French for "wartime name."

> Fred's NOM DE GUERRE in the regiment was Rookie, and he did not like it.

nom de plume *(nom duh PLOOM), noun*
An author's pseudonym or pen name.

> The writer Samuel Langhorne Clemens is better known by his NOM DE PLUME, Mark Twain.

nomad *(NO-mad), noun*
One who roams from place to place, having no real roots or home.

> Ever since Grandma and Grandpa retired and sold their home, they've lived like NOMADS, traveling the country in a reconditioned Winnebago.

nomenclature *(NO-men-klat-cher), noun*
A system of names for purposes of organization. A *nomenclature* is a technical, professional, or artistic set or system of names in a given discipline.

> Harold had a good grasp of the fundamental principles of chemistry, but his knowledge of the NOMENCLATURE of chemical compounds was weak.

nominal *(NAHM-uh-null), adjective*
In name only; not in reality.

> Mr. Goldberg is only the NOMINAL head of the firm. Everyone knows his wife's the real brains of the outfit.

non sequitur *(non-SEK-wi-tur), noun, adjective*
Something that does not follow logically. A statement that has no basis in what has gone before is considered a *non sequitur*.

> The professor pointed out the many NON SEQUITURS contained in the pamphlet.

N

nonchalance *(NON-shu-lonce), noun*

The quality of being unconcerned with worldly cares. A cool, carefree person can be said to be *nonchalant.*

> *Astaire's NONCHALANCE was appealing to the audience of the time, which was on the whole weighed down with the many cares of the Depression.*

nondescript *(non-duh-SKRIPT), adjective*

Not having a particularly distinctive or interesting appearance; hard to describe.

> *With all the cars on the lot to choose from, Peggy went and picked a NONDESCRIPT grey sedan.*

nonentity *(non-EN-ti-tee), noun*

Something that does not exist. A *nonentity* is a vacuum or a purely imaginary thing. Nonentity is sometimes used insultingly to describe a person of little importance.

> *You may safely regard this clause of the contract as a NONENTITY; it is obsolete and completely unenforceable.*

nonfeasance *(non-FEEZ-unce), noun*

Failure to perform (a given duty). Someone who is bound to act in a certain way and does not is guilty of *nonfeasance.*

> *The failure of the passersby to aid the injured woman was a heartrending example of urban apathy and NONFEASANCE.*

nonillion *(no-NILL-yun), noun*

A very large number equal to 10,000,000,000,000,000,000,000,000,000,000.

> *My parents' claim that they had asked me to clean the garage one NONILLION times struck me as the sort of irresponsible exaggeration that relieved me of any obligation to do my chores.*

nonpareil *(non-puh-RELL), noun*

A person without parallel or equal. *Nonpareil* can also mean "a flat chocolate covered with colored sugar."

> *Frank is hardly the NONPAREIL as a mystery writer he makes himself out to be.*

nonpartisan *(non-PAR-tih-zun), adjective*

Not a member of a party (political group) or association; unbiased.

> *Although the commission was supposed to be NONPARTISAN, Martin knew for a fact that three of the members were dyed-in-the-wool Democrats who would never vote against the interests of their party.*

nonplussed *(non-PLUHST)*, *adjective*
Describes a state of bafflement or perplexity.

I stood there, NONPLUSSED and bleeding, after my previously tame dog bit my hand.

nosh *(NAHSH)*, *verb*
This Yiddish word for "nibble or gnaw" has come to mean just that: the process of nibbling or snacking on something.

Before we go to the movie, let's NOSH on some of these chips.

nostrum *(NAH-strum)*, *noun*
From the Latin meaning "ours," *nostrums* originally were patent medicines, purported to cure almost anything, sold by shady characters. At present, a *nostrum* is any kind of cure-all or panacea for social ills that, in practice, would probably not really work.

Even if it could be done, Alex, giving all the poor a thousand bucks would only be a NOSTRUM.

nota bene *(NOTE-ah BEN-eh)*, *noun*
A term used to draw attention to a particular point; Latin for "note well." (Sometimes rendered as "N.B.")

Applications will be accepted until the first of the month, provided, NOTA BENE, that they are accompanied by an income tax return filed within the last two years.

notoriety *(noe-tuh-RIE-uh-tee)*, *noun*
Fame; wide publicity (particularly for sensational reasons); also, having an unfavorable reputation.

The musical gained NOTORIETY as word spread that it featured bawdy songs and plenty of nudity.

nougat *(NOO-gut)*, *noun*
A type of candy containing nuts and honey.

The new candy bar contained an appealing mixture of NOUGAT, caramel, and milk chocolate.

Nouveau riche *(noo-voh REESH)*, *noun and adjective*
Someone recently wealthy. *Nouveau riche* is often used to describe those whose newfound wealth brings with it a tactless or overbearing attitude.

The escapades of the NOUVEAU RICHE are not the concern of this column.

novice *(NOV-iss), noun*
One who is new to a profession, trade, or sport; a beginner.
> *You shouldn't take too much pride in having checkmated me in twelve moves, Steve; I'm a NOVICE and you're a nationally rated player.*

noxious *(NOK-shuss), adjective*
Harmful; injurious. That which has a corrupting or debilitating influence is *noxious.*
> *The NOXIOUS weed soon took over the entire crop, which eventually failed.*

nuance *(NOO-ahnts), noun*
A subtle difference in expression, meaning, tone, etc.
> *The NUANCES of Brenda's expression alert me to her mood.*

nubile *(NOO-bile), adjective*
Sexually mature and/or prepared for marriage. *Nubile* is used almost exclusively in reference to young women; there is no exact parallel to describe young men.
> *Art looked at his "baby" daughter Marie and realized that she had somehow become a NUBILE young woman of eighteen.*

nugatory *(NOO-guh-toe-ree), adjective*
Worthless or in vain. That which is trifling or pointless is *nugatory.*
> *I'm afraid the edict of the High Commissioner has rendered your request to have the prisoner freed NUGATORY.*

nullify *(NULL-ih-fie), verb*
To make invalid; to render null.
> *Because the league NULLIFIED the disputed home run, the two teams had to play the ninth inning over again the following week.*

numerology *(noo-muh-ROL-uh-jee), noun*
The supposed practice of divining the future through analyzing the occult significance of numbers. *Numerology* is not the same as the science of mathematics.
> *Judy's interest in NUMEROLOGY is the latest in a series of mystic doings; she was very big on Tarot cards last week.*

numismatics *(noo-miz-MAT-iks), noun*
Coin or currency collecting. *Numismatics* can also include the collecting of paper money or medals.
> *I suppose my decision to put aside my newly minted Susan B. Anthony dollar coin marked my first foray into NUMISMATICS.*

doctrinaire
abstemious
levity hubris panacea
veracity cerebellum
criterion labyrinth
nonagenarian
meticulous zither

O

erbiage quondam
colloquial
vok palpable pagination
incipient salutary
vity redact fervent
beleaguered yawnful
elixir beneficent
moose pragmatism

O

obdurate *(AHB-dur-uht), adjective*
Stubborn and unyielding to an excessive degree.
> *I left the house after our argument, determined to be just as OBDURATE as Jane.*

obeisance *(oh-BAY-suhnts), noun*
A movement, such as a bow, that shows respect for someone else. Most of the time, this word is used negatively, to indicate that one believes someone is acting like a sycophant or toady.
> *The OBEISANCE Max shows Mr. Jenkins is just revolting.*

obfuscate *(OB-fuss-kate), verb*
To muddy or confuse an issue. Someone who *obfuscates* makes every effort to muddle facts important to someone else's judgment or decision.
> *The defense has put up with enough of these attempts to OBFUSCATE, Your Honor.*

obligatory *(uh-BLIG-uh-tore-ee), adjective*
Required as an obligation. To say a duty is *obligatory* is to say that one is bound by morality, law, or tradition to perform it.
> *The coaches, who hated each other bitterly, nevertheless exchanged the OBLIGATORY handshakes at the end of the game.*

oblique *(oh-BLEEK), adjective*
Angled; indirect. To make an *oblique* reference to something is to mention it glancingly, leaving the listener unclear as to the nature or context of the thing referred to.
> *The witness's description was too OBLIQUE to be of any use to the police.*

oblivion *(uh-BLIV-ee-un), noun*
The state of being beyond memory and utterly forgotten. To say something is in *oblivion* is to say it is lost to human recollection.
> *To Tim, the fact that his book was being allowed to go out of print meant that he as an author had been consigned to OBLIVION.*

oblivous *(uh-BLIV-ee-uss), adjective*
Not mindful. Someone who is *oblivious* displays little awareness of surroundings.
> *We warned Jan about the consequences of her actions, but she was OBLIVIOUS to us.*

obsequious *(ub-SEE-kwee-uss), adjective*
Compliant and servile to superiors. Someone who takes a fawning, submissive demeanor in order to curry favor with those in authority could be said to be *obsequious*.
> *You may consider the waiter's attentions well meant; I find him OBSEQUIOUS.*

obsolescence *(ob-suh-LESS-unce), noun*

The state or condition of becoming outdated. Planned *obsolescence* is the deliberate "underdesigning" of products or systems; the items are meant to wear out sooner than they might in order to make way for new items to fulfill essentially the same function.

> *The farm machinery's OBSOLESCENCE was now hard for even Grandpa to deny.*

obsolete *(ob-suh-LEET), adjective*

No longer useful or in use; unnecessary.

> *The room-sized computers of the sixties have long since been rendered OBSOLETE by the advent of desktop and even laptop equivalents.*

obstinate *(OB-sti-nut), adjective*

Unyielding. Someone who holds firmly to an opinion, attitude, or approach despite obstacles could be said to be *obstinate*.

> *Melvin, OBSTINATE to the end, refused to talk to Mr. Smith about settling the case out of court.*

obstreperous *(ob-STREP-er-us), adjective*

Uncontrollably aggressive; defiant, boisterous.

> *Before announcing the plan for massive layoffs to his workers, the boss hired an extra security force to prevent certain OBSTREPEROUS persons from inciting a riot.*

obtain *(ub-TANE), verb*

To get or acquire.

> *With his green card set to expire in a few months, Olaf searched for an American woman who could marry him so that he could OBTAIN citizenship.*

obtuse *(ob-TOOS), adjective*

Not sharp. *Obtuse* is most often used to describe a person whose powers of intellect or observation are poor.

> *Perhaps I'm being OBTUSE, but I'd like you to explain that last point again for me.*

obviate *(OB-vee-ate), verb*

To make unnecessary. To *obviate* something is to avoid it by acting in anticipation.

> *The research department provided sufficient data; the problem was OBVIATED before it reached crisis proportions.*

occlude *(oh-KLOOD), verb*

To obstruct. Something that is closed or blocked off is *occluded*.

> *Mr. Ryan, who had a history of heart problems, died that night of a coronary occlusion.*

O

ocher *(OAK-ur), noun*
A yellow or reddish-brown clay; the color typical of this clay.
> *The shelves of the pottery shop were filled with dozens of OCHER vessels of varying sizes.*

ochlophobia *(ok-luh-FO-be-uh), noun*
An illogical fear or dread of crowds.
> *Betty never realized she suffered from OCHLOPHOBIA until she moved to the city, where she had great difficulty walking to and from work during rush hour.*

octave *(OK-tuv), noun*
In Western music, a tone eight tones above or below another tone.
> *The famous opera singer had a vocal range of three OCTAVES.*

octogenarean *(ok-tuh-juh-NARE-ee-un), noun*
A person in his or her eighties. An *octogenarean* is one who is between eighty and eighty-nine years old.
> *Mrs. Reardon, an OCTOGENAREAN, attributes her longevity to drinking a glass of fruit juice every mornig.*

odious *(OH-dee-us), adjective*
Abhorrent. Something that stirs disgust or hatred could be said to be *odious*.
> *Such ODIOUS sentiments of racial prejudice have no place in this company.*

odyssey *(ODD-uh-see), noun*
A long journey that entails danger or adventure. *Odyssey* derives from Homer's poem *The Odyssey*, which describes such a journey undertaken by the character Odysseus.
> *The film Easy Rider recounts the ODYSSEY of two counterculture motorcyclists in search of America.*

oenophile *(EE-nuh-file), noun*
A wine connoisseur.
> *Len, a lifelong OENOPHILE, shuddered as I produced a bottle of Ripple to accompany our dinner of fish sticks and macaroni and cheese.*

oeuvre *(OO-vruh), noun*
From the French meaning "work," an *oeuvre* is an artist's, writer's, or composer's body of work, treated as a whole.
> *The film was not appreciated for many years because it seemed so separate from the director's usual OEUVRE.*

off-color *(off-KUH-lur), adjective*
Questionable in taste or propriety; distasteful.

The comedienne was talented, but her frequent use of OFF-COLOR remarks kept her from getting bookings on network television shows.

officious *(uh-FISH-uss), adjective*
Prone to offering one's services and/or insight, even when they are not requested or appropriate. Someone who is *officious* is meddlesome and overbearing.

Tom was certainly a generous host, but his OFFICIOUS nature was hard for me to live with after a week or two.

off-the-record *(off-the-REK-erd), adjective*
Not intended for publication.

Senator Power's frank admission that he had never read the United States Constitution was probably intended as an OFF-THE-RECORD comment.

ogle *(OH-gul), verb*
To watch intently; to gaze at lasciviously.

Bryan's idea of an afternoon well spent was lounging around the beach OGLING women twenty years too young for him.

ogre *(O-gur), verb*
A legendary man-eating monster; a brute or wicked person.

As a child, Vern believed that a huge OGRE lived in his bedroom closet.

olfactory *(ol-FAK-tuh-ree), noun*
Relating to the sense of smell.

For me, walking past the bakery every morning on the way to school was an OLFACTORY delight.

oligarchy *(OLL-ih-gark-ee), noun*
Government by an elite few.

My father's opinion was that since the mid-Sixties the country had been operating under the pretense of democracy, and was in fact an OLIGARCHY.

ombudsman *(AHM-buds-muhn), noun*
A person who acts as a mediator between the public and an agency, university, or office, in order to resolve disputes.

After going around and around with discrepancies in my tuition bill, the OMBUDSMAN finally got involved.

O

ominous (OM-ih-nuss), *adjective*

Foreboding or menacing. Something that is *ominous* foretells the possibility of future harm or evil.

> *The day began with sunny weather, but by 2 p.m. an OMINOUS sky threatened to ruin our outing.*

omnibus (OHM-nih-bus), *noun*

Something that covers many areas or subjects; also, a bus.

> *The OMNIBUS law passed shortly after the publication of Sinclair's The Jungle was meant to assure consumers that blatant violations of basic health and quality standards would never again be seen in the food industry.*

omnidirectional (om-nee-duh-REK-shun-ul), *adjective*

Capable of receiving or transmitting from every direction.

> *Agent Warren hid a tiny OMNIDIRECTIONAL microphone in the suspected drug smuggler's hotel room.*

omnipresent (ahm-nuh-PREZ-ent), *adjective*

Occurring, or seeming to occur, everywhere at once.

> *As the day awoke, the sound of early birds was OMNIPRESENT.*

omniscient (om-NISS-see-unt), *adjective*

All-knowing. *Omniscient* refers to having absolute knowledge.

> *Contrary to what you may have heard, Professor Powers is not OMNISCIENT; he still has a thing or two to learn about chairing the biology department.*

omnivorous (om-NIV-er-uss), *adjective*

Accustomed to eating both animal and vegetable food items. *Omnivorous* (derived from the Latin for ""eating everything") can also mean "voracious," in the sense of taking all that is offered.

> *The Cantonese, I am told, are OMNIVOROUS, and it is said that the traveler is best advised not to inquire too closely into exactly what he is eating.*

oncology (on-KOL-uh-jee),

The study of tumors.

> *Abbey was worried when she found a lump in her breast, but the ONCOLOGY specialist told her it was a benign cyst.*

onerous (OWE-nur-uss), *adjective*

Troublesome and burdensome. Something that entails heavy a obligation might be considered *onerous*.

> *This contract—a thoroughly one-sided agreement—is perhaps the most ONEROUS document I have ever seen.*

onomatopoeia *(on-uh-mot-uh-PEE-uh), noun*
The development of a word whose pronunciation imitates its main reference. The words "splat" and "buzz," for instance, are examples of *onomatopoeia*.

> *Over the centuries, the process of ONOMATOPOEIA has become an accepted part of the English language.*

ontogeny *(on-TAHJ-uh-nee), noun*
The cycle of development of an organism.

> *The chapter Anne was having trouble with described the ONTOGENY of the common housefly in minute detail, with particular emphasis on the maggot stage.*

ontology *(on-TALL-uh-gee), noun*
Study of the nature of being and existence. The adjective form is *ontological*.

> *For several minutes, we had a lively conversation about the ONTOLOGY of the deep-fried Twinkie.*

onus *(OWN-us), noun*
The burden of performing a task or duty. To say that the *onus* is on a person to do something is to say that he is responsible for doing it.

> *The ONUS of completing this long-delayed project now falls to you.*

opacity *(oh-PASS-ih-tee), adjective*
Degree of imperviousness to light; level of opaqueness.

> *The paper was of a very low OPACITY, nearly transparent.*

opaque *(oh-PAKE), adjective*
Impenetrable to light. That which does not allow light to pass through is *opaque*.

> *Karl was unable to make out exactly what was happening behind the OPAQUE screen that had been set in front of him.*

operatic *(op-uh-RAT-ik), adjective*
Relating to or reminiscent of the opera; overly dramatic or difficult to believe.

> *I'm afraid my family's conflict style tends to be a little OPERATIC at times.*

operose *(OP-uh-roass), adjective*
Hard-working and industrious.

> *Jack's OPEROSE attention to detail is sure to send him quickly up the corporate ladder.*

ophidian *(oh-FIDD-ee-un), adjective*
Describes snakes or something snake-like. More broadly, it can be used as a "nice" way to call someone dishonest or mean-spirited.

> *The lawyer's OPHIDIAN eyes made me second-guess myself with every question he asked.*

opiate *(OPE-ee-ut), noun*

An addictive narcotic, especially one with numbing or sleep-inducing qualities.

Marx's well-known remark that religion is the OPIATE of the people helped make many church groups implacable enemies of Communism.

opine *(oh-PINE), verb*

To make one's opinion known. To *opine* is to state one's view.

Grant OPINED that be could take Vicksburg if the President would show patience in the undertaking.

opprobrium *(uh-PRO-bree-um), noun*

Infamy. *Opprobrium* is disgrace resulting from shameful action.

Quentin knew that dropping out of school would bring only OPPROBRIUM from his father.

optimal *(OP-tih-mul), adjective*

Best; favored. The *optimal* time for something is the best possible time.

As you know, we were not working in OPTIMAL conditions: it was snowing heavily and the wind was blowing at over 40 m.p.h.

opulent *(OP-yoo-lent), adjective*

Rich. Something characterized by wealth or affluence (an extravagant dinner party, for instance) could be considered *opulent*.

Without the money from Powers, Hans knew be would be unable to maintain his OPULENT lifestyle.

opus *(OPE-us), noun*

A major work (of art or literature). Opera is derived from one of the plural forms of *opus*. (In English, opuses is the accepted plural.)

Although be bad been working on it for over a year and a half the composer was less than halfway done with his OPUS.

oracle *(OR-uh-kul)t noun*

A means by which prophetic wisdom is imparted. *Oracle* is sometimes used figuratively to describe someone who is seen as offering completely dependable counsel or advice.

After Appomatox, Grant's words seemed (much to his surprise) to be regarded as having issued from an ORACLE.

oracular *(or-AK-yuh-lur), adjective*

Resembling an oracle; said in a solemn or cryptic manner.

My boss, Mr. Twombey, always issued his pronouncements in a gloomy, ORACULAR fashion that left us wondering whether something horrible was about to happen.

orator *(ORE-uh-tur), noun*
A gifted and persuasive professional public speaker.
> *Don's encyclopedic knowledge of the topic, combined with his ability as an ORATOR, made him the odds-on favorite to win the debate.*

ordnance *(ORD-nunce), noun*
Weapons; military supplies.
> *Though the government denied there would be a confrontation with the rebels, the reports of dramatically increased ORDNANCE shipments led the press to believe otherwise.*

orgiastic *(ore-jee-ASS-tick), adjective*
Reminiscent of or pertaining to an orgy; likely to elicit extremely intense emotions.
> *When the doors opened the shoppers streamed into the store in an ORGIASTIC frenzy, hurrying to find the sale's best bargains.*

orifice *(ORE-ih-fiss), noun*
An opening in the body.
> *The ORIFICE Prince Hamlet makes the Player King select as the receptacle for poison, his victim's ear, recalls the method Claudius used in killing Hamlet's father.*

origami *(or-ih-GAH-mee), noun*
The Japanese art of cutting and folding paper.
> *After studying ORIGAMI in her craft class, Aunt Janice decided to decorate her entire Christmas tree with miniature paper figures.*

ornate *(or-NATE), adjective*
Overwrought or decorated elaborately. That which is flashy or extravagantly ornamented is *ornate*.
> *The furniture in the living room was as ORNATE as it was uncomfortable.*

ornery *(ORE-nuh-ree), adjective*
Stubborn or unyielding; inclined toward obstinate behavior.
> *Grandma insists that Grandpa was an easygoing fellow in his youth, but since their move from the country he has become quite ORNERY.*

ornithology *(or-nih-THAHL-uh-jee), noun*
The study of birds.
> *Her lifelong love of birds led Stella to seek a degree in ORNITHOLOGY.*

orotund *(OR-uh-tund), adjective*
(Of the voice or speech) possessing a full, big sound; sonorous; (of a style of speaking) overbearing or pretentious.
> *The senator delivered an impassioned, if OROTUND, defense of the party's trade policy.*

Orwellian *(or-WELL-ee-un), adjective*
Resembling the qualities or subject matter of the writing of George Orwell, particularly the totalitarian future world of his book 1984.

My father saw the surveillance cameras in suburban supermarkets as the first sign of an ORWELLIAN clampdown on civil liberties.

oscillate *(OSS-ih-late), verb*
To sway back and forth; vacillate.

My two-year-old nephew was mesmerized by the fishtank, with its colorful fish, OSCILLATING plants, and soft lighting.

osmosis *(oss-MOE-sis), noun*
Gradual absorption, assimilation.

Jerry rested his head on the textbook and closed his eyes, as if hoping to absorb the information in it by OSMOSIS.

ossify *(OSS-ih-fye), verb*
To harden or become bonelike. Literally, *ossify* means "to change into a bone," but it is often used to describe a rigidity of outlook or opinion.

The creative team's concepts, which had originally seemed very promising, had OSSIFIED into a conventional set of ideas that no one found exciting.

ostensibly *(uh-STEN-sib-lee), adverb*
Seemingly; as represented. A reason *ostensibly* given for taking an action is the reason that, to all intents and purposes, one would associate with motivating the act.

He was OSTENSIBLY visiting the city on business; no one was aware of his espionage activities,

ostentatious *(oss-ten-TAY-shuss), adjective*
Showy. Someone who makes a boastful display, or makes constant attempts to show off talents or possessions, could be said to be *ostentatious*.

You shouldn't take the Rolls to the party; it will be seen as OSTENTATIOUS.

osteoporosis *(oss-tee-oh-puh-ROE-sis), noun*
A condition of fragile, brittle bones, particularly common in women of advanced age.

The doctor advised all of his female patients over fifty to make sure they took in plenty of calcium as a precaution against OSTEOPOROSIS.

ostracize *(OSS-truh-size), verb*
To exclude or banish. To *ostracize* someone is to exclude him from a social circle.

Desmond was OSTRACIZED from the group after the negative publicity his mother received.

otiose *(OH-she-oass), adjective*

Useless, ineffective, or idle due to laziness.

> *You're never going to lose weight, Janine, if you don't change your OTIOSE lifestlye.*

outré *(oo-TRAY), adjective*

From the French meaning "to pass beyond," *outré* describes someone or something radically unconventional or outside the limits of what most consider proper.

> *It's not OUTRÉ to go to a church picnic wearing an expletive-covered T-shirt, Sally. It's just rude!*

overarching *(oh-ver-ARCH-ing), adjective*

Central or principally important.

> *I quickly ascertained that compassion was not the OVERARCHING reason for her line of questioning.*

overweening *(OH-ver-WEEN-ing), adjective*

Overconfident, proud, arrogant.

> *Even after losing the race, the athlete retained her OVERWEENING manner.*

owlish *(OW-lish), adjective*

Describes someone who looks like an owl in that he or she has a wise, solemn appearance. In addition, the word often is used to describe someone who wears thick glasses.

> *I got contacts because I was sick of people making jokes about my OWLISH appearance.*

oxymoron *(ahk-see-MORE-on), noun*

A phrase in which contradictory or incongruous terms are used together, as in the phrase "poor little rich kid."

> *When Ted said the term "military intelligence" always struck him as an OXYMORON, he meant it as a joke, but his cousin, a lifelong army officer, took grave offense.*

P

pacify *(PASS-ih-fie), verb*

To bring to a point of peace; to dissuade from anger or hostility. Someone who eases tensions or resolves conflicts *pacifies* a situation.

> *Her suggestion that she offer a written apology to the offended client seemed to PACIFY Mr. Peters.*

pact *(pakt), noun*

An agreement or promise.

> *When they were each ten years old, Louise and Barbara made a solemn PACT to grow up together, attend the same college, work for the same company, and live in the same house.*

pagan *(PAY-gun), adjective or noun*

Someone who is not aligned with the world's major religions or a description of someone who does not belong to these major religions. Often, the word suggests someone who is hedonistic or irreligious.

> *Jean is forever telling her friends that being a PAGAN does not mean that she worships Satan.*

pagination *(paj-ih-NAY-shun), noun*

The numbers by which one marks the pages in a book. *Pagination* also refers to the sequence and arrangement of pages in a book.

> *The word processor PAGINATED Jim's document flawlessly the first time.*

palatable *(PAL-uh-tuh-bull), adjective*

Agreeable in taste. *Palatable* can also mean "acceptable."

> *You have two options, Mr. Mayor, neither very PALATABLE.*

palatial *(puh-LAY-shul), adjective*

Having the grand, luxurious characteristics of a palace; resembling a palace.

> *Mr. Laramie offered to hold the reception at his PALATIAL seaside mansion, but the social committee opted for a hotel ballroom in the city.*

palaver *(puh-LAV-er), noun*

A parley or conference. *Palaver* can also refer to charming but insubstantial talk meant to persuade or cajole.

> *Don't be taken in by Frank's PALAVER; be is not the agent for you.*

palindrome *(PAL-in-drome), noun*

A word or sentence (such as *pop* or *Not so, Boston*) that reads the same forward and backward.

> *James's dogged attempt to write a novel consisting solely of a single sixty-thousand-word PALINDROME led his relatives to wonder whether his best days as a writer of fiction were behind him.*

palisade: *(pal-ih-SADE), noun*
A defensive barrier or fence comprising a row of tall stakes driven into the ground; also, a line of steep cliffs along a river.

> *As we drove along the PALISADES of the river gorge, my wife and I lamented that we had forgotten to bring our camera.*

pallid *(PAL-id), adjective*
Wan, pale; lacking bright, deep color.

> *Frazier's PALLID complexion and inability to bear even the slightest noise led me to conclude that he was hung over.*

palpable *(PALP-uh-bull), adjective*
Touchable or able to be perceived. That which is *palpable* is tangible or undeniably present.

> *A PALPABLE sense of excitement filled the air of the city before the big game.*

palpitate *(PAL-pih-tate), verb*
To flutter; to beat more rapidly than usual.

> *Mel's heart PALPITATED wildly at the prospect of a date with Irma.*

paltry *(PAHL-tree), adjective*
Trivial; insignificant; worthless.

> *The PALTRY sum found in the cash register made us regret having picked this store for our first robbery.*

panacea *(pan-uh-SEE-uh), noun*
A cure-all; something with the ability to cure any illness or remedy any disorder.

> *According to my eighty-four-year-old grandfather, chocolate is the PANACEA to any problem life may throw at you.*

panache *(puh-NASH), noun*
A distinctive flair or style; a flamboyant manner.

> *Rosamund was swept away by the charming stranger's PANACHE—he seemed so dashing and romantic.*

pandemic *(pan-DEM-ik), adjective*
Widespread. Something that is general, common, or all-encompassing could be said to be *pandemic*.

> *We must begin to appeal not to universal fears, but to PANDEMIC human values.*

pandemonium *(pan-duh-MOAN-ee-um), noun*
Chaos. *Pandemonium* refers to wild, uproarious, and noisy tumult.

> *PANDEMONIUM broke out in the streets of the city after the local team won the pennant.*

P

pander *(PAN-der), verb and noun*

To appeal to the worst in someone. Literally, a *pander* is a pimp.

> *Despite accusations that he was PANDERING to the voters, the candidate insisted on repeatedly raising the issue of his opponent's extramarital affairs.*

panegyric *(pan-uh-JEER-ick), noun*

Formal, elaborate praise.

> *After Coach Henry retired, her former athletes filled the local paper with PANEGYRICS concerning her character and accomplishments.*

panjandrum *(pan-JAN-drum), noun*

An important person; a bigwig.

> *I was able to obtain a list of local business PANJANDRUMS to solicit for investment funds.*

panorama *(pan-uh-RAM-uh), noun*

An extensive, unobstructed view of a wide area.

> *Despite my lifelong aversion to flying, I couldn't help admiring the breathtaking PANORAMA of San Francisco below me.*

pantheism *(PAN-thee-iz-um), noun*

A doctrine that espouses God's manifestation in all things. *Pantheism* tends to identify Deity with the natural world. The word derives from the Greek roots for "all" and "God."

> *It is fair to say that although she had no formal religious upbringing Edith tended toward the PANTHEISM she associated with certain Native American religious rites.*

pantomime *(PAN-tuh-mime), verb*

The conveyance of ideas, words, emotions, or stories without the use of words.

> *My attempt to describe the accident in PANTOMIME to the villagers I encountered was pathetic; I bitterly regretted my decision not to study French before our trip.*

papal *(PAY-pull), adjective*

Of or pertaining to the pope. A *papal* decree is one issued by the pope.

> *The actor was unable to obtain a PAPAL audience, although he did meet with an archbishop while visiting the Vatican.*

parable *(PARE-uh-bull), noun*

A brief allegory or story meant to highlight an essential truth.

> *Jesus' PARABLE of the Prodigal Son is perhaps the most inspiring passage in the New Testament.*

parasitic *(pair-uh-SIT-ick), adjective*
Describes something or—more often—someone who acts like a parasite and lives off of another while doing little if anything useful.

> *My PARASITIC brother-in-law said he was just going to stay with us until he got back on his feet, but he's been sitting around on our couch for nearly a month now!*

paradigm *(PARE-uh-dime), noun*
An example. A *paradigm* is an ideal instance or a pattern worthy of study.

> *There have been a number of presidencies well suited to times of national crisis, but Lincoln's is the PARADIGM.*

paradox *(PAIR-uh-doks), noun*
A seemingly self-contradictory statement that expresses a valid idea or potentially true statement. *Paradox* can also mean "a conclusion that, while reached by conventional logical methods, nevertheless cancels itself out."

> *Before announcing the test grades, Mrs. Miller reminded her students of the PARADOX that a teacher often must be cruel in order to be kind.*

paraffin *(PARE-uh-finn), noun*
A white wax-like material used in the production of candles and wax paper.

> *So many customers had ordered Betty's homemade Christmas candles that she had to send her son Wally out to buy more PARAFFIN.*

paragon *(PARE-uh-gone), noun*
A peerless model or pattern of perfection. A *paragon*, unlike a *paradigm* (above) is an absolute—and often a hypothetical—standard.

> *Even if we could live our lives in accordance with the PARAGONS of right living, would we not still experience conflict and misunderstanding with others?*

paralysis *(puh-RAL-ih-siss), noun*
Loss or damage of movement ability; the loss of feeling in a part of the body due to disease or injury. *Paralysis* is used figuratively to refer to the inability of a person or institution to take action in a given situation.

> *Lacking firm direction from its founder, the company soon reached a state of PARALYSIS.*

parameter *(puh-RAM-uh-ter), noun*
Limit or boundary. *Parameter* also has a technical meaning within the field of statistics, but this is not in common use.

> *Within these broad PARAMETERS, you are free to act as you see fit.*

paramount *(PARE-uh-mount), adjective*
Supreme; superior; excellent
> *It is of PARAMOUNT importance that we complete this project on time.*

paramour *(PARE-uh-more), noun*
An illicit lover.
> *Although the women in her circle made high-minded speeches about her morality, Mrs. Able knew full well that most of them had had a PARAMOUR at one time or another.*

paraphernalia *(pare-uh-fur-NALE-ee-uh), noun*
One's possessions; accessory items relating to a particular profession, hobby, or activity.
> *The abundance of drug PARAPHERNALIA found in his hotel room did not do much to support the rock star's claim that he abstained from all intoxicating substances on religious grounds.*

paraphrase *(PARE-uh-frase), verb*
To restate in different words. Also, as a noun: an instance of such restating.
> *To call this work a new translation of the original Greek texts is an overstatement; it is a capable, but by no means groundbreaking, PARAPHRASE of existing English editions.*

parenthetical *(par-un-THET-ih-kul) adjective*
Contained within parentheses. Figuratively, something that qualifies or explains in a manner setting it off from a main idea is *parenthetical.*
> *I should add, as a PARENTHETICAL note, that I am donating all monies raised from these efforts to charity.*

pariah *(puh-RIE-uh), noun*
An outcast; one who is shunned, avoided, or despised.
> *After his firing, Milton had the nerve to show up unannounced at the company picnic, then seemed surprised when he was treated as a PARIAH.*

parity *(PAIR-ih-tee), noun*
Equality in terms of amount, status, position, etc.
> *Wait, wait, wait. Five for you and one for me is far from PARITY, my friend!*

parlance *(PAR-lunce), noun*
A way of speaking. Something that is in common *parlance* is familiar to most speakers.
> *The special PARLANCE of the construction workers was difficult for Mort to decipher.*

parlay *(PAHR-lay), verb*
To take something—such as talent or a small amount of money—and attempt to use it to gain great fortune or success.

> *Jackson PARLAYED a talent for poker into a lucrative career.*

parochial *(puh-ROE-key-uhl), adjective*
Limited or narrow in scope, outlook, or ideas. This meaning has become more dominant than the word's original meaning, which describes something pertaining to a parish, such as a *parochial* school.

> *My grandfather's PAROCHIAL views about "men's superiority" are not likely to change.*

parody *(PARE-uh-dee), noun*
A satirically humorous imitation or mocking interpretation of a well known work, person, or institution.

> *"Life in Hell" is an irreverent PARODY of parents, school, and the working world.*

paroxysm *(PARE-uk-siz-um), noun*
An outburst. A *paroxysm* is a sudden action or an incidence reminiscent of something explosive.

> *Joan broke out in PAROXYSMS of laughter at Pete's joke.*

parse *(PAHRSS), verb*
To break a sentence down into its component parts. In recent years, the word also has come to mean analyzing, or breaking down, anything.

> *I spent my time after our argument PARSING every cutting remark she had made.*

parsimonious *(par-suh-MOAN-ee-uss), adjective*
Stingy. Someone who is exceptionally frugal or thrifty could be considered *parsimonious*.

> *The old man's PARSIMONIOUS ways were legend: it is said that in a lifetime of restaurant dining, he never once picked up a check.*

partake *(par-TAKE), verb*
To participate and share in.

> *Your offer is kind, but I'm under strict doctor's orders not to PARTAKE of any alcoholic beverage.*

partisan *(PAR-tih-zun), adjective*
Showing a marked inclination or bias. Also, as a noun: one who is partial to a particular side or view.

> *As a Democrat, I realize that my PARTISAN role in opposing the governor's policies may cause some of the Republicans in this body to doubt my truthfulness in this matter.*

parvenu *(PAR-vuh-new), noun*
From the French meaning "upstart," a *parvenu* is someone who has recently gained wealth, prestige, or an important position but has not yet figured out how to act appropriately in that new position.

> *The Clampett family, of classic television's Beverly Hillbillies, is a great example of a PARVENU clan.*

passé *(pass-SAY), adjective*
No longer fashionable or current.

> *Marge's insistence that platform shoes were PASSÉ led me to believe that she hadn't been keeping up with fashion trends.*

passim *(PASS-im), noun*
A word used to indicate that a given source or element is used frequently throughout a written work.

> *References to a fictitious writer named Kilgore Trout appear PASSIM in a number of Kurt Vonnegut's novels.*

pastiche *(pah-STEESH), noun*
A haphazard collection of items from various sources. Also, a piece of music, writing, or art made up mostly of material taken from existing sources.

> *Some folks consider hip-hop music nothing but mindless PASTICHE, but I heartily disagree.*

pastoral *(PAS-tur-ul), adjective*
Pertaining to life in the country. *Pastoral* also has religious connotations: a *pastoral* message is one to the clergy or people in a region from a bishop.

> *To many critics, the novel's PASTORAL setting jarred against its themes of urban angst.*

pathos *(PAY-thos), noun*
A quality arousing or evoking pity or sorrow. To employ *pathos* is to act in a way meant to elicit tender sympathy from an observer.

> *Chaplin's development of pathos as a component of film comedy was one of his most significant achievements.*

patina *(puh-TEE-nuh), noun*
A film or sheen that occurs naturally on an aged surface.

> *In the antebellum mansion, I thought about the generations of hands that had left a PATINA on the banisters.*

patois *(PAT-wah), noun*
From the French meaning "clumsy speech," *patois* refers either to rural speech or to jargon . . . basically any language that deviates from standard usage.

I've given up trying to follow the PATOIS of teenagers, the teacher complained.

patriarchy *(PAY-tree-ark-ee), noun*
A group ruled by a patriarch; an organization or clan in which lines of descent and inheritance are traced through the male.

Martha accused her father of running a PATRIARCHY, arguing that she deserved to take on the leadership of the company far more than her younger brother.

patrimony *(PAT-rih-mo-nee), noun*
Heritage or legacy. Someone's *patrimony* can be either a financial inheritance or an ancestral heritage. (A *patrimony* can also be a church endowment.)

The will outlined PATRIMONY payments totaling over one million dollars.

patronize *(PAY-truh-nize), verb*
This word CAN mean simply to give a business your patronage, but "patronize" usually has a negative meaning, suggesting that one is being condescending toward another.

Just because I didn't graduate from college doesn't mean you can PATRONIZE me whenever we try to have an intellectual discussion!

patsy *(PAT-see), noun*
Someone who is set up to take the blame of a crime or wrongdoing; one who is framed.

Although conspiracy theorists have seized on Lee Oswald's description of himself as a PATSY, other observers remain unconvinced that he acted as part of an organized plot to kill President Kennedy.

paucity *(PAW-si-tee), noun*
Smallness of number. A *paucity* of something is a shortage or lack of it.

We were forced to head back down the mountain due to a PAUCITY of supplies.

pavlovian *(pav-LOW-vee-uhn), adjective*
Russian physiologist Ivan Pavlov pioneered research in conditioned responses. For example, he would give dogs food immediately after ringing a bell, and before long, the dogs would salivate just by hearing the bell . . . even if no food was given to them. Today, *pavlovian* describes any kind of conditioned response.

Roger always has this sort-of PAVLOVIAN response whenever he hears Julie's voice. He immediately starts to sweat and look flushed. At this rate, he's never going to ask her out!

peccadillo *(pek-uh-DILL-oh), noun*

A minor fault. *Pecadillo* comes from the Italian for "little sin."

> *Jane knew her PECCADILLO would be overlooked, but she could not put it out of her mind.*

peculate *(PECK-you-late), verb*

To steal something, such as public funds, that has been entrusted to one's care.

> *The city manager lost his job and was arrested after PECULATING funds set aside for employee retirement.*

pecuniary *(pi-KYOO-nee-air-ee), adjective*

Of or pertaining to money. That which consists of or concerns money is *pecuniary*.

> *Uncle Walter decided to stay with us for a few months owing, as he put it, to "PECUNIARY difficulties."*

pedagogue *(PED-uh-gog), noun*

An educator or schoolteacher. A *pedagogue* is a person who instructs.

> *Mr. Harper, a stern PEDAGOGUE, would not tolerate idle chatter in his class.*

pedant *(PED-unt) noun*

A person who displays learning inappropriately or excessively; also, someone who focuses too narrowly on rules and minor details.

> *Don't get Roland started on Shakespearean tragedy; he's a shameless PEDANT who'll dominate an entire lunch hour's discussion with observations on the time problem in Othello.*

pedantic *(puh-DAN-tik), adjective*

Intellectually showy or overblown. A pedant is a person who makes a great display of knowledge; to be *pedantic* is to act in this way. *Pedantic* can also mean "overly concerned with formal rules."

> *I found James's PEDANTIC manner quite condescending.*

pedestrian *(puh-DESS-tree-uhn), adjective*

Lacking in originality or vitality. The word also can be used to describe someone who travels on foot.

> *If you really want to advance in this company, you're going to have to come up with something better than the PEDESTRIAN ideas we've already tried and rejected.*

peerage *(PEER-ihj), noun*

Countries, empires, kingdoms, etc. considered friendly toward another empire or country.

> *The nation's PEERAGE began to shift after it launched covert attacks against formerly friendly countries.*

peerless *(PEER-luss), adjective*
Without peer; above others with regard to ability or quality; beyond compare.

> *Mrs. Reilly's PEERLESS skills as a mediator soon earned her a special position of respect on the school board.*

pejorative *(puh-JORE-uh-tiv), adjective*
Disparaging. That which downgrades or defames (usually a term or description) is *pejorative.*

> *When I said Lynn was a typical Massachusetts driver, I didn't mean that as a PEJORATIVE remark.*

pellucid *(puh-LOOSE-id), adjective*
Objects or meanings clear to the point of transparency.

> *I'll read anything by that author because her PELLUCID prose can make me interested in any subject.*

penal *(PEE-nul), adjective*
Related to or pertaining to punishment or imprisonment; having to do with a prison system.

> *President Clinton once remarked that the White House, in his view, represented the crown jewel of the federal PENAL system.*

penchant *(PEN-chunt), noun*
A liking or inclination.

> *Over dinner, Vicky, who had a PENCHANT for speaking her mind no matter what, asked the congressman what he thought his chances were of being imprisoned as a result of his recent indictment for embezzlement.*

penitent *(PEN-ih-tunt) verb*
Feeling guilty or remorseful for wrongdoing. As a noun: a person who is *penitent.*

> *Aaron made a token effort to apologize for his rude behavior, but it was evident to us all that he was not at all PENITENT.*

pensive *(PEN-siv), adjective*
Thoughtful; having wistful or dreamy thoughts.

> *My girlfriend was ready for a riotous night on the town, but I was feeling, PENSIVE, so we ended up going to a cafe and talking well into the night.*

penultimate *(pen-UL-ti-mut), adjective*
Next-to-last. *Penultimate* is often thought to mean "final," but it does not.

> *The book's PENULTIMATE chapter gave no hint of the surprise ending the novel had in store.*

penurious *(peh-NOOR-ee-uss), adjective*
Miserly. *Penurious* can also mean "lacking in means or extremely poor."
> *Joan, raised in comfortable surroundings, was not cut out for such a PENURIOUS lifestyle.*

penury *(PEN-you-ree), noun*
Extreme poverty.
> *Not many of us would be willing to exchange our lot in life for the simple life of PENURY taken on by these monks.*

peony *(PEE-uh-nee), noun*
A colorful plant bearing large petals; the state flower of Indiana.
> *The florist assembled a lovely arrangement of PEONIES for Aunt Irene.*

perambulate *(puh-RAM-byuh-late), verb*
To walk around. To *perambulate* is to stroll or saunter.
> *The elderly couple PERAMBULATED the city streets every night after dinner.*

percolate *(PUR-kuh-layt), verb*
To pass or make pass through a porous body.
> *I was dying for a cup of fresh brewed coffee, but as I didn't have time to wait for it to PERCOLATE, I had to settle for instant.*

peregrination *(pear-uh-grih-NAY-shun), noun*
Journeys or wanderings made on foot.
> *Wally's Sunday PEREGRINATIONS took him from shuttered shops to rivers spoiled by centuries of pollution.*

peremptory *(puh-REMP-tuh-ree), adjective*
Allowing for no rebuttal or overturning. A *peremptory* act is one that admits no possibility of denial or negotiation.
> *Kings may issue PEREMPTORY declarations of war, Mr. Secretary; presidents are obliged to discuss such matters with Congress.*

perennial *(puh-REN-ee-ull), adjective*
Enduring. That which gives evidence of lasting indefinitely can be considered *perennial.* (Certain plants that have a long blooming cycle are called *perennials.*)
> *The nation's PERENNIAL budget crisis took an ugly new turn this week.*

perfidy *(PURR-fih-dee), noun*
Perfidy is a calculated breach of faith or trust.
> *In wartime, such PERFIDY as you have been found guilty of yields only one sentence: death.*

perforated *(PUR-fur-aye-tud), adjective*
Featuring holes or opening, especially at regular intervals.
> *The magazine coupon was PERFORATED along the side for easy removal.*

perfunctory *(purr-FUNK-tuh-ree) adjective*
Mundane; routine. Also: showing little care. Something done with little interest is a *perfunctory* act.
> *Preoccupied, Tom went about his daily tasks with a PERFUNCTORY air.*

perjure *(purr-jer), verb*
To lie or give false and misleading testimony. To *perjure* oneself is to commit the crime of testifying to something one knows is untrue.
> *Although Mr. Frattori was not convicted on the main charges he faced, he may serve time in prison for having PERJURED himself during the trial.*

perjury *(PUR-juh-ree), verb*
To lie purposely while under oath.
> *Rather than risk PERJURY charges by lying to the Senate committee, the witness was advised to refuse to answer questions pertaining to his activities in Central America.*

perigee *(PEAR-uh-jee), noun*
The point at which a heavenly body, especially an orbiting body like the moon, is closest to the Earth.
> *People all over the country got out their telescopes to see the meteor as it reached its PERIGEE.*

perimeter *(puh-RIM-ih-tur), noun*
The outer edge of an enclosed shape or area. *Perimeter* can also refer to the distance described by this edge.
> *In the early morning hour, Jake would take a walk along the PERIMETER of the yard.*

peripatetic *(per-ih-puh-TET-ik), adjective*
Wandering. Someone who goes from one place to another is *peripatetic*.
> *These days, pursuing the presidency requires serious candidates to live a PERIPATETIC lifestyle that profoundly affects one's home and family life.*

periphery *(puh-RIFF-uh-ree), noun*
The area at the extreme of a given boundary. The outskirts of a town, for instance, are on the *periphery* of the town.
> *There among the homeless, at the furthest PERIPHERY of society, Maria found her calling.*

P

permeable *(PURR-me-uh-bull), adjective*
Porous; capable of being permeated.

> *"Only certain substances can pass through the PERMEABLE membrane," Mrs. Adams explained to her class.*

permeate *(PURR-mee-ate), verb*
To penetrate. Something that *permeates* spreads throughout.

> *Joan's stories are PERMEATED with a sense of spiritual mystery.*

permutation *(per-myoo-TAY-shun), noun*
A transformation leading to a complete change.

> *After exploring numerous PERMUTATIONS of its style, the band returned to the sound with which it had first attracted fans.*

pernicious *(purr-NISH-uss), adjective*
Tending to cause insidious harm or injury. *Pernicious* can also mean "fatal or likely to cause death."

> *A PERNICIOUS plague spread through the village.*

perpetuate *(purr-PETCH-oo-ate), verb*
To make everlasting; to prolong memory or use (of a thing). To *perpetuate* someone's memory is to cause that person's life to be recalled after his death.

> *The rumor that I am resigning has been PERPETUATED by a number of sources, all completely unreliable.*

perquisite *(PURK-wuh-zit), noun*
An incidental privilege other than payment that accompanies a position of responsibility; also, an extra payment beyond what is owed. Often shortened to "perk."

> *Among the president's PERQUISITES were two front-row seats to all the Celtics' regular-season home games.*

persnickety *(purr-SNIK-uh-tee), adjective*
Fussy and overattentive to small details. *Persnickety* can also mean "snobbish."

> *Gordon made a point of being PERSNICKETY about meals: breakfast was always served in his home at exactly 7:04, and dinner at exactly 6:42.*

perspicacity *(per-spih-KASS-ih-tee), noun*
Insightfuness. Someone who shows keen understanding displays *perspicacity*.

> *The problem was a complex one that required the analysis of someone with great PERSPICACITY.*

perspicuity *(purr-spi-KYOO-ih-tee), noun*
Clear and easy to understand. *Perspicuity* is generally used with regard to speech or writing.

> *The report from the accounting office was loaded with technical jargon; writing with PERSPICUITY is not one of the talents of the people who work there.*

pertinacious *(per-tih-NAY-shuss), adjective*
Persistent or obstinate to the point of annoyance.

> *The car salesman's PERTINACIOUS patter caused me to leave the lot immediately.*

peruse *(puh-ROOZ), verb*
To read through with attention. *Peruse* can also mean "to examine with an eye to detail."

> *The witness PERUSED the document for some time, then declared that it was not the one he had signed.*

pervasive *(purr-VAY-siv), adjective*
Having infiltrated or penetrated. A *pervasive* rumor is one that has been circulated widely.

> *The prejudice against handicapped persons is no longer as PERVASIVE as in years past.*

pestle *(PESS-ul), noun*
A tool used to grind substances into a powder in a mortar.

> *During the excavation, the crew discovered a number of ancient food preparation items, including wooden PESTLES, clay crocks, and eating utensils made of polished bone.*

petit four *(PET-ee FORE), noun*
A small decorated cake. Plural: *petits fours.*

> *Aunt Marcia always served tea and PETITS FOURS at three o'clock.*

petrified *(PET-ruh-fied), verb*
Scared to the point of losing the ability to move; scared stiff; turned to stone.

> *My aunt was so PETRIFIED of snakes that when one slithered its way onto the pool deck, my brothers and I had to carry her, lounge chair and all, into the house.*

pettifoggery *(pet-ee-FOG-er-ee), noun*
Petty dishonesty or trickery.

> *"Let's put all this PETTIFOGGERY behind us," said Mr. Powers, "and start dealing with each other in a more straightforward manner."*

petty *(PET-ee), adjective*

Describes something small and trifling, and *petty* often is used in a negative way, to suggest that someone is being small-minded and mean.

> *"I still can't believe our relationship ended over such a PETTY argument," Stewart said.*

petulant *(PET-yoo-lunt), adjective*

Impatiently peevish. Someone who shows great annoyance or irritation with minor problems could be said to be *petulant*.

> *He dismissed their questions with a PETULANT wave of the hand and quickly changed the subject.*

phaeton *(FAY-ih-tin), noun*

A lightweight four-wheeled passenger carriage drawn by horses.

> *The PHAETON, once a common sight on any city street, was eventually phased out and replaced by the automobile.*

phalanx *(FAY-lanks), noun*

From the Greek describing a military formation, a *phalanx* is a group of closely assembled people or animals, usually working together for a specific purpose, such as launching an attack.

> *The geek tried not to show his fear in the hallway, as the PHALANX of jocks walked in his direction.*

phallic *(FAL-ik), adjective*

Of or pertaining to the phallus or penis; reminiscent of a penis; also, by extension, reminiscent of the life-giving force of nature, as in ancient Dionysian festivals that made the phallus a central element.

> *According to Freud, PHALLIC symbols (such as the sword of Unferth used by Beowulf) abound in both ancient and modern literature.*

phantasmagoria *(fan-taz-muh-GORE-ee-uh), noun*

A dreamlike, constantly changing series of visions.

> *The avant-garde film had no dialogue or plot in the traditional sense; it was essentially a PHANTASMAGORIA set to music.*

phantasmagoric *(fan-tazz-muh-GORE-ihk), adjective*

Describes the type of imagery one might see in a dream: mysterious, shifting scenes, filled with incongruous elements.

> *The director's PHANTASMAGORIC images delighted some audience members, while confusing the expectations of others.*

pheromone *(FARE-uh-mone), noun*
A substance released by an animal that produces specific physiological reactions or behavioral changes in other animals of the same species.
> *The perfume company's claim that its new perfume contained PHEROMONES that would cause it to act as a human aphrodisiac was the subject of strict scrutiny by federal regulators.*

philander *(fi-LAN-der), verb*
To engage in amorous flirtations or exploits with someone who one cannot or does not intend to marry. *Philander* is used in reference to the sexual habits of men, not women.
> *These accusations of PHILANDERING, whether based in fact or not, have little to do with the question of whether the candidate will serve our state well in the United States Senate.*

philanthropy *(fih-LAN-thruh-pee), noun*
Generosity or benevolence toward mankind. Someone who acts out of *philanthropy* is someone who commits resources to the betterment of his fellow man. (A *philanthropist* is one who bestows wealth on public institutions or people in need.)
> *Toward the end of his life, Andrew Carnegie was a model of PHILANTHROPY.*

philistine *(FILL-uh-steen), adjective and noun*
In the Bible, the Philistines were opponents of the Israelites. They were quintessential bad guys. Today, a *philistine* is someone who is smug, commonplace, and conventional, and he or she often is antagonistic toward intellectual pursuits.
> *Laura always found it difficult to be an intellectual while surrounded by her childhood friends, PHILISTINES whose main concern was shopping.*

philter *(FIL-tur), noun*
A magical love potion.
> *Thinking the glass contained Evian water, Veronica drained the PHILTER to its dregs; her eyes met those of the startled butler, and she melted with tenderness.*

phlegmatic *(fleg-MAT-ic), adjective*
Having a calm, unexcitable temperament.
> *Allan's PHLEGMATIC personality was certainly helpful during the deadline crunch in keeping us all from panicking.*

phonics *(FON-iks), noun*
The study of the sounds and acoustics of language.
> *David's teacher's insistence that studying PHONICS was not necessary to develop good reading skills struck us as odd.*

phraseology *(fray-zee-ah-LO-jee), noun*
In language, the way phrases and words are employed.
> *With her excellent diction, articulation, and PHRASEOLOGY, Holly had a gift for public speaking and debate.*

physiognomy *(flz-ee-OG-nuh-mee), noun*
The human face (especially when regarded as a mirror of one's emotional state). *Physiognomy* is also the practice of determining a person's inclination or character from facial signals.
> *There was a noticeable change in Doris's PHYSIOGNOMY as Todd read her the news.*

picayune *(PIK-uh-yoon), adjective*
Petty. Something that is trifling or unimportant is *picayune*.
> *Mr. Frankl apparently couldn't be bothered with such PICAYUNE concerns as what color shirt to wear.*

pictorial *(pick-TOR-ee-ul), adjective*
Relating to or consisting of pictures.
> *National Geographic offers a PICTORIAL introduction to people and cultures we may never have known about before.*

picturesque *(PIK-chuh-resk), adjective*
Reminiscent of or suggesting a (painted) picture. A striking or unusually interesting scene can be considered *picturesque*.
> *The film's PICTURESQUE setting is not enough to make up for its scant plot.*

pidgin *(PIDJ-in), noun*
A type of language created by the interaction of two distinct languages, used to help people communicate across language barriers.
> *We spoke PIDGIN to each other, and I finally was able to understand how to get to the nearest bathroom.*

pied *(PIED), adjective*
Describes animals, plants, cloth designs, etc. featuring two or more colors.
> *The poet Gerard Manley Hopkins believed the strangeness of PIED creatures and plants was a sign of God's grace.*

piety *(PIE-uh-tee), noun*

Devotion; religious reverence. Someone who shows a marked inclination to worship God is said to show *piety*.

> *Joseph Smith—a man not noted for his PIETY—suddenly started attending religious services.*

pigment *(PIG-munt), noun*

A dry coloring substance meant to be mixed with fluid; any matter that produces color.

> *The use of PIGMENTS developed only in the late nineteenth century is proof positive that this painting is not one of Vermeer's.*

pilaf *(PEEL-af), noun*

A flavored rice dish served alone or with meat, poultry, or vegetables.

> *The restaurant is certainly trying to cater to the needs of the health-conscious, offering more chicken, fish and vegetable entrées than before, and allowing diners a choice of rice PILAF or fries.*

pilfer *(PIL-fer), verb*

To take without authorization or permission; to steal.

> *I had a feeling the tickets Wayne was trying to sell me had been PILFERED from someone, but he assured me that was not the case.*

pillory *(PILL-uh-ree), verb*

In olden days, a *pillory* was a wooden frame in which one was imprisoned and subjected to public ridicule. In modern times—and as a verb—*pillory* means to subject someone to merciless public ridicule or abuse.

> *I sipped my morning coffee as the respective party's pundits PILLORIED each other.*

pinnacle *(PIN-uh-kul), noun*

The topmost point. To reach the apex or highest point of something is to reach its *pinnacle*.

> *Fred reached the PINNACLE of his profession when he was named chairman of the history department.*

pious *(PIE-uss), adjective*

Devout; dedicated to God and the practice of one's faith or religion.

> *Joseph had always seemed to be the most PIOUS of all of us, so no one in our class was surprised when he announced that he'd found his calling in the ministry.*

P

piquant *(pi-KONT), adjective*
Stimulating; provocative, particularly to the tastebuds; spicy.

> *Normally, Mexican food is too hot for me, but Nancy's salsa dip was just PIQUANT enough to be delightful.*

pique *(peek), verb*
To injure a person's pride and thereby engender harsh feelings. Someone who shows resentful irritation at a perceived slight can be said to be *piqued*.

> *Marcia was PIQUED at not having been invited to the party.*

pithy *(PITH-ee), adjective*
Something very brief but meaningful and concise.

> *The guest speaker limited his remarks to a few PITHY observations on the impossibility of getting anything done in Washington.*

pittance *(PIT-unce), noun*
A very small amount.

> *My allowance in those days, of course, was a PITTANCE compared to my brother's.*

pixie *(PIK-see), noun*
An elf or fairy.

> *The villages believed the mysterious theft to be the work of mischievous PIXIES and trolls.*

placard *(PLACK-urd), noun*
A notice or sign set out on stiff paper or board.

> *The umpire asked us to remove our PLACARD from the bleacher wall, claiming that it obstructed the view of the hitters.*

placate *(PLAY-kate), verb*
To appease. Someone who concedes or yields in order to avoid another's anger can be said to *placate* that person.

> *Although the company was unable to raise wages, it did make an effort to PLACATE the union by extending the afternoon coffee break.*

placebo *(pluh-SEE-bo), noun*
A medicine having no fixed medical purpose or healing property given either to pacify a patient or, as a control method, to test the effectiveness of another drug. A *placebo* is administered as though it were a medication or drug, yet is neutral from a medical standpoint.

> *Scientists are still uncertain as to exactly what causes the PLACEBO effect, in which some patients taking a "fake" drug actually improve.*

placid *(PLAH-sid), adjective*
Undisturbed; smooth. That which appears calm or undisturbed on the surface can be said to be *placid*.

> *The PLACID country surroundings were just the change Caitlyn needed after three months in noisy Manhattan.*

plague *(playg), noun*
A broad-based affliction. A *plague* is a widespread calamity usually associated with a severe and sudden incidence of disease in a population. (*Plague* can refer to divine intervention or, figuratively, to any sudden and widespread reversal of fortune affecting a group: "a plague of bank closures.")

> *Fortunately, humans have not encountered a severe outbreak of the bubonic PLAGUE for centuries.*

plaintive *(PLAIN-tive), adjective*
Expressing sorrow or sadness; mournful.

> *A PLAINTIVE feeling hung over the house for weeks after our dog Sasha died.*

plaited *(PLAY-tud), adjective*
Braided.

> *Julia usually wore her hair neatly PLAITED, but she drew more than a few looks when she let it fall to its full length—nearly to her waist-for the company party.*

planar *(PLAY-ner), adjective*
Flat or level, like a geometric plane.

> *My boys spent the morning rolling a ball across the PLANAR surface of their new playhouse's floor.*

plangent *(PLAN-jent), adjective*
Describes something loud and, typically, sorrowful.

> *The PLANGENT locomotive whistle made Henry drop a tear in his beer.*

platitude *(PLAT-ih-tood), noun*
A commonplace or useless remark. A statement that is trite or unoriginal can be considered a *platitude*.

> *You have taken a speech that seemed quite promising and filled it to the brim with PLATITUDES.*

platonic *(pluh-TON-ik), adjective*
Free from sexual desire. *Platonic* also refers to the ideal form of something.

> *Emily knew that her relationship with Paul had to remain a PLATONIC one.*

P

plaudit (PLAW-dit), *noun*

An expression of gratitude or praise. *Plaudits* (in the plural) is usually taken to mean "applause."

> *I am unworthy, my friends, of the PLAUDITS you have bestowed on me this evening.*

plausible *(PLAW-zuh-bull), adjective*

Having the ring of truth, though not a proven fact.

> *Rhonda's excuse for tardiness was PLAUSIBLE, but I still think she was just out drinking all night.*

playa *(PLY-uh), noun*

The lowest area of a desert, usually flat and sometimes covered with water.

> *The desert's undrained PLAYA contained the only water for hundreds of miles.*

plebeian *(plih-BE-uhn), adjective or noun*

In ancient Rome, the *plebeians* were the common people. Today, the word still pertains to common tastes. Sometimes, the word can be used in a negative way, to suggest that someone is being common, as in vulgar.

> *"I don't get wine," Bart said. "I guess my tastes are just too PLEBEIAN."*

plebiscite *(PLEB-uh-site), noun*

A vote, open to all voters, which decides matters of public policy.

> *The annexation was voted down in a PLEBISCITE.*

plenary *(PLEE-nuh-ree), adjective*

Describes something that is absolute and unqualified.

> *Original FBI head, Edgar Hoover, did his best to give himself and his agency PLENARY powers.*

plenitude *(PLEN-ti-tood), noun*

Abundance. *Plenitude* is the standard spelling; *plentitude*, though commonly used, is generally considered incorrect.

> *The sudden PLENITUDE of supplies was certainly a welcome change for the hungry travelers.*

plethora *(PLETH-er-uh), noun*

Excessive oversupply. To have a *plethora* of something is to have a vast quantity of it.

> *The new edition contains a PLETHORA of trivia concerning the films made by Mr. Howard and his cohorts in the forties and fifties.*

pliable *(PLIE-uh-bull), adjective*
Able to be changed in shape, form, or inclination; capable of being directed or influenced.

Gold, one of the world's most valuable metals, is also one of the most PLIABLE.

pliant *(PLY-unt), adjective*
Supple. Something that is modified or altered easily is *pliant*.

You must mold papier mache quickly; it is not PLIANT for long.

plight *(plite), noun*
Predicament, especially one arising from a solemn obligation. A *plight* is an unfortunate or desperate situation.

Out of sympathy for the public television station's PLIGHT, Glenn made a large donation.

plod *(plod), verb*
To trudge along slowly, as if weighed down.

The tour guide noticed Nelson PLODDING along behind the rest of the group and guessed that he was not a big fan of Monet.

plucky *(PLUK-ee), adjective*
Brave; courageous.

It was the gnomelike Mario, the last person Sergeant Denton would have termed a PLUCKY young cadet, who ended up winning a medal for risking his own life to save his comrades.

plutocracy *(ploo-TOK-ruh-see), noun*
Rule by the rich. *Plutocracy* can also refer to the overall influence of the wealthy in social affairs.

"If PLUTOCRACY were likely to improve the nation's standard of living," Gerald said haughtily, "then I would be a plutocrat."

pneumatic *(noo-MAT-ik), adjective*
Related to air or wind; using air or compressed gas as a force.

It took Milton some time to master the controls of the huge PNEUMATIC drill, but eventually he got the hang of it and set about a gleeful, early-morning destruction of the pavement outside his absent neighbor's home.

poignant *(POY-nyunt), adjective*
Appealing to the emotions. That which is acutely painful or affecting is *poignant*.

The film's final scene is meant to be POIGNANT, but I found it cloying.

P

poise *(poyze), noun*
Stability of outlook or emotional state, especially when facing trying circumstances. Also, as a verb: to set on a potentially hazardous surface, such as a narrow edge.
Ruth-Anne's POISE during the rigorous interview impressed us all.

polarize *(PO-luh-rize), verb*
To encourage elements or components to occupy opposite ends of a spectrum. Something that divides or sows discord is said to *polarize*.
The scandal left the two wings of the party completely POLARIZED.

polemics *(puh-LEM-ik), noun*
The art of argument. Someone who is strong in the field of *polemics* is gifted in making points by means of controversial discourse with others.
The talk show host's great asset was his skill in POLEMICS—not his personality.

politick *(POL-ih-tik), verb*
To talk about or engage in politics.
Barry spends hours POLITICKING with his associates.

polity *(POL-ih-tee), noun*
A system of government. A nation's *polity* is its structure of social and political functioning.
The POLITIES of the Greek city-states, admired as they may be, cannot serve as a literal model for a modern industrial society.

polydipsia *(pol-ee-DIP-see-uh), noun*
An abnormal or excessive thirst.
The bartender, clearly uninterested in Ralph's claim to suffer from POLYDIPSIA, told him flatly that he'd had enough.

polygamy *(puh-LIG-uh-mee), noun*
The societal practice of having more than one spouse (especially, more than one wife) at a time.
The sect's advocacy of POLYGAMY and group parenting eventually brought it into bitter conflict with the stern-minded townsfolk of Harris Hollow.

polyglot *(POL-ee-glot), noun*
A person who speaks a number of languages. Someone fluent in French, German, and English would be a *polyglot*.
The President's translator, a POLYGLOT, served him well in missions to Germany, Portugal, and Mexico.

polygraph *(POL-ee-graff), noun*
A machine used in lie detection that indicates changes in pulse, perspiration, blood pressure, and respiration.

> *After the suspect passed a series of POLYGRAPH test, police formally dropped all charges.*

polymath *(PAHL-ee-math), noun*
Someone who is learned in many different areas.

> *Even though he never graduated from college, James is known as a POLYMATH.*

pompadour *(POMP-uh-dore), noun*
A male hairstyle in which the hair is set high in a wave in the front.

> *Don wore a POMPADOUR, a black leather jacket, and blue jeans to the costume party in imitation of his hero Fonzie from "Happy Days."*

pompous *(POM-puss), adjective*
Pretentious; overblown; self-important.

> *The food was good and the service was prompt, but our waiter's POMPOUS air and unceasing sneer made me consider leaving a single penny as a tip.*

pongee *(pon-JEE), noun*
A thin, unbleached variety of silk.

> *The gauze-like scarf was woven from a delicate PONGEE.*

pontiff *(PON-tiff), noun*
A high or chief priest; usually, the pope.

> *Although lately John Paul II has not made as many pilgrimages to foreign lands as he did in the late Seventies and early Eighties, the PONTIFF has made a special point of visiting one or two important cities per year.*

pontificate *(pon-TIF-ih-kate), verb*
To issue authoritative decrees (as a pontiff might). *Pontificate* usually carries a sense of self-righteous pomposity.

> *Can I assume the Senator now intends to PONTIFICATE on the many virtues of our current trade policy?*

populism *(POP-yuh-liz-um), noun*
A political movement that reaches out to "just plain folks," rather than to social or cultural elites. Someone who espouses populism is called a populist. Sometimes *populism* is used negatively, to suggest that a political candidate is appealing to the worst side of human nature in an effort to get votes. For example, prior to the Civil Rights Era, *populism* often was equated with "continuing the status quo of segregation."

> *Opponents called the candidate a populist, meaning it as an attack, but he accepted the word and turned it into one of the pillars of his successful campaign.*

porcine *(PORE-sein), adjective*
Reminiscent of or pertaining to a pig; resembling a pig.

> *Mike's constant description of his heavyset blind date as "my PORCINE companion" may have had something to do with her early departure from the party.*

portend *(por-TEND), verb*
To suggest or foretell. If A *portends* B, A signifies that B is imminent.

> *The tone of Joan's voice this morning PORTENDS trouble.*

posit *(POZ-it), verb*
To stipulate. Someone who *posits* a thing presents or assumes it.

> *In his address, the mayor POSITED the conditions he would have to meet to resolve the fiscal crisis.*

posterity *(pah-STAIR-ih-tee), noun*
Future generations, considered collectively.

> *The president believes POSTERITY will judge his administration a successful one.*

postern *(POSS-turn), noun*
A back or rear door or gate, especially in a castle or fort.

> *The fire marshall was unimpressed with our evacuation plan, which required guests, in the event of an emergency, to make their way through a dark, narrow hallway leading to a POSTERN.*

postmodern *(post-MAH-dern), adjective*
Very modern, cutting-edge, avant-garde.

> *Older audiences stayed away in droves from the director's POSTMODERN films, but young people ate them up like candy.*

postmortem *(post-MORE-tuhm), noun*
Traditionally, "postmortem" has referred to the examination of a body after death, but pundits have picked up on the word and use it to describe a political, cultural, social, etc. event, after the event's occurrence.

> *Pundits spent weeks doing POSTMORTEMS of the lengthy primaries once the primaries finally ended.*

postpartum *(post-PAR-tum), adjective*
Occurring after pregnancy and birth.

> *In the weeks following the delivery, Janice felt quite low at times, but her obstetrician assured her that hers was a standard case of POSTPARTUM depression and would soon pass.*

postulate *(PAHSS-chuh-late), verb*

To assume as self-evident something for which one has no proof.

Cindy POSTULATED that "everyone" knows that particular restaurant has terrible service.

potable *(POH-tuh-bull), adjective*

Drinkable. Something that can be drunk safely is *potable.*

No amount of boiling could make the water from the stagnant lake POTABLE.

potent *(PO-tunt), adjective*

Strong; powerful.

The poor review of Henry's play served as a POTENT incentive for him to labor more carefully over the next one.

potentate *(POT-n-tate), noun*

A powerful person. An influential political or business figure could be considered a *potentate.*

The First Lady was thoroughly at ease with foreign POTENTATES and diplomats from the administration's first day.

pragmatic *(prag-MA-tik), adjective*

Practical. Something that is *pragmatic* is useful or apt.

The governor, in this case, decided not to take the advice of the ideologues, opting instead for a PRAGMATIC approach.

prate *(PRAYT), verb*

To talk at length in a pointless manner.

As her blind date continued to PRATE about his former girlfriends, Lydia considered jumping out of the moving car to get away from the guy.

prattle *(PRAT-ul), noun*

Meaningless babble; idle chatter.

I had stopped at the diner to have breakfast and read the morning paper, but the endless PRATTLE of the waitress made it impossible for me to get beyond the front page.

precarious *(pruh-KARE-ee-us), adjective*

Insecure. Something that is *precarious* is uncertain and subject to misfortune or collapse.

The crisis has left our nation in a PRECARIOUS position.

P

precedence *(PRESS-uh-dunce), noun*
The act or right of preceding; an instance or claim of coming first in order or priority.

> *To his credit, the president of the toy company agreed that the safety of children took PRECEDENCE over profits and promptly recalled the defective item from the stores.*

precedent *(PRESS-i-dent), noun*
A previous parallel incident justifying a present action. A *precedent* is an example from the past that is either identical to a current situation or similar enough to it to use as a guide.

> *There is no PRECEDENT for the action the defense is requesting, Your Honor.*

preceptor *(pri-SEP-tur), noun*
A school principal, teacher, or instructor.

> *Our elementary school's PRECEPTOR was a stern man who handed out swift discipline to troublemakers.*

precipice *(press-ih-pis), noun*
A cliff. To be "on the *precipice*"" can also be to be on the verge of a dangerous course of action.

> *Though the view is spectacular here, I don't advise walking near the PRECIPICE.*

precipitous *(pruh-SIP-uh-tuss), adjective*
Very steep, as a precipice; rushing away headlong.

> *The prospect of learning to drive a standard shift in this city of PRECIPITOUS hills is an intimidating one.*

precept *(PREE-sept), noun*
A rule, order, or principle that sets up a standard guide for conduct.

> *I make it a personal PRECEPT never to ask my staff to do anything I would not be willing to do myself.*

precocious *(pri-KO-shuss), adjective*
Prematurely advanced, especially with regard to mental ability. A child who vies for attention by displaying adult-like social or mental skills is also said to be *precocious*.

> *Bill, a PRECOCIOUS nine-year-old, could already do algebra and geometry.*

predecessor *(PRED-uh-sess-er), noun*
Something or someone succeeded or replaced by another.

> *Jane knew it would be difficult to live up to the standards set by her PREDECESSOR.*

predestined *(pre-DESS-tind), adjective*
Controlled by the fates; governed by higher powers and foreordained.
> *After his meeting with the fortuneteller, Jim honestly believed he was PREDESTINED to meet and marry a woman from Argentina.*

predominate *(prih-DOM-uh-nate), verb*
To be the most noticeable or leading element or to have the most authority or force.
> *Brad felt that his six months in Europe gave him the right to PREDOMINATE the conversation about European customs and culture.*

preeminent *(pre-EM-ih-nunt), adjective*
Superior to others.
> *The young Stalin's plan was to reach a PREEMINENT position in the party hierarchy by any means necessary.*

preemptive *(pre-EMP-tive), adjective*
Possessing and acting on a prior right (for instance, as one who has the first claim to purchase a property.) Similarly, to take a *preemptive* action is to act before others can.
> *The old miner had a PREEMPTIVE claim to the property, and so our purchase of it was impossible.*

preen *(preen), verb*
To primp; to perfect one's appearance. Also: to take pride (in oneself or one's accomplishments).
> *The crew knew that the reason Barry arrived at the studio an hour before broadcast was so that he would have plenty of time to PREEN in front of the mirror before going on camera.*

premillennial *(pre-muh-LEN-ee-uhl), adjective*
In general, *premillennial* refers to a time just before the start of a new millennium, such as the 1990s. The word has gained increasing usage by some religious groups to describe the time just before the second coming of Jesus Christ, which they believe imminent.
> *Trudy left the church after she decided she did not subscribe to its PREMILLENNIAL views.*

premise *(PREM-iss), noun*

The idea or statement that stands as the base of a theory or argument; also, the conceit underlying the action of a work of fiction or drama.

> *The story's PREMISE—that all of us can win the lottery if we only play it enough times—is so farfetched as to be laughable, but the piece is not, alas, intended as a comedy.*

prenatal *(pre-NAY-tull), adjective*

Occurring before childbirth.

> *Dr. Ellis advised all her patients to follow a sound PRENATAL regimen that included a diet rich in protein, calcium, and iron.*

preposterous *(prih-POSS-tur-uss), adjective*

So outlandish as to be unbelievable; incredible.

> *Your suggestion that we hold the board meeting in the park in order to enjoy the warm weather is simply PREPOSTEROUS, James.*

prerogative *(puh-ROGG-uh-tive), noun*

A right or privilege limited to a particular person in a particular situation.

> *The manager exercised his PREROGATIVE to stop the bickering during the staff meeting.*

presage (press-ij) *verb*

To foretell or indicate. If A *presages* B, A serves as a warning or sign that B will occur soon.

> *Such provocation may PRESAGE armed conflict in the region.*

prescience *(PRESS-ee-unce), noun*

Foreknowledge. *Prescience* is the knowledge of events before they take place.

> *Lacking PRESCIENCE, I really can't tell you what Sally intends to do.*

presentiment *(prih-ZEN-tuh-ment), noun*

A feeling that something—especially something bad—is going to happen.

> *The flight was uneventful, despite Clyde's PRESENTIMENT that a mid-air disaster would occur.*

prestidigitation *(press-tih-dih-jih-TAY-shun), noun*

Sleight of hand, or a magician's work in general.

> *The magician's acts of PRESTIDIGITATION were a hit at my son's birthday party.*

pretense *(PREE-tence), noun*

An instance of pretending. To make a *pretense* of surprise, for instance, is to falsely act or claim to be surprised.

> *We will prove here that the lease was signed under false PRETENSES.*

prevail *(prih-VAIL), verb*

To succeed and become dominant, or to be widespread.

> *The challenger ultimately PREVAILED over the two-time heavyweight champion.*

prevalent *(PREV-uh-lunt), adjective*

Occurring often; common.

> *Although a belief that some kind of conspiracy in President Kennedy's murder is certainly PREVALENT in public opinion these days, there is no consensus on the nature of that purported conspiracy.*

prevaricate *(pri-VARE-uh-kate), verb*

To avoid revealing the true nature of one's position, actions, feelings, etcetera. Someone who "waffles" on an issue, throwing up distractions or responding to questions evasively, is said to *prevaricate*.

> *My opponent has chosen to PREVARICATE rather than address his role in the scandal.*

priapic *(pry-AP-ick), adjective*

Related to the phallus or to a man who is obsessed with his masculinity.

> *The medication's PRIAPIC warnings, that some erections could last longer than four hours, led to a series of jokes by late-night comics.*

prima donna *(PREE-muh DON-nuh), noun*

A self-centered member of a group or organization who feels that his contributions are so important as to merit special treatment. (Literally, a *prima donna* is the leading female singer in an opera company.)

> *There is no place for PRIMA DONNAS in this organization; we must work together as a team.*

primacy *(PRY-muh-see), noun*

First in order, rank, importance, etc.

> *My aging dog, Sally, kept trying to attack my new puppy, Max, because she feared he would disrupt her PRIMACY in the household.*

primer (PRIM-ur), *noun*

A basic, grade-school textbook.

> *For decades, the foundation of American schooling was the old-fashioned PRIMER, from which children studied subjects ranging from history to poetry to arithmetic.*

primordial *(pry-MORE-dee-UL), adjective*
Original. Something that is *primordial* comes at the very first position in a sequence.

> *Perhaps science can't answer such PRIMORDIAL questions as "How did the universe begin?"*

principal *(PRIN-sih-pul), adjective*
First in importance. Also, as a noun: the main performer in a dramatic production; also, the head of an elementary or high school. (See, for comparison, the entry for *principle*.)

> *My PRINCIPAL objection to your plan is that it is completely unethical, but I might also add that it is not likely to yield any significant income for our company.*

principle *(PRIN-sih-pul), noun*
A common truth or law; a standard of behavior. (See, for comparison, the entry for *principal*)

> *Melanie's assertion that our former Congressman is an overweight graft artist without a single moral PRINCIPLE was out of line; he's lost a good deal of weight in recent months.*

pristine *(PRISS-teen), adjective*
Unspoiled; primitive. Something that is *pristine* is original and uncorrupted by later influence.

> *The PRISTINE wilderness had an invigorating effect on Charles, who had never gone camping before.*

proclivity *(pro-KLIV-ih-tee), noun*
A predisposition. To have a *proclivity* to do something is to tend to do it.

> *Allen has a PROCLIVITY to untidiness that will not go over well with Ralph.*

procrustean *(pro-KRUS-tee-un), adjective*
Seeking to enforce doctrines or theories by violently eliminating all possible alternative viewpoints. *Procrustean* derives from the name of a fabled thief of ancient Greece who stretched or amputated his victims in order to make them fit a bed exactly.

> *The regime's PROCRUSTEAN tactics are designed to completely eliminate all political dissent.*

procure *(pro-KYOOR), verb*
To obtain. Someone who *procures* something gathers or collects it.

> *Susan soon PROCURED sufficient financing to close the deal.*

prodigal *(PROD-ih-gul), adjective*
Extravagant or wasteful; imprudent.

> *Helen's PRODIGAL spending habits were well known to the family, and were one of the main reasons they fought her bid to take over the business.*

prodigious *(pro-DIDGE-uss), adjective*
Impressive in size, impact, or stature; amazing.

> *Clark's PRODIGIOUS collection of old movie posters led many of his friends to ask whether he had once owned a theatre.*

prodigy *(PRAW-dih-gee), noun*
A person possessing extraordinary skill or talent. A *prodigy* can also be a wonder or marvelous example.

> *The young Mozart, a famous child PRODIGY, played the piano with the skill of a master.*

proffer *(PROF-fur), verb*
To offer; to tender or volunteer (a thing); as a noun, a thing offered.

> *Colin PROFFERED his car as a means of getting to Florida for spring break, but as none of us knew how to drive a standard, we had to decline.*

profligate *(PROFF-lih-git), adjective*
Shamelessly immoral. *Profligate* can also mean extravagantly or recklessly wasteful.

> *Cedric abandoned his PROFLIGATE ways and decided it was time to live life along the straight and narrow.*

profundity *(pruh-FUN-dih-tee), noun*
Depth of reasoning or insight. Something that shows *profundity* gives evidence of great understanding and intellectual incisiveness.

> *A paper's length is no indication of its PROFUNDITY.*

profusion *(pro-FYOOZH-un), noun*
An abundance or extravagance.

> *Jane's fiance insisted on sending her such a PROFUSION of flowers that she soon ran out of places to put them.*

progenitor *(pro-JEN-ih-ter), noun*
An ancestor who can be traced back through the direct line. A *progenitor* can also be the originator of a school of thought or organization.

> *Picasso, considered by many the PROGENITOR of Cubism, showed a mastery of conventional painting technique in his very early work.*

prognosticate *(prog-NOSS-tih-kate), verb*
To predict. Someone who foretells the future *prognosticates*.

> *As to the game's final outcome, I refuse to PROGNOSTICATE.*

progressive *(pruh-GRESS-iv), adjective*
Forward-moving, especially with regard to social or political issues. A *progressive* politician is one who is associated with reform movements or similar causes.

> *Governor Dowling's retirement is seen as a severe blow to the entire PROGRESSIVE movement.*

proletarian *(pro-luh-TARE-ee-un), adjective*
In ancient Rome, *proletarians* were the poorest class of people. Today, *proletarian* describes members of the working class. The noun form, which you may see, is *proletariat*.

> *The politician's PROLETARIAN appeals earned her many votes during the election.*

proliferate *(pro-LIF-uh-rate), verb*
To multiply or come into being rapidly. To *proliferate* can also mean to spread or become more common at an accelerated pace.

> *After the film's success, a number of cheap imitations PROLIFERATED for a time.*

prolific *(pruh-LIFF-ick), adjective*
Extremely fruitful and productive.

> *Joyce Carol Oates is one of America's most PROLIFIC writers, turning out three or four books a year.*

prolix *(pro-LIKS), adjective*
Tediously wordy. Something that is long and verbose is *prolix*.

> *The report was utterly PROLIX; I gave up trying to finish reading it.*

Promethean *(pruh-ME-THee-un), adjective*
In ancient Greek myth, Prometheus was the son of a titan, and he created humankind and then taught it how to use fire. Today, *Promethean* describes someone who is visionary, someone who produces bold new ideas.

> *Who could have foretold in the 1950s that people tinkering around with computers would be such PROMETHEAN pioneers?*

promiscuity *(prom-ih-SKYOO-ih-tee), noun*
Indiscriminate choice of sexual partners. A *promiscuity* can also be an instance of promiscuous sex.

> *The comparatively tolerant attitude toward the PROMISCUITY of the late '70s and early '80s changed dramatically with the onset of the AIDS crisis.*

promissory *(PROM-uh-sore-ee), adjective*
Suggesting a promise.

> *That night's PROMISSORY kiss left James unable to get Samantha out of his mind until he saw her again.*

promontory *(PROM-uhn-tore-ee), noun*
A piece of land that projects from a coastline or lowland, which typically offers spectacular views.

> *I spent all the time during our vacation sitting out on the balcony of our inn, enjoying the views from my PROMONTORY perch.*

promulgate *(PROM-ul-gate), verb*
To put forward publicly. To *promulgate* can also mean "to announce in an official capacity."

> *The news of the British attack was PROMULGATED by town criers.*

propagate *(PROP-uh-gate), verb*
To cause to multiply by natural processes. *Propagate* is related to the word propaganda, which means "that (information) which is disseminated for public circulation by a person or party for advantage."

> *Darwin's observations on the way species PROPAGATE and adapt were shocking to many readers.*

propensity *(pruh-PEN-sih-tee), noun*
A tendency or inclination.

> *Rhonda's PROPENSITY for chocolate did not mesh well with her diet plans.*

propinquity *(pruh-PIN-kwih-tee), noun*
Nearness, especially with regard to place, sequence, or heredity. If A is in close proximity to B, A is in *propinquity* to B.

> *Living in PROPINQUITY to constant civil conflict, as I did, is hardly a recipe for a happy childhood.*

propound *(pruh-POUND), verb*
To set forth. To *propound* is to offer (a theory) for review or consideration.

> *Dr. Richards PROPOUNDED his most complex mathematical theory yet at the conference.*

propriety *(pruh-PRY-uh-tee), noun*
Conformity to standards appropriate to a given situation.

> *My typically foul-mouthed boyfriend was a model of PROPRIETY the first time he met my folks.*

prosaic *(pro-ZAY-ik), adjective*
Commonplace or workaday. Something that is unromantic or matter-of-fact is *prosaic*.

> *Banks, whose PROSAIC outlook on life left little room for frivolity, was a stern father.*

proscribe *(pro-SKRIBE), verb*
To prohibit. To *proscribe* is also to denounce as injurious.

> *Any discussion of the fleet's battle plan was PROSCRIBED under threat of imprisonment.*

proselytize *(PROSS-ih-li-tize), verb*
To attempt to convert to one's own religious faith. Someone who proselytizes attempts (often overbearingly) to recruit others to his religion.

> *Thus it was that our main goal of PROSELYTIZING the natives was temporarily abandoned in favor of the more pressing and immediate object of surviving their raids on our settlement.*

prosthesis *(pross-THEE-sis), noun*
An artificially constructed member meant to replace a damaged or missing part of the human body.

> *Several months after the accident, Greg was fitted for a PROSTHESIS for his lower left leg that would allow him to walk again.*

prostrate *(PROSS-trait), adjective or verb*
Lying face down on the ground due to being weary, overthrown, or helpless; or the act of putting someone in such a prone position.

> *The quarterback lay PROSTRATE for several minutes after he was sacked.*

protagonist *(pro-TAG-uh-nist), noun*
The lead character in a story, play, novel, etc.

> *I stopped reading the book because I found the PROTAGONIST so unbelievable.*

protean *(PRO-te-un), adjective*
Versatile; changing form easily.

> *As further demonstration of his PROTEAN abilities as an actor, Ned agreed to appear in a six-week run of Henry IV, Part One, playing Falstaff and Hotspur on alternate nights.*

protege *(PRO-tuh-zhay), noun*
Someone aided by another influential person. A *protege* is a person who is protected, encouraged, or helped (for instance, in career matters) by another of superior status or rank.

> *Everyone expected Dean to name Bill (his PROTEGE) to the new post.*

protocol *(PRO-tuh-call), noun*
Formal etiquette, especially as practiced in diplomatic circles. *Protocol* can also
refer to established rankings followed in a social gathering.

> *Her inability to adhere to official PROTOCOL led to her dismissal from the embassy
> staff.*

prototype *(PRO-tuh-type), noun*
The original model of something. A *prototype* is the experimental or trial version of
a system or invention.

> *The PROTOTYPE underwent several modifications before Ben felt comfortable
> showing it to potential investors.*

provenance *(PRAHV-uh-nunts), noun*
Derivation, or place of origin.

> *At least three cities claim to be the PROVENANCE of "true" barbecue.*

proverbial *(pruh-VER-bee-ul), adjective*
Calling to mind (a familiar) proverb. Something that is *proverbial* shows an
immediate parallel with a well-known saying, story, or maxim.

> *Stan considered his younger brother about as useful as the PROVERBIAL fifth wheel.*

providence *(PROV-ih-dnce), noun*
Divine care. To trust in providence is to hold an assurance that God will provide
for needs or guide one's actions. (*Providence* can also mean "thrift.")

> *Despite Mother's assurance that PROVIDENCE will see to our needs, I feel I should
> try to find a job.*

provincial *(pruh-VIN-shull), adjective*
Describes people with narrow-minded, unsophisticated attitudes, such as those
considered to originate in provinces.

> *After moving to Manhattan from a small town, Phyllis quickly left behind her
> PROVINCIAL tastes.*

provocateur *(pruh-vock-uh-TURR), noun*
From the French meaning "challenger," a *provocateur* is someone who deliberately
causes trouble or sparks dissension.

> *Mick revels in being a PROVOCATEUR, often wearing to church his T-shirts
> featuring satanic rock bands.*

provocative *(pruh-VOK-uh-tive), adjective*
Stimulating or combative. Someone who is *provocative* tends to focus on controversial issues.

> *Despite Ed's PROVOCATIVE attitude—or perhaps because of it-he won the respect of his supervisor on the creative team.*

proximity *(prok-SIM-ih-tee), noun*
Close or near in time, location, or relation.

> *The PROXIMITY of my desk to Irma's meant that I would be subject to her endless, tedious stories about her crocheting classes.*

proxy *(PROK-see), noun*
One given authority to act on behalf of another. Also, the permission one gives another to act in one's place.

> *As I didn't want to reschedule my next vacation, I named Donna as my PROXY for the next stockholder's meeting.*

prudent *(PROOD-nt), adjective*
Exercising due care with regard to one's interests. Something that is *prudent* is judicious or carefully considered.

> *I believe the merger was a PRUDENT course of action, one that will solidify our cash position immediately.*

prurient *(PROOR-ee-ent), adjective*
Lewd (said of an idea, representation, account, etcetera). A *prurient* interest is one focusing excessively on sex.

> *"The idea," Judge Cotlin wrote, "that Joyce's Ulysses is designed mainly to excite the reader's PRURIENT interest is absurd."*

pseudomorph *(SOO-doh-morf), noun*
A deceptive or irregular form.

> *I thought the shape on the floor was a bug and prepared to squash it with a book, when I realized it was merely a PSEUDOMORPH . . . a piece of dirt or an oddly-colored dust bunny.*

psoriasis *(suh-RIE-uh-suss), noun*
A chronic skin disease causing the skin to become covered with red patches and white scales.

> *Emmett treated his first bout of PSORIASIS by applying copious amounts of moisturizer, but it did no good.*

psychosomatic *(sy-ko-suh-MAH-tik), adjective*
Pertaining to disorders having emotional or mental (rather than evident physical) causes. *Psychosomatic* can also refer to that which involves both mind and body.

> *Although the first doctor she consulted insisted that Jane's symptoms were PSYCHOSOMATIC, the second found signs of physical illness.*

puerile *(PYOO-ur-ul), adjective*
Juvenile. *Puerile* derives from a Latin word meaning "boyish."

> *Such PUERILE babbling is not fit to be printed in the Letters section of this newspaper.*

pugilism *(PYOO-juh-liz-um), noun*
Boxing. *Pugilism* is the science or practice of fistfighting.

> *Finally, the two PUGILISTS stepped into the ring; the match was about to begin.*

pugnacious *(pug-NAY-shuss), adjective*
Prone to quarrels or fights. A *pugnacious* person is one who is given to conflict or dispute.

> *Aaron's PUGNACIOUS attitude is the reason he is involved in so many arguments.*

pulchritude *(PUHL-krih-tood), noun*
Physical beauty.

> *Emily's easygoing attitude attracted boys' attention almost as much as her PULCHRITUDE.*

pumice *(PUM-iss), noun*
A lightweight volcanic rock used in powder form as a cleanser.

> *For three hours I scrubbed the basin with the pink, gritty PUMICE the guard had supplied, but I could not remove the orange blotches.*

punctilio *(pungk-TIL-ee-o), noun*
A fine point of etiquette.

> *"Don't use dessert forks during the main course, please," my grandmother intoned, reverting to one of her favorite PUNCTILIOS.*

punctilious *(punk-TILL-ee-uss), adjective*
Overly attentive to trifling details. Someone who takes great care to dispose of seemingly small matters in a formally correct way is *punctilious*.

> *The PUNCTILIOUS Mrs. Smith took issue with the seating arrangements we had suggested.*

pundit *(PUN-dit), noun*
An educated or authoritative person whose opinion is generally respected.

> *The political PUNDITS had all decreed that Truman would be defeated in a head-to-head contest with Governor Dewey, but the voters had other ideas.*

pungent *(PUN-junt), adjective*
Powerful or sharp (typically used with regard to odors or tastes).

> *That PUNGENT odor coming from the back of the refrigerator is what's left of the lasagna Chris made three months ago.*

puny *(PYOO-nee), adjective*
Very little; being small in stature or strength.

> *A brilliant but rather PUNY child, Jason often had to endure the taunts and abuse of the school bully.*

purge *(purj), verb*
To free (someone or something) of all that is perceived as bad; to take steps to cleanse or purify.

> *I tried to PURGE my system of the flu virus by drinking endless glasses of fruit juice, but I still ended up missing a week of work.*

puritanical *(pyoor-ih-TAN-ih-kull), adjective*
Reminiscent of the Puritans (whose strict lifestyle took an extremely narrow view of what was morally acceptable). To issue or follow overly restrictive, moralistic standards about work or socializing is to be *puritanical*.

> *Faith took a rather PURITANICAL outlook on the importance of working a full day; a simple cold was not going to stop her from showing up at work.*

purloin *(PURR-loin), verb*
To steal or to take by dishonest means.

> *Bobby PURLOINED almost all the contents of his dad's change jar before being discovered.*

purvey *(pur-VAY), verb*
To supply.

> *Beluga caviar, PURVEYED by a local gourmet shop, was set out for the guests on large silver trays.*

purview *(PURR-vyoo), noun*
A person's range of authority and control.

> *Yes, Junior, I'm afraid that taking out the garbage DOES in fact fall into your PURVIEW.*

pusillanimous *(pyoo-sih-LAN-ih-muss), adjective*
Cowardly; profoundly lacking in noble qualities of courage and mettle.

> *The actor made a career of playing PUSILLANIMOUS types in movies and on television, but he was apparently a robust and vigorous man of action in real life.*

putative *(PYOO-tuh-tive), adjective*
Reputed or generally regarded by common assent. *Putative* is sometimes confused with punitive, which means "inflicting punishment."

> *The defendant, PUTATIVE head of the city's most notorious crime family, entered the courtroom confidently.*

putrid *(PYOO-trid), adjective*
Rotten . . . either in terms of vegetables OR in terms of behavior.

> *Vivian's putrid, drunken antics got us thrown out of the fancy French restaurant.*

pyriform *(PEER-uh-form), adjective*
Shaped like a pear.

> *"If I get much more PYRIFORM, I'm going to have to rent a space in the produce section," Vivian complained.*

pyromaniac *(pye-roe-MAY-nee-ak), noun*
One who compulsively sets fires.

> *Police believe that the blaze is not the work of an arsonist out for commercial gain, as was initially suspected, but the art of a PYROMANIAC.*

pyrrhic *(PEER-ik), adjective*
Gained at an injustifiably high cost. A *pyrrhic* victory refers to the ancient King Pyrrhus of Epirus, who observed after a particularly bloody battle that another similar victory would destroy his kingdom.

> *You must admit that selling a great many products on which we will lose money would be something of a PYRRHIC victory.*

doctrinaire
abstemious
levity hubris panacea
veracity cerebellum
labyrinth
criterion
nonagenarian
meticulous zither

Q

verbiage quondam
colloquial
wok palpable paginatio
incipient salutary
evity redact fervent
beleaguered yawnful
elixir beneficent
amoose pragmatism

Q

quaff *(kwoff), verb*

To drink heavily; to engage in the robust intake of alcoholic beverages.

> *On his twenty-first birthday, Sean vowed, he would QUAFF at least one glass of beer at every tavern in the city.*

quagmire *(KWAG-mire), noun*

An entaglement that offers no ready solution or means of escape. Literally, a *quagmire* is a boggy patch of ground which wagons and caravans often cannot pass over.

> *The hostage situation, which once worked in the President's favor, now threatens to become the worst QUAGMIRE of his administration.*

quahog *(KO-hog), noun*

An edible clam found off of the Atlantic coastline of North America.

> *Every summer Grandpa would take us to his beachhouse in Maine, where we'd fish and dig for QUAHOGS in the quiet hours before dawn.*

qualm *(kwalm), noun*

A misgiving or pang of conscience (at one's course of action). To have *qualms* about a particular action is to wonder whether or not it is right.

> *He had no QUALMS about leaving his job; he had given the company three very good years.*

quandary *(KWON-duh-ree), noun*

A dilemma; a difficult or uncertain situation.

> *Alisha found herself in a real QUANDARY when she realized she'd asked two dates to the prom.*

quantum *(KWAHN-tuhm), noun*

From the Latin meaning "how great," *quantum* is a share or portion; something that can be counted.

> *Mike assumed that his bridges were burned, without assessing the QUANTUM of the changes he had brought about.*

quarantine *(KWOR-un-teen), verb*

To set apart; to isolate from others in order to prevent the spread of disease.

> *An elementary knowledge of public health procedures would have led you to QUARANTINE this area immediately, Dr. Miller.*

quark *(kwork), noun*

An elementary particle. A *quark* is one of the smallest known quantities of matter.

> *Phillip's work in applied physics focused on the behavior of QUARKS in various environments.*

quash *(KWAHSH), verb*

To repress or subdue completely.

> *The military quickly QUASHED the developing rebellion.*

quaver *(KWAY-vur), verb*

To tremble, shake, or quiver.

> *Eddie's hand QUAVERED as he extended the box containing the diamond ring across the table toward Helene.*

quell *(kwell), verb*

To subdue; to crush or extinguish; to overcome.

> *The police sought to QUELL the rioters by using tear gas, but due to equipment malfunctions were unable to do so.*

querulous *(KWER-uh-luss), adjective*

Given to complaining. Someone who makes peevish complaints is *querulous*.

> *Adrienne, a QUERULOUS young woman, complained about all her problems during lunch hours at work.*

quibble *(KWIB-uhl), verb or noun*

As a noun, "quibble" means either an instance of using evasive language to avoid the subject at hand OR an example of petty criticism. The verb is the act of using evasive language or the act of offering petty criticism.

> *"Do you love me?" Janice asked. Paul QUIBBLED for some time, pointing out how much she meant to him and how happy he was to be with her. Janice knew the answer to her question was "no."*

quid pro quo *(kwid pro KWO), noun*

A thing given in return for something else; Latin: "something for something."

> *Ryan's acceptance of a $40,000 check in return for a written promise to vote in favor of the highway project, a staggeringly obvious QUID PRO QUO, led to his indictment.*

quiescent *(kwee-ESS-unt), adjective*

Dormant; inactive.

> *The old piano that had once rung out triumph after triumph had been standing QUIESCENT in its oak-paneled room since the day of its master's death.*

quietus *(kwhy-eat-us), noun*

Something that ends or settles a situation. Also, a word for death or retirement.

> *The QUIETUS of the argument arrived when Marteeka made a point that Frieda could not refute.*

Q

quintessence *(kwin-TESS-unts), noun*

The purest and most perfect form of something.

> *"In my opinion," Howard said, "the Twinkie is the QUINTESSENCE of the snack cake."*

quirk *(kwurk), noun*

An idiosyncrasy; an odd behavioral or personality characteristic.

> *I hope you can overlook Mr. Johnson's QUIRK of using rough language with outside salespeople.*

quisling *(KWIZ-ling), noun*

One who betrays his or her own country and aids an invading one; particularly, an official who serves in a puppet government.

> *That the Vichy government in France was composed primarily of cowards, profiteers, and QUISLINGS is hardly open to dispute.*

quixotic *(kwik-SOT-ik), adjective*

Hopelessly and impractically idealistic. *Quixotic* is derived from the literary character Don Quixote, whose romantic view of the world is at odds with the harsh realities of existence.

> *Arthur's QUIXOTIC search for financial backing for his get-rich-quick schemes only amused Betty.*

quizzical *(KWIZ-ih-kul), adjective*

Puzzled.

> *Chris gave his boss a QUIZZICAL look upon being told he would not receive any pay for the next month.*

quondam *(KWAHN-dumm), adjective*

From the Latin meaning "at one time," *quondam* means one-time or former.

> *Professor Lightyear's QUONDAM assistant turned to wickedness and soon became an evil genius.*

R

R

rabbinical (*rub-BIN-ih-kul*), *adjective*

Of or pertaining to rabbis. Another acceptable form of *rabbinical* is *rabbinic*.

I intend to take up rabbinical studies in September.

rabble (*RAB-ul*), *noun*

A mob; a rowdy crowd or disorderly group.

Flashing cameras recorded the journey of the accused as the police guided him through the RABBLE that had gathered on the courthouse steps.

raiment (*RAY-munt*), *noun*

Clothing or apparel, often of the best quality.

Clyde stood uncomfortably at the party in his stiff RAIMENT.

rambunctious (*ram-BUNK-shuss*), *adjective*

Difficult to manage or control; extremely boisterous.

We love to have Roman and Marlena over for dinner, but their three-year-old is so RAMBUNCTIOUS that no one gets to relax and enjoy the meal.

ramification (*ram-ih-fih-KAY-shun*), *noun*

Eventual consequence. *Ramification* is, literally, the process of extending along branchlike progressions; an act's *ramifications*, then, are the events or situations arising from it over time.

I believe the RAMIFICATIONS of approving this bill have not been thought through fully.

rampage (*RAM-page*), *noun*

An instance reminiscent of frenzied violence; a destructive period of self-indulgent behavior.

"The tiniest mistake sends my boss on a RAMPAGE," the senior staffer moaned.

rampant (*RAM-punt*), *adjective*

Widespread; unrestrained.

The obedience trainer told us that because we had allowed our dogs to run RAMPANT through our old apartment, we would have a hard time keeping them confined to one area of the new house.

rancor (*RAN-kur*), *noun*

Intense ill-will; bitter resentment.

Mike's RANCOR toward his ex-wife was so intense that the mere mention of her name was sometimes enough to send him into a tirade.

rankle *(RANG-kul), verb*

To cause irritation or festering resentment. Someone who is peeved by a perceived slight or oversight is said to be *rankled*.

> *The criticism he received for his plan RANKLED Paul for some time.*

rapacious *(ruh-PAY-shuss), adjective*

Given to plunder or the forcible overpowering of another. *Rapacious* is related to the word rape.

> *The foe we face is a RAPACIOUS one who thinks nothing of overrunning the weak if it suits his purposes.*

rapport *(rah-PORE), noun*

A trusting and peaceful mutual relationship.

> *Although the Wilsons found their neighbors odd at first, the four soon developed a strong RAPPORT.*

rapprochement *(rap-rosh-MAWN), noun*

The repairing of damaged relations. To bring about a *rapprochement* is to improve an existing rift between two parties.

> *The process of RAPPROCHEMENT between the two countries was slow and laborious.*

rapture *(RAP-chur), noun*

Ecstatic feeling. To experience *rapture* is to be carried into a realm of joy.

> *Beethoven's Ninth Symphony, well played, is enough to send me into fits of RAPTURE.*

rarefied *(RARE-uh-fied), adjective*

Lofty or exalted. Something that is *rarefied* is refined and of high caliber.

> *I must admit I feel a little out of place in such RAREFIED company.*

ratiocinate *(rash-ee-OSS-ih-nate), verb*

To reason. To *ratiocinate* is to probe thoroughly by means of logical examination.

> *We have some of the best mathematical minds in the world working on this problem, and yet no one has proved able to RATIOCINATE with sufficient clarity to find a solution.*

raucous *(RAW-kuss), adjective*

Rowdy; boisterous; disorderly and wild. Also: harsh or grating to the ear.

> *My parents' fears that we would use their vacation as an opportunity to stage RAUCOUS parties in the den were not entirely without foundation.*

R

ravage *(RAV-ij), verb*
To wreak havoc or inflict ruinous damage upon.

My online Mongol hordes RAVAGED the simulated village.

ravenous *(RAV-uh-nuss), adjective*
Powerfully hungry. *Ravenous* can also mean intensely eager to be satisfied.

I am RAVENOUS, but fortunately dinner will be served soon.

raze *(raze), verb*
To flatten, level, or demolish.

Despite our arguments that the building had significant historical value and should be restored, the planning board authorized its demolition; within a week of the meeting, it was RAZED.

reapportionment *(re-uh-PORE-shun-ment), noun*
Redistribution. *Reapportionment* is generally used with reference to changes in political districts based on shifting population.

The REAPPORTIONMENT of voting districts dramatically affected the balance of power in the House.

rebuff *(re-BUFF), noun*
An instance of rejection or expressed disapproval. To receive a *rebuff* is to be sharply and summarily turned down.

Tim suffered his employer's REBUFF shortly after proposing the new project.

rebuke *(rih-BYOOK), noun or verb*
Sharp, stern disapproval or, as a verb, its expression.

Al's drunken behavior earned a sharp REBUKE from his wife.

recalcitrant *(ri-KAL-sih-trunt), adjective*
Resistant to authority. Someone who has difficulty working under any superior could be said to be *recalcitrant*.

Boot camp is not the best place for RECALCITRANT behavior, Mr. Diamond.

recant *(rih-KANT), verb*
To disavow (a formerly held view). Historically, people considered religious heretics have been forced to *recant* unauthorized beliefs by church authorities.

It was not until June that the Congressmen RECANTED and withdrew his support for the constitutional amendment.

recapitulate *(re-kub-PIT-yoo-late), verb*
To summarize in concise form. To *recapitulate* a story is to relate its essential points briefly.

> *Sgt. Dennis, an eyewitness, RECAPITULATED the incident to his superiors at headquarters.*

recede *(rih-SEED), verb*
To move back or away.

> *My brother is so sensitive about his RECEDING hairline that he's started wearing a hat whenever he goes out in public.*

recession *(rih-SESH-uhn), noun*
Generally speaking, the act of withdrawing. Economically speaking, a *recession* occurs when the gross domestic product declines for two or more quarters in a row.

> *Pundits could not agree on whether or not the country's poor economy was indicative of a RECESSION.*

recidivism *(rih-SID-ih-viz-um),*
Repeated relapse into a past condition or behavior.

> *The rate of RECIDIVISM for inmates in this institution is woefully high, Warden.*

reciprocal *(rih-SIP-ri-kul),*
Given in return for something else; mutually negotiated.

> *Many economists feel that the U.S. economy cannot truly improve until the United States is able to negotiate a RECIPROCAL trade agreement with the Japanese.*

reciprocate *(rih-SIP-ro-kate), verb*
To give or act in turn following the lead of another. Someone who *reciprocates* reproduces the courtesy, gift, or example of another.

> *Mr. Powers has shown evidence that he wants to end the feud; the least you can do is RECIPROCATE.*

reclusive *(ri-KLOO-siv), adjective*
Hermitlike. Someone who shuts himself off from the influences of the world could be considered *reclusive*.

> *The RECLUSIVE millionaire lived the life of a hermit, never leaving his home.*

recompense *(REK-um-pense), verb and noun*
To give compensation (for suffering or injury, for instance). As a noun, *recompense* means "that which is given in compensation."

> *There is no RECOMPENSATE for the loss you have suffered, Mrs. Williams.*

reconcile *(REK-un-sile), verb*

To settle or bring into agreement. One can *reconcile* conflicts, contradictory columns of figures, or even internal emotions that seem at odds with each other.

> *How is the White House to RECONCILE these conflicting signals from the Kremlin?*

recondite *(RECK-un-dite), adjective*

Describes something, such as knowledge, that is difficult, obscure, and beyond ordinary knowledge.

> *I made it through only five pages of the author's RECONDITE prose before turning to the latest thriller.*

reconnaissance *(ri-KON-uh-sunce), noun*

A search (of an area) made for the purpose of gaining information likely to yield military advantage. *Reconnaissance* is borrowed from the French.

> *The pilot knew that a RECONNAISSANCE mission such as this one would be difficult and dangerous.*

reconnoiter *(rek-uh-NOY-ter), verb*

To engage in reconnaissance. (See above.) *Reconnoiter* is from an old French verb meaning "to explore."

> *Your mission is to RECONNOITER the area and meet back here at 0800 hours.*

recoup *(rih-KOOP), verb*

To regain or recover the equivalent of something lost.

> *John robotically placed coins in the slot machine, trying desperately to RECOUP his losses.*

recrimination *(rih-krim-ih-NAY-shun), noun*

An accusation made in response to an accusation; a countercharge.

> *Bo knew that divorce proceedings often degenerated into endless, bitter rounds of seemingly pointless RECRIMINATION.*

rectify *(REK-tih-fie), verb*

To put right. Someone who *rectifies* a calculation corrects the mathematical errors it contains.

> *Ellen RECTIFIED her previous mistakes and filed the report.*

rectitude *(REK-ti-tood), noun*

Righteousness and moral virtue.

> *Myra demonstrates an astounding amount of moral RECTITUDE for one so young.*

recumbent *(ri-KUM-bent), adjective*

Lying down. *Recumbent* can also mean "inactive."

> *Oscar lay on the beach, RECUMBENT beneath the warm Hawaiian sun.*

redact *(rih-DAKT), verb*

To revise or edit a manuscript into publishable form. *Redact* can have a negative connotation, suggesting that edits are made against a writer's probable wishes.

> *Julie was livid when she found how the editors had REDACTED her careful, polished prose.*

redolent *(RED-uh-lent), adjective*

Either having a pleasant fragrance OR being suggestive or reminiscent of something else, such as a writer's work that shows clear evidence of another writer's influence.

> *The song's dominant theme was REDOLENT of well-known works by Beethoven.*

redoubtable *(rih-DOUT-uh-bull), adjective*

Inspiring wonder or awe; worthy of respect.

> *The REDOUBTABLE Saint George mounted his charger and set off in search of his next dragon.*

redundant *(rih-DUN-dunt), noun*

Superfluous. That which fulfills the role of something already in place and functional is *redundant*.

> *Many of the functions of the shuttle vehicle are deliberately designed to be REDUNDANT in order to provide backup systems in case primary systems fail.*

refulgent *(rih-FUL-junt), adjective*

radiant.

> *A REFULGENT smile crossed Anna's face when she learned that her loan had been approved.*

refurbish *(re-FUR-bish), verb*

To renovate or repair. To *refurbish* is to restore to a state of attractive completion.

> *The housing project's volunteers REFURBISHED the abandoned apartments in record time.*

regale *(rih-GALE), verb*

To entertain; to give delight. Also, to provide pleasure, particularly by means of food, spectacle, or the like.

> *In this film, although the millionaire REGALES the innocent country girl with beautiful gifts and a lavish week on the town, money isn't enough to win her heart in the end.*

regime *(ruh-ZHEEM), noun*
A government or ruling system in power. *Regime* tends to have a negative connotation.

> *The fascist REGIME was toppled by freedom fighters.*

regimentation *(rej-uh-men-TAY-shun), noun*
Discipline and uniformity of action and appearance, typical of the military.

> *Fred passed the exit that would take him to his job, ripped off his tie and threw it out the window, and generally rebelled against the REGIMENTATION of his daily life.*

regress *(rih-gress), verb*
To return to an earlier state of being.

> *Every time Dan gets around Lydia he REGRESSES to some sort of infantile state.*

regurgitate *(rih-GURJ-ih-tate), verb*
To vomit; to cast (something) back again.

> *Frankly, the prospect of working all night on the project made me want to REGURGITATE, but the deadline was near and it had to be met.*

reiterate *(re-IT-uh-rate), verb*
To restate or say again; to repeat.

> *Let me REITERATE: There will be no exception to the official policy on removing unauthorized recordings from the studio.*

rejoinder *(rih-JOIN-der), noun*
An answer to a reply, especially a clever or witty answer.

> *I stood there silently, racking my brain for a suitable REJOINDER to Mike's rude remarks.*

relapse *(RE-laps), noun*
A return or slip back into an old condition, state, or mindset.

> *Mom warned me that I'd have a RELAPSE of the flu if I stood out in the cold watching the football game for three hours, and she was right.*

relegate *(REL-uh-gate), verb*
To assign or place in a position, often one of low prestige or power; to set out of sight; banish.

> *Although the press release described Lou's new position as a promotion, he and everyone else in the organization knew he was being RELEGATED to a less prominent spot in the hierarchy after the fiasco of the Darwin project.*

relentless *(ri-LENT-lis), adjective*
Unceasingly harsh. Something that is unyieldingly intense or severe is *relentless*.

> *Under the RELENTLESS questioning of the prosecutor, Diane lost her composure.*

relevance *(REL-uh-vence), noun*

The quality of being pertinent. That which has a connection or apt association has *relevance*.

> *These sales figures have no RELEVANCE for our purposes; they are at least six years old.*

relevant *(REL-uh-vunt), adjective*

Pertaining to or having bearing, influence, or relation to the matter at hand.

> *The defense attorney argued vehemently—but in vain—that the accused's past history was not RELEVANT to the case.*

relinquish *(ri-LING-kwish), verb*

To give up. Someone who surrenders or forswears a thing *relinquishes* it.

> *The King RELINQUISHED his throne to marry the woman he loved.*

relish *(REL-ish), verb*

To enjoy heartily; also, an instance of great enjoyment. (Also: a sweet pickle dish composed of various vegetables.)

> *On particularly difficult days, Barbara RELISHED a private fantasy of kicking Mr. Wilkins in the shins.*

remand *(rih-MAND), verb*

To send back.

> *The judge REMANDED the case much more quickly than had been expected, issuing an unusually thorough set of instructions for the lower court to follow.*

reminisce *(rem-uh-NISS), verb*

To recall the past; to remember; to have memories.

> *I used to like to sit on the porch swing with Grandma on those cool summer nights and listen to her REMINISCE about her childhood in Italy.*

remiss *(rih-MISS), adjective*

Negligent; unreliable or careless in one's duties.

> *I hired Ted because he was my friend, but if he continues to be REMISS in his duties I'm afraid I'm going to have to let him go.*

remonstrate *(rih-MON-strate), verb*

To protest, object, or offer disapproval; to offer objection or specific complaint.

> *Neighborhood parents packed the meeting to REMONSTRATE with the school committee for voting to close the local elementary school.*

remunerate *(ri-MYOO-ne-rate), verb*

To pay (in consideration of another person's expense or action). To *remunerate* is to settle an existing financial obligation by means of payment.

> *The insurance company REMUNERATED the accident victim only after months of delaying.*

remuneration *(rih-myoon-uh-RAY-shun), noun*

Something provided in exchange for goods or services; payment.

> *Fred was quite comfortable with the general idea of working in the automotive industry; it was the low level of REMUNERATION he couldn't get used to.*

remunerative *(rih-MYOON-er-uh-tive), adjective*

Describes something that is profitable.

> *Jane quit her day job after she found her online business was more REMUNERATIVE than she'd expected.*

renaissance *(REN-uh-sonce), noun*

A rebirth or revival. Also (when capitalized) the period of artistic and cultural renewal in Europe that extended from, roughly, the fourteenth to seventeenth centuries; (when lower-case) a similar reawakening of dormant interests, spirits, or abilities.

> *Leonardo Da Vinci is recognized by most historians as the preeminent scientific and artistic genius of the RENAISSANCE.*

rendezvous *(RON-day-voo), noun*

A meeting; especially, a secret meeting between lovers.

> *Claire knew that if her mother found out about her RENDEZVOUS with Elton, she would be grounded for at least a week.*

renege *(ri-neg), verb*

To go back (on one's word). Someone who breaks a promise or commitment *reneges* on an agreement.

> *Dalton was supposed to have been named vice president in exchange for his support, but Peterson RENEGED on the deal after assuming control.*

renounce *(re-NOWNCE), verb*

To abandon or deny any connection with. Someone who *renounces* something severs all ties to it.

> *Only by RENOUNCING all desire for possessions, the monks believed, could one attain enlightenment.*

renowned *(rih-NOWND), adjective*
Famous or well-known.

> *We were all thrilled to learn that a RENOWNED author of your caliber had agreed to teach at the university this semester, sir.*

repartee *(rep-er-TAY), noun*
Conversation characterized by witty banter.

> *The REPARTEE of the new late-night host seemed rehearsed rather than spontaneous.*

repercussion *(ree-per-KUSH-un), noun*
An echo; reverberation; also, the result of an action, often negative.

> *The REPERCUSSIONS of Ben's cheating were more severe than he had expected: a failing grade for the class and a two-week suspension.*

replete *(ri-PLEET), adjective*
Full. To say A is *replete* with B is to say A is supplied to the highest possible level with B.

> *The market was REPLETE with everything the holiday shopper could have wanted.*

replica *(REP-lih-kuh), noun*
A copy, imitation, or facsimile of an original.

> *While Steve was in Paris he bought a REPLICA of the Mona Lisa for his mother.*

replicate *(REP-li-kate), verb*
To reproduce (an event or action). *Replicate* can also mean "to bend back."

> *Dr. Yate believed he had made an important discovery, but he was unable to REPLICATE his experiment for the other scientists in his group.*

repose *(rih-POSE), noun*
An instance of resting after exercise or strain; also, tranquil rest reminiscent of eternal or heavenly ease.

> *We hiked in the Blue Hills from sunrise to sunset, stopping only for a brief REPOSE by the lake around midday.*

reprehensible *(rep-ri-HEN-sih-bull), adjective*
Abhorrent. That which is morally inexcusable is *reprehensible*.

> *I agree that the crimes were REPREHENSIBLE; they were not, however, committed by my client.*

reprieve *(ri-preev), verb*
A suspension or delay from imminent proceedings. A *reprieve* is a respite.

> *The inmate won a last-minute REPRIEVE from the governor.*

reproach *(ri-PROACH), verb and noun*

To express stern disapproval of. As a noun, *reproach* means scornfully stated disdain.

> *Your many efforts to get on Harvey's good side have succeeded only in winning his REPROACH.*

reprobate *(REP-ruh-bate), noun*

An unprincipled person. A *reprobate* is someone who has crossed an accepted line describing morally sound behavior.

> *From that day on Johnson was considered a REPROBATE, and was shunned in the town.*

reprove *(re-PROOV), verb*

To censure. Someone who corrects or finds fault *reproves*.

> *REPROVING children can only go so far; you must set a good example for them, as well.*

repudiate *(rih-PYOO-dee-ate) verb*

To disprove and thereby render obsolete. A theory that has been *repudiated* is one that is accepted as invalid.

> *This survey totally REPUDIATES the findings Geraldson claims in his earlier paper; his model can no longer stand.*

repugnance *(ri-PUG-nunce), noun*

Disgust. To show strong aversion for something is to show *repugnance*.

> *We can greet the news of the terrorist bombing only with REPUGNANCE.*

requisite *(REK-wi-zit), adjective*

Necessary. That which is required or essential is *requisite*.

> *Having failed to fill out the REQUISITE forms, Lydia missed the opportunity to enter her work in the fair.*

requite *(rih-KWYTE), verb*

To seek retribution or revenge for an actual or assumed wrong.

> *You have wronged me for the last time! My thirst for revenge will not be REQUITED until you, too, are suffering!*

rescind *(ri-sind), verb*

Reverse (for instance, an order, command, or edict). To *rescind* an instruction is to overrule it.

> *The order of detention is hereby RESCINDED; you may return to your native country at your earliest convenience, Mr. Dawson.*

resilience *(ri-ZIL-yunce), noun*

The ability to rebound. That which bounces back shows *resilience*.

> *Joanne's RESILIENCE was remarkable; she recovered from the operation in record time.*

resilient *(rih-ZIL-yunt), adjective*

Having the ability to survive; likely to rebound, particularly from hardship.

> *Although Rudy failed to make the team during his freshman year, he was RESILIENT and dedicated enough to earn a spot the next year.*

resolute *(REZ-uh-loot), adjective*

Unyielding in determination. Someone who is firm of purpose is *resolute*.

> *We remain RESOLUTE on the question of the hostages: they must be released without precondition.*

resonant *(REZ-uh-nunt), adjective*

Pertaining to or reminiscent of a sound (often deep and pleasant) that echoes or continues.

> *The calm, RESONANT tone of the professor's voice was, after a night without sleep, very nearly enough to put me asleep.*

resonate *(REZ-uh-nate), verb*

To vibrate or sound in a way similar to something else. In addition, that which matches or complements an existing pattern can be said to *resonate* with that pattern.

> *The sound of clicking footsteps RESONATED through the cavernous hallway.*

respite *(RESS-pit), noun*

A reprieve; an instance of temporary relief.

> *Mark had worked on the book for six weeks straight without RESPITE.*

resplendent *(ri-SPLEN-dent), adjective*

Brilliantly shining. That which is splendidly lustrous is *resplendent*.

> *A sky RESPLENDENT with stars awaited Norman and his telescope.*

restaurateur *(reh-stuh-ruh-TUR), noun*

A person who manages and owns a restaurant.

> *The Andersons had no one to complain to when they discovered their rude waiter was none other than the RESTAURATEUR himself.*

restitution *(res-ti-TOO-shun), noun*

The act of compensating for a past misdeed. To make *restitution* for something is to acknowledge to wrongness of a past act and attempt to repair the damage caused by it.

> *A bill authorizing RESTITUTION to the citizens interned in the camps recently cleared Congress.*

resurgence *(ri-SUR-jents), noun*

Reappearance or revival. Something that has a *resurgence* returns to a position of prominence or visibility.

> *A RESURGENCE of popularity for bell-bottom slacks is not expected this season, but the experts have been wrong before.*

restive *(RES-tive), adjective*

Uneasy; impatient with delay. Someone who is impatient or uncomfortable with present surroundings could be said to be *restive*.

> *The RESTIVE players gathered around the coach, eager to get the game underway.*

resurrect *(rez-uh-REKT), verb*

To bring back from the dead. Figuratively, to *resurrect* something (a fashion, for instance) is to reintroduce it after it has been dismissed as no longer relevant or appropriate.

> *It astounds me that you have gone to the trouble to RESURRECT these completely discredited ideas.*

resuscitate *(rih-SUS-ih-tate), verb*

To revive someone after he or she has passed out or died.

> *The crowd cheered as the lifeguard RESUSCITATE the drowning victim.*

reticent *(RET-ih-sent), adjective*

Reserved. Someone who prefers silence to conversation in social settings could be said to be *reticent*.

> *Little Amy was RETICENT at the party, staying close to her mother and avoiding all talk with strangers.*

reticulate (rih-TIK-yoo-lit),

Like a net or network. Also, as a verb (rih-TEK-yoo-late), to cause to take the form of a network.

> *The maple leaf's fibers are RETICULATE in structure.*

retinue *(RET-n-oo), noun*
A group of companions or followers (of a person of great importance). A *retinue* is an entourage.

> *The President and his RETINUE are expected here just before noon.*

rhetoric *(RET-ur-ik), noun*
The art of the effective use of language. *Rhetoric* is also speech or writing calculated to arouse passion.

> *Are we ever going to move from empty RHETORIC to a sound plan of action on this issue?*

retort *(rih-TORT), verb*
To reply in a sharp, sometimes retaliatory fashion; (as a noun:) a biting reply.

> *"Well, if you're so smart," Frank RETORTED, "why did you drop the ball on the five-yard line?"*

retraction *(rih-TRAK-shun), noun*
A formal renunciation of statements considered or determined to be false or injurious to reputation.

> *After erroneously linking Mr. Vining to organized crime figures, the paper was forced to issue a front-page RETRACTION explaining and acknowledging its mistake.*

retribution *(ret-ruh-BYOO-shun), noun*
Punishment (as from God) for past wrongdoing. *Retribution* can also refer to divine reward for the just, but the negative sense is more common.

> *Some saw the mafia don's debilitating illness as a form of divine RETRIBUTION for a life of crime.*

retroactive *(ret-ro-AK-tiv), adjective*
Effective back to a stated point in time. Something that is made *retroactive* is extended as though it had been taking place since a certain past date.

> *We will be raising your salary to $100,000 a year, Perkins, RETROACTIVE to January 1.*

retrograde *(REH-truh-grade), adjective*
Of withdrawing, retreating, or moving backward.

> *I wouldn't say you're in a slump. I'd say you're making RETROGRADE progress.*

retrospect *(RET-ruh-spekt), noun*
Hindsight. *Retrospect* derives from the Latin roots for "backward" and "vision."

> *In RETROSPECT, the decision to launch the attack at night now seems like a catastrophic error.*

revamp *(re-VAMP), verb*

To redo. To *revamp* is to renovate thoroughly.

> *The playwright decided to REVAMP several of the weaker scenes in the first act.*

revelry *(REV-ul-ree), noun*

Uninhibited celebration.

> *Although Allan had a lot of work to do, he couldn't resist joining in the REVELRY that accompanied the office Christmas party.*

reverberate *(rih-VUR-buh-rate), verb*

To echo back and forth, rebound, or recoil.

> *The sound of the gunshot REVERBERATED throughout the canyon.*

revile *(rih-VILE), verb*

To curse or abuse in harsh language. Someone who is *reviled* by another is denounced or hated by that person.

> *Realizing that he was REVILED by those opposing his stand on the military buildup, the Senator decided to cancel his appearance at the campus.*

ribald *(RIB-uld), adjective*

Amusingly coarse or lewd. A *ribald* story is one that is off-color.

> *The young boys often retired to a spot behind the gym where they would pretend to smoke cigarettes and exchange RIBALD jokes none of them understood.*

rife *(rife), adjective*

Widespread; commonly occurring.

> *Unimaginably poor sanitary conditions, RIFE in London at the time, were the chief cause of the sufferings of the plague years.*

riff *(RIFF), noun*

In music, especially jazz and rock, a short melodic phrase repeated as background or used as a main theme.

> *Once the bass player started playing the insistent opening RIFF to "My Girl," people poured out onto the dance floor.*

rigmarole *(RIG-muh-role), noun*

Nonsensically complicated procedure. *Rigmarole* is also misleading and incomprehensible doubletalk.

> *I have had enough of this author's RIGMAROLE; I want a book with some substance to it.*

riposte *(rih-POAST), noun*

In fencing, the thrust made in response to an opponent's parry; also, a retaliatory remark or retort.

> *I thought Newman was good-natured enough to handle my jokes about his receding hairline, but his heated RIPOSTE about my weight problem indicated otherwise.*

risible *(RIZZ-uh-bull), adjective*

Capable of causing laughter due to its ludicrous nature.

> *Will someone please tell Sean that the hairstyle he thinks is so cool is really just RISIBLE?*

rogue *(roag), noun*

A scalawag. A *rogue* is a person (usually a man) known to have low morals and habits.

> *Everyone in Savannah knew that Rhett was a ROGUE, but somehow he managed to use that fact to his advantage.*

roman à clef *(ro-MON ah KLAY), noun*

A purportedly fictional work that only thinly veils the actual experiences of the author or of characters based on real personages.

> *Capote was ostracized by those in his circle when he published a devastating excerpt from a ROMAN À CLEF, Answered Prayers, that lampooned the frailties and indiscretions of the people who had been closest to him.*

rote *(ROAT), noun*

A habit or mechanical routine.

> *The children learned their multiplication tables by ROTE.*

roué *(roo-AY), noun*

A licentious man; a libertine or lecher.

> *Although Ernest's dalliances might have been understandable when he was a young man, they were more difficult for his family to forgive in his later years, when he came to resemble nothing so much as a tired and lonely old ROUÉ.*

rube *(ROOB), noun*

Slang for an unsophisticated person; a bumpkin.

> *"Look at those RUBES over there," Charlie scoffed; "they wouldn't know a good restaurant if it smacked them in the face"*

R

rubicon *(ROO-bih-kon), noun*
A point beyond which permanent change is unavoidable. The word comes from the name of a river (the *Rubicon*) once crossed by Julius Caesar in an act that led irrevocably to war.

> *In signing the bill, the Governor may have crossed the RUBICON and forever closed the door on his prison reform program.*

rudimentary *(roo-duh-MEN-tuh-ree), adjective*
Basic. That which is elementary is *rudimentary*.

> *This thesis is full of RUDIMENTARY errors in grammar, to say nothing of several significant lapses in style.*

rue *(roo), verb*
To be sorrowful; to mourn or regret bitterly.

> *After spending prom night at home watching movies by herself, Susan began to RUE the day she had rejected Mark so cruelly.*

rueful *(ROO-ful), adjective*
Regretful. *Rueful* can also mean pitiable.

> *In the terminal, Jean gave a RUEFUL sigh as she stared at the plane that was to carry her away from San Francisco forever.*

ruminate *(ROO-muh-nate), verb*
To ponder or review mentally. Someone who *ruminates* over something tosses it over in his mind.

> *Elaine was still RUMINATING over whether or not to attend college in the fall.*

rusticate *(RUSS-ti-kate), verb*
To move (a person) to the country. *Rusticate* can also mean "to accustom to country living."

> *I am afraid you will be unable to RUSTICATE Ken; he is a city boy through and through.*

doctrinaire
abstemious
levity hubris panacea
veracity cerebellum
labyrinth
criterion abyrinth
nonagenarian
meticulous zither

S

erbiage quondam
colloquial
vok palpable pagination
incipient salutary
evity redact fervent
beleaguered yawnful
elixir beneficent
amoose pragmatism

sacrilege *(SACK-ruh-lij), noun*
The violation of anything sacred or anything someone may consider sacred.

The bar patrons found Dan's negative words about the Yankees a SACRILEGE.

sacrilegious *(sak-ruh-LIDJE-uss), adjective*
Profane; blasphemous toward something considered holy or sacred.

Some in the audience considered the director's decision to omit the famous "to be or not to be" speech nothing short of SACRILEGIOUS.

sacrosanct *(SACK-roh-sankt), adjective*
Beyond criticism because it is considered sacred.

You can't criticize the Beatles, Steve. They're SACROSANCT.

sadistic *(suh-DISS-tick), adjective*
The French count, Donatien A.F. de Sade (1740–1815), wrote novels that depicted cruel sexual practices. Over time, his name became synonymous with cruelty and with describing those who delight in being cruel to others.

Only a SADISTIC creep would give out as much homework as Mr. Thomas.

saffron *(SAFF-ron), noun*
A variety of crocus that blooms in the autumn. Also: a spice. Also: yellow-orange in color.

The September page of my calendar is my favorite: trees with leaves of red, orange, and gold, surrounded by a field of purple SAFFRON.

sagacious *(suh-GAY-shuss), adjective*
Perceptive; showing sound judgment.

Brian is the perfect candidate for chairman of the board; experienced, patient, and SAGACIOUS enough to help us counter the threat from our competitor.

sake **(SAH-kee),**
A wine-like Japanese beverage made with fermented rice.

When he returned from California, my father and I dined on sushi and drank warm SAKE at his favorite Japanese restaurant.

salacious *(suh-LAY-shuss), adjective*
Lewd or off-color. *Salacious* is generally used in reference to deliberately provocative pictures or writing.

Most magazines sent by family members to the troops were entirely innocent; who could find anything SALACIOUS in a copy of Golf Digest?

salient *(SAY-lee-unt), adjective*
Striking, obvious.

> *Let's not get bogged down in the details of the bonus plan; the SALIENT point is, we've provided our editors with a measurable financial incentive to do the very best acquisitions work they can.*

salivate *(SAL-ih-vate), verb*
To secrete saliva. To *salivate* over something is to eagerly anticipate eating it; the word has seen some figurative use in this sense.

> *We now know that dogs will SALIVATE upon hearing a bell they associate with food, even if the food is not present.*

sallow *(SAL-low), adjective*
Colorless; sickly-looking.

> *The SALLOW tone of Melanie's skin led us to wonder whether she was ill.*

salubrious *(suh-LOOB-ree-uss), adjective*
Healthful; promoting or contributing to good health.

> *Working out at the health club was definitely a more SALUBRIOUS use of my spare time than sitting at home in front of the television eating potato chips.*

salutary *(SAL-yoo-tare-ee), adjective*
Promoting physical soundness. That which is conducive to good health is *salutary*.

> *The medicine Dr. Catton gave to Mother seems to have had a SALUTARY effect.*

sanctimonious *(sank-tih-MONE-ee-uss), adjective*
Hypocritical; two-faced, especially with regard to matters of morals or religion.

> *Despite his SANCTIMONIOUS brayings on issues of "family values," Reverend Wilton certainly seems to know his way around a certain part of town, according to the reporter who trailed him there last night.*

sanctum *(SANK-tum), noun*
A holy, sacred place.

> *Brandon's small home office contained little more than a computer, an encyclopedia, and a few pieces of furniture, but it was in this unprepossessing SANCTUM that he wrote his Pulitzer Prize–winning play.*

sangfroid *(san-FRWA), noun*
The state of being supremely composed or self-assured, especially in the face of adversity or danger.

> *I always marveled at Janie's SANGFROID before taking exams; I usually got so nervous I could hardly hold a pencil.*

S

sangria *(sang-GREE-uh), noun*
A cocktail of Mexican origin consisting of wine and fruit juices.

> *The cool cantina, with its seemingly endless supply of enchiladas and SANGRIA, was just what we needed after a long day of sightseeing in the hot Acapulco sun.*

sanguinary *(SANG-gwuh-nare-ee), adjective*
Marked by bloodshed.

> *They awoke the next morning to find that the battle had been won, but not without cost: it had been the most SANGUINARY encounter of the two-year conflict.*

sanguine *(SAN-gwinn), adjective*
Possessing a positive attitude. *Sanguine* usually carries the sense of being cheerful despite obstacles or potential problems.

> *Despite the many setbacks she had faced, Ellen remained SANGUINE.*

sans *(sans) preposition*
Without.

> *On the MTV show "Unplugged," rock artists perform their songs SANS electric instruments and amplifiers.*

sardonic *(sar-DON-ik), adjective*
Bitter or sarcastic. That which is derisively scornful is *sardonic*.

> *Milton gave a SARDONIC laugh when asked if he would mind stepping aside to let someone else have a turn at the pinball machine.*

sartorial *(sar-TORE-ee-uhl), adjective*
Pertaining to tailors and their trade.

> *Jake arrived at the job interview in SARTORIAL splendor.*

sate *(sate), verb*
To satisfy completely or to excess.

> *Our hunger for television SATED for the evening, we switched off the set and looked for a good book to read aloud.*

satiate *(SAY-shee-ate), verb*
Satisfy beyond reasonable expectation. To be *satiated* is to consume to excess.

> *If this Thanksgiving dinner doesn't SATIATE your appetite, nothing will.*

satire *(SA-tire), noun*
A humorous work employing sarcasm or irony in order to ridicule, expose, or make light of a person, institution, or practice.

> *I wonder how many of the young children now streaming to theaters to watch this cartoon are accompanied by adults who can appreciate its subtle SATIRE of consumer culture.*

saturnalia *(sat-uhr-NAIL-yuh), noun*
Risque merrymaking, possibly including an orgy. The festival for the Roman god, Saturn, was marked by unrestrained merrymaking.

> *Anyone looking at the party's aftermath the next day would have thought it was a SATURNALIA, not a fairly quiet reunion of five old friends.*

saturnine *(SAT-ur-neen), adjective*
Moody and morose. Someone who is *saturnine* is gloomy.

> *For some months after the death of his cat, Cosgrove maintained a SATURNINE front.*

satyr *(SAY-ter), noun*
A lecherous man. In Greek mythology, *satyrs* were part-man, part-horse (or part-goat) creatures noted for their high spirits and lasciviousness. The word "satirical" also is derived from the mythological *satyrs*.

> *Everyone knows Professor Roth is a SATYR. He puts all the girls with the most cleavage in the front row.*

saunter *(SON-tur), verb*
To walk leisurely or for pleasure.

> *On Sunday afternoons, Mr. Weeks would SAUNTER through Central Park gathering material for his short stories.*

savoir faire *(SAV-whah FAIRE), noun*
Tact or social skill.

> *I'm afraid Helen just doesn't have the SAVOIR FAIRE necessary to build coalitions in such a fractious organization.*

scalene *(SKAY-leen), noun*
In geometry, having no two equal sides.

> *In geometry we learned about the six kinds of triangles: right angle, acute, isosceles, obtuse, equilateral, and SCALENE.*

scanty *(SCAN-tee), adjective*
Insufficient; noticeably lacking.

> *The food at this restaurant is certainly good, but the portions are a little too SCANTY for the price we're paying.*

scapegoat *(SKAPE-goat), noun*

A person considered responsible for a fiasco or mishap who was not in fact totally responsible for it. *Scapegoat* derives from an ancient practice of selecting a goat to accept the sins of a community.

> *I will not act as SCAPEGOAT in this affair; you all had a vote in the matter, and you all voted yes, just as I did.*

scarify *(SKARE-ih-fie), verb*

To wound with harsh criticism.

> *The drill instructor SCARIFIED recruits for the slightest deviation from protocol.*

scathing *(SKAY-thing), adjective*

Violently critical. *Scathing* usually refers to speech or writing about another's conduct or performance.

> *The SCATHING review by the Times theater critic had the anticipated effect: the show closed within two weeks.*

schadenfreude *(SHAH-dun-froy-duh), noun*

An instance of rejoicing at the misfortune of another.

> *Wilson's conviction on perjury charges set off a festival of SCHADENFREUDE among his many conservative detractors.*

schematic *(skuh-MAT-ik), adjective and noun*

Having to do with a diagram or scheme. As a noun, *schematic* can mean "a fully diagrammed plan or drawing."

> *Will you please refer to the SCHEMATIC design I have reproduced on page twelve of your handbook?*

schism *(SKIZ-um), noun*

A division; a break or rupture of relations, especially one due to ideological or political differences.

> *The SCHISM in the party over the issue of slavery reflected a division in the country itself.*

schizophrenia *(skits-uh-FREEN-ee-uh), noun*

A mental condition that often causes sufferers to hallucinate, to be disoriented, and often to withdraw from society.

> *It is a common misconception that the term "SCHIZOPHRENIA" refers to the condition of multiple personalities.*

schlemiel *(shluh-MEEL), noun*

An unlucky or awkward individual who can never seem to get the best of a situation.

> *My guess is, that used car salesman had Mike pegged for a SCHLEMIEL the second he stepped onto the lot.*

schlimazel *(shluh-MOZ-ul), noun*

Someone who endures constant bad luck.

> *Over the past year, Jonah's car was stolen, his house burned down, he lost his job, and he broke his leg—all of which earned him an impromptu "SCHLIMAZEL of the Year" award from his coworkers at the company party.*

schmaltzy *(SHMALT-see), adjective*

Overly sentimental (especially with regard to music or art); tastelessly overdone.

> *Although Libby loved her great-grandfather, she found his SCHMALTZY taste in music hard to bear.*

scintilla *(sin-TILL-uh), noun*

The smallest imaginable portion.

> *Your Honor, the prosecution's case, which is based entirely on hearsay, is unsupported by a SCINTILLA of hard evidence.*

scintillate *(SIN-til-ate), verb*

Giving off sparks. Something of remarkable interest that sets off a sudden reaction among people can also be said to *scintillate*.

> *News about the new film has been hard to come by, but a few SCINTILLATING details have leaked out.*

scion *(SIE-on), noun*

A person directly descended from a given line.

> *My professor told me my claim to be a SCION of William Shakespeare's line was totally at odds both with the existing genealogical information and with the quality of writing in my term paper.*

scourge *(SKUHRJ), noun*

A *scourge* either is a whip used to torture, or it is a cause of affliction.

> *Famine is one of humanity's most horrific SCOURGES.*

scrutinize *(SKROOT-n-ize), verb*

To review extremely closely. Someone who examines an object or document in minute detail *scrutinizes* it.

> *It is your job to SCRUTINIZE these applications carefully for any inaccuracies or misleading statements.*

S

scull *(skull)*, *noun*

A long oar used in the stern of a boat; also, a light racing rowboat. As a verb: to propel a boat with a *scull*.

Stewart loved to get up early in the morning and SCULL around the calm lake.

scurrilous *(SKUR-ih-luss)*, *adjective*

Offensive to civilized discourse; verbally abusive.

Because they were made on the floor of the Senate, the Senator's SCURRILOUS accusations against me were protected, but if he should dare to repeat them in another setting I will sue him for every penny he's worth.

sear *(SEAR)*, *verb*

To burn or scorch, or to cause to dry up and wither.

While I was on vacation, the heat SEARED my plants, leaving them nothing but lifeless brown stalks.

seasonable *(SEE-zun-uh-bull)*, *adjective*

Timely; in keeping with or appropriate to the season. (See, for comparison, the entry for *seasonal*.)

In December, the outside of our building is done up in SEASONABLE green and red lights.

seasonal *(SEE-zun-ul)*, *adjective*

Happening as a result of regular and anticipated changes occurring at a specific time of the year.

Don't worry; that dramatic drop in sales for February is a SEASONAL dip experienced to one degree or another by everyone in our industry.

secede *(sih-SEED)*, *verb*

To withdraw officially and formally from an organization or union; to renounce one's membership.

After Lincoln's election to the presidency, the southern states, with South Carolina leading the way, began to SECEDE from the Union.

seclude *(sih-KLOOD)*, *adjective*

To hide or keep apart; to keep in isolation.

The two met in a woody, SECLUDED area of the estate to be sure their conversation would not be overheard.

sectarian *(seck-TEAR-ee-un)*, *adjective*

Narrow-minded and limited in outlook.

The competing cliques' SECTARIAN squabbles captured the interest of the entire school.

secular *(SEK-yuh-lur), adjective*

Not religious in form or content; worldly.

> *Although the Cardinal had a long list of ecclesiastical issues to review with me, he began our interview with a few wholly SECULAR remarks on the poor fortunes of the Red Sox this year.*

sedentary *(SED-un-tare-ee), adjective*

Involving the act of sitting; accustomed to a lack of movement or exercise.

> *Although I have nothing against watching television during the work week, I do like to engage in less SEDENTARY activities on weekends.*

sedimentary *(sed-uh-MEN-tuh-ree), adjective*

Characterized by being settled in one's ways or habits. *Sedimentary* usually has a negative connotation. Sediment is rocks and minerals that have settled over millions of years.

> *Your SEDIMENTARY lifestyle is just going to lead you to an early grave!*

sedition *(sih-DISH-un), noun*

Words or actions directed against public order; the incitement of disorder or rebellion.

> *The dictator's charges of SEDITION against his political opponents were met with skepticism by the international press.*

sedulous *(SED-yuh-luss), adjective*

Done or crafted with skill, diligence, and care.

> *The teen's SEDULOUS labors at the desert site were rewarded by the discovery of triceratops bones in the third week of the dig.*

seethe *(seethe), verb*

To boil. In addition, someone who internalizes agitation or anger can be said to *seethe.*

> *Still SEETHING from his defeat at the hands of the Dodgers on Tuesday, Gibson took the mound with a look of unwavering determination last night.*

segregate *(SEG-ruh-gate), verb*

To separate or keep apart from others.

> *As the judge seemed doomed to have to point out for the rest of his life, his order affected only those school districts whose officials deliberately practiced SEGREGATION in violation of law—not SEGREGATION that was purely the result of existing demographic patterns.*

segue *(SEG-way), noun*

In music, to pass from one section to another; also, as a noun, any connective matter linking, for example, otherwise unrelated thoughts or observations.

> *Tomlin's mature routines, which featured random observations on the eccentricities of life with few or no SEGUES, were risky but always rewarding.*

semantics *(suh-MAN-tiks), noun*

The science of the way meaning is communicated through language. A *semantic* distinction is one focused on the way something is phrased, rather than its underlying reality.

> *Whether we say the compensation will be "appropriate" or "competitive" is really a matter of SEMANTICS; we know exactly how much we intend to pay the person we finally hire.*

semaphore *(SEM-uh-fore), noun*

A method of (usually seafaring) communication or signaling based on the positionings of the arms of a standing person or the similar positioning of flags (with one held in each hand).

> *Mark's attempt to render the complete works of Goethe in SEMAPHORE makes for a dedicated, if not exactly enthralling, piece of long-term performance art.*

sententious *(sen-TEN-shuss), adjective*

Tending to use many cliches or maxims in order to enlighten others. Someone who shares many sayings or stories in a sanctimonious or preachy way is *sententious.*

> *Polonius's SENTENTIOUS manner of speaking clearly irritates Hamlet in this scene.*

sentient *(SEN-shunt), adjective*

Having consciousness and use of the senses.

> *Until he's had his morning coffee, Mike cannot even be classified as a SENTIENT being.*

septuagenarian *(sep-tuh-juh-NARE-ee-un), noun*

A person in his or her seventies. A *septuagenarian* is one who is between seventy and seventy-nine years old.

> *Grandmother, now 69, is not looking forward to becoming a SEPTUAGENARIAN.*

sepulchral *(suh-PUHL-kruhl), adjective*

Describes something that is characteristic of a tomb because it is hollow and deep.

> *Anyone who's watched old reruns of The Addams Family will never forget Lurch's SEPULCHRAL voice saying, "You rang?"*

sequential *(sih-KWEN-shul), adjective*
An order of arrangement or succession; one after another in arrangement.

> *The class graduation proceeded in SEQUENTIAL order from the beginning of the alphabet to the end, which Jane Zsilow found disheartening.*

sequester *(si-KWES-ter), verb*
To set apart (from outside influence). That which is protected from the prejudices of the external world is *sequestered*.

> *The jury was SEQUESTERED, due to the extraordinary amount of publicity the trial generated.*

seraphic *(sih-RAFF-ick), adjective*
Characteristic of an angel.

> *The music's SERAPHIC tones left me feeling spiritually uplifted.*

serendipity *(sare-un-DIP-ih-tee), noun*
The quality of coming upon important insights or discoveries by accident. To experience *serendipity* is to encounter fortunate coincidence.

> *It was pure SERENDIPITY that, nearly fainting with hunger, I came upon the stock of supplies that night.*

serenity *(suh-REN-ih-tee), noun*
Peacefulness in outlook; a lack of agitation.

> *Although she had always been a whirlwind of activity while we were growing up, my sister Alice seems to be enjoying the SERENITY of convent life.*

serf, *(SURF) noun*
A member of the lower feudal class bound to the land in medieval Europe; a slave.

> *At times, Rufus felt he was moored to his little computer like a SERF to his plot of land.*

seriocomic *(seer-ee-oh-KOM-ik), adjective*
Having both serious and humorous characteristics.

> *Like many of today's successful dramatists, Erica employs SERIOCOMIC themes in her work.*

serpentine *(SUR-pun-teen), adjective*
Snakelike. That which is reminiscent of serpents is *serpentine*.

> *Most salespeople resent the stereotype of their profession as SERPENTINE and ruthless.*

serriform *(SAIR-uh-form), adjective*
Shaped like a saw-edge; having ridges reminiscent of saw-teeth.

> *The two SERRIFORM pieces fit together perfectly, making a solid joint.*

sesquipedalian *(ses-quih-puh-DAY-lee-un), adjective*
Appropriately, this word describes someone who uses really big, ponderous words. From the Latin meaning "a foot and a half."

> *"That commentator uses such SESQUIPEDALIAN language that I doubt anyone knows what he's talking about," my father complained.*

servile *(SUR-vil), adjective*
Overly eager to serve; slavish.

> *Marion's uncharacteristically SERVILE demeanor can only mean one thing: He wants a raise.*

severance *(SEV-uh-runce), noun*
A division; a breaking away, as of a relationship.

> *Bill was able to negotiate a handsome SEVERANCE package when he left the company.*

severity *(suh-VARE-uh-tee), adjective*
Great force or concentration; harshness.

> *The SEVERITY of Milton's remarks about my proposal's deficiencies came as a shock to me; he had told me before the meeting that he liked the idea.*

shako *(SHACK-oh), noun*
A stiff, tall piece of military headgear, resembling a fez with an upright plume.

> *The guard's SHAKO trembled as he advanced toward us angrily.*

shear *(sheer), adjective*
To clip or cut. (See, for comparison, the entry for *sheer*.)

> *I'm afraid I'm not much good at SHEARING sheep; I can't cut the fleece evenly.*

sheer *(sheer), adjective*
Absolute; utter. Also: transparent. (See, for comparison, the entry for *shear*.)

> *To work on a project for twenty-four hours straight is SHEER madness, Roland.*

shibboleth *(SHIB-uh-leth), noun*
A special term not widely known that, when used, identifies the user as a member of a group. *Shibboleth* (a word with biblical origins) can also refer to a peculiarity of fashion or lifestyle common to a single group.

> *The more cynical in the department will tell you that career advancement has less to do with ability than with contacts and memorizing SHIBBOLETHS.*

shogun *(SHO-gun), noun*
Before 1868, the commander of the Japanese military.

> *The SHOGUNS of ancient Japan are considered among the most notable strategists in military history.*

shun *(shun), verb*

To keep away from or avoid.

> *Wade's parents thought he would be glad they had agreed to chaperone the school dance, and seemed surprised when he SHUNNED them for the entire evening.*

shunt *(SHUNT), verb*

To change the direction of; to divert.

> *When his proposal was dismissed after less than a minute of discussion, Mark felt more than ever that his ideas were being SHUNTED aside without due consideration.*

simile *(SIM-uh-lee), noun*

A comparison in speech or writing. "Her smile is like the morning sun" is an example of a *simile*.

> *By asking, "Shall I compare thee to a summer's day?" Shakespeare initiates a SIMILE he will develop fully in succeeding lines of the sonnet.*

similitude *(sih-MIL-ih-tood), noun*

Likeness or similarity. If A is a *similitude* of B, a is similar to B.

> *Bea and Rosa have a SIMILITUDE of habits when it comes to cooking.*

simulacrum *(sim-yuh-LAY-krum), noun*

An minor, unreal or eerie similarity. A *simulacrum* can also be an effigy.

> *The boy possessed only the barest SIMULACRUM of the classic DeBerris brow, but something told me his claim to be a descendant was valid.*

sine qua non *(SEE-nay kwa NON), noun*

An essential feature (of something). *Sine qua non* is Latin for "without which not."

> *Many people consider a happy ending to be the SINE QUA NON of a proper comedy.*

sinecure *(SIN-uh-kyoor), noun*

A job that is profitable although it requires only a marginal amount of work.

> *Everyone's annoyed that the boss gave her do-nothing son a SINECURE just to keep him from getting into trouble.*

singsong *(SING-song), adjective*

Rendered chantingly or with a musical air; spoken in a manner reminiscent of singing.

> *Bert taunted Arthur with a SINGSONG recitation of his most embarrassing incidents at school.*

singularity *(sing-you-LAIR-ih-tee), noun*

A peculiarity or unique quality.

> *Fiona's SINGULARITY in fashion makes her—for good or ill—the talk of most parties she attends.*

sinister *(SIN-uh-ster), adjective*

Describes or suggests something unfavorable and potentially harmful. Southpaws of the world will be unhappy to learn that the word is Latin for "left."

> *The SINISTER music gave me gooseflesh.*

Sisyphean *(sis-uh-FEE-uhn), adjective*

Describes something, such as a task, that is tortuous and seems endless. In classical mythology, Sisyphus was a king noted for his trickery. He was punished by having to roll a stone uphill. Just before the stone got to the top of the hill, it would roll back down, and Sisyphus would have to start the arduous task all over again.

> *Some days, keeping paperwork under control seems a SISYPHEAN task.*

site *(site), noun*

A place or spot. (See, for comparison, the entry for *cite.*)

> *We will build the new library and treasure hall on this SITE.*

skepticism *(SKEP-tih-siz-um), adjective*

An instance of doubt or uncertainty.

> *Your SKEPTICISM that we will be able to finish the work on time is understandable, given our history of delivering material late.*

skittish *(SKTT-ish), adjective*

Nervous and lacking confidence. Someone who is uneasy about approaching a task can be said to be *skittish* about it.

> *Lisa is still a bit SKITTISH about the computer, George; perhaps you can give her a hand.*

skulk *(skulk), verb*

To move about furtively or quietly.

> *After she lost her job, Lea SKULKED around the town at odd hours, hoping to avoid her former colleagues.*

skullduggery *(skull-DUG-uh-ree), noun*

Dishonest actions; cheating.

> *Mike accused me of throwing copying my answers to the math quiz; I replied that I had never engaged in such SKULLDUGGERY, or at any rate had never been caught, which in my view amounted to much the same thing.*

slander (SLAN-dur), verb

An untrue and malicious statement intended to damage the reputation of another. (As a legal term, *slander* refers to oral, rather than written or pictorial, defamation.)

If I hear any more of your SLANDERS against my father, Mr. Caen, you will be hearing from my attorney.

sloe (SLO), noun

A small fruit resembling a plum.

Many people like the taste of SLOE gin, but Jennifer prefers the traditional variety flavored with juniper berries.

slough (SLUFF), verb

To become shed or cast off, like the slough—or outer skin layer—of a snake.

I did my best to SLOUGH off my feelings of uncertainty and to move ahead optimistically.

slovenly (SLUHV-in-lee), adjective

Dirty or untidy in one's personal habits.

Burt's SLOVENLY room is at odds with his tidy personal appearance.

sluggish (SLUG-gish), adjective

Lacking vitality or alertness; lethargic.

As the hours drew on, I pecked away at my keyboard dutifully; toward morning, however, I could tell that I was getting SLUGGISH.

smarmy (SMAR-mee), adjective

Insincerely earnest.

In between syrupy love songs, the SMARMY lounge singer repeatedly assured the crowd they were by far the best audience he'd ever performed for.

smattering (SMAT-er-ing), noun

A little bit. A *smattering* is a small amount of something.

Dean picked up a SMATTERING of Italian during his visit to Venice.

smitten (SMIT-uhn), adjective

Very much in love, or struck, as though by a hard blow.

Warren is so SMITTEN with Ellen that he's practically stopped getting anything productive done.

snafu (sna-FOO), noun

An egregious but common error.

Supposedly, the word "SNAFU" is an acronym of the phrase "Situation normal, all fouled up."

snit *(snit), noun*

An angry or nasty mood; an irritated state.

> *After his roommate spilled grape juice all over his favorite coat, Jay was in a SNIT for weeks.*

sobriety *(so-BREYE-uh-tee), noun*

Clear-headedness. *Sobriety* is generally used to signify freedom from the influence of alcoholic drink.

> *My guess is that W.C. Fields had as few moments of SOBRIETY in real life as he had in the movies.*

sociometry *(so-see-OM-uh-tree), noun*

The determination of preference among members of distinct social groups. *Sociometry* can also refer to distinctions accountable to social differences.

> *What we found is that the brand's success or failure in a given area was due not mainly to income level, but to SOCIOMETRY.*

sociopath *(SO-see-uh-path), noun*

A person who, because of mental illness, lacks restraint or moral responsibility toward fellow members of society.

> *Although motion pictures and popular fiction have shown an unending fascination with serial killers, the fact is that such SOCIOPATHS are quite rare.*

sociopolitical *(so-she-oh-puh-LIT-uh-kuhl), adjective*

Describes the combination of social and political factors that affects certain people, groups, classes, etc.

> *Depending on his audience, the politician either emphasized or distanced herself from the SOCIOPATHIC background of her family.*

solace *(SOL-uss), noun*

Consolation. To give *solace* is to sympathize with and console.

> *The fact that he had thrown three touchdowns was little SOLACE to Jim: all he could think about was losing the game.*

solecism *(SOL-ih-siz-um), noun*

An act that breaks formal rules. *Solecism* is generally taken to mean "a transgression of established standards" (for instance, with regard to etiquette or writing.)

> *She told her husband not to worry, that forgetting a host's name was only a minor SOLECISM and certainly nothing to be concerned about.*

solicitious *(suh-LISS-ih-tuss), adjective*
Openly concerned or worried (about the condition of another). Someone who is attentively eager to help is *solicitous*.

> *Joan could not have been more SOLICITIOUS to Peter while he was sick.*

solidarity *(sol-uh-DARE-ih-tee), noun*
Unity arising from a common purpose or situation.

> *As the project's deadline got closer and closer, the assembled team showed an amount of SOLIDARITY that it earlier had lacked.*

soliloquy *(suh-LIL-uh-kwee), noun*
In drama, a speech given by a character when no one else is present on stage. A *soliloquy* can also be any discourse a person gives to himself, or an account of a person's interior thoughts.

> *Hamlet's third act SOLILOQUY was delivered in a strange, choppy manner that I found most unsettling.*

solipsism *(SOL-ip-siz-um), noun*
The idea that one's own perceptions are the only meaningful reality. *Solipsism* was once used to describe a philosophical doctrine, but it has also been taken to mean "the practice of extreme self-centeredness."

> *To the store manager, bringing thirteen items to the twelve-items-only line at the supermarket was an example of unforgiveable SOLIPSISM.*

solipsistic *(sawl-up-SIS-tik), adjective*
Believing that the self is the only reality.

> *It's difficult to achieve the give-and-take qualities of a good discussion with Sandy, whose arguments tend to be a little SOLIPSISTIC.*

solstice *(SOL-stiss), noun*
Either of the two yearly times during which the sun is furthest from the celestial equator; the longest and shortest days of the year in the Northern Hemisphere. (The longest day, known as the summer *solstice*, occurs in June; the shortest day, or winter *solstice*, is in December.)

> *During the Roman winter SOLSTICE festival, known as Saturnalia, revelers would put candles on trees and hold massive celebrations intended to persuade the fading sunlight to return.*

S

somber *(SOM-ber), adjective*

Depressing; joyless.

> *The SOMBER expression on my boss's face before our meeting made me wonder whether the long-rumored layoff was finally to be ordered, but as it turned out he had simply slept poorly.*

somnambulist *(som-NAM-byoo-list), noun*

A person who walks during sleep.

> *My father, the most notorious SOMNAMBULIST in our family, once emptied out the contents of the refrigerator before proceeding back upstairs to bed.*

somniferous *(som-NIFF-er-us), adjective*

Describes something, such as drugs, that induces sleep.

> *The professor's SOMNIFEROUS voice caused many students to fall asleep during her lectures.*

somnolent *(SOM-nuh-lunt), adjective*

Tired, sleepy.

> *Having worked all night on the paper, Gaylord dragged himself into the lecture hall and spent the hour casting a well-meaning but SOMNOLENT gaze in the direction of his professor.*

sonorous *(SON-uh-russ), adjective*

Deep or rich in sound; also, overblown or conceited in language.

> *The chairman's SONOROUS but mercifully brief remarks brought the long meeting to a close.*

sophistry *(SOF-iss-tree), noun*

A seemingly convincing argument that is logically flawed. To accuse someone of *sophistry* is to say he is practicing sly doubletalk.

> *I believe this jury is too sophisticated to be taken in by the SOPHISTRIES the defense has offered.*

sophomoric *(sof-uh-MORE-ik), adjective*

Immature; overbearing in a conceited or pretentious way; characteristic of one with little learning but convinced that he or she is brilliant.

> *Preston was intrigued by the fraternity's offer of fun and games, but I found their SOPHOMORIC initiation rituals and elitist attitudes tough to take.*

soporific *(sop-uh-RIF-ik), adjective*
Causing or likely to cause sleep or drowsiness; anything likely to induce sleep.

> *Rick's endless speech on the social habits of the grouse was a poor choice for after-dinner entertainment, but, judging by the reaction of the group, an excellent SOPORIFIC.*

soprano *(suh-PRAN-oh),*
The uppermost singing voice in boys and women.

> *Every woman in the a capella group had a good voice, but to me the tall SOPRANO in the blue sweater stood out as an exceptional musical talent.*

sordid *(SORE-did), adjective*
Tawdry. That which is base or undignified is *sordid*.

> *Desmond brought everyone up to date on all the latest gossip, omitting not a single SORDID detail.*

sovereignty *(sov-rin-tee), noun*
Power or legitimacy as a nation. A nation's *sovereignty* refers to its self-determination and right to exist as a separate, independent entity.

> *The border incursion should be accepted for what it is: an affront against the SOVEREIGNTY of our country.*

spartan *(SPAHR-tin), adjective*
Self-disciplined, frugal, and stoic. People who lived in the ancient Greek city of Sparta were known for their discipline and austerity.

> *Paul lives such a SPARTAN life that his apartment has more exercise equipment than furniture.*

spasmodic *(spaz-MOD-ik), adjective*
Characteristic of a spasm; brief and fitful.

> *The regime's SPASMODIC attempts at reform had yet to bring prosperity to the nation's citizens.*

spate *(spayt), noun*
A sudden outpouring; a flood or deluge.

> *My request for a raise was greeted by a SPATE of hysterical laughter and occasionally obscene rantings from my boss, Mr. Walker.*

spatial *(SPAY-shull), adjective*
Of or pertaining to physical space.

> *The cover artist's use of varying widths of type leaves the viewer with an intriguing sense of SPATIAL disorientation.*

spay *(spay), verb*

To render (an animal) infertile by removing the ovaries.

After she had whelped three litters, Myron decided that it was about time to have Queenie SPAYED.

specious *(SPEE-shuss), adjective*

Something that appears to be good or right, but upon closer examination is not; superficially convincing but unsound.

My opponent's arguments may seem sound at first hearing, but if you will grant me five uninterrupted minutes, Mr. Moderator, I will show them to be SPECIOUS.

spectral *(SPEK-trul), adjective*

Reminiscent of ghosts or spirits; gruesome and otherwordly.

Scrooges SPECTRAL visitors take different forms, but each is interested in the same thing: the redemption of the old man's heart.

spiel *(shpeel), noun*

A long, extravagant argument or speech designed to persuade.

I let the salesman recite his SPIEL just to be polite, but the guy impressed me so much I ended up buying a vacuum cleaner.

spinster *(SPIN-ster), noun*

A single woman, especially a middle-aged one. *Spinster* usually carries negative connotations of unattractiveness and being past one's prime; there is no parallel expression that carries the same sense about an unmarried man.

Although Charles had expected a gathering of SPINSTERS at the club meeting, be was greeted at the door by none other than the starting quarterback for the local college football team.

spoonerism *(SPOO-ner-iz-uhm), noun*

The transposition of initial consonants of two or more words. For example, one might intend to say, "The bloom is off the rose" but say instead, "The room is off the blose." English clergyman, W.A. Spooner (1844–1930), was well known for committing this linguistic "sin."

My mother's frequent, unintended SPOONERISMS make her an endless source of mirth at our family reunions.

sporadic *(spo-RAD-ik), adjective*

Irregular. That which occurs at unpredictable intervals is *sporadic*.

SPORADIC gunfire echoed down the streets all night.

spurious *(spyoor-ee-uss), adjective*

Inauthentic. Something that is not genuine is *spurious*.

> *There were many in the academic community who were ready to accept the SPURIOUS manuscripts as coming from Shakespeare's own hand.*

spurn *(spurn), verb*

To reject with disdain.

> *Ginger had thought of trying to locate the child she had given up for adoption fifteen years before, but she was afraid he would SPURN her attempts to see him.*

squalid *(SKWAHL-id), adjective*

Filthy and foul from lack of care or neglect.

> *I shoved old banana peels and cigarette butts from the passenger seat of Mickey's SQUALID car.*

squall *(skwall), noun*

A sudden, violent burst of wind often accompanied by snow or rain.

> *Although it wasn't snowing all that hard, we had to delay our trip because the SQUALLS made visibility too poor for safe driving on the hill's narrow roads.*

squalor *(SKWAL-ur), noun*

The state or quality of being filthy.

> *My mother knew full well that my roommates were not the tidiest men in the world, but she still seemed shocked when confronted with the unrepentant SQUALOR of our apartment.*

staccato *(stuh-KAH-toe), adjective*

Made up of abrupt, separate parts.

> *Suddenly we were awakened by STACCATO bursts of gunfire in the next street.*

staid *(stayed), adjective*

Serious and dignified.

> *Bert's fluorescent pinstripes and huge bow tie were not at all what his new supervisor had in mind when he called for STAID attire.*

stalactite *(stuh-LACK-tite), noun*

An icicle-shaped deposit hanging from the top of a cavern, formed by drips of water containing calcium or other minerals.

> *STALACTITES hang from the tops of caves; an easy way to remember this is that the second half of the word begins with a "t" for "top."*

stalagmite *(stuh-LAG-mite), noun*
A deposit, typically found on a cave floor, formed from the drippings of a stalactite.
> *STALAGMITES are found at the bottoms of caves; an easy way to remember this is that the second half of the word begins with a "g" for "ground."*

stalemate *(STALE-mate), noun*
In chess, a condition in which neither side is in checkmate and the game cannot proceed because no legal move can be made; also, any situation in which progress, movement, or negotiation has becomes impossible.
> *I thought I had beaten Joreth when I captured the knight he had left undefended, but he was such a strong player that he was able to maneuver a STALEMATE.*

stalwart *(STOL-wert), adjective*
Firm of purpose; steadfast. *Stalwart* can also mean courageous.
> *Because the flight had been delayed by more than ten hours, only the most STALWART fans stayed up to greet the rock group at the airport.*

stanch *(stanch),* **verb**
To stop a liquid's flow (usually said of the bleeding accompanying a wound).
> *Dr. Cooper tied a tourniquet around Mark's injured arm to STANCH the flow of blood.*

status quo *(STAH-tus KWO), noun*
The existing state of affairs or condition.
> *Although Bill desperately wanted to get married, Melanie was more interested in preserving the STATUS QUO.*

staunch *(stonch), adjective*
Firm in resolution or belief; fixed.
> *Mr. West, a STAUNCH conservative, believed that government waste was the main problem requiring attention in Washington.*

stationary *(STAY-shun-air-ee), adjective*
Unmoving; fixed in place. (See, for comparison, the entry for *stationery*.)
> *Although the cart was designed to be wheeled freely, a set of clamps could be engaged that would allow it to serve as a STATIONARY post for nurses' supplies.*

stationery *(STAY-shun-air-ee), noun*
Writing paper. (See, for comparison, the entry for *stationary*.)
> *Following her wedding, Amy had STATIONERY embossed with her married name.*

stentorian *(sten-TORE-ee-uhn), adjective*
A sound characterized as loud and powerful.

> *The announcer's STENTORIAN voice could be heard even after a storm knocked out the power to his microphone.*

stereotype *(STAIR-ee-o-type), noun and verb*
A commonly accepted notion that presents an oversimplified or inaccurate viewpoint (of a racial group's behavior, for instance). As a verb, to *stereotype* someone is to assign him characteristics in keeping with a popular image of the group he belongs to, whether or not he possesses those characteristics.

> *Most salespeople resent the STEREOTYPE of their profession as serpentine and ruthless.*

stigma *(STIG-muh), noun*
A sign of disgrace or low status. *Stigma* derives from a Greek word meaning "tattoo;" presumably the sense of disgrace arose from the practice of physically marking someone to distinguish him as belonging to a lower class.

> *I was unprepared to deal with the social STIGMA of bankruptcy, yet it seemed my only available course of action.*

stigmatize *(STIG-muh-tize), verb*
To mark as wicked or infamous.

> *Many people with AIDS find that coping with the physical trauma of their disease is only part of their difficulty; another part is being STIGMATIZED by others as somehow deserving of punishment.*

stilted *(STILL-tud), adjective*
Stiff and formal; rigid and unspontaneous in nature.

> *The letter was composed in such STILTED, elaborately correct language that Sergeant Ryan surmised it was written by someone whose native language was not English.*

stipend *(STIE-pend), noun*
A periodic payment, such as a scholarship or other allowance; remuneration for a service.

> *A small monthly STIPEND from the Institute made it possible for Vernon to continue his biography of Yeats.*

stipulation *(stip-yoo-LAY-shun), noun*
A condition. A *stipulation* is an essential point (of an agreement or arrangement) that must be satisfied.

> *The will does feature one important STIPULATION: you must wait until you are thirty years old to receive the money.*

stodgy *(STAHJ-ee), adjective*

Dull, uninteresting, and tediously commonplace.

> *I could only spend five minutes in the STODGY club before I left for a rowdier place.*

stoic *(STO-ik), adjective*

Above succumbing to sensations of pain or pleasure. *Stoic* originally referred to a philosophy that advocated putting aside unjust thoughts and indulgences and attending first and foremost to the duties of life.

> *Paul remained STOIC when given the news that his father had finally succumbed to the illness.*

stoke *(stoke), verb*

To poke or feed (a fire); to supply with fuel.

> *My opponent's remarks are meant to STOKE the fires of intolerance, not help us learn to live with one another.*

stolid *(STOL-id), adjective*

Unemotional; impassive.

> *The witness retained her STOLID, professional demeanor in the face of some intense cross-examination.*

stopgap *(STOP-gap), noun*

A temporary expedient.

> *We knew that keeping Dad inside the house by suggesting he watch the football game while we mowed the lawn was nothing more than a STOPGAP; sooner or later he'd have to see the huge dent Billy put in the car.*

straitlaced *(STRAYT-LAYST), adjective*

Describes someone with a prudish nature and very strict morality.

> *Before she went to college and began to loosen up a little, Wendy was best known for being the most STRAITLACED girl in her graduating class.*

straits *(STRAYTS), noun*

A position of difficulty and challenge, often brought on by making bad decisions.

> *After a series of bad investments, I found myself in dire financial STRAITS.*

stratum *(STRA-tum), noun*

From the Latin meaning "cover," *stratum* is a layer or level within a larger substance, object, idea, etc. The plural is "strata."

> *As his apology tumbled out, STRATUM after stratum of Carl's mistakes came to light.*

striate *(STRY-ate), verb*

To mark with stripes or streaks. The adjective form, which you may see, is *striated*.

> *I think I'll try to liven up the appearance of this room by STRIATING one of its walls with white and yellow.*

strident *(STRY-dnt), adjective*

Harsh. Speech that is obtrusively grating is *strident*.

> *Dennis's appeals for money became more common—and more STRIDENT—as the year wore on.*

stringent *(STRIN-junt), adjective*

Imposing strict standards, rigid.

> *It was very difficult for Bonnie to adhere to such a STRINGENT diet, but she managed to do it.*

stucco *(STUCK-oh), noun*

A plaster or cement wall finish.

> *The real estate agent explained that STUCCO homes were very popular in this area of southern California.*

stultify *(STUL-tih-fy), verb*

To render foolish or unable to act intelligently. That which *stultifies* causes a decrease in mental power.

> *The intense heat had a STULTIFYING effect on Melanie; she found she had difficulty thinking clearly.*

stultifying *(STULL-tih-fie-ing), adjective*

Likely to stifle or cause to be futile or ineffective.

> *It was on a STULTIFYINGLY hot August day in Memphis, Tennessee, that the idea of scaling back my daily running routine first occurred to me.*

stupefy *(STOO-puh-fie), verb*

To make numb with amazement; to stun into helplessness.

> *The prospect of working until the morning hours left me STUPEFIED, but there was no alternative.*

stymie *(STIE-mee), verb*

To thwart; to prevent (another) from achieving a goal.

> *The reporter's attempts to get to the bottom of the scandal were STYMIED by the refusal of the principals to talk to him—either on or off the record.*

subaltern *(sub-AWL-turn), adjective*
Low in position or rank; secondary in importance.

> *Stop giving me all these SUBALTERN reasons for your behavior and tell me what your true motivation is!*

subjective *(sub-JEK-tiv), adjective*
Originating in one's personal observation. To say that something is *subjective* is to say that it may be influenced individual prejudice and represents only a particular person's viewpoint.

> *Mind you, this is only a SUBJECTIVE observation, but my feeling is that that restaurant serves the worst Chinese food in the city.*

subjugate *(SUB-juh-gate), verb*
To cause to become subservient. To *subjugate* another is to make him perform your will.

> *The dictator's attempts to SUBJUGATE his country's smaller neighbors will end in failure, mark my words.*

sublimate *(SUB-lih-mate), verb*
To transfer the force of an unacceptable inclination or impulse to a pursuit considered proper. To *sublimate* an urge is to redirect it to a wholesome purpose.

> *There is a popular—but unproven—notion that butchers are secretly violent, and that they choose their profession as a means of SUBLIMATING their passions.*

sublime *(suh-BLYME), adjective*
Grand or lofty. That which is splendid is *sublime.*

> *Many people can make a pretty good pot of spaghetti; mine, however, is SUBLIME.*

subliminal *(sub-LIM-ih-nul), adjective*
Operating below the level of conscious perception.

> *The advertising industry has long been suspected of using SUBLIMINAL implants in advertisements for cigarettes and liquor, but scientists and industry insiders have always scoffed at the notion.*

subsequent *(SUB-suh-kwunt), adjective*
After; following in time.

> *The butler at first denied that he'd had anything to do with the murder, but the SUBSEQUENT testimony of three witnesses eventually convinced him to confess.*

subservient *(suh-SER-vee-unt), adjective*
Bending to the will of another. Someone who is *subservient* is servile.

> *Stan always became meek and SUBSERVIENT in his boss's presence.*

subsistence *(sub-SIST-unce), noun*

The means required to support one's existence.

> *Mr. Best, I've gone five years without a raise, and inflation has turned what was once a reasonable wage into a SUBSISTENCE-level compensation.*

substantiate *(sub-STANT-chee-ate), verb*

To provide proof or evidence; to give validity to.

> *The soft-drink company sought to SUBSTANTIATE the claim that their soda was the best tasting by holding blind taste tests in shopping malls across the country.*

substrate *(SUB-strayt), noun*

An underlying layer that serves as a foundation or basis.

> *Doodling on notepads during office meetings became the SUBSTRATE for Phil's successful cartooning career.*

subterfuge *(SUB-tur-fyoodge), noun*

A misleading ruse or cunning evasion; a strategic avoidance employing deceit.

> *Nick knew he would have to come up with a clever SUBTERFUGE to get out of going to another boring Sunday dinner at his grandparents' home.*

subvert *(sub-VUHRT), verb*

To undermine, corrupt, or overthrow.

> *Sherry considers herself a rebel because she loves to SUBVERT society's traditions.*

succinct *(suck-SINKT), adjective*

Brief; pithy; concise.

> *Norman preferred to say a SUCCINCT goodbye to his brother before getting into the cab, rather than engaging in a long, drawn-out scene at the train station.*

succor *(SUCK-ur), noun*

Aid or assistance; relief.

> *Although she did not participate in the crime, Mrs. Helm was sentenced to five years in prison for giving SUCCOR to men she knew to be kidnappers.*

suffrage *(SUFF-rudge), noun*

The right to vote.

> *Today's apathetic voters (or, more precisely, nonvoters) seem to have little appreciation of how hard previous generations had to fight for the principle of universal SUFFRAGE.*

sui generis *(SOO-ee JEN-er-us), adjective*
From the Latin meaning "of its own kind," *sui generis* describes someone or something that is completely unique, something that seems to have sprung fully formed into existence.

> *Andrea's SUI GENERIS writing style seemed far removed from anything I have read before or since.*

sully *(SUL-ee), verb*
To besmear or make foul. Figuratively speaking, to *sully* a person, group, or institution is to cast aspersions on it.

> *I will not allow you to SULLY the good name of my family with such baseless accusations.*

sultry *(SUL-tree), adjective*
Very hot and moist; characterized by heat. Also: likely to arouse passion or romance.

> *I passed the SULTRY summer evenings in a beach chair with a margarita in hand, staring out at the expanse of tropical ocean.*

sumptuous *(SUMP-choo-us), adjective*
Extravagant. That which is lavish is *sumptuous*.

> *A SUMPTUOUS feast awaited the couple at the hotel.*

sundry *(SUN-dree), adjective*
Various. *Sundry* can also mean "an unspecified number more than two."

> *SUNDRY inexpensive plastic items were spread out on a table at the front of the store.*

supercilious *(soo-per-SIL-ee-uss), adjective*
Disdainful or haughty. Someone who is overbearingly proud could be said to be *supercilious*.

> *Randy can take on a SUPERCILIOUS air at times; you mustn't let his highminded behavior bother you.*

superdelegate *(SOO-per-del-uh-get), noun*
An elected party official or a party leader chosen to a national political convention as an uncommitted delegate.

> *SUPERDELEGATE had to decide the winner of the hotly-contested primary.*

superfluous *(soo-PER-floo-uss), adjective*
Unnecessary. That which exceeds what is essential is *superfluous*.

> *The film's long production number was eventually cut from the final version because test audiences felt it was SUPERFLUOUS to the main plot.*

superlative *(soo-PER-luh-tiv), adjective*
To the highest possible degree. Something that is *superlative* is of surpassing quality or power.

> *Boris's SUPERLATIVE skills as a chess player are well known around campus.*

supersede *(soo-per-SEED), verb*
To supplant or replace. If A now fulfills the function of B and makes B obsolete, A *supersedes* B.

> *This form, which SUPERSEDES the old version, has been made much easier to read and fill out.*

supine *(SOO-pine), adjective*
Lying down with the back to the floor. *Supine* can also mean "passive."

> *Damon found the marketing department SUPINE when it came to implementing ideas.*

supplant *(suh-PLANT), verb*
To replace with something—or someone—else.

> *After Linda moved in, Roy found many of his most-treasured pieces of unique—some might say ugly—artwork SUPPLANTED with tasteful, traditional watercolors.*

suppliant *(SUH-plee-unt), noun or adjective*
One who asks humbly for something, or a description of someone who asks humbly.

> *After he had an affair, Steve's SUPPLIANT behavior toward his wife became almost nauseating to his friends.*

supplicate *(SUP-lih-kate), verb*
To make a humble, sincere, and earnest request of someone.

> *The department heads decided their best bet was to assemble as a group in the president's office and SUPPLICATE her to approve the budget increases.*

surcease *(sur-SEESE), noun*
End. A *surcease* is a cessation.

> *It was only with the SURCEASE of hostilities that life began to return to normal for the region's civilian population.*

surcingle *(SUR-sing-gul), noun*
A strap that holds a saddle or other apparatus on a domesticated animal.

> *The worn leather SURCINGLE snapped, and Dan was thrown from the galloping horse.*

surfeit *(SUR-fit), noun and verb*

Excess. To have a *surfeit* of something is to have too much of it.

> *We have had a SURFEIT of proposals and analysis; the time has come for us to act.*

surly *(SUR-lee), adjective*

Sullen; gruff; morose.

> *Shiela, in the SURLY mood that accompanies her every working morning since the divorce, barked that I had no right to ask her for the report that was due last week.*

surmise *(sur-MIZE), verb*

To guess; to come to a conclusion (often without strong evidence).

> *We SURMISED that Leanna had declined the invitation to Arthur's birthday party simply because she didn't want to buy him a gift.*

surrealism *(suh-REE-uh-liz-um), noun*

A twentieth-century movement in art and literature that emphasized the subconscious or irrational nature of perceived forms through the illogical placing and presentation of subject matter.

> *Dali's "The Persistence of Memory," which features the now-famous melting watches, was immediately hailed as a masterpiece of SURREALISM.*

surrealistic *(suh-ree-uh-LISS-tik), adjective*

Unreal. *Surrealistic* art focuses on images or emotions that are otherworldly or profoundly removed from everyday experience.

> *The astronauts made their way across the SURREALISTIC landscape of Mars.*

surreptitious *(sur-up-TISH-uss), adjective*

Undertaken in stealth. That which is done in hiding is done *surreptitiously.*

> *I have reason to believe our conference room has been fitted with "bugs" designed to monitor our conversations SURREPTITIOUSLY.*

surrogate *(SUR-uh-gut), noun*

One who acts in the place of another. *Surrogate* is derived from a Latin verb meaning "to nominate in one's place."

> *Although he was not related to Eric, Dean found himself acting as a SURROGATE brother to him.*

surveillance *(sur-VAY-lunce), noun*

An instance of watching something closely, usually in a scrutinizing fashion.

> *The police set up SURVEILLANCE in the house across the street from the escaped con's girlfriend, as they were sure he would try to visit her.*

sustenance *(SUS-tuh-nunce), noun*
Means of supporting life.
> *After the bombing, the city's hungry occupants wandered through nearby wooded areas in search of SUSTENANCE.*

susurration *(suss-uh-RAY-shun), noun*
A soft, whispering sound.
> *I sat there on the porch of my parents' farmhouse, listening to the SUSURRATION of wind-driven stalks of wheat.*

sward *(swored), noun*
Land covered with thick grass.
> *We decided that the large, flat SWARD would make an excellent location for a game of touch football.*

swelter *(SWEL-tur), verb*
To suffer from extreme heat.
> *Jasmine and I found ourselves lost in the middle of the jungle, SWELTERING in the tropical heat.*

sybarite *(SIB-er-ite), noun*
A person enamoured of luxury and pleasure.
> *Rodney lived the life of a SYBARITE, driving his Rolls-Royce around his summer cottage in Nice and wintering at his Virginia mansion.*

sycophant *(SIK-uh-funt), noun*
One who tries to gain favor by flattering excessively.
> *Any film star used to being surrounded by an entourage of SYCOPHANTS is likely to find it difficult to keep things in perspective when questioned by an unsympathetic journalist.*

syllogism *(SIL-uh-jiz-um), noun*
A form of logical argument that features three propositions and finishes with a conclusion. An example of a *syllogism* would be "All elected Republican officials will be at the meeting; all the members of Congress from my state are elected Republican officials; therefore all the members of Congress from my state will be at the meeting."
> *Aristotle's formulation of the SYLLOGISM as a tool for logical analysis is one of the most significant contributions to Western thought.*

sylph *(SILF), noun*
A slim, graceful girl or woman.

> *Although the fashion industry now considered her to be the most exotic SYLPH on the scene, the fashion model had thought herself clumsy and awkward as a teenager.*

sylvan *(SIL-vuhn), adjective*
Of, about, or characteristic of the woods. Sylvanus was the god of the woods for ancient Romans.

> *The bed and breakfast deep in the forest was a SYLVAN paradise.*

symbiotic *(sim-bee-OTT-ik), adjective*
Characteristic of an intimate or mutually advantageous relationship, especially (in biology) one between dissimilar organisms.

> *In ocean life you often see SYMBIOTIC relationships between large and small fish, in which the smaller feed off of organisms existing on the larger, thereby keeping the larger fish clean and healthy.*

symmetry *(SIM-ih-tree), noun*
The quality of showing complementary forms or aesthetically pleasing proportions. *Symmetry* is structural balance.

> *The sculpture's lack of SYMMETRY is unnerving to the casual observer, and that is exactly what the artist has in mind.*

symposium *(sim-POSE-ee-um), noun*
A meeting for discussion; especially, a gathering of experts before an audience whose members may pose questions.

> *The SYMPOSIUM was a disaster; both professors arrived an hour late, after most of the audience had given up and left.*

synchronize *(SINK-ruh-nize), verb*
To cause something to take place at the exact same time (as another event); to cause to occur in unison.

> *As this is an operation requiring the utmost accuracy from all team members, I suggest we SYNCHRONIZE watches now before beginning our assignments.*

syncretize *(SINK-rih-tize), verb*
To combine or unite varying parties, ideas, principles, etc.

> *As the denomination's local attendance began to fall sharply, several churches SYNCRETIZED their efforts to improve overall attendance.*

synergy *(SIN-er-gee), noun*
The situation that exists when two or more groups, agents, businesses, etc. join forces to accomplish a common goal. *Synergy* is a word commonly used in today's corporate culture.

The SYNERGY demonstrated by the two departments quickly sparked amazing results.

synonym *(SIN-uh-nim), noun*
a word with a meaning similar or identical to that of another word in a language.

"Masculine" and "male" are SYNONYMS.

synopsis *(sih-NOP-sis), noun*
A summary. A *synopsis* is a brief recounting of the principle points of something.

A full SYNOPSIS of the play's plot would give away a delightful surprise ending, so I will not attempt one here.

synthesis *(SIN-thuh-suss), noun*
A combination of elements to form a new whole.

The writer's latest book is an intriguing SYNTHESIS of classical Greek tragedy and cyberpunk elements.

T

tableau *(ta-BLOW), noun*
A memorable scene created by the grouping of objects and people.
> *When I walked into the room, the TABLEAU of angry faces let me know we were about to resolve the family argument.*

taboo *(tuh-BOO), noun*
Anything deemed absolutely unacceptable or immoral by a social order. Also: forbidden or off-limits.
> *Anthropologists have found that incest is a universal TABOO in human culture.*

tacit *(TASS-it), adjective*
Implied; understood without being openly explained or expressed.
> *The men took their sergeant's harsh language toward Ned as TACIT approval of their own abusive behavior toward him.*

taciturn *(TASS-ih-turn), adjective*
Quiet. Someone who tends to avoid speech is *taciturn*.
> *You must understand that Betty can be quite TACITURN after a day at work; her silence is not because of anything you have done.*

tactile *(TACK-tul), adjective*
Of or pertaining to the sense of touch.
> *At this stage, your baby's need for TACTILE stimulation is intense; she must be held, stroked, and cuddled regularly.*

tai chi chuan *(tie jee chwan), noun*
A martial art of China that emphasizes slow, meditative movements.
> *Each morning, I saw Erica in the park practicing the gentle, fluid movements she'd learned in our TAI CHI CHUAN class.*

talisman *(TAL-iss-mun), noun*
A lucky charm; an engraved object believed to possess occult powers.
> *Justin was all set for the big game until he reached into his pocket and found that his TALISMAN—a small piece of stone from the shores of Ireland, given to him by his mother—was missing.*

talkathon *(TALK-uh-thon), noun*
An extended speech or discourse, especially one featuring excessive posturing.
> *I was told that this meeting was meant to explore the pros and cons of locating the waste site near our town, but I see we've moved toward a TALKATHON on the long-term benefits of the nuclear power industry.*

tam-o'-shanter *(TAM-o-shan-ter), noun*
A floppy Scottish hat with a tight headband.

> *Angus MacGregor, a man fiercely proud of his heritage, usually took the opportunity of a company picnic to don a kilt and TAM-O'-SHANTER and play his bagpipe.*

tandem *(TAN-dum), adjective*
One after another. To walk in *tandem* is to walk in single file.

> *We gave Mom and Dad a TANDEM bicycle for Christmas this year.*

tangelo *(TAN-juh-lo), noun*
A kind of citrus fruit; hybrid of a tangerine and a grapefruit.

> *The corner fruit market specialized in stocking the more exotic fruits and vegetables, and for most of the year was the only place in town where one could regularly purchase TANGELOS.*

tangential *(tan-JEN-chull), adjective*
Divergent or digressive; only slightly connected (to a more important matter).

> *After reviewing the financial outlook for the coming year, the chairman closed the meeting with a few TANGENTIAL remarks on some new software the accounting department would be purchasing.*

tangible *(TAN-juh-bull), adjective*
Real; touchable. That which exists corporeally is *tangible*.

> *The prosecution has offered many theories and speculations, but no TANGIBLE evidence linking my client to the murder.*

tantalize *(TAN-tuhl-ize), verb*
To tease or taunt by keeping something desired just out of reach. Tantalus was a mythical king whose bad deeds caused him anguish in the afterlife. He was made to stand in a lake with boughs of fruit just out of his reach. When he tried to get a drink, the water disappeared, and he could never quite reach the fruit in order to satisfy his hunger.

> *Lotteries TANTALIZE people with their implied promise of instant wealth. Of course, most people don't win.*

tantamount *(TAN-tuh-mount), adjective*
Equivalent to in all meaningful respects. *Tantamount* derives from an old verb meaning "to amount to as much."

> *Please remember that, since this is a tight race, a vote for the third-party candidate is TANTAMOUNT to a vote for my opponent.*

Taoism *(DOW-is-um), noun*

A system of philosophy identified with the sage Lao-Tzu, and embodied most notably in his work *Tao-te-ching*, that holds that life lived simply and in accordance with natural laws and events is most in keeping with the Tao, or way, that underlies all existence.

> *Scholars may debate the fine points of a rational understanding of TAOISM, but a true practitioner probably expresses it best when she gracefully and thankfully accepts a proffered cup of tea.*

taphephobia *(taff-uh-FOE-bee-uh), noun*

The abnormal fear of being buried alive.

> *After seeing the final scene of that horror film, The Grave Claims Its Own, I couldn't sleep, and I had an inkling of what it must be like to suffer from TAPHEPHOBIA.*

tarantella *(tar-un-TELL-ah), noun*

A spirited Italian dance in 6/8 time.

> *Al, a dedicated foxtrotter, had a tough time dealing with his new wife's seemingly endless fascination with the TARANTELLA.*

tariff *(TEAR-if), noun*

Duties or taxes placed on imports or exports.

> *In an effort to balance trade, the government levied a TARIFF on most imported goods.*

taurine *(TAW-rine), adjective*

Of or pertaining to bulls. *Taurine* can also refer to the zodiacal sign Taurus.

> *Brian could display a certain TAURINE tenacity when it came to completing a project on time.*

taut *(taut), adjective*

Tight; firm.

> *This toy telephone will not work unless you pull the tin cans far enough apart to make the string TAUT.*

tautology *(taw-TOL-uh-gee), noun*

Unnecessary repetition—in different words—of an already stated idea. To describe someone as an "wealthy member of the city's upper class" would be a *tautology*.

> *Your description of Brian as a "foreign illegal alien" is a TAUTOLOGY: every illegal alien is a foreigner.*

tawdry *(TODD-ree), adjective*
Cheap and tasteless; also, ostentatious and gaudy.
> *Although many in the publishing world considered the actress's tell-all book to be a sleazy foray into the TAWDRIEST kind of name-dropping, there were few who didn't envy its sales totals.*

taxonomy *(tak-SON-uh-mee), noun*
The science of formal classification and naming. In biology, *taxonomy* also has a more formal meaning related to the classification of organisms.
> *The newly discovered insect was dubbed "Liliput" by the researchers, although its formal name was a question of TAXONOMY that no one felt hurried to resolve.*

technocracy *(tek-NOK-ruh-see), noun*
Government by engineers, technicians, or other highly skilled members of society. *Technocracy* (a theory popularized in the 1930s) gave us the word technocrat, which refers to a person skilled in (economic or managerial) technique who holds a position of power and influence.
> *The claim that I would institute some sort of TECHNOCRACY simply because I am a skilled manager ignores my years of service as a District Attorney.*

teem *(TEAM), verb*
To abound or swarm.
> *I was nauseated by the sight of ants TEEMING all over a discarded hot dog bun.*

teetotaler *(tee-TOE-tuh-ler), noun*
Someone who does not drink alcohol under any circumstances. *Teetotaler* was formed from the verb teetotal, coined during the Temperance movement of the nineteenth century.
> *No wine for me, thanks; I've been a TEETOTALER since high school.*

telegenic *(tell-uh-JEN-ic), adjective*
Likely to make a good appearance on television.
> *When he's not doing his newscast, he's awkward and withdrawn, but once the camera is on, Lenny comes across as appealing, confident, and incredibly TELEGENIC.*

telekinesis *(tel-uh-kuh-NEE-siss), noun*
The supposed ability to move objects by means of mental energy. *Telekinesis* derives from the Greek roots for "from a distance" and "movement."
> *Geller's claim to possess powers of TELEKINESIS has been thoroughly discredited.*

teleologic *(tel-ee-uh-LAHJ-ick), adjective*
Describes the belief that there is an intelligent design or purpose discernible in nature.

The natural camouflage some animals develop would seem to be proof that we live in a TELEOLOGIC universe.

telepathy *(tuh-LEP-uh-thea), noun*
The supposed ability to read minds or communicate mentally. *Telepathy* is a form of ESP (extrasensory perception).

I hope you're not suggesting that I cheated on the exam by using TELEPATHY.

teleprompter *(TEL-uh-promp-tur), noun*
An automated means of displaying lines to be read by actors. The *teleprompter* is a device used in place of cue cards.

The show's most amusing moment—the failure of the TELEPROMPTER that forced actors to improvise—had had nothing to do with its script.

temblor *(TEM-blor), noun*
An earthquake. *Temblor* is derived from a Spanish verb meaning "to quake."

Because residents had considered earthquakes unlikely to occur in the region, few structures had been built to withstand a major TEMBLOR.

temerity *(tuh-MARE-uh-tee), noun*
Rashness; reckless disregard of danger or unpleasant consequences. To take a bold action is to show *temerity*.

You have the TEMERITY to ask for a raise after showing up late forty percent of the time over the last three months?

temper *(TEM-per), verb*
To moderate or lessen the impact or harshness of something.

Tom TEMPERED his harsh words with a warm smile.

tempera *(TEM-pur-uh), noun*
A paint medium popularized during the Renaissance, generally composed of egg, oil, water, and pigment.

Raphael's early TEMPERA works have disintegrated badly over the centuries and are in need of restoration.

temperance *(TEM-puh-runce), adjective*
Self-restraint; moderation; specifically, the act of abstaining from consuming alcohol or other intoxicating substances.

Although Mr. Bedford had been a model of TEMPERANCE for most of his adult life, he relented when I pleaded with him to try some of the punch we had made for the party.

tempestuous *(tem-PESS-choo-uss), adjective*
Stormy, violent.
> *Lear's own rage and madness, far more than any artificial theatrical storm effects, are the truly TEMPESTUOUS elements of these scenes.*

tempo *(TEM-po), noun*
The speed or pace of something (particularly, of music).
> *Our aerobics instructor will only play music with a fast TEMPO and a strong beat, although there are times, generally after a hard day at work, when I feel like introducing her to the wonders of Mantovani.*

temporal *(TEM-puh-rul), adjective*
Pertaining to or limited by time; characteristic of worldly (rather than celestial or heavenly) endeavor.
> *My father believed that TEMPORAL joys and sorrows were of little consequence in the grand scheme of things.*

temporize *(TEM-puh-rize), verb*
To gain time by being evasive or indecisive.
> *I stuttered and unleashed a flurry of "um's" in an effort to TEMPORIZE and come up with a logical explanation for my earlier behavior.*

tenable *(TEN-uh-bull), adjective*
Capable of being maintained. That which is *tenable* can be held.
> *The general warned the mayor that the troops' position was no longer TENABLE, and that preparations should be made to evacuate the city immediately.*

tenacious *(tuh-NAY-shuss), adjective*
Unyielding; stubborn. Someone who is *tenacious* is hard put to give up.
> *Bill was a tough campaigner who put up a TENACIOUS fight for the nomination, but in the end he came up short.*

tendril *(TEN-dril), noun*
A threadlike organ of leafless plants that often attaches itself to other objects or surfaces to support the plant.
> *The shrub's tendrils had wound themselves around the wooden pole and were threatening to crush it.*

tenebrous *(TEN-uh-bruhss), adjective*
Dark and gloomy.
> *The TENEBROUS forest began to frighten some of the youngest hikers in the group.*

T

tenet *(TEN-ut), noun*

A principle. Something held to be true, valid, or essential by a group or organization is a *tenet*.

> *I think you will agree with me that the primary TENET of this company is that the customer must come first.*

tentative (TEN-tuh-tiv),

Given to or showing hesitation; lacking in resolution or consistency.

> *The parents were able to capture their child's first TENTATIVE steps on videotape.*

tenuous *(TEN-yoo-uss), adjective*

Not solid (in terms of logical connection); insubstantial. Literally, *tenuous* means "slender (as a thread)."

> *The connection between the performance of the stock market and the result of the yearly Super Bowl game might seem TENUOUS at best, but there is evidence of some strange correlation between the two.*

tenure *(TEN-yur), noun*

The holding of a post or property, especially with regard to status as a permanent employee. *Tenure* can also refer the period such a post is held.

> *After sixteen years in the department, Professor Milligan was finally granted TENURE.*

tepid *(TEP-id), adjective*

Lukewarm in temperature; also, unenthusiastic.

> *Although he expected a loud and long ovation from the crowd in appreciation of his work, the playwright had to make do with a few pockets of TEPID applause and a low buzzing sound distinctly reminiscent of snoring.*

terpsichorean *(turp-sih-KORE-ee-uhn), adjective*

Having to do with dancing. Terpsichore is the ancient muse of dancing.

> *Our awkward post-wedding dance could hardly be called an example of TERPSICHOREAN splendor.*

terra cotta *(tare-uh KOT-uh), noun, adjective*

A reddish clay modeling compound that hardens when exposed to extreme heat. *Terra cotta* is used primarily for pottery, the exterior facings of buildings, and sculpture.

> *The exhibition is notable for several gorgeous TERRA COTTA sculptures of birds dating from the 1890's.*

terrestrial *(tuh-RESS-tree-ul), adjective*
Of or pertaining to the earth, or to life on earth.

> *Although life on a space station is interesting to read about, I still believe I'd be most comfortable in a TERRESTRIAL setting.*

terse *(turce), adjective*
Pithy; brief; concise.

> *Although I tried to pump Jim for information about his new girlfriend, his TER.SE answers were a polite way of letting me know it was none of my business.*

tertiary *(TUR-shee-are-ee), adjective*
Third in succession. That which follows the second item in a list, sequence, or progression is *tertiary.*

> *The disease had progressed beyond its first two phases, and even showed signs of worsening beyond the TERTIARY stage.*

testator *(TESS-tay-tur), noun*
A male who sets out his wishes in a legal will. The female form of *testator* is *testatrix.*

> *The TESTATOR, I'm afraid, made a serious mistake in failing to have the will witnessed.*

testatrix *(tess-TAY-triks), noun*
A female who sets out her wishes in a legal will. The male form of *testatrix* is *testator.*

> *Let's keep one thing in mind: Mother is the TESTATRIX, not you two, and she can dispose of her property in any way she sees fit.*

tete-a-tete *(TET ah tet), noun*
A meeting in which two people meet face-to-face. *Tete-a-tete* is French for "head-to-head."

> *You and Millie have done enough talking behind each other's back; I think the time has come for you to have a TETE-A-TETE and work this problem out once and for all.*

tetragrammaton *(tet-ruh-GRAM-uh-ton), noun*
The written Hebrew word for God consisting of the four letters yod, he, vav, and he, and usually rendered YHVH. *Tetragrammaton* is Greek for "having four letters."

> *The sight of the TETRAGRAMMATON carved in stone above the altar always filled Paul with a sense of inner peace.*

T

than *(than or then), conjunctive*
A conjunction used to introduce the second element of an unequal comparison. (See, for comparison, the entry for *then*.)
> *Bert is shorter THAN Velma is.*

their *(thare), pronoun*
Belonging to that group. (See, for comparison, the entries for *there* and *they're*.)
> *Many celebrities zealously guard THEIR privacy.*

then *(then), adverb*
At that time. (See, for comparison, the entry for *than*.)
> *You should have known me back THEN!*

theocentric *(the-oh-SEN-trik), adjective*
Placing God at the center (of a system of beliefs). That which focuses on God is *theocentric*.
> *You'll find this writer's philosophies a little more THEOCENTRIC than the last one we studied.*

theocracy *(thee-OK-ruh-see), noun*
Government by religious leaders. *Theocracy* is the concentration of political power in the hands of church figures.
> *It was to prevent the excesses of THEOCRACY (or its cousin, government by divine right) that the Founding Fathers forbade establishment of a formal state religion.*

therapeutic *(thare-uh-PYOO-tik), adjective*
Having to do with cures for illness. That which is remedial is *therapeutic*.
> *The problem is not physical illness, but stress; I think you will find that a weekend in the country will have a strong THERAPEUTIC effect.*

there *(thare), adverb*
In that place. (See, for comparison, the entries for *their* and *they're*.)
> *Although I've always wanted to visit Barcelona, I've never found the time or money I needed to vacation THERE.*

thespian *(THESS-pee-un), noun*
An actor. *Thespian* refers especially to a person who performs onstage in a play.
> *Sir Laurence Olivier was rightly regarded as the most versatile THESPIAN of his era.*

they're *(thare), pronoun contraction*
They are. (See, for comparison, the entries for *their* and *there*.)
> *Mom and Dad just told me that THEY'RE planning to renovate the dining room.*

threshold *(THRESH-old), noun*

An entranceway; a piece of stone or wood positioned under a doorway; also, the beginning or initiation of anything.

> *Those who were present for the final meeting agreed afterward that the countries had reached a new THRESHOLD in trade relations.*

throng *(throng), noun*

A large crowd.

> *As the desperate editor stood on the tenth-floor ledge, a THRONG of spectators gathered on the street below.*

tiered *(teerd), adjective*

Constructed or arranged in layers or levels.

> *In talking to bakeries about a wedding cake for my daughter, I was flabbergasted to learn that some of the elaborate TIERED cakes cost over a thousand dollars.*

timbre *(TAM-bur), noun*

A quality of sound, usually musical, determined by its overtones; a distinctive quality or tone.

> *I feel that the haunting TIMBRE of the oboe, when played by a master, is more moving than that of any other musical instrument.*

tincture *(TING-churr), noun*

A trace amount or slight tinge.

> *The drama was leavened with a TINCTURE of comic relief.*

tint *(tint), noun*

A color or a degree of a color; a slight variation in shade. As a verb: to add or alter color, generally in a subtle way.

> *My mother was aghast when my sister Cassandra came back from her first semester at college with her golden-blonde-hair TINTED a pale orange.*

tintinnabulation *(tin-tin-ab-yoo-LAY-shun), noun*

The ringing of bells. *Tintinnabulation* derives from a Latin word meaning "bell."

> *The TINTINNABULATION from the center of the village left no one in doubt: Christmas had come at last.*

tirade *(TIE-raid), noun*

An extended outburst of harsh talk. Someone who delivers a *tirade* gives a lengthy, overblown speech.

> *I did not come here to listen to a TIRADE about how inconsiderate my son is in class.*

titanic *(tie-TAN-ic), adjective*

Of enormous strength, influence or size.

> *The TITANIC explosion in the movie's final scene required several hundred pounds of dynamite and was filmed from eleven different angles.*

titillate *(TIT-ih-late), verb*

To arouse or excite in a pleasing way. Something that *titillates* tickles one's fancy.

> *These stories about the sex lives of past presidents may be TITILLATING, but they wouldn't have passed for hard news in my day.*

titular *(TICH-uh-lur), adjective*

By title only. The *titular* head of a group is a person who is technically designated as the leader, but who lacks real power.

> *Ed may be the TITULAR head of the organization, but I have a feeling that Bill has more influence in day-to-day matters.*

tome *(toam), noun*

A thick or heavy book. *Tome* applies especially to long, academically oriented books.

> *I had been hoping to read something light that I could finish over my vacation, not a TOME like this.*

toothsome *(TOOTH-sum), adjective*

Pleasant or appealing (especially with regard to taste.) *Toothsome* can also mean "alluring."

> *We concluded the feast with a TOOTHSOME banana split.*

topical *(TOP-ih-kuhl), adjective*

Having to do with issues of current or local interest.

> *Glenda is always reading magazines so she can keep up with TOPICAL issues and have something to say when encountering new clients.*

torpid *(TORE-pid), adjective*

Sluggish; inactive; reminiscent of an in hibernation.

> *My sister Helen was always involved in torrid romances; my boyfriends were invariably TORPID and uninteresting.*

torpor *(TOR-pur), noun*

Indifference, sloth or inactivity. *Torpor* is a state calling to mind the hibernation of animals.

> *Gregg's TORPOR on the job has been troubling me; I can't help wondering if he may be having trouble at home.*

torque *(tork), noun*

In mechanics, the force that causes twisting or rotation in a body.

The screwdriver was too small to generate enough TORQUE for the job.

torrential *(to-REN-shul), adjective*

Reminiscent of or pertaining to severe storms. That which is intense or unyieldingly powerful is *torrential*.

A TORRENTIAL rain kept the children inside all day.

torrid *(TORE-id), adjective*

Parching and burning, like desert heat, or ardent and passionate, like love.

Their TORRID affair began when they met at a business convention.

tort *(tort), noun*

In law, a civil misdeed requiring compensation. *Tort* is a legal term sometimes misspelled as torte (see below.)

You are incorrect in assuming this would be a criminal case; we are looking at a TORT, not a crime.

torte *(tort), noun*

A cake made with eggs and very little flour. A *torte* has nothing to do with a tort (see above.)

Mrs. Carrigan's Linzer TORTES are the best I have ever tasted.

tortuous *(TORE-choo-uss), adjective*

Winding; full of twists and turns,

Drive safely; the road leading from the center of town up the side of the mountain is a TORTUOUS one.

totalitarian *(toe-tahl-ih-TARE-ee-un), adjective*

Characteristic of a system of government in which political power is highly centralized and in which authorities tolerate no dissent, punishing efforts at pluralistic discourse; of or pertaining to a governmental system that controls or dictates many aspects of life.

Although the worldwide fall of Communism has been widely discussed, several of its familiar TOTALITARIAN governments—notably those of China and North Korea—are still alive and kicking.

totem *(TOTE-um), noun*

An animal, plant, or other natural object believed to be an ancestor of a tribe of peoples; a representation of such an object.

The tribe had an impressive collection of carved wooden TOTEMS.

totter *(TOT-tur), verb*

To walk or move with unsteady steps; to sway at ground level.

> *The sight of Mr. Bass TOTTERING home from another night at Mulvaney's Pub was enough to make a teetotaler out of anyone.*

tousle *(TAU-zul), verb*

To muss up or dishevel.

> *Lynne admired the model's TOUSLED hair, but she knew that what looked sexy on a long, elegant face like that would look like an accident with a blender on her.*

tout *(TOWT), verb*

To publicize in a boastful, extravagant manner.

> *The studio TOUTED its latest picture as "the greatest story ever told."*

tractable *(TRAK-tuh-bull), adjective*

Manageable or easy to control. Someone who takes instruction or guidance easily is *tractable.*

> *Jane was a willful and disobedient little girl, but her sister Annie was more TRACTABLE.*

traduce *(truh-DOOCE), verb*

To slander or defame; to speak falsely of or with malice toward (a person).

> *I was flabbergasted to learn that your campaign has tried to TRADUCE my character by offering cash payments to my ex-wife in return for her stories about me.*

tragedian *(truh-JEE-dee-un), noun*

An actor noted for performing tragic parts.

> *Richard Burbage was the premier TRAGEDIAN of the Elizabethan era.*

traitorous *(TRAY-tur-uss), adjective*

Reminiscent of or pertaining to a traitor; perfidious.

> *The third chapter of the book covered Benedict Arnold's TRAITOROUS acts and his eventual exposure as a British agent.*

trajectory *(truh-JEK-tuh-ree), noun*

The curving path followed by a projectile in flight.

> *The bullet's TRAJECTORY from the warehouse window would be completely consistent with the injury suffered by the victim, Your Honor.*

transcendental *(tran-sun-DEN-tl), adjective*

Beyond the realm of normal experience or understanding. That which transcends our customary bounds of perception is *transcendental.*

> *While the astronauts reacted in different ways to the TRANSCENDENT experience of space travel, all were profoundly affected by the experience.*

transfiguration *(trans-fig-yuh-REY-shun), noun*

An extreme change in appearance; a metamorphosis.

> *I was fascinated by the time-lapse video of a caterpillar's TRANSFIGURATION into a butterfly.*

transgression *(trans-GRESH-un), noun*

A violation of a rule. To break a law or guideline is to commit a *transgression*.

> *David was perhaps a little too eager to cross over into Mr. Peterson's yard to play ball, but this was a minor TRANSGRESSION.*

translucent *(tranz-LOO-sunt), adjective*

Capable of allowing some light to show through, but not transparent. A gauzy shower curtain, for instance, is *translucent.*

> *From my bed, through the TRANSLUCENT hospital curtains, I could dimly make out that a scuffle of some kind was taking place in front of the building.*

transmogrify *(trance-MOG-rih-fy), verb*

To change into a different shape or form.

> *Drink this and I promise you you'll be TRANSMOGRIFIED into a poet for the ages.*

transubstantiation (tran-sub-stan-shee-AY-shun), *noun*

The theology that the bread and wine of the Eucharist became the actual body and blood of Jesus Christ, while retaining their original appearance.

> *The doctrine of TRANSUBSTANTIATION became a main focus of disagreement between Protestants and Catholics during the Reformation.*

transvestism *(tranz-VEST-iz-um), noun*

The act or practice of dressing for pleasure and gratification in the clothing of the opposite sex; especially, the practice of men dressing in women's garments.

> *Milton Berle's televised drag humor had far more to do with his willingness to do anything for a laugh than with any TRANSVESTISM on the comedian's part.*

tranquility *(tran-KWIL-ih-tee), noun*

Peacefulness; the state of being undisturbed.

> *After all the insanity of the deadline week, I was looking forward to the TRANQUILITY of my annual vacation in Vienna.*

transcend *(tran-SEND), verb*

To rise above common levels.

> *The young violinist's performance at the recital TRANSCENDED all of his teacher's expectations.*

transgress *(trans-GRESS), verb*

To violate a principle or moral law.

> *After having TRANSGRESSED once, an agonized Henry knew he would never violate the club's rules again.*

transient *(TRAN-zee-unt), adjective*

Existing only temporarily; brief; fleeting; transitory.

> *With seven children to care for, my wife and I knew that tranquility in the house was a TRANSIENT thing.*

transition *(tran-ZISH-un), noun*

A change; a passage from one state or form to another.

> *Mark made the TRANSITION from actor to director with relative ease.*

transpire *(tran-SPIRE), verb*

To take place. That which happens *transpires*.

> *Mrs. Potter, please tell the court exactly what TRANSPIRED that night as you remember it.*

transpose *(trans-POZE), verb*

To reverse or change the position of. To *transpose* A and B is to put A in B's place, and vice versa.

> *The two frames of the film had been mysteriously TRANSPOSED, so that it now looked as though the man's head moved forward suddenly instead of backwards.*

traumatize *(TRAW-muh-tize), verb*

To cause to undergo mental or physical distress.

> *Many of the patients in the ward had been TRAUMATIZED over the years by abusive staff.*

travail *(truh-VALE), noun*

Hard work, especially work causing physical pain. *Travail* is sometimes used to describe the labor of childbirth.

> *It is not surprising that, given the TRAVAILS of the long journey westward, some settlers opted to return East rather than try to make a life on the frontier.*

travesty *(TRAV-ih-stee), noun*

A grotesque parody (of something). That which presents an insulting mockery (of a cherished institution, for instance) is a *travesty*.

> *Let's face it: the way Congress deals with overexpenditure is a TRAVESTY of its own budget reduction legislation.*

treacle *(TREE-kul), noun*
Overly contrived sentiment; unrestrained mawkishness.
> *The movie's plot, which concerned a little blind girl's search for her puppy, represented perhaps the most unapologetic TREACLE of the year.*

treatise *(tree-tiss), noun*
A scholarly essay or written argument. A systematic written examination of a subject is a *treatise*.
> *Mill's TREATISE on the equality of women was revolutionary for its time.*

tremolo *(TREMM-uh-lo), noun*
A quality of musical sound marked by rapid repetition of one or two notes.
> *The pianist played extravagantly, adding embellishments and trills of TREMOLO far too often for my taste.*

tremulous *(TREM-yuh-luss), adjective*
Describes someone or something trembling as a result of fear or timidity.
> *As Brock steeled his courage to ask out Alice, his TREMULOUS voice exposed his trepidation.*

trenchant *(TREN-chunt), adjective*
Incisive and discerning.
> *Mart's TRENCHANT observations on Scorsese's films were a welcome addition to our discussion of major American directors.*

trepidation *(trep-ih-DAY-shun), noun*
A state of fear or agitation. To have an apprehension is to have a *trepidation*.
> *At first, I approached the task of writing this book with some TREPIDATION.*

triage *(TREE-ozh), noun*
The procedure of prioritizing victims (of a battle or accident, for instance) to determine which will receive medical care first; of or pertaining to this procedure.
> *Nurse Victoria's single day in the TRIAGE unit of the mobile hospital left her so exhausted that she found herself wondering how the others worked there day after day.*

triennial *(tri-EN-ee-ul), adjective*
Ocurring every three years. That which occurs once in a three-year cycle is *triennial*.
> *The TRIENNIAL Shakespeare festival takes place in April of every third year.*

trifling *(TRY-fling), adjective*
Insignificant. That which is unimportant is *trifling*.
> *The fact is, you are unlikely to be called in for an audit over such a TRIFLING amount of money.*

T

trigamy *(TRIG-uh-mee), noun*
The condition of being married to three husbands or three wives simultaneously.

> *As a result of two identical filing errors on the part of the county clerk in the years before her third marriage, Beth learned to her dismay that she was, technically at least, guilty of TRIGAMY.*

trimester *(try-MESS-tur), noun*
A period spanning three months.

> *For Beth, as for most women, the last few weeks of the final TRIMESTER of pregnancy was a challenging time.*

tripartite *(try-PAR-tite), adjective*
Consisting of three elements; involving three participants.

> *The TRIPARTITE trade agreement was signed by representatives of Canada, Mexico, and the United States.*

trochee *(TROE-kee), noun*
In poetry, a metrical element consisting of a two-syllable unit, the first stressed and the second unstressed.

> *The word "given" is a TROCHEE.*

troglodyte *(TROG-luh-dyte), noun*
One who behaves in a beastly, savage, or primitive manner. Literally, a *troglodyte* is a cave-dweller.

> *I knew that Sebastian would be uncommunicative after his ordeal, but I did not expect him to act like such a TROGLODYTE at work.*

troika *(TROY-kuh), noun*
A group of three individuals acting in concert to exert authority.

> *The photos he took at the historic conference included a memorable image of the victorious TROIKA: Churchill, Stalin, and Roosevelt.*

trompe l'oeil *(tromp LAY), noun,*
An instance of visual trickery, as, for instance, an optical illusion giving the impression of three dimensions in a two-dimensional artistic medium.

> *The painter specialized in TROMPE L'OEIL murals that often fooled passersby into thinking they were walking toward a storefront.*

trooper *(TROO-pur), noun*
A military or police officer. (See, for comparison, the entry for *trouper*)

> *I tried to talk my way out of the speeding ticket, but the TROOPER wouldn't hear any of it.*

troubadour *(TROO-buh-dore), noun*

A traveling medieval poet and singer; also, any wandering singer or minstrel.

After college, Ivan fancied himself something of a TROUBADOUR, and wandered from town to town in search of a coffeehouse willing to let him play.

trouper *(TROO-pur), noun*

An actor, especially a veteran performer who is able to come through no matter what; also, any person who is remarkably dependable. (See, for comparison, the entry for *trooper*.)

Nancy drove through a snowstorm to man the desk on Saturday—what a TROUPER!

truckle *(TRUCK-le), verb*

To yield lamely or obsequiously.

I begged you not to TRUCKLE to that real estate agent's outrageous demands, but you wouldn't listen.

truculent *(TRUCK-yuh-lunt), adjective*

Inclined toward conflict; eager to fight.

I had a run-in with a rather TRUCULENT sales clerk, who insisted, despite my receipt, that I had not bought the defective blender at his store.

trumpery *(TRUMP-uh-ree), noun*

Worthless stuff; a thing or things without value; nonsense.

Mark's paper, composed between 3:00 and 6:00 a.m. on the day it was due, used complicated language to disguise its poor construction, but the instructor had seen such TRUMPERY often enough to recognize it instantly.

truncate *(TRUN-kate), verb*

To shorten by cutting (a segment).

The director left the long passage about the "willow that grows aslant the brook" intact, but decided to TRUNCATE an earlier scene that had something to do with Hecuba.

truncheon *(TRUN-chun), noun*

A stick carried by police officers. A *truncheon* is a billy club.

The sight of the policemen beating the young demonstrators with TRUNCHEONS, when beamed to the nation on television, was more than enough to ruin the convention for the party.

tryst *(trist), noun*

A prearranged meeting, especially one between lovers. *Tryst* derives from an old verb meaning "to make an arrangement with."

We've decided to celebrate our second honeymoon with a weekend TRYST at the Ambassador Hotel.

tumescent *(too-MESS-unt), adjective*
Swollen or beginning to swell.

> *The yellowjacket stung Rhoda on the thumb, leaving a TUMESCENT welt she felt compelled to show everyone in the office.*

tumid *(TOO-mid), adjective*
Swollen, like a body part, or pompous, like some human beings.

> *Stephen's TUMID, purple bruise was a source of fascination on the playground.*

tumultuous *(too-MUL-choo-uss), adjective*
Chaotic, especially as a result of a popular outcry. That which is in a violent uproar is *tumultuous*.

> *After the board of trustees rejected the students' proposal, there were TUMULTUOUS protests on campus.*

tundra *(TUN-druh), noun*
A treeless arctic plain.

> *For days the members of the search team trekked through the frigid TUNDRA, but they at last they had to abandon the expedition without locating any survivors.*

turgid *(TUR-jid), adjective*
Swollen and overinflated. This word typically is used in a negative manner because it serves as a slightly nicer way to call someone a blowhard.

> *The speaker's TURGID rhetoric caused many in the audience to develop drooping eyelids.*

turncoat *(TURN-kote), noun*
One who reverses sides in a conflict or changes principles easily.

> *At the risk of being labeled a TURNCOAT, I've decided to support your candidacy— even though you're a Democrat.*

tutelage *(toot-l-ij), noun*
The act of providing guided instruction or protection. *Tutelage* can also mean "close instruction."

> *It was under Dr. Clay's TUTELAGE that he came to understand how much craft was required to write a solid play.*

tutorial *(too-TORE-ee-ul), noun*
A software program offering step-by-step instruction and demonstration in the use of another program; a component of a software program that offers instruction in the main program's use. Also: of or pertaining to tutors.

> *The manual that came with the software was woefully inadequate, but, fortunately, the program featured an excellent TUTORIAL.*

tyranny *(TEER-uh-nee), noun*

The abusive and unrestrained exercise of power.

Paine's bold arguments against the TYRANNY of George III made Common Sense powerful reading.

tyro *(TIE-roh), noun*

From the Latin meaning "recruit," a *tyro* is a beginner or novice.

Far from being a TYRO, my five-year-old has been playing baseball since he was only two.

doctrinaire
abstemious
levity hubris panacea
veracity cerebellum
labyrinth
criterion
nonagenarian
meticulous zither

U

erbiage quondam
colloquial
vok palpable pagination
incipient salutary
evity redact fervent
beleaguered yawnful
elixir beneficent
amoose pragmatism

U

ubiquitous *(yoo-BIK-wi-tuss), adjective*
Seemingly everywhere at once. That which is *ubiquitous* is so common as to appear to be all places.

> *By the early fifties, that UBIQUITOUS symbol of independence, the automobile, had influenced virtually every facet of American life.*

ulterior *(ul-TEER-ee-ur), adjective*
Being beyond what is obvious or put forth; lying beyond a recognized boundary.

> *I flatly reject the notion that my proposal to your daughter is occasioned by any ULTERIOR motive, sir.*

ultimatum *(ul-tih-MAY-tum), noun*
One's last set of demands. To issue an *ultimatum* is to outline a set of terms that cannot be compromised.

> *Either pay the rent by midnight on the thirty-first, or be thrown out in the street: that was Simon's ULTIMATUM.*

ultimo *(ul-TEE-mo), adjective*
Of or in the calendar month preceding the current one.

> *On the 23rd ULTIMO, I was informed by counsel that an indictment would be forthcoming.*

ultrasaurus *(ul-truh-SORE-us), noun*
A recently discovered of dinosaur that is believed to have stood five stories high.

> *A dinosaur that would make a T. rex look like a pipsqueak may seem a farfetched notion, but scientists are now certain that the ULTRASAURUS was such a creature.*

ululate *(UL-yuh-late), verb*
To howl.

> *Late at night, Bert sometimes thought he heart faint sounds of the old house's former occupants ULULATING plaintively, as if imprisoned there.*

umbrage *(UM-brij), noun*
Resentful annoyance. To take *umbrage* is to express irritation.

> *I take UMBRAGE at the suggestion that I have used my position here for illicit personal gain.*

umlaut *(OOM-laut), noun*
A symbol (ü) used, especially in German, to indicate special pronunciation of vowels.

> *The German sportswriters in town for the race were unhappy with the typewriters we had provided, as they did not have UMLAUTS.*

unanimity *(yoo-nuh-NIM-ih-tee), noun*
Agreement without dissent.

> *I was genuinely surprised at the UNANIMITY with which my proposal was accepted by the board.*

unassuming *(un-uh-SOOM-ing), adjective*
Modest; humble.

> *Sam is the UNASSUMING type who refuses to take credit after a job well done, preferring to cite the contributions of others.*

unbecoming *(un-bee-KUM-ing), adjective*
Unseemly; likely to detract from one's reputation or character.

> *I think your use of street language during the confirmation hearing was most UNBECOMING, George.*

unblinking *(un-BLINGK-ing), adjective*
Not displaying emotion or response. Also: unwavering in devotion.

> *Victor's UNBLINKING reaction to the judge's sentence left observers with no further insights on the motives that led him to commit the crime.*

uncalled-for *(un-KALD-for), adjectival phrase*
Improper or unjustified; also, superfluous.

> *That reference to my father's bankruptcy was UNCALLED-FOR, Senator.*

uncanny *(un-CAN-ee), adjective*
Strange; mysterious or otherwordly.

> *Greg's shooting ability is UNCANNY; I've seen him sink twenty foul shots in a row.*

unceremonious *(un-sare-uh-MONE-ee-uss), adjective*
Rude or abrupt; tactlessly hasty; inappropriate.

> *June made an UNCEREMONIOUS exit just as the chairman was beginning his remarks on the Fentworth project.*

unconscionable *(un-KONSH-un-uh-bul), adjective*
Lacking in principles our conscience; beyond any reasonable boundary.

> *Your decision to destroy those letters without attempting to get permission from the poet's widow was UNCONSCIONABLE.*

uncouth *(un-KOOTH), adjective*
Crude, without manners, unrefined.

> *Carl had an unfortunate way of belching loudly in public places, guessing (accurately and loudly) whether or not someone he just met had undergone plastic surgery, and otherwise acting in an UNCOUTH manner in front of strangers.*

unctuous *(UNK-choo-us), adjective*

Oily; falsely and exaggeratedly earnest; unpleasantly smooth.

> *An UNCTUOUS salesman glided across the lot and shook us both by the hand, telling us what a pleasure it was to meet such intelligent and discriminating customers.*

underdog *(UN-dur-dog), noun*

A person or entity expected to fail or to fare poorly.

> *San Diego, a decided UNDERDOG, somehow managed to pull out a win against the division-leading Miami team.*

underhanded *(UN-dur-hand), adjective*

Devious or deceitful in nature; not open, but crafty.

> *Who knows what UNDERHANDED means were used to turn the decision in Milton's favor?*

undermine *(UN-dur-mine), verb*

To defeat or destroy, as by sabotage.

> *Little did I know that Wells was UNDERMINING my efforts to win a contract for the project.*

underwhelm *(un-dur-HWELM), verb*

To fail to impress or excite. (Informal.)

> *After all the hype money could buy, the play opened to a wave of reviews written by unanimously UNDERWHELMED critics.*

underwrite *(UN-dur-rite), verb*

To support as by subsidy. Also, to support in full as though undertaking (a risk or venture) oneself.

> *A group of philanthropists UNDERWRITES our drama department's annual playwriting competition.*

undisposed *(un-dis-POZED), adjective*

Not inclined; not favoring.

> *Jim was not crazy about having to find a job, but he was also UNDISPOSED to letting his children go hungry.*

undulate *(UN-dyoo-late), verb*

Move in a wavelike motion. That which *undulates* moves in regular wavy patterns.

> *After a hard day at work, Ellis would sit on the seashore stare ahead at the UNDULATING ocean to ease his mind.*

unequaled *(un-EE-kwuld), adjective*
Unmatched; without serious competition.

> *The salesman bragged of the car's "UNEQUALED level of trouble-free performance," but it broke down within two weeks of the time we bought it.*

unequivocal *(un-ee-KWIV-uh-kul), adjective*
Unambiguous; unadorned; blatant or obvious in expression.

> *My response to your suggestion that we lie to the judge is an UNEQUIVOCAL one: absolutely not.*

unfaltering *(un-FALL-tur-ing), adjective*
Unwavering; steadfast.

> *Frank's UNFALTERING composure on the witness stand, even under intense cross-examination, impressed us all.*

ungainly *(un-GANE-lee), adjective*
Graceless.

> *Wilma, who had always thought of herself as UNGAINLY, was surprised at the ease with which she and Clive moved across the dance floor.*

ungrammatical *(un-gruh-MAT-ih-kul), adjective*
In violation of grammatical rules.

> *Fred's use of such UNGRAMMATICAL sentences as "Him and me want to talk at you" didn't score him any points with the college president.*

unguent *(UNG-gwunt), noun*
A locally applied ointment or salve.

> *In treating poison ivy, calamine lotion or some similar UNGUENT is usually recommended.*

unicameral *(yoo-nih-KAM-uh-rul), adjective*
Featuring a single chamber or body.

> *The new constitution provides for a UNICAMERAL legislature, rather than an upper and lower house.*

unilateral *(yoo-ni-LAT-ur-el), adjective*
Undertaken independently, although likely to have implications for others (for instance, allies, associates, or family members). A *unilateral* decision is one made with no consultation of affected parties.

> *The allies resolved that no member country would take any UNILATERAL act that might threaten mutual security.*

U

unimpeachable *(un-im-PEECH-uh-bul), adjective*
Exemplary; beyond reproach or suspicion.

> *My alibi for the night in question comes from an UNIMPEACHABLE source, Sergeant Miller; I was helping Father White at the homeless shelter.*

unique *(yoo-NEEK), adjective*
Singular; alone in a particular class.

> *Professor Watson would always scold me when I described something as "very UNIQUE" as something that is UNIQUE is by definition unparalleled, and therefore cannot be modified with a word like very.*

unkempt *(un-KEMPT), adjective*
Disheveled or messy; lacking care in aspect or look.

> *The witness's story was believable, but the defendant's lawyer worried about his UNKEMPT appearance.*

unmitigated *(un-MIH-tih-gay-tud), adjective*
Complete and without exception; unalloyed; sheer or outright.

> *Ron, who had worked on his article for six months, read the acceptance letter from the New Yorker with UNMITIGATED joy.*

unobtrusive *(un-ub-TROO-siv), adjective*
Not easily seen or noticed; not showy in nature.

> *The guards dressed in civilian clothes, taking seriously the pop star's request that his security detail be as UNOBTRUSIVE as possible.*

unorthodox *(un-ORTH-uh-docks), adjective*
Characterized by breaking with custom and tradition due to independence of spirit.

> *The teacher's UNORTHODOX methods got many students to develop an appreciation for learning.*

unprecedented *(un-PRESS-uh-dent-ud), adjective*
New; unparalleled; not having been done before.

> *The studio granted Lewisohn UNPRECEDENTED access to the group's session tapes and related recording materials.*

unremitting (**un-ruh-MITT-ing**), **adjective**
Persistent; relentless.

> *An UNREMITTING rain spoiled our plans for a picnic.*

untenable *(un-TEN-uh-bull), adjective*
Impossible; unsupportable.

The paper's central thesis, that Hamlet is a transvestite, is UNTENABLE to say the least.

unsavory *(un-SAY-vuh-ree), adjective*
Likely to give social or moral offense. Also: unpleasant or distasteful.

I have no patience for biographers who concern themselves only with the number of UNSAVORY episodes they can uncover.

unseemly *(un-SEEM-ly), verb*
Inappropriate; unbecoming.

The family felt that Bill's presence at the memorial service would have been UNSEEMLY, as he had been my sister-in-law's bitterest business rival.

untold *(un-TOLD), adjective*
Not counted. Also: not revealed.

Greg used UNTOLD pads of paper in constructing the first draft of his epic.

unwarranted *(un-WORE-un-tud), adjective*
Groundless; lacking factual basis.

The defense will prove each and every one of these UNWARRANTED accusations to be false, Your Honor.

unwieldy *(un-WEELD-ee), adjective*
Hard to handle or manage.

The deliveryman had a tough time getting that UNWIELDY package to our front door.

unwitting *(un-WTT-ting), adjective*
Unaware; unintentional. Also: unintended.

Greg was shocked to learn that he had been the UNWITTING stooge of a foreign espionage organization.

unwonted *(un-WAHNT-id), adjective*
Not typical, habitual, or ordinary.

January's UNWONTED warm weather was far from unwanted!

upbraid *(up-BRAID), verb*
To criticize and assign blame (to a person). To *upbraid* is to scold.

I did not spend thirteen years at this firm to be UPBRAIDED by a junior clerk, Mr. Franklin.

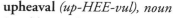

U

upheaval *(up-HEE-vul), noun*
A sudden, violent change.

> *Given the sense of UPHEAVAL in the department after the director's resignation, it's not too surprising that productivity has fallen.*

uprear *(up-REER), verb*
To lift or raise up.

> *At the sound of the siren, our dog UPREARED her head and howled.*

upside *(UP-side), noun*
The positive aspect of a situation; particularly, the potential profit in a business proposal.

> *The UPSIDE of investing in the Russian company was considerable, but there were considerable risks as well.*

upstage *(up-STAYJ), verb*
To distract attention from (a person undertaking an act supposedly of primary interest). To *upstage*, in the theatrical sense, is to stand behind the main action of a scene and distract the audience.

> *I am not accustomed to being UPSTAGED during a presentation, Peter.*

upthrust *(UP-thrust), noun*
Quick, strong upward movement in the national economy or in the stock market.

> *This financial writer feels that the current UPTHRUST in the market cannot be sustained.*

urbane *(ur-BANE), adjective*
Suave; sophisticated; debonair.

> *Clive, Linda's URBANE English cousin, was pleasant company for us all during his stay here.*

ursine *(UR-sin), adjective*
Bearlike. *Ursine* derives from the Latin word for "bear."

> *Mr. Hess was so glad to see me that be ran across the hall and gave me a fierce (I might say URSINE!) embrace.*

usurious *(yoo-ZHOOR-ee-us), noun*
Charging excessive interest on money loaned; characterized by usury.

> *The rates we agreed to when we bought the house seem positively USURIOUS by today's standards.*

usurp *(yoo-SURP), verb*

To assume forcibly and/or without right. To *usurp* is to take over.

> *The authority of Congress was indeed USURPED by Lincoln during the war, but legislators briskly reasserted themselves once the crisis was past.*

usury *(YOO-sur-ee), noun*

Excessive interest on a loan. Someone who demands extravagant payment in exchange for money lent out practices *usury*.

> *The rates you are charging for this loan you consider "fair," sir, border on USURY.*

utilitarian *(yoo-til-ih-TARE-ee-un), adjective*

Characterized by a concern for the practical or useful. That which is *utilitarian* is pragmatic.

> *I propose we take a UTILITARIAN approach to the problem: since it no longer runs, why not scrap the old car completely and sell it for parts?*

utopia *(yoo-TOE-pee-uh), noun*

A (theoretical) perfect society or paradise. *Utopia* was coined by using Greek forms to produce a word meaning "nowhere."

> *Any notion that granting eighteen-year-olds the right to vote would turn the country into a pastoral, strife-free UTOPIA was quickly disproven.*

uxoricide *(uk-SOR-ih-side), noun*

Tthe crime of murdering one's wife.

> *Eventually, the defendant was acquitted of UXORICIDE; his wife's death was ruled a suicide.*

uxorious *(uk-SORE-ee-us), adjective*

Submissive or doting towards one's wife.

> *Although Grandpa makes a show of rebellion against Grandma's strictures every now and then for our sake, he's as UXORIOUS as they come.*

doctrinaire
abstemious
levity hubris panacea
veracity cerebellum
criterion labyrinth
nonagenarian
meticulous zither

V

erbiage
colloquial quondam
vok palpable paginatic
incipient salutary
evity redact fervent
beleaguered yawnful
elixir beneficent
amoose pragmatism

V

vacillate *(VAS-uh-late), verb*

To waver between options. A person who cannot decide which course of action to settle on *vacillates*.

> *Mr. Mears's principal weakness is that he is seen as a VACILLATING leader, one who cannot choose one path and stick to it.*

vacuity *(va-KYOO-ih-tee), noun*

Empty; without content.

> *Staring out at the VACUITY of the Atlantic, Stan forgot for a moment the hazards of the journey ahead.*

vacuous *(VAK-yoo-uss), adjective*

Lacking content or substance. That which is empty is *vacuous*.

> *Televised debates are so potentially dangerous that most candidates settle for offering VACUOUS recitations of campaign speeches rather saying something new and unexpected.*

vagabond *(VAG-uh-bond), adjective*

Leading the life of a person who has no home; transient.

> *Ivan's VAGABOND existence was not easy, but he was inured to it.*

vainglorious *(vane-GLORE-ee-uss), adjective*

Given to self-absorption; inclined to view oneself excessively or too highly.

> *Although some are entranced by Anais Nin's diaries, they always struck me as the narcissistic, VAINGLORIOUS observations of a woman totally unable to look beyond herself.*

valedictory *(val-uh-DDC-tuh-ree), adjective*

Saying farewell; of or pertaining to departing.

> *Karen was selected to give her class's VALEDICTORY address.*

valetudinary *(val-uh-tood-uhn-AIR-ee), adjective*

Sickly to the point of being an invalid.

> *After catching the disease, Val stayed at home for three months in a VALETUDINARY state.*

valiant *(VAL-yunt), adjective*

Courageous, bold; brave.

> *I made a VALIANT effort to complete the project by the deadline, but in the end I had to get an extension from my boss.*

validate *(VAL-ih-date), verb*

To substantiate or confirm; to make valid.

> *I won't VALIDATE your accusations with a response.*

valise *(vuh-LEECE), noun*
A small piece of luggage; a carry-on bag.
> *The stewardess asked me to stow my VALISE in the overhead cabin.*

vamoose *(vah-MOOSE), verb*
To depart in haste; to leave hurriedly.
> *We've got a full day of travel ahead of us; let's VAMOOSE.*

vanguard *(VAN-gard), noun*
The most advanced groups (of a military force or social movement, for instance.)
That which is at the forefront is in the *vanguard*.
> *Dali was the first to admit that he took full financial advantage of his position at the VANGUARD of the Surrealist movement.*

vanquish *(VAN-kwish), verb*
To defeat, as in combat.
> *Having VANQUISHED the enemy, the general returned victorious to his native land.*

vapid *(VA-pid), adjective*
Insipid; flat, dull, or lifeless.
> *The movie's scenery was appealing, but its VAPID characters made it hard for one to care about what was going on.*

variegated *(VAR-ee-uh-gay-tid), adjective*
Changing in color. That which alters hue is *variegated*.
> *June's latest needlework project uses VARIEGATED thread to achieve a rainbow effect.*

variorum *(var-ee-OR-ee-um), noun*
A version of a literary work that may contain several different versions of the work as well as notes and criticism.
> *For the introductory course on Chaucer, we were required to purchase an unabridged VARIORUM edition of The Canterbury Tales.*

vaticide *(VAT-uh-side), noun*
The act of murdering a prophet.
> *Tom took the reviewer's negative article on his religious poetry as an act tantamount to VATICIDE.*

vegan *(VEH-jun), noun*
A person who eats only vegetables, fruits, and grains and no animal products whatsoever.
> *VEGAN since college, Wanda had a hard time finding restaurants that offered entrees she could eat.*

vehement *(VEE-uh-ment), adjective*

Strongly felt or marked by high emotion. That which is forceful and emphatic is *vehement*.

> *Congress overrode the President's veto after many members had openly expressed their VEHEMENT dissatisfaction with Administration policy.*

venal *(VEE-nul), adjective*

Corruptible or excessively devoted to selfish interests (as opposed to public interests); susceptible to bribes. (See, for comparison, the entry for *venial*)

> *The problem with politics by scandal, of course, is that it eventually leaves voters with the impression that all officeholders, regardless of ideology or experience, are VENAL, contemptible scalawags.*

vendetta *(ven-DET-uh), noun*

A bitter feud or grudge.

> *Mark's arguments against my proposed project had less to do with its merits than with the VENDETTA he has held against me since I was hired for the job he wanted.*

veneer *(vuh-NEER), noun*

A thin surface layer; a coating; a superficial surface or deceptive appearance.

> *Though it was not readily apparent to those who hadn't seen the supervisor in action, his VENEER of calm and approachability masked the temper and tolerance of a three-year-old.*

venerable *(VEN-er-uh-bul), adjective*

Commanding reverence; sacred.

> *"Ladies and gentlemen" Bob intoned, "it is my privilege to introduce tonight's guest of honor, the VENERABLE Dr. Mildred Flint"*

venerate *(VEN-uh-rate), verb*

To regard or treat with the reverence due to one's god / God or holy leader.

> *"The way the United States VENERATES celebrities can be quite annoying," Sylvia said.*

venial *(VEE-nee-ul), adjective*

Forgivable; excusable. (See, for comparison, the entry for *venal*)

> *Mom told us that occasionally missing curfew was only a VENIAL offense, but lying to her about why we'd missed it was not.*

vent *(VENT), verb*

To relieve pressure by giving expression to something, in the way a vent allows steam to escape.

> *The boss made me so mad that I didn't feel back to normal until I was able to VENT to my wife about the situation.*

veracious *(vuh-RAY-shuss), adjective*
Honest; truthful.

> *Your Honor, I ask that the defense's assertion that none of the prosecution's witnesses are VERACIOUS be stricken from the record.*

verbiage *(VER-bee-uj), noun*
Unnecessary words. Superfluous or overwrought language is *verbiage*.

> *Like many novelists, Robert overwrote: he would let everything fly in one session and then come back and pare away at VERBIAGE in another.*

verbose *(ver-BOSE), adjective*
Wordy. That which uses unnecessary language is *verbose*.

> *This is not Hemingway's best work: long passages of the manuscript are strangely VERBOSE and—let's face it—downright boring.*

verdant *(VUR-dnt), adjective*
Green (with plant life). That which is lush with vegetation is *verdant*.

> *The VERDANT surroundings give one the feeling of being a million miles from the city, but from where we are standing now Nashville is only fifteen minutes away by car.*

verification *(veh-rih-fih-KAY-shun), noun*
Something that confirms.

> *I could find no VERIFICATION of the author's claim that he had met with Hemingway in the early twenties.*

veritable *(VER-ih-tuh-bull), adjective*
Authentic; true. That which is undeniably legitimate or actual is *veritable*.

> *The cardboard boxes contained a VERITABLE treasure trove of Civil War artifacts, probably worth tens of thousands of dollars.*

vermilion *(vur-MILL-yun), noun*
Scarlet red; bright red.

> *In her trademark VERMILION pantsuit, Carrie really stood out in a crowd.*

vernacular *(ver-NAK-yoo-lur), noun and adjective*
The mode of expression in language accepted in a given circle. As an adjective, *vernacular* describes the quality of being common to a particular group's or region's speech.

> *I saw that Clement was once again intoxicated—or "blasted," to use the VERNACULAR he seems to prefer.*

versatile *(VER-suh-tl), adjective*
Capable of doing many tasks, or prone to frequent changes.

> *Mike is a VERSATILE baseball player because he can play the infield or the outfield with equal aplomb.*

vertiginous *(ver-TIJ-uh-nuss), adjective*

Having to do with whirling, spinning, or feeling dizzy. "Vertigo" is a dizzying sensation, sometimes inspired by heights, that can make you feel like you're about to fall.

The cliff's VERTIGINOUS face was awe-inspiring . . . and a little bit frightening.

vertigo *(VUR-tih-go), noun*

A sensation of dizziness and disorientation. *Vertigo* is a feeling of tilting or spinning.

Jane was overcome with a sudden bout of VERTIGO as the ship left port.

verve *(vurv), noun*

A spirited and enthusiastic manner, particularly when embodied in an artistic performance; an air of vitality.

The critics were unanimous in their opinion that, although the plot of the play was implausible and its production values poor, the actress playing the librarian brought a unique VERVE to the role.

vestige *(vess-tij), noun*

A remaining sample of something no longer common. That which represents something now lost is a *vestige*.

The last VESTIGE of truly nomadic Indian life was wiped out at Wounded Knee; from that point on, Native Americans would be forced either to assimilate with the settlers or to live on the reservation.

vet *(VET), verb*

To appraise or evaluate for authenticity.

The campaign manager thoroughly VETTED the short list of vice-presidential candidates.

vex *(vex), verb*

To irritate or bother.

Although his school friends constantly teased him about his ballet lessons, Ken never allowed their comments to VEX him.

vexation *(vek-SAY-shun), noun*

Irritation. That which aggravates causes *vexation*.

"Where on earth is my horse?" Scarlett demanded in VEXATION.

viable *(VIE-uh-bul), adjective*

Capable of being performed or occurring.

Mike argued quite persuasively that the only VIABLE solution to the company's financial dilemma was for it to go public and raise money by selling stock.

vial *(VTE-ul), noun*
A small container (usually glass) used to hold liquids, medicines, and the like.

> *The doctor gave me a small VIAL of the drug for use over the weekend, and a written prescription so I could get more from the pharmacy on Monday.*

viand *(VIE-und), noun*
An article of food.

> *Chef Jacques thought that any VIAND, whether prime rib or meatloaf, should be served to the customer in a visually appealing way.*

vicarious *(vi-KARE-ee-uss), adjective*
Arising from the experiences of others rather than one's own experience. To gain *vicarious* pleasure is to gain pleasure from actions not one's own.

> *I think Paul derives some VICARIOUS thrill from making us fight; every spat we have seems to spring from something he's said to us.*

vicissitude *(vih-SISS-ih-tude), noun*
A fateful obstacle or turn of events.

> *Aware that most of us are hurt by love's VICISSITUDES at some point during our lives, Max tried to forget the past and find someone new.*

vigilant *(VIJ-uh-lunt), adjective*
Alert and watchful in order to detect danger.

> *My VIGILANT watchdog barks at the slightest sound.*

vilify *(VIL-ih-fie), verb*
To defame; to slander.

> *My opponent's ceaseless attempts to VILIFY me during this campaign reached a new low when she accused me of being on the side of the neo-Nazi movement.*

vindicate *(VIN-dih-kate), verb*
Proven correct or innocent despite previous indications to the contrary. To be *vindicated* is to have one's name cleared after being falsely suspected of something.

> *The test results VINDICATED the athlete: there was no trace of any illicit substance in his bloodstream.*

vindictive *(vin-DIK-tiv), adjective*
Mean-spirited; eager for revenge. A *vindictive* person is motivated by a desire for vengeance.

> *When angered, Lynn can be quite VINDICTIVE; those who work with her know that the most painless course is to stay cm her good side.*

virile *(VIR-ul), adjective*
Forcefully masculine. Someone who is *virile* is characterized by the drive and energy thought to be common among men.

It was hard for me to picture my grandfather as the VIRILE young man beaming out from that old photograph.

virtually *(VUR-choo-uh-lee), adverb*
Existing in effect, although not in actual fact or form.

Paul had been worried about his first day at work for weeks, so it came as a surprise to him when he passed his first day in the office with VIRTUALLY no nervousness.

virtuoso *(vur-choo-OWE-so), noun*
A supremely skilled artist.

Geena is a piano VIRTUOSO who has won dozens of competitions.

virulent *(VIR-yuh-lent), adjective*
Something or someone poisonous or intensely hostile. *Virulent* shares the same root as the word "virus."

Marla's VIRULENT words were meant to hurt her sister deeply.

visage *(VIZ-uj), noun*
The face. *Visage* can also mean "appearance."

It was a grim-VISAGED Roosevelt who addressed Congress the day after the Japanese attack.

visceral *(VISS-er-ul), adjective*
Deeply felt. *Visceral* means "from the viscera," or bodily interior.

A VISCERAL wave of panic ran through Clark's body as he listened to the air-raid siren blare.

viscosity *(vis-KOSS-ih-tee), noun*
The thickness of a liquid.

The mechanic working on my car recommended I switch to a brand of motor oil with a higher VISCOSITY.

viscous *(VIS-kuss), adjective*
Having a gluey nature and consistency.

I could barely gulp down the VISCOUS concoction my personal trainer called an "energy drink."

vitiate *(VISH-ee-ate), verb*
To corrupt or impair the quality or effectiveness of something or someone.

My boss's constant criticism, far from improving my performance, actually VITIATED it.

vitriolic *(vit-ree-OL-ik), adjective*
Acidic (literally, but also in tone). *Vitriolic* speech or writing is harsh and caustic.
> *McCarthy's VITRIOLIC attacks on organizations with no actual Communist ties went completely unchallenged in the Senate.*

vituperative *(vie-TOO-per-uh-tive), adjective*
Scathing and harshly abusive, as criticism.
> *You can't hide your VITUPERATIVE attack behind a few surface pleasantries!*

vivacious *(vy-VAY-shuss), adjective*
Spirited. That which is full of life is *vivacious*.
> *The novelist's characters are saucy and VIVACIOUS, but the situations they face are, alas, deadly dull.*

vivid *(VIV-d), adjective*
Brilliant; resplendent and gaily colored. Also: described or capable of describing with great precision and detail; related in such a way as to leave a distinct impression.
> *Julius, a boy with a VIVID imagination, could amuse himself in his room for hours making up stories and adventures for his toy soldiers.*

vivify *(VIV-ih-fie), verb*
To bring to life; to make lively or active.
> *The characters in Keillor's stories are VIVIFIED through his almost uncanny sense of human nature and his knowledge of the importance of seemingly small events.*

vivisection *(viv-uh-SECK-shun), noun*
The practice of cutting on living animals to learn new physiological information.
> *Animal-rights activists carried signs outside the clinic in which VIVISECTIONS took place.*

vociferous *(vo-SIF-er-us), verb*
Crying out loudly; noisy, especially in anger.
> *Anticipating a VOCIFEROUS reaction, I waited until we were well outside of the crowded restaurant before telling my father I had totaled the car.*

volatile *(VOL-uh-tull), adjective*
Potentially unstable. That which is likely to shift or change suddenly is *volatile*.
> *We should have known that asking those two to work together after the divorce would lead to a VOLATILE work environment.*

volition *(vo-LISH-un), noun*
The mental faculty associated with free will and unhindered, uncoerced choice.
> *Nothing you can say or do will be able to transform your father overnight; he will have to admit of his own VOLITION that he needs help and then make a commitment to work toward a recovery.*

voluble *(VOL-yuh-bul), adjective*
Talkative; gregarious.

> *Muriel's little girl is the most VOLUBLE two-year-old I've ever met. She rattled on endlessly until her mother sent her upstairs to play.*

voluminous *(vuh-LOO-mih-nuss), adjective*
Possessing great volume or fullness.

> *Michelle's wedding dress was so VOLUMINOUS that there was barely room for Jon to stand next to her at the altar.*

voluptuous *(vuh-LUP-shoo-uss), adjective*
Sensually enjoyable. *Voluptuous* can also refer to that which calls to mind sensual pleasure.

> *The bestselling writer showed up fashionably late in a long black limousine, accompanied by a VOLUPTUOUS companion whose name we never learned.*

voracious *(vo-RAY-shuss), adjective*
Greedily hungry. Someone who is gluttonous or ravenous is *voracious*.

> *Tom is a VORACIOUS reader; I believe he has been through every volume in our public library.*

vortex *(VOR-tex), noun*
A whirlpool or whirlwind; a spinning mass of liquid or flame capable of drawing objects into it; something regarded as capable of drawing other entities into its current with great strength.

> *Even as the two nations slipped inexorably toward the VORTEX of war, the mainstream press focused on trivialities.*

vouchsafe *(vouch-SAFE), verb*
To deign or to condescend; to agree, in a condescending manner, to grant a request or do something; to offer as a favor or privilege.

> *James's show of superiority to everyone else in the family was so blatant that I'm surprised he VOUCHSAFED to spend a few minutes with me at the reunion.*

vox populi *(VOKS POP-yoo-lie), noun*
The voice of the people: public opinion.

> *I reject the idea that any ideologue who phones up a radio talk show represents the VOX POPULI.*

vulpine *(VUHL-pine), adjective*
Cunning or crafty, like a fox.

> *My son's VULPINE grin let me know he was up to something of which I would not approve.*

W

waft *(WAFT), verb*

To carry lightly, as if caught in a breeze.

The scent of bread WAFTED from the corner bakery.

waggish *(WAG-ish), adjective*

Joking, witty, and mischievous. The noun form, which you might see, is "wag."

Kent's WAGGISH comments got him in trouble with the boss.

wallow *(WALL-lo), verb*

To immerse oneself in utterly. Literally, to *wallow* in something is to roll around in it.

Joan's reviews were certainly unflattering, but in my opinion, she WALLOWED in self-pity after opening night and did the cast and crew of the show a disservice.

Walter Mitty *(WAHL-ter MIH-tee), noun*

A timid person who compensates for his or her timidity by having a rich fantasy life; someone who is self-aggrandizing. *Walter Mitty* is the titular character of a short story by humorist James Thurber. Thurber's character is, not surprisingly, the quintessential *Walter Mitty*.

You've always got all these grandiose plans, but it's time for you to stop being a WALTER MITTY and actually do something!

wan *(wahn), adjective*

Without color; pallid; pale.

Frankie looked thin and WAN after his long bout of mononucleosis.

wanderlust *(WAN-dur-lust), noun*

A strong, innate desire to travel.

While Jerry told his family each Thanksgiving that he would someday settle down and raise a family, his irrepressible WANDERLUST kept him from putting down roots until he was well into his sixties.

wane *(wane), verb*

To decrease in size, power, or intensity; to diminish; to decline.

Stanley took up French, dancing, backgammon—he even learned the basics of horticulture—anything to rekindle his girlfriend's WANING interest in their relationship.

wangle *(WANG-gul), verb*

To get one's own way by using manipulation or clever means.

Franz WANGLED two tickets to the concert by pretending to be the son of the city's premier entertainment critic.

wanton *(WON-tun), adjective*

Completely unrestrained. *Wanton* can also mean "done without any justification."

> *Such WANTON, pointless cruelty, even in the name of science, is inexcusable.*

wary *(WARE-ee), adjective*

On guard; watchful of danger; leery; suspicious.

> *Although the new project has undeniable potential, I'm WARY about Ted's claim that he can bring the product to market by the first of January.*

waspish *(WAH-spish), adjective*

Easily irritated and annoyed and likely to "sting"—or act spitefully—in return for perceived slights.

> *Wanda's WASPISH behavior puts everyone in the office on eggshells.*

watershed *(WAH-ter-shed), noun*

An important event that serves to distinguish two separate phases. Literally, a *watershed* is a ridge that diverts water in a new direction.

> *The new arms agreement is being touted as a WATERSHED in East-West relations.*

waver *(WAY-vur), verb*

To sway; to quiver or flutter; also, to move back and forth on an issue before making a final decision.

> *Although the administration did its utmost to secure legislative support for the controversial initiative, three WAVERING senators announced their opposition to it last night, thus guaranteeing that the bill will never make its way out of committee.*

wayfaring *(WAY-fare-ing), adjective*

Tending to travel by foot. A *wayfaring* person is one who walks as a means of conducting a journey.

> *My father, like many other men of his generation, spent some time as a WAYFARING laborer during the depths of the Depression.*

weal *(WEEL), noun*

Happiness and well-being, typically as a result of being financially secure.

> *The public WEAL greatly improved under the successful policies of the president.*

wean *(WEEN), verb*

To withdraw from a habit or form of enjoyment. The phrase "wean on" suggests accustoming someone to something at an early age.

> *Sasha is a great pianist because she was practically WEANED on Beethoven.*

W

weltschmerz *(VELT-schmayrtz), noun*
From the German meaning "world pain," *weltschmerz* is a kind of lingering sorrow that some believe is a given in life.
> *Mike likes to say he's in the grip of WELTSCHMERZ, but the rest of us just say he's a total drag.*

wend *(wend), verb*
To go forward. To *wend* one's way is to proceed along a given course.
> *Hansel and Gretel, WENDING their way through the forest innocently, had no idea what awaited them at journey's end.*

whelp *(hwelp), noun*
The offspring of a female dog or of certain other animals. Also, as a verb: to give birth to (used in connection with a female dog, wolf, lion, or similar animal).
> *Where is that little WHELP—he's taken my slipper again!*

whet *(hwet), verb*
To stimulate; also, to sharpen a knife or a similar object by honing on a stone.
> *Worried that I had eaten so little over the past few days, Mom tried to WHET my appetite by cooking my favorite foods: chicken fingers and mashed potatoes.*

whey *(whay), noun*
In cheesemaking, the liquid that separates from milk curd during coagulation.
> *Many parents, when asked by their children to identify exactly what Miss Muffet is eating in the famous nursery rhyme, are at a loss to explain "curds and WHEY."*

whilom *(HWHY-lum), adjective*
Former, erstwhile.
> *I'm afraid our WHILOM friendship will not survive this latest betrayal.*

whimsical *(WIM-zih-kul), adjective*
Fanciful; given to acting on sudden notions or ideas.
> *John is known as a real sourpuss around the office, but as his college roommate I can tell you he has his WHIMSICAL side.*

whippet *(WIP-it), noun*
A short-haired, fast-running dog similar to a greyhound.
> *Like WHIPPETS straining before a race, the swimmers tensed at the edge of the pool, toes curled over the smooth stone of the starting line.*

whittle *(HWIT-ul), verb*
To shape a piece of wood and make it smooth by shaving or carving off pieces.
> *I thought WHITTLING was a pretty useless activity until I saw the beautiful walking stick Uncle Zeke had whittled for Grandpa.*

who's *(hooze), contraction*
Who is. (See, for comparison, the entry for *whose*.)
> *WHO'S going to the fair with me tonight?*

whose *(hooze), possessive pronoun*
Belonging to whom. (See, for comparison, the entry for *who's*)
> *WHOSE idea was it to go to the fair tonight?*

wile *(wile), noun*
A clever trick meant to attain a goal; an instance of or talent for beguiling deceit.
As a verb: to lure, entice, or beguile.
> *Headquarters trusts, as always, that the information with which you have been entrusted is secure even from the WILES of a spy of the opposite sex.*

wily *(WILE-ee), adjective*
Cunning; shrewd; clever or crafty.
> *Our WILY little puppy quickly learned that he could escape from the yard by digging a hole under the fence.*

winnow *(WIN-oh), verb*
To analyze carefully in order to separate valuable parts from worthless parts.
> *I WINNOWED through the stack of personal papers, looking for the ones I needed to present to the IRS.*

winsome *(WIN-sum), adjective*
Pleasant; charming.
> *Although he had overslept and been in a terrific rush to get out of the house, a WINSOME glance from the vaguely familiar woman at the toll collection booth helped put Milton's morning back on track.*

wiseacre *(WIZE-ake-ur), noun*
A know-it-all; one who professes to know everything.
> *"Listen, you little WISEACRE," Sergeant Artemis howled at Corporal Budworth, "if you think you can train these recruits better than I can, you ought to try it sometime."*

withered *(WITH-urd), adjective*
Shriveled; wrinkled and dried up.
> *It made Tim sad to realize that the oak tree he had such fun climbing as a child was now too WITHERED and old for his son to ascend safely.*

witticism *(WIT-ih-siz-um), noun*
A witty saying or remark.
> *We like to invite Roger to our cocktail parties, as he is able keep other guests entertained for hours on end with his stories and WITTICISMS.*

wizened *(WIZ-und), adjective*
Old; shriveled.

> *The subject of the documentary was a WIZENED old man of ninety-seven who happened to be the oldest living Bolshevik.*

woeful *(WOH-ful), adjective*
Filled with sorrow; in a sorry state, filled with woe.

> *When the home team lost the game in the final seconds, the WOEFUL crowd gasped then went silent.*

wok *(wok), noun*
A bowl-shaped skillet used in Oriental cooking.

> *Jeb, who could work wonders in the kitchen with his WOK, treated us to an excellent stir-fried vegetable and chicken dish.*

wonk *(WONK), noun*
A person who spends what many would consider too much time studying information in great detail. *Wonk* is a favorite word of pundits, who often use it to describe politicians who supplant personal experience with intense study of an issue.

> *One candidate touted his experience and said that his opponent was a policy WONK whose only knowledge of issues came from her ability to read.*

wont *(wont), noun*
A habit or custom.

> *As was his WONT, Jeb took a walk to the sidewalk cafe near his home and bought a copy of the New York Times to read.*

wrest *(rest), verb*
To take away; to pull away forcefully.

> *When it comes to dealing with friends who are drunk and want to drive home by themselves, Mr. Powell advocates tactful suggestions, shrewd negotiation, and, if all else fails, an outright attempt to WREST the keys away from the person.*

writhe *(rythe), verb*
To twist (the body), especially in reaction to pain or strong sensation. To *writhe* is to twist the body or squirm.

> *The injured dog WRITHED in agony, but soon calmed down when the vet administered a local anesthetic.*

wunderkind *(VOON-dur-kind), noun*
Child prodigy.

> *Although he died young, Mozart, a WUNDERKIND whose career in music began at the age of six, had a career that spanned two and half decades.*

X, Y, & Z

Xanadu *(ZAN-uh-doo), noun*

A place of great beauty and luxury. *Xanadu* is the setting of Samuel Taylor Coleridge's poem, "Kubla Khan."

> *The Caribbean resort, with its palm trees ocean breezes, was a XANADU of earthly delights.*

Xanthippe *(zan-TIP-ee), noun*

A scolding, shrewish, ill-tempered woman or wife. *Xanthippe* was the wife of the philosopher, Socrates.

> *Listen, Esther, I know you say you want what's best for our son, but your tone has more than a hint of the XANTHIPPE in it.*

xenophobe *(ZEE-nuh-fobe), noun*

One who fears anything foreign or different; one who regards people, places, or customs that differ from one's own as inherently dangerous.

> *I don't believe my opponent is really a XENOPHOBE, despite his rhetoric against foreigners; he is simply a canny, wealthy, and extremely dangerous demagogue.*

yabber *(YAB-bur), verb*

To jabber; to chatter meaninglessly.

> *I am not interested in any of your YABBERING about how busy you've been at home; I want to know why this work is a month and a half late.*

yammer *(YAM-mer), verb*

To complain loudly; to whine.

> *While Diane was YAMMERING about how hard it was to get the office plants watered properly, I was trying to make a deadline.*

yarmulke *(YAR-mul-kuh), noun*

A skullcap-like headpiece worn by Jewish men (especially those following Orthodox or Conservative traditions). The *yarmulke* is worn during religious services or prayer.

> *Winston was unsure whether he was supposed to wear a YARMULKE at the wedding; after all, he was a Gentile.*

yaw *(YAW), verb*

To deviate temporarily from course, as a ship in rough waters or as an airplane encountering turbulence.

> *The ship YAWED in the strong winds.*

yearling *(YEER-ling), noun*
An animal that has entered its second year; also, a horse that is one year old, dating from the beginning of the year following its foaling.

> *Mr. Tompkin's prize YEARLING is a thoroughbred Clydesdale.*

yeoman *(YOH-mun), adjective*
Characterized by performing a difficult task with a great deal of effort, loyalty, and valiance. *Yeoman* was a social class during the Middle Ages.

> *The boss praised me for doing such a YEOMAN job on the McKenzie Account.*

yeshiva *(yuh-SHEE-vuh), noun*
A place of instruction in the Orthodox Jewish tradition for children of elementary school age.

> *When the YESHIVA released its children in the afternoon, the sounds of laughter echoed through the neighborhood.*

yeti *(YEH-tee), noun*
The (legendary) Abominable Snowman.

> *Carl claims to have photographic evidence of the Loch Ness Monster, several UFOs, and a large grey YETI, but I have yet to see any of it.*

yippie *(YIP-pee), noun*
A participant in a radical youth movement of the 1960s, the Youth International Party; one whose actions are reminiscent of the rebelliousness and irreverence of that time.

> *The YIPPIE protestors were on a collision course with Mayor Daley's riot police that night.*

yob *(yob), noun*
A hooligan or ruffian.

> *The first YOB may have been a tough customer from Liverpool, where the phrase originated.*

yokel *(YOE-kul), noun*
A bumpkin; a rustic person.

> *That one-set show may have impressed the YOKELS where you come from, but here in the big city we require a little more flash and stardust from our musicals.*

yore *(yore), noun*
Former days; an era long past.

> *In days of YORE, scribes sat in their chambers copying out long manuscripts, and dreaming, I like to believe, of copiers and word processors.*

your *(yore), possessive pronoun*
Belonging to you. (See, for comparison, the entry for *you're*.)
> *Where is YOUR jacket, David?*

you're *(yore), contraction*
You are. (See, for comparison, the entry for *your*.)
> *Are you sure YOU'RE going to go to the party tonight?*

zealot *(ZEL-ut), noun*
A fervent or fanatical partisan (in favor of a certain cause). A *zealot* is a person who shows great zeal.
> *Although he did not mind overlooking an occasional error in procedure, Mr. Fallow was a ZEALOT when it came to posting correct numbers for an accounting period.*

zeitgeist *(TSIGHT-Giced), noun*
A German contraction meaning "time spirit," *zeitgeist* refers to the taste and outlook—the "spirit"—common to a particular time.
> *That band has survived for decades because it always seems to make an accurate assessment of the current ZEITGEIST.*

zenith *(ZEE-nith), noun*
The highest point attained. A *zenith* is the apex of something.
> *Koufax's career reached its ZENITH in 1963, when he won 25 games and was awarded the Cy Young Award unanimously.*

zephyr *(ZEFF-ur), noun*
The west wind; any gentle wind.
> *Mike christened his new boat the ZEPHYR, even though he planned to use it primarily during the rugged winters of his native Massachusetts.*

zest *(zest), noun*
gusto; vigor; spice; enjoyment.
> *Annabel's ZEST for life led her enthusiastically into modern dance, mountain climbing, and untold hours of volunteer work.*

zither *(ZITH-ur), noun*
A small, harp-like stringed instrument.
> *An autoharp is similar to a ZITHER in that it has many strings and is strummed; because it has keys, however, the autoharp is easier to play.*

zymurgy *(ZIE-mur-jee), noun*
The branch of chemistry concerned with fermentation.
> *Though not true chemists, brewers and winemakers could be considered lay experts in the field of ZYMURGY.*